TO BIND THE NATION

Solomon Nkayishana Maphumuzana kaDinuzulu Zulu

TO BIND THE NATION

*Solomon kaDinuzulu and
Zulu Nationalism
1913–1933*

Nicholas Cope

UNIVERSITY OF NATAL PRESS
PIETERMARITZBURG
1993

ISBN 0 86980 888 5

This book is printed on acid-free paper

Typeset in the University of Natal Press
Printed by Kohler Carton and Print
P.O. Box 955, Pinetown 3600
South Africa

For my parents

Contents

Illustrations

Acknowledgements

The author and publishers would like to thank the following individuals and institutions for their assistance and permission to reproduce illustrations

> Killie Campbell Africana Library (Durban), 1, 3, 6, 10, 11, 14; Local History Museum (Durban), 9 (left); Natal Archives Depot (Pietermaritzburg), 9 (right), 15; State Archives (Pretoria), 2, 12; Don Africana Library (Durban), 16; S.B. Bourquin, 4, 5, 13; I. Edwards, 7.

Thanks are also due to Helena Margeot, Cartographer at the University of Natal, Pietermaritzburg, for producing the map.

Abbreviations

In the Text

ALU	Abaqulusi Land Union
ANC	African National Congress (formerly SANNC)
CNC	Chief Native Commissioner (Natal)
CP	(South African) Communist Party
CPSA	Church of the Province of South Africa (Anglican)
DNC	District Native Commissioner
ICU	Industrial and Commercial Workers' Union
MNA	Minister for Native Affairs
NAD	(Union) Native Affairs Department
NNC	Natal Native Congress
SANNC	South African Native National Congress (subsequently ANC)
SNA	Secretary for Native Affairs
ZNTI	Zululand National Training Institution

In the Footnotes

AWGC	A.W.G. Champion Collection, University of South Africa
CK	Carter/Karis Collection of South African Political Materials (microfilm)
CNC	Chief Native Commissioner's Correspondence, 1910–19, Natal Archives
CNC PMB	Chief Native Commissioner's Correspondence, 1919–50, Natal Archives
DZ	Records of the Diocese of Zululand, Diocesan Offices, Eshowe
EGJ	E.G. Jansen Collection, University of the Orange Free State

JUS	Archives of the Secretary for Justice, State Archives
KCAL	Killie Campbell Africana Library, Durban
MS CAMP	Sir Marshall Campbell Collection, KCAL
MS CHAM	Champion Papers, University of the Witwatersrand
MS LUG	H.C. Lugg Collection, KCAL
MS MAR	J.S. Marwick Papers, KCAL
MS NIC	George Heaton Nicholls Collection, KCAL
NEC	Evidence of the Native Economic Commission, 1930–32, State Archives
NTS	Archives of the Department of Native Affairs, State Archives
SAP	Archives of the Commissioner of the South African Police, 1901–60, State Archives
SNA	(Natal) Secretary for Native Affairs' Records, Natal Archives
UG	Union Government

Glossary

The following Zulu words and phrases are listed alphabetically in the form in which they are first used in the text.

amabutho	age-set regiments (sg. *ibutho*)
amakhanda	royal military homesteads (sg. *ikhanda*)
(i) beshu	traditional loin skin
(i) bhinca	a wearer of traditional clothing, a 'heathen'
hamba kahle	'go carefully' (a parting salutation), also used to describe political moderation or conservatism
ibandla yesizwe	national council
ihlambo	purification ceremony marking the end of mourning
imbongi	bard, or reciter of praises (*izibongo*)
impi	Zulu military force
indaba	official meeting
induna enkulu	principal headman
inkatha	sacred coil symbolising Zulu unity and power, comprising substances of metaphysical significance bound circularly in woven grass
inqina	ritual hunt to 'wash the spears', conducted during *ihlambo* ceremony
insila	body servant of a chief, or body matter containing the 'essence' of a person
isibaya	cattle enclosure
isibongo	clan name, surname
isigodlo	royal seraglio
izangoma	diviners (sg. *isangoma*)
izibongo	praises, praise poem
izikhulu	great leaders of the nation
izinceku	personal attendants (sg. *inceku*)
izinduna	headmen (sg. *induna*)
izinyanga	herbalists (sg. *inyanga*)

(i) kholwa	Christian or Westernised African; aspirant middle class
(i) lobolo	brideprice, marriage contract
ukubuthwa	to enrol *amabutho*, referring to the proceedings of an enrolment ceremony
ukukhonza	to pay respects to
umnumzana	homestead head, head of family
umphathi	organizer
utshwala	Zulu beer

Note on Zulu pronunciation

What follows is a brief guide for the reader who is unfamiliar with the Zulu language, and who may consequently feel perplexed when confronted with Zulu names and terms in the text, not knowing how they should be read.

Every syllable is pronounced: 'Dube' (Du-be) does not rhyme with 'cube'. The stress falls on the penultimate syllable: 'Gumede' (Gu-**me**-de) does not rhyme with 'remedy' (**re**-me-dy).

The vowels are short, and correspond to the following English vowel sounds:

'a' as in the article 'a' (a pen), not as in 'apple' or 'name'

'e' as in 'egg', not as 'ee' (see) or 'é' (café)

'i' as 'ee' (see)

'o' as in 'nor', not as in 'on' or 'no'

'u' as 'oo' (food)

The consonants are as in English, except:

'c', 'q', 'x' represent clicks (dental, palatal, lateral)

'hl' represents lateral fricative (written 'll' in Welsh)

'dl' represents 'hl' with vocalisation (written 'dhl' in old Zulu orthography)

'ph', 'th', 'kh', 'bh' represent 'p', 't', 'k', 'b' with aspiration (a distinction not shown in old Zulu orthography, so that *umphathi* was written *umpati*)

Note on Zulu orthography

Modern Zulu orthography has been used in the text (thus 'Thukela' and not the old spelling 'Tugela'), except in the case of the first names of people (thus 'Mnyaiza' and 'Matole', which would now be written 'Mnyayiza' and 'Mathole'), because these are the spellings by which the individuals were referred to during their lives. In regard to clan names (*izibongo*), however, modern Zulu orthography has been used (thus 'Mthethwa' and 'Buthelezi', which would previously have been written 'Mtetwa' and 'Butelezi'). There are, nonetheless, certain exceptions in the cases of particular families; the Zulu literary family 'Dhlomo' (of H.I.E. Dhlomo and R.R.R. Dhlomo fame) has retained the old spelling; there are, too, certain 'Ndlovu' families which have retained the old spelling 'Ndhlovu'.

Isigijimi sikaZulu ngeNkata

Mahashini Royal Kraal,
Nongoma P.O.
ZULULAND.

UKUHLANGANA KU NGAMANDHLA

Kini nonke maduna [Chiefs] bafundisi zikulu, nabantu nibikelwa ukuti Inkata ka Zulu nonyaka iyakuugena ngo :-

6th October 1925

Komkulu eMahashini Royal Kraal, emzini kaSolomon ka Dinuzulu. Njengoba engatikanga amaduna kulo ka 17th August nawoke ase yakufika ku wo lo wonyaka 6th October 1925.　　　　:　　　　:　　　　:

Kumenywa onganeno no pesheya ko Pongolo noTukela

　　　Bonke abatumela izimali ze Nkata abazitume nge gama lika Gilbert Zulu.　　Ukuputa koka 5th August kwafika abakwa Ndabazabantu ngezentela wozanike.

Bonke abafuna izimoto zokuya Emahashini nxase behle Esitimeleni kwa Somkele nome eVryheid ababhalele ku Mr. W. Bhulose, Native Market Victoria Street, Durban, ngapambi kuka 25th Sept ufake istembu

Ngabenu ngenhlonipo,
Wm. F. Bhulose Umongameli,
Rev. S. D. Simelane Umbhali.

Advertisement for the 1925 Inkatha meeting bearing the legends 'Ukuhlangana ku Ngamandhla' and 'Unity is Strength', Zulu and English renditions of the South African state motto 'Ex Unitate Vires'.

Preface

This book is based on a doctoral dissertation completed in 1985, for which I began research in 1981 at the University of Natal. I commenced my research with the aim of answering a beguilingly simple question: What happened to the Zulu royal family after the death of Dinuzulu in 1913? In my undergraduate studies I had become aware that, while much was known about Zulu kings and their political role in the nineteenth century, very little was known about Zulu royalty in the early twentieth century.[1] I set out, therefore, to fill what I perceived to be a gap in historical knowledge. The history that follows is a pared-down version of the doctoral dissertation, less 'academic' and more literary in style, less thematic and more narrative in structure, and hopefully more readable to the non-specialist.

Before 1913, the institution of Zulu kingship repeatedly acted as a rallying point for Zulu taking up arms against the prospect or practice of colonial overrule. The political role played by Cetshwayo kaMpande Zulu (Cetshwayo, son of Mpande, of the royal Zulu clan) during the Anglo-Zulu War of 1879 is illustrative in this respect, as is the political role of Dinuzulu kaCetshwayo Zulu during the post-conquest Zulu civil war and the 'Zulu rebellion' of 1906. After each of these periods of violent confrontation between Zulu and forces of imperialism or colonialism, colonial authorities responded by banishing the head of the Zulu royal family from Zululand. The imprisonment and exile of Dinuzulu after the 1906 rebellion, however, was the third and last occasion on which the head of the Zulu royal family was banished from Zululand.

Since Dinuzulu's death in exile in 1913, the heirs to the Zulu royal house have been domiciled in Zululand without interruption: Solomon Nkayishana kaDinuzulu (1913 to 1933); Cyprian Bhekuzulu kaSolomon (1948 to 1968 – Arthur Mshiyeni kaDinuzulu having acted as regent during Cyprian's long minority); and Goodwill Zwelithini kaCyprian (1971 to the present – following a brief regency period under Israel Mcwayizeni kaSolomon). Their political influence has remained an important theme in Zulu history throughout the twentieth century. But their political role has become increasingly distanced from the politics of protest, and ever closer to the politics of compromise. This has been most manifest in current times, in which the Zulu king acts out the ceremonial role of a Zulu 'constitutional monarch', the initiative in Zulu national affairs having shifted to Chief Mangosuthu Gatsha Buthelezi (Chief Minister of KwaZulu) and the Inkatha organisation (formed in 1975, resuscitating the name of a Zulu national organisation that had existed in the 1920s).

The period 1913 to 1933, when Solomon kaDinuzulu was head of the Zulu royal family, was a dynamic period of transition in the political role of the Zulu kingship. The restoration of the head of the Zulu royal family to Zululand in 1913, and the restoration of the political prominence of the Zulu kingship in Zulu politics that followed, which are crucial themes in this book, did not entail simply a restoration of the 'old' Zulu kingship. The Zulu kingship in the early twentieth century no longer represented what it had represented in the nineteenth century, during the existence of the independent Zulu kingdom.

Nor can the Zulu nationalist sentiment associated with Solomon kaDinuzulu in the 1920s be equated with the politicised Zulu nationalism of today. It is true that Zulu politics in the 1920s evince some clear connections with present political developments in Natal, and there is no doubt that an understanding of the present is assisted by an understanding of the past. However, the 1920s in Natal were different from the present: the Inkatha of the 1920s was regional, rather than national in its ambitions, and was neither as controversial nor as influential as the present Inkatha. It lasted for less than a decade; although its political future appeared secure in the late 1920s, the organisation disintegrated in the early 1930s, having been undermined by corruption and a loss of political direction, and by its association with an increasingly erratic royal figurehead, Solomon kaDinuzulu. It is with this history that this book is concerned; and it is to history that this book is committed.[2]

When describing the evolution of Zulu nationalism in South Africa in the early twentieth century, this book searches 'beneath the skin' of ethnic nationalism to identify the social forces that shaped it. It shows how, in the early twentieth century, nationalism among the Zulu-speaking people was neither innate nor inevitable. Rather than being seen as an immutable objective 'fact' of Zulu political consciousness, inherited directly from the pre-colonial period, twentieth-century Zulu nationalism is better understood as a modern political force, reconstructed principally by Zulu social and political elites in the altered circumstances of post-industrial South Africa.[3] Twentieth-century Zulu nationalism is also better understood as a malleable political force, for at different times it has meant different things to different people. The text's main theme is not ethnic Zulu nationalism itself, however; it is the life and political role of Solomon kaDinuzulu Zulu, the head of the Zulu royal family between 1913 and 1933. Although set in a detailed political context, which throws incidental light on both the origins of Apartheid and moves for devolution in the Natal/ KwaZulu region, this book is essentially a biography and ends with Solomon's death. The story of the Zulu kingship and Zulu nationalism continues, but will have to await a further book.

In preparing my doctoral dissertation, I depended on and was inspired by two earlier histories: Jeff Guy's *The destruction of the Zulu kingdom* (1979), which focuses on the post-conquest civil war in Zululand, and Shula Marks's *Reluctant rebellion* (1970), which focuses on the 1906 rebellion in Natal. This present book follows on from these histories, taking the story into the early 1930s, complementing Marks's more recent text, *The ambiguities of dependence in South Africa* (1986).[4] I am moreover indebted to both authors for offering me advice and encouragement over the years. Attending Shula Marks's 'Southern Africa' seminar at the Institute of Commonwealth Studies, University of London, has been a privilege and also a vital means of keeping in touch with academic research. Jeff Guy's perceptive and detailed reader's report on my doctoral dissertation provided very important guidance in planning the conversion of the dissertation into a book. I must also acknowledge another source of inspiration in revising the dissertation for publication. Brian Willan's *Sol Plaatje* (1984), which also deals with black South African history in the early decades of the twentieth century, focusing on the life of a contemporary writer and founder of the African National Congress, alerted me to the potential in a biographical approach to the writing of history.[5]

Among the very many people that I am indebted to for assistance and encouragement, there are others that deserve special mention. Paul Maylam, at the time Associate Professor of History at the University of Natal, Durban, supervised the preparation of my doctoral dissertation under difficult circumstances: since I had left South Africa in 1983, supervision of the writing-up stage had to be conducted through the cumbersome medium of long-distance correspondence. Throughout what was a long and arduous task, I was able to depend on him as an unfailing source of encouragement and advice. My father, Trevor Cope, Professor of Zulu Language and Literature at the University of Natal, Durban, prior to his retirement, has been an immeasurable help in assisting me to edit this text, suggesting where cuts could be made, and championing the interests of readability. He has assisted, too, with numerous linguistic queries. Jeffrey Horton, Professor Emeritus of History at the University of Natal, contributed much to the final presentation of the manuscript. During his annual retirement pilgrimages to London, he read through what I had so far written paying much-appreciated attention to usage and expression. I would like also to acknowledge the contribution of Jo Beall, similarly ex-University of Natal but now at London University, for her political insight and overview discussion of the manuscript in its final stages. Finally I am very grateful to Margery Moberly, publisher, and Jenny Edley, editor, at the University of Natal Press, Pietermaritzburg, for the guidance they have offered.

Writing is nonetheless inherently a lonely task. The writing work that resulted in both dissertation and book has been carried out essentially on my own, intermittently, while working as a teacher of English language in adult education, and while living in London, Chester, Paris and once again in London. Any errors of interpretation or fact in the historical reconstruction that follows must therefore remain my responsibility.

NOTES

1. An important exception was provided by Shula Marks, 'Natal, the Zulu royal family and the ideology of segregation', *Journal of Southern African Studies*, vol. 4, no. 2 April 1978.

2. The historical focus distinguishes this study from two illuminating recent publications on Zulu politics: Gerhard Maré and Georgina Hamilton, *An appetite for power: Buthelezi's Inkatha and South Africa* (Braamfontein, 1987); and Mzala, *Gatsha Buthelezi: chief with a double agenda* (London, 1988). While both these studies refer to the past, their focus falls on the conflicts of the present.

3. There have been two important recent publications on the dynamics of nationalism and ethnic nationalism in southern Africa: Shula Marks and Stanley Trapido (eds), *The politics of race, class and nationalism in twentieth century South Africa* (London, 1987); and Leroy Vail (ed.), *The creation of tribalism in southern Africa* (London, 1989). For the Zulu case during the 1920s in particular, see Shula Marks, *The ambiguities of dependence in South Africa: class, nationalism and the state in twentieth-century Natal* (Braamfontein, 1986); and Nicholas Cope, 'The Zulu petit bourgeoisie and Zulu nationalism in the 1920s: origins of Inkatha', *Journal of Southern African Studies*, vol. 16, no. 3, September 1990.

4. Jeff Guy, *The destruction of the Zulu kingdom* (London, 1979); and Shula Marks, *Reluctant rebellion: the 1906–1908 disturbances in Natal* (Oxford, 1970). For Marks's more recent text (1986), see note above.

5. Brian Willan, *Sol Plaatje: South African nationalist, 1876–1932* (London, 1984).

Prologue

The independent Zulu kingdom existed for approximately six decades, little more than half a century, in the mid-nineteenth century. Shaka Zulu, the first Zulu king, assumed leadership of the Zulu clan in around 1816; Cetshwayo Zulu, Shaka's nephew and the fourth Zulu king, was captured by British military forces in 1879, and sent into exile. Despite this comparatively short existence, the Zulu kingdom had been a centralised and militarily powerful state, with an intricate set of customs, ceremonies and beliefs which served to legitimise the rule of the Zulu king. Self-sufficiency and national unity had been highly valued in the ideology of the Zulu kingdom, as had political independence. These principles, which had been personified by the successive Zulu kings Shaka, Dingane, Mpande and Cetshwayo Zulu, were not successfully defended in the Anglo-Zulu War.

The imperial invasion of the Zulu kingdom was mounted from the neighbouring British territory, the Colony of Natal, which had been annexed in 1845. Natal colonial officials, at whose behest the Anglo-Zulu War of 1879 had been waged, saw the exile of the Zulu king as an essential step in the suppression of Zulu military capability and national unity, and in the subordination of the Zulu people to colonial rule. It was they, rather than British officials in London, who were to exert the weightiest influence on official policy in post-conquest Zululand. The Zulu king was accordingly denied a role in the post-war 'settlement' of Zululand. The system of 'native administration' that had gradually evolved in the Colony of Natal, south of the Thukela river, was now applied north of the Thukela river, in the territory of the old Zulu kingdom.

The Colony of Natal's system of native administration, was named after Natal's first Secretary for Native Affairs, Sir Theophilus Shepstone. 'Shepstonism' was a system of indirect rule, based on the recognition of African customary law and institutions, and the employment of African chiefs as officers of local government. It was also based on the resilience of the African agricultural and pastoral economy, because the extraction of surplus from the African homestead, mainly in the form of hut tax, provided an essential source of revenue for the colonial state. Natal's African population was generally allowed continued access to land on which to cultivate and herd in accordance with pre-colonial habits, either on the basis of communal tribal tenure in the African reserves that Shepstone demarcated, or as tenants on Crown Land and white-owned farms. Shepstonism, especially in its earlier stages, therefore provided for a certain continuity with the African past, in law, politics and the economy. An important difference was that the African inhabitants of Natal were now made responsible for supporting an overarching colonial administration. Greater demands were made on the African homestead to produce a regular surplus, and to supply labour to the emerging colonial economy so as to earn money to pay taxes.[1]

Shepstone's administrative system essentially superimposed British authority on African political institutions that already existed at a local level. At the apex of the administrative hierarchy was the office of 'Supreme Chief', automatically occupied by the colonial Governor of Natal, in which office was vested the autocratic powers that an African king was presumed to wield – though none had previously existed south of the Thukela. In the hands of the Supreme Chief rested ultimate power, to be delegated as he wished through Natal's Secretary for Native Affairs, the white magistrates beneath him, and, in turn, the African chiefs and headmen beneath them. It was in the lower reaches of the hierarchy that the essence of indirect rule lay. Chiefs were to function, on the one hand, as civil servants who were ultimately responsible to the Supreme Chief; on the other hand, in accordance with African customary law and usage, they were to perform their traditional chiefly duties in representing and governing their adherents – or 'tribes'. Shepstone and Natal colonial officials, however, were in no doubt as to where the primary responsibilities of chiefs should lie when the interests of the colonial state and local people conflicted.

In Natal, where Shepstonism had evolved, Shepstone's task was to administer an African population which, prior to annexation in 1845, had been subject to various disruptive influences, the most devastating of which had been the periodic influx of raiding parties from the Zulu kingdom. The Natal African population was somewhat dependent and malleable, many in fact being refugees from Zulu rule, and hence Shepstone's ideas of 'government tribes' under 'appointed chiefs' could be fairly readily implemented. This proved not to be the case north of the Thukela river, where the Zulu population had a recent history of centralised rule, focused on the Zulu royal house, and of independence.

After the Anglo-Zulu War, Sir Garnet Wolseley, the High Commissioner then recently appointed for South Eastern Africa, addressed the Zulu people as follows:

> Only yesterday you yourselves have seen [Cetshwayo] carried away as prisoner, never to return again to Zululand . . . His country is now to be divided up into different chieftainships, and I hope his fate will be a warning to all chiefs not to follow in his footsteps, but to act according to the commands and terms given by the British Queen . . . Zululand now belongs to the Queen of England. She has, however, already enough land in Africa, and so has, through me as her representative, appointed certain chiefs to rule over the districts which I shall presently name.[2]

Thus were Shepstonist principles, in the form of Wolseley's infamous 'settlement', ushered into Zululand. Shepstone and Shepstonists characterised the Zulu royal family as a fearsome and disruptive remnant of a 'pure military despotism', unequivocally 'opposed to the quiet of the country and the peace of the people'. Shepstone himself regarded monarchical authority within a unitary political structure as an imposition on the Zulu people, who, 'composed originally of conquered and incorporated tribes', yearned for their 'ancient and separate existence, relieved of the terrible incubus of the Zulu royal family'.[3] The aim of colonial administrators was to impress upon the Zulu that the powers and pretensions of Shaka's heirs had permanently expired, and to replace the rule of the Zulu king with the rule of a number of lesser Zulu chiefs, who were appointed by, and therefore beholden to, the colonial administration.

The period of civil wars that ensued north of the Thukela proved disastrous for the political status of the Zulu royal family and the idea of Zulu national unity, more disastrous than the Anglo-Zulu War itself. The most immediate adherents of the Zulu royal house, the Usuthu, were dealt their heaviest blow by the appointment of two disaffected Zulu of the royal lineage itself, Hamu and Zibhebhu, to rule as chiefs over Zululand's northern regions. Both Hamu and Zibhebhu had been closely connected with the colonial world before the war, through European advisers, commerce and labour recruiting, and Hamu was the only Zulu of note to defect with his followers to the British side during the war. Hamu was awarded a large district in the north-west that included not only his own adherents, the Ngenetsheni, but also the staunchly royalist Qulusi and a large part of the Buthelezi. Hamu's district also included the personal homestead of the Buthelezi leader, Mnyamana, who had been Cetshwayo's principal adviser. To the east of Hamu, Zibhebhu was awarded a district that included not only his own adherents, the Mandlakazi, but also the core of the Usuthu, including Cetshwayo's son and heir-apparent, Dinuzulu.

In seeking to consolidate the new positions that they had been accorded under the terms of Wolseley's 'settlement', both the Ngenetsheni and the Mandlakazi turned on the Usuthu and other royalist groups; the colonial administration threw its weight behind them, especially the Mandlakazi, who emerged as the Usuthu's most devastating enemies of the Zulu civil war. Yet the Zulu royalist cause was undermined not only by the military successes of its opponents and the partiality of colonial officials. Towards the end of the civil-war period, there was also a waning determination within the royalist camp. Most importantly, in the late 1880s, a rift developed between the Usuthu and the Buthelezi, apparently as a result of disagreement over strategy. This rift was to linger for more than three decades.

A further factor which undermined the status and influence of the Zulu royal house was the loss of territory: in the mid-1880s, approximately one-third of the territory of the old Zulu kingdom was claimed from the Usuthu by Boers from the Transvaal. The alienation of the north-western districts, which included the best grazing lands, came as a consequence of an alliance the Usuthu had temporarily formed with Boer leaders in 1884, in order to defeat the Mandlakazi. Important royalist groups, including the Qulusi and leading sections of the Buthelezi and the Usuthu, thus found themselves subjects of the Boer 'New Republic' − as did the Ngenetsheni under Hamu. The Zulu lost their traditional rights to the land in the New Republic, which became 'Northern Natal', part of the Colony of Natal, following the Boer defeat in the Anglo-Boer War of 1899−1901. Consequently, the demands for labour and rent made by the new landlords brought about an accelerated process of impoverishment and social fragmentation.

More broadly, in the wake of the formal annexation of the remainder of the original Zulu country in 1887 (British 'Zululand' was subsequently incorporated into the Colony of Natal in 1897), Zulu society as a whole was drawn increasingly into the labour and commodity markets of a growing capitalist sector in southern Africa; industrialisation and commercial expansion had gathered pace since the mineral discoveries in the interior, during the last third of the nineteenth century. New needs and aspirations were evolving among the Zulu as a consequence of this process, and new social divisions were emerging.

By the turn of the century, Zulu society was no longer what it had been during the time of the old Zulu kingdom, and it seemed that the Zulu royal family might gradually fade into insignificance, having been transformed into little more than an ideological remnant of past Zulu independence. Overall, the thirty-four years that elapsed between the capture of Cetshwayo in 1879 and the death of Dinuzulu, Cetshwayo's son and heir, in 1913 were dark years for the royal cause. Twenty of these years, indeed, had been years of imprisonment or exile for the head of the Zulu royal family – imprisonment in Cape Town and Pietermaritzburg, and exile in the Cape, on St Helena and in the Transvaal. And of those years during which the head of the Zulu royal family had been permitted to live in the Zulu country, many had been years of civil war or civil disturbance. Cetshwayo had died while in hiding from the Mandlakazi; Dinuzulu died in exile. These were dark years, too, for those ideals of Zulu unity, nationhood and independence that Zulu kings had symbolised in the time of the old Zulu kingdom.

* * * * *

By the early twentieth century, nevertheless, there were signs that the Zulu royal family could play a new unifying role in African politics in Natal. More specifically, there were signs that the Zulu royal family was being perceived in a new light in certain quarters of the Zulu-speaking population – which included not only Zulu north of the Thukela river in the territory of the old Zulu kingdom, but also Natal Africans in Natal proper (the territory of the original Colony of Natal, as distinct from the subsequently included territories of Zululand and Northern Natal). These signs showed themselves clearly in 1906, the year of the 'Zulu rebellion'.[4]

The 1906 rebellion originated in Natal proper and spread north of the Thukela to Zululand only after retreating rebels had taken refuge there. There was little evidence that Dinuzulu deliberately involved himself in the 1906 rebellion; yet there was no doubt that he did play a role, even if that role was an unwelcome imposition from the rebels themselves. For the rebels, the Zulu royal family became a source of inspiration and focus for unity, and a living reminder of a powerful and independent African past. In the course of hostilities, they adopted royal symbols as rallying calls to battle, and looked to the Zulu royal family as a rallying point for a united offensive against colonial rule. The association of Dinuzulu's name with their cause served as a potent boost to morale.

The great majority of the rebels of 1906 were Natal Africans. They were thus descendants of the very people that had been subjected to repeated Zulu raids during the early years of the Zulu kingdom's existence, prior to the British annexation of Natal, and whom Zulu of the Zulu kingdom had regarded with some scorn.[5] It was significant too that the social base of the rebellion was not limited to 'tribal' Africans in the rural areas. Considerable numbers of workers deserted their employment in urban areas to join the rural rebels. Kholwa (Christian African) communities in Natal proper, moreover, were clearly ambiguous about the rebellion. Hitherto the kholwa had tended to identify strongly with the colonial order and Victorian 'civilisation', distancing themselves from tribal society, but in 1906 many forebore to condemn the rebels and some went so far as to join them. The 1906 rebellion was therefore not merely an example of 'tribal' resistance to colonisation, but reflected an early development of African nationalism in the modern sense.[6] The undercurrents that briefly broke through to the surface in 1906 revealed that the Zulu royal family had a wider base of potential support, both territorially and socially, than it could have claimed in 1879.

These political developments must be understood in their socio-economic context, which for Natal's African population was one of accelerated impoverishment.[7] In Natal proper, the twin pressures of hut tax and decreasing land availability were intensified at the turn of the century. Hut tax in the African reserves increased dramatically between 1902 and 1905; a new £3 tax was levied on inhabitants of African mission reserves in 1903, and in the same year rentals for tenants on Crown land increased from £1 to £2. More and more Africans were being forced off the land to seek wage labour – which was in fact one of the main objectives of colonial tax and land policy. The immediate spark for the 1906 rebellion came in 1905, when a £1 poll tax was imposed on all African males who did not already pay hut tax.

Although their effect was delayed in comparison with neighbouring Natal proper, these trends were mirrored in Zululand. Large-scale labour migration in Zululand has been dated from 1888, the year following British annexation, when hut tax was imposed. Labour migration accelerated after 1897, when the territory was incorporated into Natal and taxes levied in Natal proper were similarly levied in Zululand. In 1904, moreover, the report of the Zululand Lands Delimitation Commission made 40 per cent of Zululand available for purchase by private buyers – the balance being demarcated as Zulu reserves, following the Shepstonist precedent set in Natal proper.[8] In practice, purchaseable land in Zululand fell almost exclusively into the hands of British settlers. For the Zulu inhabitants of Northern Natal, conditions were yet more adverse: there, since the days of the Boer 'New Republic', no land at all had been set aside for African occupation. All Zulu had summarily become tenants of white landlords, and were required to pay substantial rents or render labour for their tenure. At the turn of the century, the rate of African labour migration from Northern Natal's Vryheid district was the highest in the whole of Natal.[9]

To add to these burdens there came a devastating series of natural disasters that wrought havoc on African agriculture: the locust plague of 1896, the rinderpest epidemic of 1897, and then the lingering cattle disease known as east coast fever. In addition, several years of poor rains culminated in a severe drought in 1903. Immediately before the rebellion, therefore, many were faced with the spectres of poverty and insecurity, and proportionately more were forced into the labour market to provide subsistence for their rural families. The hardship and ferment occasioned by this accumulation of factors were expressed politically in the events of 1906. The pervasiveness of African social distress had the effect of promoting a sense of unity among a population, where previously there had been none. In casting about for a rallying point, these pan-Natal sentiments of an early African nationalist character came to focus on the Zulu royal family. While some chiefs had become identified as servants of the colonial government, this was manifestly not so in the case of the Zulu royal family. That it, too, had been 'maltreated' by colonial rulers was certainly one reason why the rebels of 1906 looked to Dinuzulu for inspiration and leadership.

Rather than devising a more accommodating policy towards the Zulu royal family after the 1906 rebellion, however, the Natal government instead applied a policy that was yet more repressive. Dinuzulu was deprived of his position as chief of the Usuthu, taken into custody, and tried for high treason. The judgment of the treason trial, while exonerating Dinuzulu on the majority of the charges, found him guilty of harbouring rebels at various stages of the rebellion. For this he was incarcerated in Pietermaritzburg gaol in 1909. Mankulumana kaSomaphunga Ndwandwe, Dinuzulu's principal headman, was also imprisoned, and on his release just before Union was prohibited from returning to Zululand. Shingana kaMpande Zulu, Dinuzulu's uncle and guardian during his minority, was banished to an area south of Durban where he was shortly to die. In making administrative arrangements for the Usuthu, who now had no chief, the Natal Government redoubled its efforts to apply the dictum of 'divide and rule'. R.H. Addison, who was then Natal's District Native Commissioner (DNC) for Zululand, 'abolished' the Usuthu and parcelled out its members among four local chiefs, only one of whom was a member of the Zulu royal family proper, and all of whom had in some way seceded from the royal cause. Indeed, one was a Mandlakazi, and another was a Buthelezi.[10]

On the other side of the coin, one of the first actions of the newly constituted Union government of 1910 was to order the release of Dinuzulu from gaol. This was partly a result of Harriette Colenso's long campaign for justice and sympathy for Zulu royalty, which had been especially vigorous since the 1906 rebellion. Harriette was a daughter of John William Colenso, the renowned Anglican Bishop of Natal, and like her father she had been a tireless champion of Zulu rights from 1879. It was nonetheless Louis Botha himself, the Prime Minister of the Union of South Africa, who was primarily responsible for Dinuzulu's release. Botha knew Dinuzulu personally, since he and Dinuzulu had fought alongside each other during the 1884 Boer-Usuthu alliance against the Mandlakazi; and Botha was convinced that Dinuzulu had not been responsible for the 1906 rebellion. Presumably wishing to avoid offending Natal officials, Botha arranged for a farm in the Transvaal to be set aside for Dinuzulu and his immediate retinue rather than suggesting his repatriation to Zululand. Mankulumana was allowed to accompany Dinuzulu into exile. Even so, as Dinuzulu left gaol for the relative freedom of the Transvaal, Natal officials tried to force him to sign a declaration stating that he would never return to Natal. He refused, and only signed when Botha wired him asking him to comply. Dinuzulu was settled on the farm 'Rietfontein' in the Middelburg district, and his annual government stipend was restored to him.[11] African opinion all over the Province of Natal and beyond applauded the action of the Union government. Significantly, however, there were reports from Zululand that Zulu 'loyal' to the government were concerned that Dinuzulu might be repatriated.[12] This reflected the continuing division in Zulu society between those who supported the government and those who supported the royal cause.

The release of Dinuzulu from prison in 1910 attracted widespread news coverage. Apart from the major British dailies, regional British newspapers such as the *Bristol Times*, *Cork Examiner*, *Glasgow News*, and *Manchester Courier* carried reports, all of which welcomed the action of the Union government and very often explicitly condemned the Natal government's treatment of Dinuzulu. In general, Dinuzulu's release was not an important issue in the minds of Natal's whites; after all, he had been released only to be permanently exiled. Perhaps, as the *Plymouth News* perceptively reasoned, because Natal was now no longer 'alone' but part of the larger white-controlled Union of South Africa, she could afford to be less fearful of the Zulu royal family.[13]

Dinuzulu's death in exile three years later caused greater consternation in white Natal, for it raised the questions of whether it would be permitted to return Dinuzulu's body to Zululand for burial and whether Dinuzulu's heir would be allowed to live there.[14] Natal officials, however, no longer had ultimate control over 'native administration' in Natal; Natal was now a province of the Union of South Africa, and not a self-governing colony. The death of Dinuzulu in effect provided officials of the Union's Native Affairs Department (NAD) head office with the opportunity to 'wipe the slate clean' and review official policy towards the Zulu royal family. Dinuzulu's heir, who was yet to be named, indeed had signed no 'self-denying ordinance' as had Dinuzulu.

* * * * *

On news of Dinuzulu's death on 18 October 1913, the Union government immediately extended its condolences to the bereaved family through the magistrate at Middelburg. The government went on to offer the services of the local magistrate, for 'the sake of Dinuzulu's memory', to help make arrangements for the welfare of Dinuzulu's dependants at KwaThengisa – the Zulu name for Dinuzulu's Transvaal residence in exile, abbreviated from KwaThengisangaye, meaning 'the place where he was sold'.[15] The Secretary for Native Affairs (SNA) offered an assurance that, if the total of Dinuzulu's debts were 'reasonable', he would recommend that the government settle them; the government would also pay for the education of Dinuzulu's two eldest sons, David Nyawana kaDinuzulu Zulu and Solomon Nkayishana Maphumuzana kaDinuzulu Zulu, at Lovedale College.[16] The question of whether it was permissible to return Dinuzulu's body to Zululand for burial was not even raised. For the Zulu royal family it never was a question. Barely a day after Dinuzulu's death, his body was being transported by train to Vryheid station, *en route* to the ancestral heartland of royal Zululand, Emakhosini, 'the place of the kings', where the heads of the Zulu royal house had been buried since the turn of the seventeenth century.[17]

Native Affairs Department officials in the Province of Natal (Natal NAD) had no time to raise objections. The personal influence of Louis Botha, whom Dinuzulu apparently regarded as his 'best friend in the government', was evident in all these developments.[18] Indeed, when Dinuzulu died there were some suggestions that Botha and Harriette Colenso were making secret arrangements for the repatriation of Dinuzulu to Zululand, contrary to the document that Natal had induced Dinuzulu to sign in 1910.[19]

The news of Dinuzulu's death was brought to the royal family in Zululand by Ndabankulu kaLukhwazi Ntombela, an aged chief and one of Dinuzulu's headmen who had been an aggressive member of the Usuthu since the wars with the Mandlakazi. Mnyaiza kaNdabuko Zulu (whose father, Ndabuko kaMpande Zulu, was Dinuzulu's uncle and had acted as Dinuzulu's guardian) then sent messengers out into the countryside to report the news to Zulu chiefs and dignitaries. He further informed them that the funeral was shortly to take place at Nobamba, the historic royal homestead established three generations before Shaka and situated in the midst of Emakhosini.[20] Thus, when the train bearing Dinuzulu's body pulled into Vryheid station, a large concourse of Zulu mourners had assembled to meet it. These mainly comprised members of the Qulusi, Mdlalose and Ntombela sections which inhabited the Vryheid district. Together they accosted the magistrate at Vryheid, Mr Colenbrander, and spoke 'very disparagingly of the Government', accusing it of causing Dinuzulu's ruin and death.[21]

At Vryheid, Dinuzulu's body was transferred to a wagon for the journey to Nobamba. There were many signs that Dinuzulu's body was returning to a Zululand substantially different to the Zululand in which he had been born. The body had arrived in a European-style coffin rather than wrapped in skins as was customary. It had moreover arrived by train, a symbol of industrialisation which, to many local Zulu, was the vehicle that transported sons and daughters away to distant labour centres and townships, perhaps never to return. This translation of the *izibongo* (praises, praise poem) of 'The European Railway Train', transcribed between 1910 and 1920 by a retired Natal NAD official and dedicated recorder of Zulu history, James Stuart, vividly encapsulates the train's image and effect:

> Go thou metal of the white people!
> Take them and transport them.
> . . . .
> Go with them and put them out of sight yonder far!
> Loose woman that causes people to wander,
> Who takes women and men and sends them to Johannesburg,
> When they get there they will be swallowed by the dumps.
> . . . .
> Drive them that they may go,
> And make for a far-away land.
> Let them go to where ploughing is no longer done,
> Beans are no longer planted,
> And the ones at home will wait awhile
> Until the tears rain down.
> Because it takes them and transports them,
> And sends them where it is far away.[22]

Heading the large funeral procession *en route* to Nobamba was an entourage of dignitaries whose presence reflected how the beliefs and values of western civilisation, together with its dynamic – capitalist production – had penetrated Zulu life. Despite the scant enthusiasm that the Zulu royal family, especially Dinuzulu, had shown for Christianity, an African cleric from Pretoria, the Revd Twala, attended the funeral. His role was to intervene and officiate where necessary, so as to ensure that the essentially traditional ceremony also satisfied Christian belief. In a wagon directly behind the one bearing Dinuzulu's coffin sat Harriette Colenso or 'Musihelu', the missionary, philanthropist, critic of government policy, and most trusted white adviser to the Zulu royal family. At one stage her visits to Dinuzulu's residence had become so frequent and prolonged that Zulu royalty had expected her to settle permanently among them.[23] Next to Harriette Colenso sat two white labour agents from Johannesburg, known to the Zulu as 'Muhle' and 'Zithulele', both of whom were employed by Transvaal mining houses to secure a supply of African labour for the gold-fields. One was J.S. Marwick, who had earned his name 'Muhle' ('the good one') when, as Zululand Native Agent and Transvaal representative of the Natal NAD, he had organised the evacuation of an estimated seven thousand Zulu labourers from Johannesburg back to their homes on the outbreak of the Anglo-Boer War. Since 1907 he had been employed by the Farrar Group of mines with a particular brief to secure labour from Zululand and Swaziland.[24] Although positive identification is lacking, it is likely that 'Zithulele' was Lt.-Col. Morris, a veteran Transvaal labour agent and an associate of Marwick.[25]

Members of the Zulu royal family who were working on the mines when Dinuzulu died had travelled to Vryheid with Marwick and his colleague. They, together with Dinuzulu's wives from KwaThengisa, followed the wagons on foot. Among them, too, were Dinuzulu's children who had been at KwaThengisa when he died, including his sons David Nyawana and Arthur Edward Mshiyeni. The funeral procession took three days to reach Nobamba. Early on the third day it was met by a group of Zulu who had set out from Nobamba to intercept it. Among them was another of Dinuzulu's sons, Solomon Nkayishana Maphumuzana. When this enlarged funeral procession finally arrived at Nobamba, the chiefs and headmen who together represented the core of traditional and royal Zululand were reunited. Apart from Mankulumana kaSomaphunga Ndwandwe and Ndabankulu kaLukhwazi Ntombela, there was Zidunge kaNtshingwayo Khoza (lineage head of the Khoza, and heir of Ntshingwayo who had died leading Cetshwayo's army against Zibhebhu); Masimba kaNokhokhela Buthelezi (leading headman of Nobamba); Mbuzini and Zinyo kaNtuzwa Mdlalose (both their father Ntuzwa and their uncle Seketwayo had been leading Usuthu since 1879), and many other 'great men of the nation'.[26] Also present were Dinuzulu's personal attendants: Lokotwayo kaZembe Mangadini, Mvingana kaNompanda Manzimeleni and Nobiyana kaMholo Manzimeleni. Notable members of the Zulu royal family itself – all of Dinuzulu's generation, the grandsons of Mpande – were Mnyaiza kaNdabuko; Mgixo, Mpikanina and Citekana kaZiwedu; Mkebeni, Franz (or France) and Mdumela kaDabulamanzi; and Dotela (or Dokotela) kaMgidlana.

The traditional status of these men, however, belied the strong links that some had established with precisely those social forces that had undermined

Zulu independence. Mnyaiza, for example, was employed as a recruiter of mine labour by Col. Royston, an independent labour agent who also attended the funeral.[27] Similarly, Franz was employed on the gold mines as a labour supervisor, eventually to hold the position of 'Head Induna of Brakpan Compound'.[28]

After the main body of mourners had arrived with the funeral procession, latecomers continued to pour into Nobamba. It might seem incongruous that some of these latecomers had travelled such distances to attend a display of Zulu tradition and past monarchical grandeur. One was Pixley Seme, born to a Natal kholwa family and brought up by American missionaries. Having trained in law at the universities of Columbia (New York) and Oxford, he returned to South Africa to be accepted as an attorney of the Supreme Court and to establish a legal practice in Johannesburg. There he became the driving force behind the formation of the South African Native National Congress (SANNC, later the African National Congress). He also established links with Swazi and Zulu royalty. During Dinuzulu's final illness, Seme had brought a Johannesburg doctor to attend him, and had also established a fund to send Dinuzulu to Europe for treatment.[29] A small group of local officials had also arrived to be 'the eye of the government', including a few Nongqai mounted policemen from Eshowe, even though it was official policy in Natal to pretend that the Zulu kingship was defunct.[30] The funeral party was said to number seven thousand in total.[31]

The variety of individuals present at the funeral ceremony provides an insight into the variety of social forces at work among the Zulu, and underlines the impossibility of conceptualising the Zulu royal family in the twentieth century in accordance with the role it had played in the nineteenth. Many changes had occurred in the economic and social life of the Zulu people, and it is only in the context of these that developments in their political life can be more fully understood.

NOTES

1. My observations on Shepstonism and the post-conquest administration of Zululand are based principally on the following sources: Edgar H. Brookes and Colin de B. Webb, *A history of Natal* (Pietermaritzburg, 1965); Norman Etherington, 'The origins of "indirect rule" in nineteenth-century Natal', *Theoria*, no. 47, 1976, and 'The "Shepstone system" in the colony of Natal and beyond the borders', in Andrew Duminy and Bill Guest (eds), *Natal and Zululand from earliest times to 1910: a new history* (Pietermaritzburg, 1989); Henry Slater, 'The changing pattern of economic relationships in rural Natal, 1838–1914', in Shula Marks and Anthony Atmore (eds), *Economy and society in pre-industrial South Africa* (London, 1980); Jeff Guy, *The destruction of the Zulu kingdom* (London, 1979), and 'The destruction and reconstruction of Zulu society', in Shula Marks and Richard Rathbone (eds), *Industrialisation and social change in South Africa: African class formation, culture, and consciousness, 1870–1930* (London, 1982); Shula Marks, *Reluctant rebellion: the 1906–8 disturbances in Natal* (Oxford, 1970), and *The ambiguities of dependence in South Africa: class, nationalism and the state in twentieth-century Natal* (Johannesburg, 1986); Ruth Edgecombe, 'Sir Marshall Clarke and the abortive attempt to "Basutolandize" Zululand, 1893–7', *Journal of Natal and Zulu History*, vol. 1, 1978; John Laband, 'Dick Addison: the role of a British official during the disturbances in the Ndwandwe district of Zululand, 1887–1889' (MA, University of Natal, Pietermaritzburg, 1980); and John Laband and Paul Thompson, 'The reduction of Zululand, 1878–1904', in Duminy and Guest (eds), *Natal and Zululand*.

2. Wolseley's address, quoted by J. S. Marwick in *Natal Mercury*, 5/1/1917. See also Guy, *Destruction of the Zulu kingdom*, p. 69.

3. Memoranda by Shepstone, 1887–88, quoted in Edgecombe, 'Sir Marshall Clarke', p. 44; and Laband, 'Dick Addison', p. 10. Though Wolseley's 'settlement' clearly embodied Shepstonist principles, Shepstone himself was not fully satisfied with its terms. See Laband and Thompson, 'The reduction of Zululand'.

4. For the 1906 rebellion, Dinuzulu's role, and the subsequent treason trial, see Marks, *Reluctant rebellion*, (this is the most authoritative source); Brookes and Webb, *Natal*; L. Swart, 'The work of Harriette Emily Colenso in relationship to Dinuzulu kaCetshwayo culminating in the treason trial of 1908–9' (unpublished MA thesis, University of Natal, Durban, 1968), chs 3–6; D. Hemson, 'Class consciousness and migrant workers: dockworkers of Durban' (unpublished Ph.D. thesis, University of Warwick, 1979), pp. 121–23; and, for a Zulu view, Magema Fuze, *The black people and whence they came* (Pietermaritzburg, 1979), ch. 64.

5. Guy, *Destruction of the Zulu kingdom*, p. 18.

6. The word 'tribal' used here is a descriptive term, like the Zulu term *ibhinca*, which in its narrowest sense refers to those Africans who still wore traditional clothing. More broadly, 'tribal' refers to those who still lived on the land, herding and cultivating according to the custom of their ancestors, and were still closely enmeshed in the social and cultural traditions of pre-colonial African

society. It does not, however, suggest that the lives of 'tribal' Africans had been left fundamentally unaffected by the colonial order, 'indirect rule' and industrialisation.

7. See Henry Slater, 'Land, labour and capital in Natal: the Natal Land and Colonisation Company, 1860–1948', *Journal of African History*, vol. 16, 1975, pp. 257–83, and 'Changing pattern', pp. 148–70; Guy, *Destruction of the Zulu kingdom*, especially pp. 231–46, and 'Destruction and reconstruction', pp. 167–94; and John Lambert, 'From independence to rebellion: African society in crisis, *c.*1880–1910', in Duminy and Guest (eds), *Natal and Zululand*. See also Colin Bundy, *The rise and fall of the South African peasantry* (London, 1979), ch. 6.

8. See T. R. H. Davenport and K. S. Hunt, *The right to the land* (Cape Town, 1974), p. 29; and H. Rogers, *Native administration in the Union of South Africa* (Johannesburg, 1933), pp. 96–97, 284–88.

9. Hemson, 'Dockworkers of Durban', p. 53 and Fig. 2.1.

10. Blue Book on Native Affairs, U17–1911, pp. 43 (quotation), 15, 20, and 33. Other sources for this summary of the period 1907–10 were Natal Archives Depot, Chief Native Commissioner's Correspondence 1910–1919 (hereafter CNC) 144; memorandum by J. Y. Gibson, DNC for Zululand, 5/8/1914, pp. 4–6; and *Natal Mercury*, 5/1/1917. The four chiefs appointed to administer the Usuthu were: 1. Mciteki kaZibhebhu, acting chief of the Mandlakazi during the minority of Bokwe. 2. Mpikanina kaZiwedu, one of Dinuzulu's uncles, who had broken with Dinuzulu during the disturbances of 1888. 3. Moya kaMgojana, a descendant of Zwide of the Ndwandwe whom Shaka had expelled from Zululand. Mgojana had been one of Wolseley's chiefs under the 1879 'settlement', and was killed by the Usuthu in 1888 as an adherent of Zibhebhu. 4. Mkandumba kaTshanibezwe, a grandson of Mnyamana Buthelezi. The latter had been chief counsellor to Cetshwayo, but had fallen out with Dinuzulu in 1888. Mkandumba was soon to be sentenced to death for murder, and was replaced as chief by his brother, Acting Chief Muzimubi.

11. Blue Book on Native Affairs, U17–1911, p. 45; *Daily News*, 2/6/1910; and Swart, 'Harriette Colenso', p. 151. See also Killie Campbell Africana Library (hereafter KCAL), Zulu Society Collection, MS 16665, Zulu Society's transcription of Maphelu kaMkhosana Zungu's verbal account of his life and Zulu history, n.d. but evidently 1930s (hereafter Account of Maphelu), pp. 96–97. I worked from a private translation of this document, but all page references refer to the original Zulu typescript. Maphelu had been one of Cetshwayo's most trusted aides, and had served with distinction during the Anglo-Zulu War. After 1884 he became a close confidant of Dinuzulu. For a biographical outline of Maphelu, see MS 16662, notes by Zulu Society secretary, C. Mpanza, n.d.

12. See Blue Book on Native Affairs, U17–1911, pp. 35, 336–37; and CNC 54, 97/1912, Acting Magistrate, Nkandla to DNC, Eshowe, 8/2/1912. A Cape-based Xhosa newspaper expressed the more widespread African opinion that Dinuzulu's release was to Botha's 'lasting credit', and that Botha stopped short of repatriating Dinuzulu only to appease 'the susceptibilities of [Botha's] Natal enemies'. *Imvo*, 21/10/1913, Dinuzulu's obituary.

13. *Plymouth News*, 3/6/1910. A cutting of this report, along with cuttings from the other British newspapers mentioned, is located in KCAL, Miss (Harriette Emily) Colenso Newscutting Book, vol. 2, ref. 20026, pp. 121–26.

14. See, for example, *The Star*, 18/10/1913.

15. The suggestion here is that Dinuzulu had been sold by the Zulu people into the hands of foreigners. Account of Maphelu, p. 95; and Fuze, *Black people*, p. 145.

16. CNC 144, 1985/1913, notes of interview between SNA and Magistrate, Middelburg, and Mankulumana, three headmen of the late Dinuzulu, the Revd Twala, and Miss Colenso, 12/12/1913.

17. See Natal Archives Depot, Chief Native Commissioner's Correspondence 1919–1950 (hereafter CNC PMB) 72, 57/29, map and notes of Emakhosini, 1910; KCAL, H.C. Lugg Collection (hereafter MS LUG) 1.09, MS 1406, notes by Charles Mpanza; and A.T. Bryant, *Olden times in Zululand and Natal* (London, 1949), pp. 35, 45. Some Zulu kings were not buried here, on account of civil disturbance at the time of their deaths.

18. CNC 144, 1985/1913, Pixley kaI. Seme to Dr Bok, Prime Minister's private secretary, 8/12/1913.

19. CNC 144, 1985/1913, report of Socwatsha and Nongejeni, Natal NAD political intelligence messengers, 28/11/1913 (hereafter Report of Socwatsha and Nongejeni), reporting Chief Moya's (p. 6) and Chief Mciteki's (p. 8) accounts of Miss Colenso's statements at Dinuzulu's funeral.

20. Nobamba means 'stronghold of unity' and 'preserver'. MS LUG 1.09, MS 1406, notes recorded by Mpanza, annotated by H.C. Lugg.

21. Report of Socwatsha and Nongejeni, p. 1. This report, together with Account of Maphelu, pp. 98–103, were my principal sources for the events surrounding the arrival of Dinuzulu's body at Vryheid, and the funeral procession to Nobamba. Other sources are noted in the text.

22. University of Natal, Durban, Department of Zulu Language and Literature, unpublished collection of Zulu praise poems recorded by James Stuart and translated by D. McK. Malcolm and A.T. Cope.

23. 'Musihelu' is a Zulu corruption of 'Miss Harriette'. She was also known as 'uDhledhlwe' ('the staff') because in the later years of her father Bishop Colenso's life, she sat at his right hand, acting as interpreter and secretary during his interviews with Zulu. See Account of Maphelu, p. 99; KCAL, Harriette Colenso Collection, ref. 13083, notes on the life of Harriette Colenso by Alice Werner, 1932, p. 12; Shula Marks, 'Harriette Colenso and the Zulus, 1874–1913', *Journal of African History*, vol. 4, 1963; and Pers. Comm., Princess Magogo kaDinuzulu, KwaPhindangene, Zululand, 6/1/1982, Part I, p. 3. (All page references to interviews conducted by the author refer to the transcripts now stored in KCAL.)

24. KCAL, J.S. Marwick Papers (hereafter MS MAR) 2.08.1, File 6, KCM 2551 (a), Marwick's testimonial; 2.08.4, KCM 3074, unsigned noteform biography, *c.* 1918; and 2.08.5, File 7, KCM 2747, Mr Chamberlain to Sir W.F.

Hely-Hutchinson, 24/11/1899. See also Brookes and Webb, *Natal*, p.204. Regarding the origin of the name 'Muhle', Pers. Comm., Commandant S. Bourquin, Manager of Durban Municipal Native Administration Department 1954–1973, 1981; and MS MAR 2.08.5, File 7, KCM 2576 (b), 'Marwick's memorable march – a story of early Natal written by Mrs Edith Clark from records in her possession', n.d.

25. In approximately 1915 Marwick and Morris registered, as co-directors, an agency to supply labour on contract to the Native Recruiting Corporation. MS MAR, File 21, KCM 3155 (a). Although the magistrate at Eshowe in the mid-1920s, A.D. Graham, was known as 'Zithulele', it seems unlikely that it was he to whom Maphelu referred in this context. See *Natal Mercury*, 6/5/1927.

26. Account of Maphelu, p.99.

27. CNC 144, 1985/1913, notes of interview between CNC and Mnyaiza kaNdabuko, 19/2/1914.

28. CNC 254, 1557/1916, Detached Assistant Magistrate, Babanango to Magistrate, Vryheid, 21/9/1916; and CNC PMB 81, 58/7/1, H.M. Taberer, Native Labour Adviser, Johannesburg, to Major H.S. Cooke, Director of Native Labour, Johannesburg, 4/3/1930.

29. R.V. Selope-Thema, 'The life of the late Dr Pixley Seme', *Drum*, July 1953; Carter/Karis Collection (University of South Africa microfilm) (hereafter CK), Reel 14 A, various documents catalogued between 2:X514:47 and 2:X515:96; and CNC 144, 1985/1913, notes of interview between SNA and Mankulumana, 12/12/1913. For Seme's role at the funeral, see Account of Maphelu, p.101.

30. Account of Maphelu, p.99.

31. CNC 144, 1985/1913, Magistrate, Vryheid to CNC, 12/11/1913.

Part One: 1913–1925

1

Zulu society after the Act of Union, 1910

Four years after the establishment of the Union of South Africa, and at approximately the same time as Dinuzulu's funeral, the imperial commentator, Sir Rider Haggard, toured Zululand. He did so in the company of J.Y. Gibson (District Native Commissioner for Zululand) and James Stuart (formerly Assistant Secretary for Native Affairs in the Natal government), both dedicated recorders of Zulu history and both fluent in Zulu. In the course of the tour, Haggard recorded his impressions of the country and its people, comparing it to the Zululand he had known when he had last visited in 1876. Ideas of 'Social Darwinism' had been popular in some late-Victorian intellectual circles, and the patronising and elitist attitudes that flowed from them found expression in Haggard's essay. The essay's observations on economic changes and the evolution of new social divisions in Zulu society are nonetheless illuminating, and they form a useful starting point and framework for further comment.

Overall, Rider Haggard's impressions were not positive: 'Since the year 1879', he wrote in 1914, 'the history of the Zulus has been a long tale of misfortune'. In seeking to identify factors that had contributed to this misfortune, Haggard drew a sharp distinction between the policies of the Colonial Office in London and those of the Natal colonial government. It was the settler government that had been responsible for imposing the £1 poll tax on the African population (the spark for the 1906 rebellion), he recorded, and, following the report of the 1902–4 Zululand Lands Delimitation Commission, the settler government had declared 40 per cent of Zululand 'open' for white ownership.

> [In 1897] Zululand and its people were handed over to Natal instead of being allowed to remain under the direct control of the Imperial Government like Basutoland, which, of course, they would have preferred, as it is a matter of common knowledge that self-governing

colonies look at their responsibilities to native races from a very different standpoint to that which has always been adopted by the Home Government.[1]

Focusing attention on the problem of Zulu land loss, it deeply concerned Haggard that, since he had first known the Zulu, 'about two thirds of territory . . . including many of the best lands' had passed into 'the hands of white men, Boers and English together'. He then referred to the new 1913 Natives' Land Act, the first piece of land legislation to be passed by the Union government. The 1913 Act would be particularly onerous to those Zulu whose lands had passed into the private ownership of white men, he stressed, because it laid down that in future all African tenants on 'white land' would have to be 'labour tenants', performing labour service for the landowner, and that all other types of African tenancy on white-owned land would be phased out.[2] These other types of tenancy to which Haggard alluded fell under the generic term 'squatting'. 'Squatters' were African tenants who did not supply labour but instead paid for their tenure, either in the form of a cash rent or in the form of agricultural produce. From the point of view of the African tenant, squatting was considerably more attractive than labour tenancy because of the greater independence it permitted.

Labour tenants, in return for the labour service that they performed, received grazing rights for a few head of cattle or goats, a small area of arable land, some rations and sometimes a small amount of cash. Generally, however, labour tenants were trapped in a cycle of rural poverty and exploitation, and to cover their subsistence needs they depended heavily on cash earned in urban areas during the non-service period. In pursuit of its objective to ensure that Africans on white farms were henceforth farm labourers, the 1913 Act laid down that each landowner should keep only as many tenants as his need for farm labour warranted − all 'surplus' tenants he was called on to evict.[3]

As the Union government's first step towards a uniform South African 'native policy', the 1913 Act established the principle of territorial segregation. The deeper purpose of the 1913 Act, however, was not to eliminate the mingling of black and white in the rural areas, but to reduce the ability of Africans to maintain rural economic independence, and so force them to become wage labourers either on white farms or in the urban areas (mainly the gold mines). Of the two most influential capitalist sectors of the South African economy − agriculture and gold mining − it was the former that had become implacably opposed to squatting (especially large-scale 'Kaffir farming' by absentee white landlords) and African land purchase, since this locked up labour and denied it to white farms.[4] John Dube, president of the SANNC and a political figure of special influence in Natal and Zululand, perceptively observed that

> it is abundantly clear to us . . . that the authorities know perfectly well that the natives cannot leave private lands entirely . . . the Bill simply aims at compelling the natives to say they will rather remain on the [white] farms and live under those irksome conditions than to leave the [white] farms . . .[5]

Zulu living on white-owned land were primarily located in Northern Natal, which had been the Boer New Republic before being incorporated into Natal after the Anglo-Boer War. No African reserves, on the Shepstonist model, had been demarcated in this region; white landlords were consequently able to impose high demands on their African tenants, either in the form of cash, produce or labour, and hence the cost of Zulu land tenure in Northern Natal compared very unfavourably with the Zululand reserves. This higher cost was reflected socially in the considerably higher rate of labour migration from Northern Natal in comparison with the adjacent Zululand reserves, which were ecologically similar and equally distant from employment centres.[6]

During the nineteenth century and even into the early years of the twentieth century, rural capital in Northern Natal, as in Natal proper, had been more interested in land speculation than in the development of commercial agriculture. Large tracts had fallen into the hands of absentee landlords who engaged in what became known as 'Kaffir farming' by renting their holdings out to African squatters in order to gain a return on their investments, rather than working the land themselves. Around the turn of the century, however, the rapidly growing market for agricultural produce, generated by the development of new urban centres and the mining industry, stimulated among Northern Natal's white landowners a change-over from 'Kaffir farming' to commercial agricultural production. Thus arose an increased demand for farm labour, but since Natal's white farmers were generally undercapitalised they were unable to compete with the wages offered by the gold mines. Hence they depended on labour tenants for a labour supply, and their policy was to attempt to undermine African options to labour tenancy.[7]

The move against rent-paying squatters in Northern Natal, either by evicting them or by transforming them into labour tenants, was nonetheless an uneven process. Renting out rather than farming the land remained an attractive option for many landowners − and they raised objections to the 1913 Act for this reason. The District Native Commissioner (DNC) for

Northern Natal reported in 1910 that African squatters were sometimes paying the 'exorbitant' rate of £5 per hut (hut tax in the reserves was 14 shillings) as rental on white farms.[8] Thus, as the magistrate at Vryheid observed in 1915, certain landowners 'really do not want the rent-payers to turn to labourers'.[9] It is significant that W.H. Beaumont, the only Natalian on the Natives Lands Commission (appointed to report on the implementation of the 1913 Act) submitted a minority report in 1916, stating that there had been 'no [unanimous] demand in Natal for the enforcement of a Squatters Act or for any further segregation of the natives'.[10] Although rentier interests were strong in Northern Natal, white landowners there generally made increasing labour demands on their tenants as commercial agriculture expanded in the region after Union. Those tenants who were determined to avoid the constraints of labour service obligations were subject to increasing rents – or eviction. The 1913 Act accelerated these processes. Indeed, it imposed the state hut tax on squatters (previously exempt) on top of their rental commitments. This on its own reduced Zulu alternatives to labour tenancy. Especially for Zulu on white farm land, the overall impact of the 1913 Act was increased subjection, poverty and insecurity.

In the wake of the 1913 Act, the Natal NAD became so concerned about the insecurity of Zulu tenure on white farms that it sometimes felt compelled to intervene on the Zulu tenant's behalf. This was particularly so in regard to the NAD's employees, the officially recognised chiefs, whose political status and influence over their followers stood to be undermined by unsympathetic and authoritarian landlords. Because Chief Kambi kaHamu Zulu of the Ngenetsheni, whose ward in the Ngotshe district included 1250 homesteads, was 'being harassed by his landlord', the NAD stepped in and provided him with a section of government land on which to live.[11] Similarly, once Solomon kaDinuzulu Zulu had been officially recognised as chief of the Usuthu, as Dinuzulu had been prior to the 1906 rebellion, the NAD also intervened on behalf of the Zulu royal family itself. The issue of rental arrears for the two important royal residences of Nobamba and Zibindini, which were situated on the farm 'Koningsdal' owned by S.B. Buys, was a continuing cause for litigation during the early years of Solomon's chieftainship. In 1916, Buys issued Solomon with a final notice to vacate the twenty-seven huts that comprised Nobamba and Zibindini, and a court order for £100 which had allegedly accrued as unpaid rent. When the case came to court a year later and the judgment was made against Solomon, however, the CNC and SNA quickly arranged for the government to settle the Zulu royal family's rental arrears as well as the costs of the case. The NAD moreover prevailed on Buys to withdraw his notice of eviction, to sign a document formally defining the terms of Solomon's tenure, and even to reduce the rent from £3 to £2 per hut per annum.

Solomon's altercations with Buys represented only one example of his problems with land tenure in the Vryheid district. In 1917, Anton Potgieter, a rentier landlord with property adjoining that of Buys, petitioned the government to induce the Zulu royal family to settle up for cultivating part of the farm 'Welgekozen'. The farm had been ploughed without payment, he complained, and he added that he was a 'poor man and should like to live as a white man'. To counteract the administrative difficulties that ensued when an NAD chief experienced such problems of tenure, the NAD initiated arrangements to purchase a number of farms on which to settle Solomon and his dependants. The issue eventually faded when Solomon took up permanent residence at Mahashini, one of Dinuzulu's old residences, which lay in the Zululand reserves in the Nongoma district.[12]

For Zulu 'commoners', on whose behalf the NAD was less inclined to intervene, the position was worse. They were subject to a variety of obligations; the state exacted hut tax, while the landlords required labour service and sometimes a share of agricultural produce as well as rentals for huts and for arable and grazing land. But the increasing insecurity of tenure itself was yet more disruptive than the increasing costs of tenure. In 1914 Chief Nkantini kaSiteku Zulu, a grandson of Mpande who lived on reserve lands in the Emtonjaneni district, reported that some of his ward lived

> on what is known as Proviso 'B' [Babanango sub-district]. We are troubled because we are on private lands. We who are in charge of tribes do not know what to do with our natives because they are turned off one private farm and not allowed to go to another. Having been conquered we are as the Government's fowls and we therefore look to the Government to give us a piece of land on which we can go.[13]

For those who remained as labour tenants, the quality of life deteriorated. Shortly after the 1913 Act, the Babanango sub-district became known as 'Ekuhlupekeni' – the place of trouble. At a meeting with the CNC in 1920, every chief's representative from this area complained of the conditions of tenure on white farms. One observed that the 'Natives [are] loyal – they pay taxes' but was dismayed that they also had to make payments to their landlords for their huts. Chief Zombode's representative lamented that landlords were 'turning people off farms, not being satisfied with work and rents rendered to them by tenants'. 'We shall never get accustomed to tenure on farms, Sir', another said; 'Our children work and are not paid. Even our chiefs are in the same position'. Another added, 'We cry continually, trusting ever in our rulers'. To these lamentations the CNC 'responded suitably' and 'emphasized the need for adherence to contracts'.[14]

Zulu resident in Zululand (rather than Northern Natal), who had access to land in the Shepstonist 'African reserves', were less immediately afflicted by the 1913 Act. Indeed, the 1913 Act confirmed the existing boundaries of the Zululand reserves, as marked out by the 1902–4 Zululand Lands Delimitation Commission, and land there continued to be held, distributed and administered by Zulu chiefs on the basis of communal tribal tenure. However, the 1913 Act's effects were felt insofar as reserve dwellers would henceforth be much less able to rent or purchase additional – and often more fertile – land beyond reserve boundaries. But most importantly, the number of evictions from white-owned land greatly increased after the 1913 Act resulting in an influx of evicted squatters into the reserves. In 1914, chiefs in the Zululand reserves complained of increasing land congestion – Chief Mfungelwa of Eshowe district, for example, flatly observed that 'natives have been turned off private farms and we are now overcrowded'. More graphically, Headman Nfuzewa stated that 'the [Zulu] country is being taken up by farms. We are living on the edge of cliffs'.[15] Complaints were especially strong in the Eshowe, Nkandla and Emtonjaneni reserves which were absorbing evictions from both the expanding sugar estates on the coast and the white farms in Northern Natal. As the reserves became increasingly congested, they became increasingly unable to provide for the subsistence needs of their inhabitants. Consequently, Zulu in the reserves became more dependent on outside sources of income – primarily money earned by migrant labourers on the gold mines.

*   *   *   *   *

Among those Zulu who lived outside the reserves, there were some who were neither labour tenants nor squatters on white-owned land: a small but significant group owned the land on which they lived. African land purchase had begun in Natal proper as long ago as the 1860s, and had become an important means through which Africans could seriously set about cultivating crops for the open market, thus avoiding entering into labour relationships and remaining economically independent. Some African landowners even achieved a certain prosperity. The significance of African land purchase, however, went beyond purely material considerations: the concept of private land ownership was fostered in the African population by white missionaries, and formed part of a broader process of 'converting' African people to the religious and secular values of European civilisation. Thus, while residents on African mission lands absorbed Christianity, they simultaneously tended to discard their ancestors' secular values, material culture, technology, production techniques and economic practices in favour of those of European origin. Hoes gave way to oxen and ploughs, round huts to rectangular upright houses, subsistence agriculture to agriculture geared to the production of a marketable surplus, and the hierarchical yet communal ethos of tribal society gave way to one of individual advancement and accumulation.

The kholwa (Christian African) landowning establishment, in many senses an establishment of 'black Englishmen', represented the core of a new and self-consciously distinct social group in Zulu-speaking society. This emerging African middle class included not only landowning commercial farmers, however, but also ecclesiastics, teachers, lawyers, interpreters, clerks, traders, craftsmen and rent-paying cash-crop cultivators. Through the church and literacy, the kholwa were in contact with a broad set of beliefs in which the importance attached to Christian faith for spiritual life was matched in social and political life by the importance attached to the values of Victorian liberalism. Christianity and 'civilisation', on the industrialised model, were held to be inseparable. In this world, 'tribalism' and pre-industrial traditions were rejected as outdated if not barbaric, and moreover as contrary to 'progressive' and 'respectable' aspirations. Kholwa political priorities, expressed through representative organisations like the Natal Native Congress (NNC, formed in 1900), were the extension of the franchise, freehold land tenure, and overall their inclusion as full members in a non-racial South African middle class.[16]

The more established African kholwa communities were based in Natal proper, the territory of the original Colony of Natal, south of the Thukela river and outside the direct domain of the old Zulu kingdom. Similar communities developed later – in the early years of the twentieth century – among the Zulu north of the Thukela, who until 1879 had been subjects of a politically and economically independent Zulu state.

When the 1902–4 Zululand Lands Delimitation Commission set aside 40 per cent of Zululand as land available for purchase on the open market, it did so on the understanding that Zulu 'in common with other British subjects will be allowed to purchase if they wish to do so . . . we do not see how they can in common fairness be prohibited from purchasing land, notwithstanding the fact that reserves are now being delimited for their occupation'.[17] In practice, however, the purchaseable land went into the hands of white settlers predominantly of British descent, and opportunities for Zulu to own land in Zululand barely existed. Nonetheless, by 1910 a kholwa community at Eshowe, the colonial administrative centre of Zululand, had already inaugurated a 'closer settlement' scheme to promote the development of a 'progressive' township of Zulu landowners.[18] And, as further evidence of kholwa development in Zululand, two hundred Zulu from the Emtonjaneni district, 'many from the mission station', met to declare their displeasure with the 1913 Act's provisions against African land purchase.[19]

In comparison with Zululand, the development of kholwa communities in Northern Natal was more advanced. There, since the turn of the century, a small but confident Zulu middle class had grown rapidly. This was substantially because in Northern Natal, immediately following the Anglo-Boer War and the incorporation of the territory into Natal, Zulu had been able to buy small properties. By 1905, for example, there was a growing settlement of Zulu landowners three miles to the east of Vryheid, all of whom held their land on an individual title-deed basis. A syndicate had been formed to raise sufficient capital to buy property, which was subsequently divided up as individual allotments. Most of the residents of Vryheid East Township were employed in the town of Vryheid, though some were cash-crop cultivators.[20]

The fact of individual land ownership was in itself a significant indication of Zulu social change. In pre-conquest Zululand all land in theory belonged to the Zulu king, who delegated land distribution and use down through the kingdom's chiefly hierarchy. At a local level, individual Zulu had rights to certain areas of land, but these rights were given by the local chief who also had the authority to revoke them. In practice, land was thus held by the local inhabitants, collectively represented by their chief, on the basis of communal tenure. These notions of land tenure continued to operate in the Zululand reserves under the Shepstonist policy of indirect rule. The notion of individual and private ownership was a European one – and this was not the only European notion that distinguished the residents of Vryheid East Township from the Zulu rank and file.

Speaking about the kholwa community at Vryheid amongst others, the 1910 NAD report for Northern Natal recorded that 'this class has adopted European clothing, and they live in square houses, divided into rooms and suitably furnished . . . they have separated themselves as much as possible from the raw native.' In the same year, 12 per cent of all Zulu marriages in the Vryheid district were Christian marriages.[21] The relationship between Christianity, land ownership and westernisation was very evident in Vryheid East Township. William Washington Ndhlovu, an 'exempted' Zulu (i.e. exempted from the 'Natal Code' of African customary law, and assimilated into Natal colonial law), gave an illuminating description of the settlement in 1915:

> I think it is a good thing for the native people to have such a place in which we can make our homes. We have planted trees and put up

respectable houses to live in, and we have tried to improve our holdings in every possible way . . . We have one Lutheran Church, which was erected some two years ago. The Wesleyan Methodist Church are also putting up a small church . . . The majority are Christians and hardly without exception they are Zulus.

It was Ndhlovu's belief that the system of 'individual tenure' was essential if the 'progressive native' were to reap all the benefits that education had made due to him.[22]

African land purchase was, however, strongly opposed by white commercial farming interests in Natal – as elsewhere in the Union. Land purchase was a means by which Africans could free themselves from both labour and rental obligations to white landlords; and, moreover, African cash-crop cultivators, who mainly used family labour rather than hired labour, were able to produce for the market at a price with which white farmers found difficulty in competing. For rural whites, however, the fact that Africans could successfully compete in the open markets for land and agricultural produce seemed to be not simply an economic threat. There seemed also to be a deeper, more emotional, element to colonist insecurity in the face of African competition, as was obliquely expressed in a statement made by a contemporary Natal farmer. Before the 1913 Act, he said, he had been so much in 'fear of being forced off his land by powerful Native Syndicates who were committed to buying up as much land as possible' that he had considered 'yielding' and leaving the country. Xenophobic sentiments such as these were also to be found in Northern Natal, among the Boer settlers.[23]

Reflecting the interests of white farmers, the 1913 Act prohibited Africans from purchasing land outside the reserves except where the land in question was already in African hands. Otherwise, applications for African land purchase could only be granted by the Governor-General, and permission was not readily granted. In the wake of the 1913 Act, there was a desperate unanimity on the land issue in African kholwa circles throughout the Province of Natal. Giving evidence before official boards of enquiry in 1917, the province's leading kholwa, including the Revd John Dube (greater Durban), the Revd Abner Mtimkulu (Pietermaritzburg), Chief Stephen Mini (Edendale), Chief Martin Luthuli (Groutville) and W.W. Ndhlovu (Vryheid) all forcefully denounced the severe legislative restrictions recently visited on African land ownership.[24]

The clampdown on African land purchase in Natal after the 1913 Act, coupled with the increasing tendency among white farmers to demand labour rather than rent from their African tenants, tended to stifle the further development of the Zulu-speaking middle class. While those who had already bought land and had entered 'respectable' professions (for example in the church or education) remained relatively secure, the kholwa generation that came of age after Union found difficulty in realising the ambitions that a mission education had inspired. This led to profound tensions within kholwa communities, not only in Natal but also elsewhere in the Union where similar processes were at work, as the insecurities and frustrations of the new and marginalised kholwa generation were given political expression.

*   *   *   *   *

In his essay on the state of Zululand, Rider Haggard was struck by the paucity of cattle in Zululand. 'The great herds are no more,' he observed.[25] This he ascribed to two successive scourges: herds had had only six years in which to recover from the devastation of rinderpest (1897–98) before east coast fever swept Natal and Zululand and lingered until after Union. Zululand had, moreover, been struck by a severe drought in 1912.

At the time of Union, the DNC for Zululand reported that the 'deadly course' of east coast fever had left Zululand 'pitifully denuded', and the DNC for Northern Natal similarly reported that his region was 'almost depleted of its cattle'.[26] Local magistrates and the Zulu held that the disease was a consequence of the game laws which prohibited the hunting of wild game.[27] In the low-lying regions of Zululand, which had been densely populated during the nineteenth century, the spread of east coast fever had been accompanied by the spread of malaria; the latter was becoming endemic on the coast as the sugar plantations expanded there.[28] The double impact of east coast fever and malaria caused an efflux of Zulu from the stricken areas to the healthier uplands. This, coupled with the influx of evicted tenants to the latter area, exacerbated land congestion in the early years of Union. Explaining the high rate of human and livestock mortality and homestead removals within his district, the magistrate at Mahlabatini told the Natives Lands Commission in 1915 that the lower reaches of Mahlabatini 'had gradually become uninhabitable. First of all it is the loss of their cattle, and then they get the fever one after another.'[29]

Local officials pointed to one directly economic consequence of the loss of cattle: some homesteads were no longer able to plough, and could not cultivate the same acreage as efficiently by hand with hoes. On account of smaller crop yields, Zulu cash income was being stretched to cover the purchase of food from local trading stores as well as the payment of rents and taxes. This was particularly true in Northern Natal. Cash income alone could not cover the deficiencies of Zulu homestead production during the drought of 1912, however. The NAD thus permitted homesteads to kill a quota of protected game each week for subsistence purposes.[30]

Because cattle played such a vital role in both the economic and social life of the Zulu people, the devastation of the large cattle herds had pervasive consequences. Haggard referred to two of these. First, 'considerable infant mortality' because of the diminishing availability of milk – a staple nutriment.[31] The accelerated rate of infant mortality had concerned local officials for some years before Haggard's visit in 1914. While they agreed that cattle loss and malnutrition were primarily responsible, they identified another cause which deserves incidental mention here: venereal disease. As labour migration from Zululand and Northern Natal accelerated from the end of the nineteenth century, syphilis spread through the countryside 'caused principally by natives who have been working on the mines in Johannesburg'. The Zulu term *isimpantsholo*, describing venereal disorders, dates from the first years of the twentieth century. In 1910, syphilis in Zululand and Northern Natal had reached 'epidemic' proportions – and Zulu toddlers were already suffering the consequences of secondary infection.[32]

Second, Haggard reported that *lobolo* (brideprice) was now being exchanged in the form of money rather than cattle. This new development, he observed, was detrimental to the Zulu economy: money was liable to be spent, whereas cattle were a more permanent form of wealth. The transfer of *lobolo* from the family of the groom to that of the bride was only confirmed and concluded when the wife had borne children for her husband. In hard terms of property exchange, *lobolo* was a consideration for the bride's potential to produce children rather than for the bride herself. If the marriage broke up or the wife proved to be infertile, *lobolo* was refundable. Haggard recounted the situation in which his personal servant, Mazooku, found himself when his daughter's marriage dissolved. Being in difficulties following the death of his cattle from east coast fever, Mazooku had spent the £10 he had received as *lobolo*, and was unable to repay it. He was on the point of being imprisoned under the provisions of the Native Code, as applied through the courts, when Haggard intervened.[33]

In the hands of the overwhelming majority of the Zulu, money was only useful as a medium of exchange. By contrast – and apart from their role as a medium of exchange – cattle produced valuable by-products (milk, hide, dung for fertilizer), could be used for ploughing, and could be slaughtered for food. Moreover, cattle could reproduce themselves and thus they were a potentially generative form of wealth. Money, to the Zulu, was not: capitalist enterprise was extraneous to Zulu cultural traditions. The change in the form of *lobolo* from cattle to cash (a gradual and uneven process) exacerbated the economic difficulties in which its origins lay. It simultaneously reflected the decline of homestead production and a greater Zulu dependence on monetary wealth. Furthermore, since some young men were now having to earn money in order to marry, a greater need was imposed upon them to divert their labour to the industrial and commercial sectors of the economy. The outlook for independent production in Zululand at the time of Union was bleak.

The economic effects of the change in the form of *lobolo* describe only part of its impact on Zulu society. At a deeper and more subtle level, the consequences were neither solely economic nor uniformly experienced throughout Zulu society. H.C. Lugg, veteran native commissioner, Zulu linguist and scholar, emphasised that the custom of *lobolo* was not the mere exchange of property: 'the Natives have always appreciated the wider implications of the term [*lobolo*], and, to avoid confusion, refer to the cattle actually handed over as *amabeka*.'[34] As the more visible features of the *lobolo* custom changed, so too did its 'wider implications'. The changing social significance of *lobolo* both reflected the existence of important social changes and promoted their further development. In an attempt to specify the nature of these social changes, it will first be necessary to describe the social significance of cattle and *lobolo* in traditional Zulu society.

Everyday social and economic life in the Zulu kingdom effectively centred on cattle, since by architectural tradition the individual huts of the Zulu homestead were grouped around the central cattle enclosure (*isibaya*). The importance that the Zulu attached to cattle was reflected culturally in the rituals associated with their care, their sacrificial uses, and the pride with which they were held. In language, moreover, the men of the homestead could call on an extensive specialised vocabulary to describe the individual qualities of the heads of cattle that they tended. In accordance with the *lobolo* custom, it was through the transfer of cattle from the homestead of the groom to the homestead of the bride that marriage was formally settled, so enabling a young man and wife to establish their economic independence with their own homestead and family. In the same way, a man already married (*umnumzana* – homestead head) could increase the number of his wives and children, and hence the size of the productive community under his authority. Indeed, if homesteads were the productive units on which Zulu life was based, wives and children provided the homestead with productive labour. Cattle, as *lobolo*, were the way in which this labour and these productive units were given substance, and were thus essential elements in the process of production in the community. At a political level, moreover, the exchange of cattle between 'patron' and 'client' underpinned the hierarchy of authority – and since the daughters of a chief commanded more *lobolo* cattle than those of commoners, the material foundations of the chief's political authority was perpetuated. Generally, the size of a homestead's herds offered a clear reflection of its social and political status, and its material wealth. As the principal form of storable wealth in Zulu society, it was cattle that were passed down through the generations, from father to son, to perpetuate the lineage and ensure its material well-being.[35]

The devastation of the Zulu cattle herds around the turn of the century, combined with the pressures that the colonial order had placed on homestead production (primarily through requiring homesteads to raise cash to pay hut tax), was a development that necessitated considerable social adjustment. The changes that consequently took place within and around the custom of *lobolo*, which will be described below, acted as a mirror to the broader changes that were taking place in Zulu society at large.

In pre-conquest Zululand, young men had laboured in their fathers' homesteads, and when the time came for them to marry it was their fathers who supplied the *lobolo* cattle for them to do so. Subsequently, when hut tax was imposed after the annexation of Zululand, increasing numbers of young men sought wage labour to pay their fathers' hut tax, while their fathers fulfilled their side of the obligation by raising *lobolo* for their sons. From the late nineteenth century, however, when fathers found difficulty in providing *lobolo* for their sons because of cattle losses, young men began to prolong their periods of wage labour to earn sufficient money to buy their own cattle. The Natal Code (which was applied in Zululand after incorporation) laid down that a maximum of ten cattle could be demanded as *lobolo*, and allowed claims arising from *lobolo* disagreements to be heard before the courts. This maximum figure soon became the standard rate, and a heavy burden.

During the 1890s, the custom of *lobolo* gradually changed in three important ways. There developed a tendency for the bride's father to demand a fixed number of cattle, whereas previously the matter was subject to negotiation. Furthermore, these cattle were payable before the marriage took place, whereas the transfer of cattle had previously taken place over an extended period of time. Perhaps most importantly, the number of cattle doubled or even trebled. In the words of Jeff Guy, these changes signified an 'increasing concern for individual accumulation and a shift from a practice based on reciprocal obligation to one based on direct exchange', and the consequence was to sharpen the division between Zulu with property (cattle and daughters) and those without.[36]

It was in 1914 that Haggard observed the substitution of money for cattle in the *lobolo* transaction. This represented a further development of the changes identifiable in the 1890s. Indeed, it suggested that *lobolo* was being provided by the migrant labourer himself – and hence that the custom no longer depended on reciprocal obligations between the generations of father and son. In the light of the social implications that attached particularly to the transfer of cattle, it also suggested that the laterally integrative functions of the custom – the establishment of ties between the lineages of groom and bride – were weakening. Together, these developments both reflected and further promoted the decay of Zulu social integration. More broadly, the payment of *lobolo* in cash rather than cattle was testimony to the incursions made by the cash economy into Zulu society, and to Zulu acculturation generally.

The change in the purpose and significance of the *lobolo* transactions was to become increasingly marked in the early twentieth century. Although cattle were usually to be regarded as a necessary component of the property that changed hands as *lobolo* – particularly after cattle herds had recovered from the scourges of the period 1890–1910 – this did not signify a reversion to the original essence of the custom. Increasing emphasis was placed on the material value of the property that was exchanged, even at the cost of estranging rather than uniting the lineages between which the marriage was taking place. Such developments so concerned one NAD official in Zululand that, in 1927, he published an article contrasting the 'real Zulu customs' with innovations in the practice of *lobolo*. H.P. Braatvedt, the author of the article, was born the son of a Zululand missionary in the 1880s and had lived and worked among the Zulu all his life. He referred to a new practice which required a young man to present a beast to each of the prospective bride's parents at the time when the marriage proposal was made. Thereafter, the groom was required to send the bride numerous small presents, named *izibizo* ('things by which to summon') and 'mostly cash', in order to 'call' her to his home for the wedding ceremony. These *izibizo*, which amounted to as much as £10, ultimately went to the bride's father over and above the *lobolo* payment. These practices, Braatvedt argued, 'are utterly foreign to the real Zulu custom and are resented by the great majority of Zulus'.[37] This resentment arose because the value of the 'social contract' in the *lobolo* custom was being subordinated to the value of the property that was exchanged (daughters for cattle and cash). More specifically, it seems that the generation of fathers increasingly regarded the *lobolo* custom as a means whereby they could extract wealth from the generation of sons.

It was primarily the young men of Zululand who proceeded to distant labour centres to earn money. The periods that they served at these centres not only imparted a material basis for a certain independence, but also served to instil a new set of social values and aspirations derived from a different economy and a different society. The fissure that had developed between age and youth was expressed in the complaints made about the breakdown of morality and the lack of respect among youth for the authority and customs of the older generation. Something of a 'youth subculture' was developing in the reserves of Zululand. In 1910, the magistrate at Nongoma complained of 'beer-drinking parties' held by young men and women; this was an 'evil practice', he believed, since it lessened the authority of men over boys and increased female immorality.[38] In 1914, Haggard was struck by the desire 'among the young' in Zululand for European education − or 'the knowledge of how to make use of the resources of civilization'. This aspiration, he argued, had been inspired 'by observation in Johannesburg and other cities'. Haggard continued:

> Of course this is not the view of the older men who served under Cetywayo and perhaps under Panda. Indeed, one of these amused me much by a remark he made at an indaba I attended, which I quote as representative of the opinions of his generation. 'Our children try to be white', he said, alluding to the young Zulus and their aping of the garments and manners of the English, 'but they will never be'.[39]

The older generation was not only concerned about the social distance that they saw developing between their own generation and that of their sons, but complained that young men were disregarding their obligations to their fathers and dependants at home and were treating the money that they earned as their own. Labour migrants, Absolom Vilakazi has written, entered into employment contracts and earned money

> as individuals rather than as members of families or tribes. This insidious individualism which was being insinuated into their lives far away from the tribal setting and the close kinship of family group, began the destruction of the strong sense of social solidarity . . . There developed a new class of Africans . . . characterised by his absolute lack of respect for old traditions.[40]

The 'individualism' and 'lack of respect' that characterised this new class among African youth was a form of resistance to the demands of the homestead in its need to pay hut tax or, on white-owned land, to pay rent or provide labour. This resistance sometimes took a more radical form: the cutting of ties with 'home' and permanent residence in the urban areas. The disaffection of youth was especially evident among labour tenants. The labour tenancy contract was made with the homestead head, who was required to bind his sons to labour service. As a Northern Natal missionary commented, 'a boy deserts and gives up his home largely because he does not see that he has any chance . . . because he is not working directly for himself'.[41]

Chiefs, homestead heads and their dependants on the one hand, and government officials on the other, had common ground in opposing this new class of disaffected African youth – whose existence worsened economic fragility in the rural areas, and prejudiced the prompt payment of hut tax. In the drought year of 1912, during which homestead production over practically the whole of Zululand failed to provide for basic nutritional requirements, the DNC for Zululand lamented the 'growing tendency on the part of the Zulus proceeding to distant labour centres to entirely forget the claims of those dependent upon them at their homes . . . [and to] waste their substance to the detriment of their dependants.'[42] As representative of the Natal Native Affairs Department and Zululand Native Agent at the turn of the century, it was J.S. Marwick's job to ensure that wages were safely remitted to Natal and Zululand, and to trace tax defaulters. Between 1895 and 1899, the system he devised – described as a 'system of Native thrift' – reportedly secured the remittance of an average of £30 000 per annum to Natal. Significantly, Marwick was assisted by Sikonyela, previously *induna* to Mnyamana, chief of the Buthelezi.[43]

Marwick's later career contains further evidence of links between the Zulu 'establishment', labour agents and the state. When he evacuated Zulu labourers from Johannesburg on the outbreak of the Anglo-Boer War, he was assisted by Hlobeni Buthelezi who described himself as a descendant of Masiphula, chief counsellor to Mpande, and as 'well known to all the Zulus'.[44] In 1916, as newly appointed manager of the Durban Municipal Native Affairs Department, in charge of large numbers of migrant labourers, Marwick was assisted by Pika kaSiteku Zulu, a grandson of Mpande, who had been among those evacuated from Johannesburg by Marwick in 1899.[45] Similarly, in 1908 Colonel H.F. Trew of the Johannesburg police employed a grandson of Mpande known as 'Stephen Matambo', an authoritarian and violent character who had previously been a personal attendant to Lord Selbourne on the High Commissioner's train. Matambo was specifically enlisted to assist in the destruction of a Zulu gang in Pretoria whose 'speciality' was the robbery of mineworkers returning from the gold mines. This he did with such brutal efficiency that the police were shortly afterwards compelled to dismiss him.[46]

Overall, for the early twentieth century, a picture emerges of Zululand and Northern Natal becoming increasingly enmeshed as a dependent periphery in an expanding capitalist economy. With homestead production undermined by cattle disease, drought, rising cash needs, migrant labour and, most importantly, land shortage, the Zulu had become correspondingly more dependent on money for survival. Nonetheless, as this chapter has shown, the processes of rural impoverishment were by no means equally felt throughout the Zulu speaking population. Zulu society was adapting and restructuring, new social values were evolving, and new classes were in the process of formation.

$$* \quad * \quad * \quad * \quad *$$

During his tour of Zululand, Haggard attended a number of meetings between administrators and Zulu chiefs. His impression was that 'the people are crushed and bewildered'. He reported chiefs saying that they 'wander and wander' and 'have no head'.[47] In pre-conquest Zululand, it had been the Zulu king who was the Zulu 'head'. The king stood at the apex of the social and political structure, symbolised the unity of the Zulu people and the ancestral land on which they lived, ensured their spiritual well-being and acted as father and redistributor. Although the death of Dinuzulu had in effect restored the heir to the Zulu royal house to Zululand, the heir was no longer the Zulu king and Zululand could no longer naturally look to a single 'head'. Even among the tribal Zulu deep in the reserves, the image of the Zulu king had suffered in the prolonged series of civil wars between the Usuthu of Dinuzulu and the Mandlakazi of Zibhebhu. Furthermore, Zulu society was now being corroded by economic hardship and the evolution of new social divisions – developments which were transforming the role of tribal leaders themselves. There was the small, repressed, yet important aspirant middle class. And there was a tendency among the youth to become 'detribalised' and 'selfish'. Rather than having no 'head', one could suggest that the Zulu now had many heads: it was just that to the older and more conservative Zulu these 'heads' were neither as visible as the Zulu king had been, nor representative of anything with which they could identify.

Many of these social contradictions were expressed at Dinuzulu's funeral ceremony. A variety of individuals and representatives of social groups, both black and white, mixed together to pay their respects to the dead king and observe the succession of his heir. Particularly significant were royal individuals like Mnyaiza and Franz: while both were entrenched in the Zulu establishment by birth, they were also trading in and controlling Zulu labourers for the gold mines. Although many representatives of the old Zulu establishment still held positions of authority in Zululand as chiefs and *izinduna*, the continuities in form belied the shifts that had occurred in practice. This was subtly revealed in the case of the Zulu royal family by a rumour that was in circulation at the time. When speaking of Dinuzulu's funeral, one Madikana revealed what expectations some Zulu held about the political role of his successor. He referred to the 1913 Act and reported that he had heard that the Government had given out that there would be a territorial separation of the two races, the white and the black . . . [and] that there would be a competition between the white inhabitants of Natal and the Zulus as to who should purchase the ground.

In order that they may purchase land, he said, two sacks had been set aside and 'the black race was to fill these with money'. The Zulu royal family would transfer to these sacks all 'those contributions which were given as condolences' on Dinuzulu's death.[48] There was a basis of truth in this rumour: the architects of the 1913 Act had envisaged that both black and white would be permitted to purchase in certain 'released areas' (or 'neutral areas'), and the collections made by the Zulu royal family on Dinuzulu's death were associated with a project to buy land. But the Zulu royal family had no intention either of contributing this money to a communal fund for the benefit of the 'black race' in general, or of redistributing the land it bought, as Madikana and others imagined. It was intended to buy land in the Vryheid district for the use of Solomon and his dependants to free Solomon from the burdens and insecurities that he – like many other Zulu – suffered as a tenant on a white farm.[49]

The pomp and splendour of the funeral ceremony and the expressions of sympathy and loyalty made at it were nevertheless by no means hollow. For many Zulu, the Zulu royal family still had a very positive role to play in instilling a sense of continuity, identity and unity at a time when social realities did not.

NOTES

1. Colonial Office Confidential Print, Africa South, 879/115, Sir Rider Haggard to Rt. Hon. Lewis Harcourt, 1/6/1914, relating his impressions of Rhodesia and Zululand during his recent tour (hereafter Haggard's impressions), pp. 7–8. For an innovative view on Rider Haggard see Annie McClintock, 'Maidens, maps and mines: King Solomon's Mines and the reinvention of patriarchy in colonial South Africa', in Cherryl Walker (ed.), *Women and gender in southern Africa to 1945* (Cape Town, 1990).

2. Haggard's impressions, pp. 7–8.

3. Marian Lacey, *Working for boroko* (Johannesburg, 1981), pp. 126–27. Squatters who were not evicted were henceforth to pay the state hut tax as well as rentals to their landlords, which would in any case render the cost of their land tenure highly uneconomic.

4. The precise objectives of the 1913 Act have been the subject of controversy and re-evaluation. See, for example, the analyses of Lacey, *Boroko*, pp. 18–19, and 124ff; Mike Morris, 'The development of capitalism in South African agriculture: class struggle in the countryside', *Economy and Society*, vol. 5, 1976, pp. 293ff; Stanley Greenberg, *Race and state in capitalist development* (New Haven, 1980), pp. 79ff; T. R. H. Davenport, *South Africa: a modern history* (Johannesburg, 1977), pp. 334–35; Harold Wolpe, 'Capitalism and cheap labour power in South Africa: from segregation to apartheid', *Economy and Society*, vol. 1, 1972, p. 437; M. Legassick, 'Gold, agriculture and secondary industry in South Africa, 1885–1970: from periphery to sub-metropole as a forced labour system', in R. Palmer and N. Parsons (eds), *The roots of rural poverty in central and southern Africa* (London, 1977), pp. 179–81; and Bundy, *Peasantry*, ch. 8.

5. Natal Natives' Land Committee Evidence, UG35–18, evidence of the Revd John Dube, 24/3/1917, p. 100.

6. See Hemson, 'Dockworkers of Durban', pp. 51–54, and Fig. 2.2. Regarding the ecology of the region, see Guy, *Destruction of the Zulu kingdom*, pp. 4–8.

7. See Slater, 'Changing pattern', pp. 152–63; Morris, 'Capitalism in South African agriculture', pp. 308ff; and Bundy, *Peasantry*, pp. 168ff.

8. Blue Book on Native Affairs, U17–1911, p. 38.

9. Natives' Land Commission Evidence, UG22–16, p. 615.

10. Debates of the House of Assembly as reported in the *Cape Times* (hereafter *Cape Times*), which provided comprehensive coverage of parliamentary proceedings between 1915 and 1923 when these were not officially published, 4/4/1916.

11. Natives' Land Commission Evidence, UG22–16, p. 28.

12. CNC PMB 72, 57/29, Anton Potgieter to General Botha, 18/1/1917 (quotation). From the time of his succession in 1913 until his death in 1933, Solomon was almost continually in conflict with Boer landlords in the Vryheid district and Babanango sub-district. The voluminous Natal NAD correspondence concerning Solomon's tenancy problems is grouped into two files: CNC 221, 1628/1915 (which covers the period until late 1915) and CNC PMB 72, 57/29 (which covers the period 1916 onwards).

13. Natives' Land Commission Evidence, UG22–16, p. 486.

14. Natal Archives Depot, Archives of the Secretary of Native Affairs (hereafter SNA) I/9/5, minutes of meeting at Babanango, 25/5/1920.

15. Natives' Land Commission Evidence, UG22–16, evidence of Chief Mfungelwa and Headman Nfuzewa, Eshowe, 16/7/1914, pp. 489–90. For other illustrative observations from Zulu sources, see pp. 458ff and 488ff.

16. For an excellent description of Natal kholwa society see Marks, *Ambiguities of dependence*, pp. 51ff; and, for broader South African kholwa life, Brian Willan, *Sol Plaatje: South African nationalist* (London, 1984). See also Bundy, *Peasantry*, pp. 172, 179; and Slater, 'Changing pattern', p. 163.

17. Commission Report, 1905, quoted in E. H. Brookes and N. Hurwitz, *The native reserves of Natal*. Natal regional survey, vol. 7 (Cape Town, 1957), p. 13.

18. Blue Book on Native Affairs, U17–1911, p. 42.

19. Natives' Land Commission Evidence, UG22–16, evidence of G. H. Hulett, Eshowe farmer, p. 483.

20. See *ibid.*, pp. 629–30; Natal Natives' Land Committee Evidence, UG35–18. p. 235; and State Archives, Native Economic Commission, 1930–1932, Evidence (hereafter NEC) Box 4, p. 1523.

21. Blue Book on Native Affairs, U17–1911, pp. 39–40 (quotation), and p. 313.

22. Natives' Land Commission Evidence, UG22–16, evidence of W. W. Ndhlovu, p. 630 (quotation); NEC Box 4, evidence of W. W. Ndhlovu, p. 1528, and see also p. 1523.

23. SNA II/5/2, Natal Natives' Land Committee, evidence of George Coventry, Bergville farmer, 27/2/1917 (quotation); and Bundy, *Peasantry*, pp. 174–83.

24. Natal Natives' Land Committee Evidence, UG35–18, evidence of Ndhlovu, 24/3/1917, pp. 76 and 235; Stephen Mini, pp. 98–99; John Dube, pp. 99–101; Martin Luthuli, pp. 101–3; and Select Committee on Native Affairs, 1917, SC6A–17, evidence of Mini, Josiah Gumede and Abner Mtimkulu, 5/6/1917, pp. 618ff.

25. Haggard's impressions, p. 7.

26. Blue Book on Native Affairs, U17–1911, pp. 42 and 37.

27. See Guy, 'Destruction and reconstruction', p. 183; Natives' Land Commission Evidence, UG22–16, evidence of Magistrate, Mahlabatini, p. 623, and Chief Mqiniseni, Vryheid, p. 636.

28. See the magisterial reports under 'Health' in Blue Book on Native Affairs, U17–1911, pp. 96ff.

29. Natives' Land Commission Evidence, UG22–16, evidence of Magistrate, Mahlabatini, p. 623.

30. Haggard's impressions, p. 7.

31. Blue Book on Native Affairs, U17–1911, Health report for Mahlabatini and Nqutu, pp. 97–98 (quotation). See also the Health reports for other Zululand districts, pp. 96ff; and the DNC's reports, pp. 37 and 41. Regarding the Zulu term *isimpantsholo*, see A. Werner, 'Native affairs in Natal', *Journal of African Society*, vol. 17, October 1905, p. 83. Alice Werner, an academic at the University of London, was an associate of Harriette Colenso.

32. Report of the Native Affairs Department, 1912, UG33–13, CNC's report, p. 57.

33. Haggard's impressions, p. 7.

34. H. C. Lugg, 'The practice of lobolo in Natal', *Bantu Studies*, vol. 4, 1945, p. 23.

35. These observations on *lobolo* rely heavily on Guy's analyses in 'Production and exchange in the Zulu Kingdom', *Mohlomi*, vol. 2, 1978; 'Ecological factors in the rise of Shaka and the Zulu Kingdom' in Marks and Atmore, *Economy and society*; and 'Destruction and reconstruction', especially pp. 168–72 and 181ff. See also P. J. Colenbrander, 'Warriors, women, land and livestock: Cetshwayo's kingdom under stress?' (paper presented at the Workshop on Production and Reproduction in the Zulu Kingdom, University of Natal, Pietermaritzburg, 1977).

36. Guy, 'Destruction and reconstruction', pp. 181–82.

37. H.P. Braatvedt, 'Zulu marriage customs and ceremonies', *South African Journal of Science*, vol. 24, December 1927, p. 553.

38. Blue Book on Native Affairs, U17–1911, p. 315. See also pp. 313–14.

39. Haggard's impressions, pp. 8–9.

40. A. Vilakazi, *Zulu transformations: a study in the dynamics of social change* (Pietermaritzburg, 1965). The imposition of the poll tax in 1905 accelerated these developments, which began at the turn of the century, since it placed a tax on individual young men. The hut tax, by contrast, was a tax on the productive community, as a social unit, in the Zulu homestead. See Guy, 'Destruction and reconstruction', pp. 185–90.

41. Natives' Land Commission Evidence, UG22–16, evidence of the Revd J. Hallowes, Vryheid, 3/6/1915, p. 619.

42. NAD Report, 1912, UG33–13, p. 63.

43. MS MAR 2.08.4, KCM 3074, noteform biography. See also Guy, 'Destruction and reconstruction', p. 187.

44. MS MAR 2.08.5, KCM 2570(b), notes on Marwick's march, unsigned, n.d.; and KCM 2576(b), 'Marwick's memorable march'.

45. MS MAR 2.08.5, File 7, KCM 2661, J.N.D. Mkwanazi to Marwick, 20/6/1953; File 19, KCM 2887(a), Marwick to H.A. Robson, Manager of Durban Municipal Native Affairs Department, 30/11/1948; and KCAL, Killie Campbell's Newscutting Book no. 36, ref. 20438, p. 88, article reporting a letter from Pika to Marwick, 10/10/1948.

46. KCAL, Killie Campbell's Newscutting Book no. 10, KC 19701, pp. 137–38, article by Col. H.F. Trew in *Natal Advertiser*, 23/1/1937. For details of similar relationships elsewhere in the Union, see A.H. Jeeves, 'Migrant labour in the political economy of the mines: the Native Recruiting Corporation and its rivals, 1903–1919' (paper presented at the Conference on South Africa and the West, University of Natal, Durban, 1982).

47. Haggard's impressions, p. 8.

48. Report of Socwatsha and Nongejeni, p. 8.

49. The collections were also intended to liquidate Dinuzulu's debts, some of which were unpaid rentals for the use of white-owned land. The influence of Harriette Colenso and Pixley Seme was considerable here. See Natives' Land Commission Evidence, UG22–16, evidence of Miss H.E. Colenso, pp. 522–23; and CNC 144, 1985/1913, SNA to CNC, 23/12/1913.

2

Solomon's succession

As the deceased king's *induna enkulu* (principal headman), Mankulumana kaSomaphunga Ndwandwe was in charge of proceedings at Dinuzulu's funeral. It was not essential that the heir be announced before the burial took place, yet it was customary that if the heir had already been nominated, he should symbolise his succession by taking his father's spear and with it turning the first sod in his father's grave.[1] Dinuzulu's funeral was held up from the outset, however, because no heir had been nominated and there were fears on the part of the royalist Usuthu that if they did not do so quickly 'the Government would raise Kambi, the son of Hamu [of the Ngenetsheni], to the position'.[2] The turning of the first sod was thus a vital issue – and for two days Dinuzulu's body was to lie in his principal hut at Nobamba while outside the succession dispute remained unresolved. The two potential heirs were David Nyawana kaDinuzulu and Solomon Nkayishana Maphumuzana kaDinuzulu.

Since Dinuzulu had not named his successor, Mankulumana sought the advice of Dinuzulu's *izinceku* (personal attendants), Lokhotwayo, Mvingana and Nobiyana, whom the king had relied on as loyal and discreet confidants. They all reported that while the king had been seriously ill before his exile to KwaThengisa, he had confided that the heir was David. Mankulumana announced this to the assembly, and he was supported by other 'great men of the nation', including Ndabankulu kaLukhwazi Ntombela and Zidunge kaNtshingwayo Khoza, who publicly expressed the opinion that there was no reason to doubt the words of Dinuzulu's attendants. The assembly thereupon rose and acclaimed the new king, David, with the royal salute, 'Bayede'.[3]

Even as the acclamation subsided, dissenting voices were heard from the central cluster of dignitaries. 'You, son of Somaphunga [Mankulumana], is the family of the King always to be spoilt by headmen?' accused Mbuzini Mdlalose, brother of Solomon's mother.[4] Others, including Dotela kaMgidgidlana Zulu and Mnyaiza kaNdabuko Zulu, voiced their disapproval of Mankulumana's role in settling the succession, and heated discussion ensued. In the midst of this, however, the unusual decision was made to authorise David's full sister, Victoria Mpatshana, to turn the first sod of the grave. The digging of the grave was thus started as the succession dispute continued unabated. Late in the day Harriette Colenso intervened and, taking David by her right hand and Solomon by her left, led the two claimants back to the Nobamba huts.[5] As dusk fell, Mnyaiza announced that a meeting of Dinuzulu's *izinceku*, *izinduna* and Mpande's grandsons (Dinuzulu's generation) would decide the matter the following morning. He added that Harriette Colenso and Pixley Seme would be consulted because they had had access to Dinuzulu's correspondence, in which he might have named an heir.

Apart fom the testimony of Dinuzulu's *izinceku*, David's claim rested on his being the eldest of Dinuzulu's sons. Dinuzulu had moreover given him the name Nyawana − 'the feet that will walk for me'.[6] But there were many who argued that Dinuzulu had subsequently cancelled his nomination of David. It also emerged clearly that Dinuzulu's wishes were not the only consideration: the majority of those in the royal inner circle, together with those commoners who personally knew the claimants, did not want David to succeed. By all accounts he had developed into an unpleasant character. Reports received by the CNC from Zulu sources suggested that David was 'of violent morose temperament, and addicted to drink', while Solomon was by contrast 'modest, sober and intelligent'.[7] Zulu oral tradition similarly stresses the differences of character between David and Solomon. Speaking in 1981, Ndesheni kaMnyaiza Zulu recalled of David that 'this young man used to ride on horseback. If he found a white man's fence he would put a pair of pliers to it. He would not follow the official road.' Princess Mkandandhlovu, a daughter of Dinuzulu born in the year of her father's death, on the other hand emphasised Solomon's humility, gentle disposition and 'knowledge of the people'. She related how Solomon had personally cultivated his fields when he was a boy, which was remarkable for a royal youngster, and moreover he had shared the produce with his brothers and attendants. 'It was found that there was so much integrity in the younger one [Solomon] and not because he had his eye on the kingship. It was just his nature.'[8]

Addressing the meeting of dignitaries and royal attendants the following morning, Mnyaiza sharply reprimanded Mankulumana for interfering in the private affairs of the Zulu royal family, and for making David's succession public without first referring to all the *izikhulu* (great leaders of the nation) and *izinduna*. He then summoned Pixley Seme and Harriette Colenso. Seme had no specific evidence to give, but nonetheless said that he had understood that Solomon was to be the heir. Colenso then reported that she did indeed have evidence of Dinuzulu's wishes but, no doubt wary of a possible furore should David be deposed, she refused to divulge the information until Dinuzulu had been buried. It later transpired that, during the night, Solomon had produced a letter from Dinuzulu nominating him as heir, and had given it to Colenso for safekeeping. Urging that the burial go ahead without further delay, Colenso also explained that the two white labour agents known to the Zulu as 'Muhle' (J. S. Marwick) and 'Zithulele' (evidently Lt.-Col. Morris) would shortly need to return to Johannesburg to work, taking with them the Zulu mineworkers in their charge. She might also have added that Dinuzulu had by then been dead for eight days in the heat of a highveld summer.

The burial ceremony was thus set under way: royal cattle were slaughtered and Dinuzulu's body was lowered into the grave. After the assistant magistrate at Babanango had expressed the government's condolences, it fell to Mankulumana to make a reply:

> It is you [the government] who killed the one we have now buried. You killed his father and you killed him. We did not invade your country, but you invaded ours . . . The one whom we now mourn did no wrong. There is no bone that will not decay. What we now ask is, as you have killed the father, to take care of the children.[9]

While these sentiments were cause for great consternation in NAD circles, it was the way in which Mankulumana ended his speech that caused uproar among the Zulu. 'Oh! Here I have buried the son of the King. Now I die with him, as I died with him yesterday', Mankulumana concluded, deeply upset by the succession dispute, 'I am now going away . . . back to my Ndwandwe people' – and, by implication, breaking off his relationship with the Usuthu. At this a voice interjected 'And with whom are you leaving your mistakes?'; thus once more the ceremony was brought to a standstill as various *izikhulu* and *izinduna* insisted that the heir be established, for it was he who should be the first to put a stone into Dinuzulu's grave.[10] Faced with a hostile assembly and intense pressure for the succession dispute to be settled, Mankulumana referred the whole matter to Harriette Colenso. Discreetly, she told the keeper of the royal homesteads, Mandlenyatha kaNobetha Zulu, to take Solomon's hand and let him select a stone to place on Dinuzulu's coffin. This symbolic act was carried out in front of the whole assembly. No letter verifying Solomon's claim to the succession was ever produced – at least not in public. David was then led to the grave to do the same. After him followed all the other men of importance, and the grave was presently filled.

The Revd Twala, the Zulu cleric who had come down from Pretoria to officiate, thereafter conducted a Christian funeral service, which was immediately followed by the traditional Zulu counterpart. Songs were sung, Dinuzulu's *izibongo* (praise poems) were intoned, and finally 'Cetshwayo's song' was sung, as it had been when Cetshwayo was buried at Nkandla in 1884. Mankulumana then rose to announce that it was to be Solomon Maphumuzana ('the shelter' or 'giver of rest') kaDinuzulu who 'will be our comfort', at which the whole assembly roared 'Bayede', 'as if the whole world shook with their praise'.[11]

In his report on the funeral ceremony, the magistrate at Vryheid outlined three 'outstanding features'. He was struck by the 'lavish attention . . . bestowed on the funeral party and mourners by all sections of the Native Labour Recruiting Agencies', which he found 'undesirable and unedifying'. He continued that 'one might aptly apply Verse 28, Chapter 24, St Matthew', which reads 'For wheresoever the carcase is, there will be eagles gathered together.' Another feature was the sympathy shown by the 'rank and file of natives', some 7000 attending the funeral. But in contrast to this, he noted a third feature: the reluctance on the part of certain chiefs and headmen in both Natal and Zululand to attend. While the rank and file regarded Dinuzulu as their 'King and Leader', he said, most chiefs and headmen were government appointees and were therefore afraid that expressions of sympathy would weaken their positions.[12]

*   *   *   *   *

Dinuzulu's funeral ceremony showed that the division between those loyal to the government and those loyal to the Zulu royal house was very clear. Socwatsha and Nongejeni, who assembled the NAD intelligence reports on which much of this account is based, were too afraid to visit royal homesteads in Zululand even though they were not known to be NAD agents, and had visited many other homesteads without a qualm. This was especially well illustrated in the case of Chief Mpikanina kaZiwedu Zulu, who was one of the four chiefs to accept jurisdiction over members of the Usuthu when they were divided up by the Natal government. He had been despised – especially as he was a grandson of Mpande – for accepting this appointment, and had proceeded to attract other 'traitors' to him. Nobiyana, who had once been a trusted servant of Dinuzulu, but who had been discovered conveying information about matters at the Usuthu homesteads to government officials during the 1906 rebellion, was now an *induna* to Mpikanina. Dinuzulu's children had 'verbally set upon' Nobiyana when he visited the royal homestead, Nsindeni, in 1911; he was called a 'spy for the

Government' and told that he had no business on the property since he now 'belonged to Mpikanina'.[13] Although Mpikanina arrived to attend the funeral, he stood 'quite alone', and after an altercation with Mankulumana on the subject of the 1906 rebellion, he became fearful and left before the ceremony was completed.[14] So too in the case of Acting Chief Muzimubi of the Buthelezi, who had also accepted jurisdiction over a portion of the Usuthu. He chose not to attend, though he did send some men to express condolences, and 'a beast in the form of money'. He alluded to the estrangement that had come about between the Usuthu and Buthelezi, complaining that in the old days the Zulu royal house would not have nominated a successor without the presence of the Buthelezi.[15]

There were other examples. Chief Zombode, who had recently been appointed in the place of a deposed chief, was waved away from the mourners before Mankulumana intervened. Despite the efforts of Mankulumana and Mnyaiza to unite as many people as possible in the mourning, Natal NAD spies reported that 'Dinuzulu's cousins and relatives never spoke to any of the people who came to mourn who were known to be loyal to the Government. They only addressed people who they knew were still supporters of the Usuthu cause'.[16]

The conflict between the Mandlakazi and Usuthu, which had been the principal conflict of the Zulu civil war of the 1880s, nonetheless showed some signs of repair. On the part of the Usuthu, there had been moves towards a reconciliation for some time; soon after his return from exile on the island of St Helena, Dinuzulu had visited the Mandlakazi leader, Zibhebhu, and said that he wished to 'forget past animosity'.[17] Following the death of Zibhebhu in 1905, the Mandlakazi had dissipated some of their energy and unity in a succession dispute. A government commission of inquiry ultimately decided that Bokwe was the heir, and set aside the claim of Msenteli. Because Msenteli had a large following and civil war was imminent, he and some of his leading supporters were removed to the Eshowe and Nkandla districts. Bokwe was still very young, and another son of Zibhebhu, Mciteki, was appointed as regent and chief during Bokwe's minority. Despite Mnyaiza's invitation to attend the funeral, Mciteki himself refused to do so. He nonetheless did permit a few of his *izinduna* to attend, some of whom did not go themselves but merely sent representatives. When the Mandlakazi representatives arrived, they were brusquely asked why they had brought no beast with which to mourn, but Mankulumana was quick to soothe by expressing particular thanks that the Mandlakazi had sent mourners at all. The mere fact that Usuthu and Mandlakazi representatives came together and mixed was cause for special comment by observers.[18]

The dispute now lived on mainly in the minds of those who had experienced the tragedies of the 1880s, and in the minds of people like Msenteli, who in 1917 proclaimed:

> My father gave orders that we had to meet the Usuthu only at stores and at the Court House. I know it is the intention to bring about a reconciliation . . . that will never be. We must clean our guns . . . the paths will soon run red with blood if we are forced to a reconciliation.[19]

Although such violence lurked beneath the surface, in practice animosity henceforth waned − soothed as much by time as by the diplomatic approaches of the Usuthu. This was also true of the split between the Ngenetsheni and Usuthu, which similarly could be traced back to the Zulu civil war. The Ngenetsheni chief, Hamu's heir Kambi, sent mourners to Dinuzulu's funeral, and there was no mention of ill will. But overall the funeral showed that there was still considerable animosity towards chiefs and sections regarded as government collaborators.

Solomon's succession also brought to light new divisions within the Zulu royal family itself. These were to be an annoyance in the first few years of Solomon's chieftainship, but in comparison with the ruptures during Dinuzulu's time, they were of small significance. Most worrisome was the truculence of David, who had been 'king' for a day. David's uncharacteristically meek acceptance of his loss of the succession indicated that he knew he did not have the support to hazard a showdown. However, when the *izikhulu* met shortly after the funeral to set the internal affairs of the Zulu royal family in order, an attempt was made to placate David by awarding him the pre-eminent Nobamba homestead and the care of both sections of the traditionally royalist Qulusi people, under the royal *izinduna* Mnyaiza Mthethwa and Hali Mdlalose. For the time being, Solomon's principal homestead was to be Zibindini in the Babanango sub-district, where his mother had been placed by Dinuzulu. Solomon was also awarded the dilapidated Mahashini homestead in the Nongoma district, in the ward of Chief Moya Ndwandwe who was one of the four chiefs appointed over the Usuthu.[20] Mankulumana, who made these arrangements, earned widespread censure because the Qulusi had been personally administered by the king since Shaka had first incorporated them, and Nobamba had been the property of the king since the time of Ndaba, Shaka's great-grandfather.[21] The ensuing tension between the homesteads Nobamba (David's) and Zibindini (Solomon's), which lay not more than three hundred yards distant from each other, is recorded in the *izibongo* of Solomon's mother, Silomo, daughter of Ntuzwa Mdlalose:

> Wild person that is barked at by the Nobamba dogs
> Likewise those of Zibindini greet her
> They say 'Good day, daughter of the chief' [meaning Ntuzwa]
> 'You must turn your back on those who reject you
> Since those who love you are facing them'.

The circumstances of the succession dispute also receive mention in the *izibongo* of Solomon, who is referred to poetically as 'our own eater-up from Zibindini':

> The matter [dispute] was started by the men of Nobamba
> It was started by Mankulumana son of Somaphunga
> It was begun by Ndabankulu son of Lukhwazi
> It was promoted by Lokhotwayo son of Zembe
> It was urged by Mvingana son of Nompanda
> They took the cattle of the Mahashini kraal [homestead]
> And mixed them with those of Nobamba.[22]

The other division within the Zulu royal family was a consequence of the succession dispute that had followed the death of Cetshwayo in 1884. Manzolwandle's claim had been passed over in favour of Dinuzulu, who was the son of one of Cetshwayo's low-ranking wives. Manzolwandle had thereafter become 'a wanderer, shunned by nearly all his old relatives and therefore practically an orphan dependent on the Supreme Chief'. In 1907 he was appointed as a chief in the Nqutu district – which evidently annoyed Dinuzulu – and was given a hundred head of cattle by the Natal Government 'to enable him to maintain the prestige and dignity attaching to the position to which he had been appointed'.[23]

On news of Dinuzulu's death, Manzolwandle reopened his claim to the estate of Cetshwayo, which included claims for unpaid *lobolo* for several of Cetshwayo's daughters who had married subsequent to Cetshwayo's death. The government, however, refused to take up the case because, it argued, all Cetshwayo's property had become the government's property after the Anglo-Zulu War. Moreover, the government reminded Manzolwandle that it was a condition of his appointment as chief in 1907 that he renounce all claims to being heir to Cetshwayo. Despite Manzolwandle's futile but divisive rumblings, Mankulumana telegraphed him three times informing him of Dinuzulu's funeral – which was further evidence of the conciliatory efforts of the Usuthu leadership. Manzolwandle nonetheless did not attend. At Nobamba, it was said that 'Manzolwandle had been unable to attend the funeral as his trap had broken down. Then he had got onto a horse, and it, also, broke down, but the people were still expecting him.'[24]

These were some of the tensions that faced the new head of the Zulu royal house. In the space of one week, Solomon had had to endure the death of his father, the trauma of a succession dispute, the jealousies of his siblings and uncles, the lurking antagonism of the enemies of his father and grandfather, a break in the trust which had obtained between Dinuzulu and his chief counsellor, Mankulumana, the attentions of a wide range of courtiers, and the pressures imposed by a great multitude of people who had felt his succession to be an event of both public and deeply personal importance. He had also succeeded to the particular loyalty of a section of the Zulu people, the Usuthu, who were still divided among four separate chiefs. Their recognition of Solomon as Dinuzulu's successor had taken place regardless of the administrative arrangements imposed by the Natal NAD, and the contradictions so generated made Solomon's position yet more complex.

Solomon had also inherited the attentions of the many creditors of Dinuzulu's estate. Although he was allowed a £100 stipend from the government to care for Dinuzulu's widows and dependants (of which £5 per annum was paid directly to Potgieter for the lease of 20 acres of 'Welgekozen'), this was nowhere near sufficient. Apart from any other expenses, Solomon was obliged to pay about £60 per annum for hut rentals on Buys's 'Koningsdal' alone, apart from dues for grazing and arable land.[25]

*   *   *   *   *

As might have been expected of a child of Dinuzulu, Solomon had not had a secure childhood. He was born sometime between 1891 and 1893 on the island of St Helena while Dinuzulu was in exile there. Dinuzulu had taken two wives with him to St Helena: Silomo (or okaNtuzwa), daughter of Ntuzwa Mdlalose, and Zihlazile (or okaQethuka), daughter of Qethuka Magwaza. OkaNtuzwa's first child died, but while at St Helena she bore two sons, Solomon Nkayishana Maphumuzana and Arthur Edward Mshiyeni. OkaQethuka bore two sons and a daughter, David Nyawana, Samuel Bhekelendoda and Victoria Mphaphu.[26]

Life on St Helena was easy. The children 'roamed' and 'played' − and it was said that they soon lost their milk teeth on account of the number of sweets given to them by whites on the island.[27] More importantly, strong European influence was brought to bear on their upbringing through the media of elementary education and the Church. After Dinuzulu was sent into exile, Harriette Colenso arranged for Bubi Mthuli to go to St Helena to educate Dinuzulu and the royal youngsters. When Mthuli fell out with the interpreter, Colenso sought a replacement from among those who had been educated at the school of her father, Bishop Colenso. Magema Magwaza Fuze was selected and went out to St Helena to relieve Mthuli and join the Revd Barraclough in teaching the Zulu royal family.[28]

Dinuzulu was given instruction in the speaking, reading and writing of English. The youngsters' education, however, was informal. They were instructed to be literate only in Zulu, and did not achieve any great proficiency. Nonetheless, they were educated in a broader sense through the Church, which infused into them the habits and beliefs of European life. As Magogo kaDinuzulu related, Solomon and the other youngsters were

> never educated. [Solomon] never went to school. They merely learnt to read a little Zulu. In our home . . . from the beginning we were educated for the Lord, so that we may be able to read the Bible [in Zulu] . . . We were not concerned with education for speech. We were being educated to Christianity.[29]

Every Sunday they attended church where they heard services conducted by Bishop Welby and the Revd Barraclough. It was in this church that they were all baptised, and received their intriguing blend of British royal and Old Testament first names. They also learnt such skills as horse-riding.[30] Elderly members of the Zulu royal family, interviewed in the early 1980s, all emphasised that Solomon was 'Christian' and 'civilised' – the fact that he was brought up in European clothes and not a *beshu* (loin skin) was regarded as sufficient evidence of this.[31]

After Dinuzulu was repatriated to Zululand in 1898, Solomon was moved back and forth between the Usuthu royal homestead, which lay in the Nongoma district, and the European-style house Dinuzulu had constructed near the magistracy at Eshowe – where the Natal Government obliged him to live. Immediately there followed two periods of upheaval: the Anglo-Boer War and then the 1906 rebellion. The latter was more disruptive for the boy princes: as white hostility to Dinuzulu mounted in 1906, they were taken into hiding for their own safety.[32] After the lengthy treason trial and Dinuzulu's subsequent period of imprisonment, the royal youngsters spent their time alternately at their respective mothers' homesteads near Nongoma and Babanango, or with their father at his Transvaal residence in exile, KwaThengisa. It was at KwaThengisa that Solomon met Pixley Seme, who was to be a strong influence on him immediately after his succession. Also during this period, Solomon was duly enrolled by Dinuzulu as a member of the Vukayibambe *ibutho* (age set or 'regiment'), and given instruction in the traditions of the *amabutho* of pre-conquest Zululand. Despite – or perhaps partly because of – the complexities and insecurities of his early years, Solomon by various accounts grew up to be an essentially modest young man, easygoing and approachable in manner, with a sense of social concern. Something of his character emerges in the following lines of his *izibongo*:

> The honeybird that drinks from deep pools
> If he drank from shallow pools his beak would be muddied
> Tuft of soft hair he speaks not, neither has heavy words.[33]

Overall, the western influences on Solomon had sunk deep. The following description made by an American journalist, who conducted a series of interviews with Solomon's first wife during the early 1930s, refers to Solomon a few years after his succession:

> He wore underwear, shoes, military uniforms, and cocked hats; his riding breeches and boots were made to order. He preferred the soft outlines of a chair, to rest on a mattress, sit at a table for meals, have a light cast upon him after nightfall; to cover himself with ample blankets rather than skins, and lie between clean sheets; to use warm water, and soft towels to dry with, and the feel of a sponge after riding.[34]

Solomon's personal living quarters at Zibindini took the form of a traditional Zulu hut, surrounded by a finely built reed stockade. Inside, however, there was a 'brass bed, with its hand embroidered spread, some chairs, an open cupboard with brightly patterned china, and a table covered with a gleaming patterned oilcloth'.[35]

*　　*　　*　　*　　*

On his succession, Solomon immediately fell under a number of different – and sometimes contradictory – influences. One was the result of the initiative of a local African priest, William Afrikander, of the (Anglican) Church of the Province of South Africa (CPSA). Within a couple of months of Solomon's succession, Afrikander had 'converted' Solomon and David, and in February 1914 Solomon was confirmed by the Bishop of Zululand, Wilmot Vyvyan. In a fund-raising appeal published in the missionary journal, *The Net*, the Revd L.E. Oscroft of central Zululand emphasised that the church initiative should not end there:

> I was at Afrikander's station [Emtonjaneni] a fortnight ago and had several talks with Solomon and his brother David (older than Solomon

but not chosen by the people). One of the chief Royal Kraals is at a place called KwaNobamba in the midst of a large heathen population. At present we have no station there, but we are hoping to start there within the next three months. It will be a great task – there is strong heathen opposition to meet, especially from the boy king's advisors . . . Think what it means for the Church. The head of the Zulu nation, worshipping in his own church, at or near his own home . . . Afrikander has great influence over Solomon and David, and I know from their own mouths that they look to him for guidance. We must not fail them . . . despite many disappointments, there does seem at the present time a special movement towards Light taking place amongst the Zulu people. We have created their hunger – now we must satisfy it.[36]

Christian and 'enlightened' influence on Solomon issued not simply from the CPSA establishment, but more broadly from the stratum of mission-educated Zulu, the kholwa, which provided the embattled Zulu-speaking middle class with its most influential spokesmen. For some Zulu-speaking kholwa, Solomon's succession was an event of considerable significance well beyond the borders of Zululand, and even beyond the borders of Natal: it rekindled those nascent African nationalist sentiments that had flared briefly in Natal at the turn of the century and subsided after the 1906 rebellion. Amos Nxumalo, a landowner and son of a 'Kholwa house' in Pietermaritzburg, held that Solomon 'has been made King of all us black people – the whole black race'.[37] The 'black people' were not so much in need of leadership to provide political direction, as of identity, pride and inspiration. Kholwa interest in Solomon was not passive. If Solomon was to provide the image that was required of him he would have to do more than symbolise blackness, power, independence and romanticised tradition; he would also need to reflect kholwa social, cultural and political aspirations. It was a matter for concern that Solomon should not transpire to be a 'backward' tribal chief.

The views expressed in early 1914 by a leading mission-published Zulu newspaper, *Izindaba Zabantu*, which was published in Natal proper, are especially illuminating. It is in itself significant that the editor chooses to identify himself and his readership as 'Zulu', whereas in practice Natal Africans were often scorned by the 'real' Zulu of Zululand, and described as the *amakhafula* ('those who have been spat out' by the Zulu kingdom) of *esilungwini* ('the place of the whites', meaning Natal proper).

> [Dinuzulu] once held the position of King, but he was misled by his elders and fought with the English Government. The kingdom was

taken away from him . . . What was left with him was just the dignity with which he was born . . . With the Zulus Dinuzulu was their King until he died. His son, Solomon, will be recognized as King even if he is nothing to the Government and white people's eyes.

It's that dignity and power which Solomon will have among Africans that we want to talk about today. Is this power and dignity to be just nothing at all, of no use to its owner and his people? We think there is plenty he can do that is wise. We don't think he will ever see the Kingdom of Zululand, no! That Kingdom is dead and will never be again. There is another good position he can take for his people . . . the position of leading his people to Light. This position can be the same as a King's position indeed, because of its dignity, because of its help to the Zulus.

If our hopes and other people's hopes are to come true with this child, it will depend on how he is guided . . . It is up to the relatives to narrate the mistakes [of Dinuzulu] to this son who is taking up this high position . . . He must be taken away from foolish people . . . and be brought up in a westernized respectable manner which is correct for a King these days . . . We are aware that Mankulumana and Mnyaiza are men in high positions in the Royal family, but even so they are still raw, they are still in a dark pit and they don't want to go out of it so that they can see the light. If you want to see good from Solomon, these are not the people to lead him and teach him.[38]

In a leading article eighteen months later, the same newspaper expressed both dismay that its earlier advice had not been well heeded, and displeasure with Solomon's advisers. 'There are people who have asked us when we are to hear that our King Solomon is being taught the way of light . . . If all that we hear is truth, then it is obvious that he will follow his father's footsteps. Where his father went you all know.'[39] The paper in fact had no cause to be so despondent.

Apart from the initiatives of William Afrikander, which were soon to be followed by vigorous CPSA support, the 'raw' and 'unenlightened' influence of Mankulumana and Mnyaiza was being balanced by the attentions of leading kholwa spokesmen. Although his influence was to be more pronounced later, John Dube was quick to show interest in Solomon. Born to a Natal kholwa family in 1871, Dube had been educated at Inanda and Amanzimtoti Theological College before furthering his studies at Oberlin College in America. In America, Dube raised the funds that enabled him to establish the 'Zulu Christian Industrial School' at Ohlange, in the Inanda district near Durban, in 1901. Dube's Christian beliefs and concern for education and 'social progress' – in western terms – were intimately intertwined. Inspired by the American Negro educationist and political theorist Booker T. Washington, Dube at least initially felt that Christianity and education took priority over political action in terms of both short- and long-term benefits. He told a white audience: 'Christianity will usher in a new civilization and the 'Dark Continent' will be transformed into a land of commerce and Christian institutions. Then shall Africa take her place as a nation among nations.'[40]

In Natal, Dube's optimism was misplaced; white colonists were especially distrustful of the attempts of the kholwa to master the beliefs and practices of European life, and erected barriers against their progress. Shortly after the turn of the century, Dube became politically active through *Ilanga lase Natal*, a Zulu-English newspaper, and the Natal Native Congress. These were both primarily vehicles for the aspirations of the westernized kholwa elite, and both tended to express disdain for the 'backwardness' and 'stagnancy' of 'unimproved kraal life'. Nonetheless, with his 'recollections of pride in the Zulu past', Dube had campaigned on Dinuzulu's behalf during the treason trial that followed the 1906 rebellion.[41]

In 1912 he became the first president of the SANNC, and one of his first actions in this capacity testified to his desire to garner the support of the same tribal Africans whose beliefs and customs he largely rejected. At a meeting with the Zulu at Eshowe in November 1912, he made an impassioned appeal for black political unity and 'beneficial representation' in view of the forthcoming segregationist legislation. He further spoke glowingly of white industriousness and disparagingly of black laziness and sensual gratification (beer, women and food), and urged his audience to educate themselves and their children. Mtonga kaMpande Zulu was present, and he agreed to support Dube.[42]

Shortly after Solomon's succession, Dube was concerned about the way in which Solomon was being guided by his advisers. When, in December 1913, Harriette Colenso intended to present Solomon to Louis Botha for recognition (presumably as successor to Dinuzulu's one-time position as chief of the Usuthu), Dube denounced the idea on the grounds that it was improper so soon after Dinuzulu's death – the customary period of mourning had not yet been observed. This period of mourning was approximately one year in length, at the end of which an *ihlambo* was held: a ceremonial meeting of the *amabutho* and a ritual hunt (*inqina*) during which the spears of the nation were cleansed in the blood of the prey. That Dube was anxious for the mourning period to be correctly observed reflected his ambiguity about the customs and traditions of the Zulu; this was especially marked when it came to royal traditions. Harriette Colenso wrote a deferential letter to Dube, agreeing with his views and adding that Mankulumana had been of the same opinion. She added, incidentally, that she and Seme were presently at KwaThengisa, attempting to sort out Dinuzulu's financial affairs.[43]

Soon afterwards, Dube contacted Solomon, requesting his support for a fund-raising scheme to send a deputation to England to protest against the 1913 Act. The native commissioner at Piet Retief saw links between Dube's activities and the collections that were currently being made for the Zulu royal family:

> I claim that it is not unreasinable [sic] to suppose and to assume that such educated and enlightened natives as Mr John Dube and Mr P. kaL. Seme [sic] are labouring quietly and diplomatically amongst the Zulu speaking peoples with the object of achieving a complete reunion of the Zulu Nation and thereby a resuscitation and revival of the Zulu Royal House and power.[44]

It was Seme who came to be the greatest 'outside' influence on Solomon immediately after his succession. As a lawyer, Seme provided professional assistance in settling the claims of Dinuzulu's numerous creditors and in guiding the financial affairs of the Zulu royal house towards solvency. Describing himself as 'legal advisor to the late Chief Dinuzulu' and as acting in that capacity 'on behalf of his heir Solomon', Seme wrote to the office of the Prime Minister in December 1913 requesting permission for Solomon to visit Johannesburg to receive 'voluntary gifts' to settle Dinuzulu's estate. Seme's request was refused. Four days after Seme's request, the SNA similarly instructed Mankulumana that no one was to 'exploit Solomon for the purposes of settling debts'.[45] A massive tribute-collecting campaign was nonetheless launched by Seme and Solomon's influential uncle, Mnyaiza, during which Solomon was made aware that of all the people that were willing to pay tribute to him, it was Zulu migrant workers and urban residents that were most able to do so. Thus, while being advised by *kholwa* leaders, Solomon gained an early insight into the 'political economy' of his 'kingship'.

Royal tribute-collectors did not confine their attentions to the urban areas, for they were also at work deep in the rural districts. Here their activities threw light on two factors crucial to the political fortunes of the royal house. On the one hand, the response of the rural districts to the tribute-collectors showed that past divisions were breaking down and a sense of unity was being established under the figure of Solomon. This was important, for it was in the rural areas that the numerical core of Solomon's political constituency lay. On the other hand, the reaction of the NAD to this development was negative – largely because a sense of political unity among the inhabitants of the rural districts was anomalous to an administration that was based on the notion of 'divide and rule'.

In the Piet Retief district of the eastern Transvaal, despite the opposition of the local native commissioner, Chief Tunzi collected £20 from his ward (which numbered only 200 tax-paying adults, all of whom were labour tenants or squatters) and handed this to Seme and Mnyaiza for transmission to Solomon. In a state of consternation, the native commissioner reported that Chief Tunzi and his ward were the descendants of a small section which had been expelled from Zululand by Cetshwayo after an altercation, but

> today they are contributing to a fund for the benefit of the heir to the Zulu Royal House, against which they actively bore arms in the Anglo-Zulu war of 1879. Though Tunzi and his small following may only be an infinitesimal unit there are other tribes in which the feeling of resentment against the Zulu Royal House is dying out . . .[46]

The magistrate at Nongoma similarly reported that Solomon was receiving presents from 'all over Zululand, both in money and in kind'. Contributions from individuals had been as high as £10, and Mnyaiza had collected a 'considerable amount' for Solomon when he stopped off at Charlestown on his way between KwaThengisa and Zululand. Tribute was pouring into the royal homesteads in Zululand, and Phikisile, one of Solomon's sisters, had been instructed to keep an account of the money received. The magistrate concluded with a plea to the CNC that Solomon should not be allowed to reside in the locality, as Solomon's being 'paraded about as a chief of great standing' had 'considerably unsettled' his district.[47]

The CNC, Dick Addison, responded by summoning Mnyaiza to his office. 'Where are you leading this boy [Solomon]?', he asked, and proceeded, 'Look here, you know what these lawyers are. This man Seme is a Natal man. I know his father who lives at Richmond. Lawyers want money only. They will end by leaving you in the lurch.' Mnyaiza replied that 'the people' wanted to see Solomon, and that he had indeed gone about to solicit money even though he knew the government had forbidden it. Mnyaiza also referred to his duties as a labour recruiter which, he said, required him to travel around the country. There was little the CNC could do. He could hardly forbid Mnyaiza himself to move about the country since he was committing no wrong in doing so, and he could hardly forbid the collection of subscriptions that were by all accounts voluntarily given. All he did do was reiterate that 'Dinuzulu's children [have] been given away to others [appointed chiefs] and it is wrong to act as you have been acting.'[48]

As the CNC related to the SNA, the activities of Seme and Mnyaiza, and of Solomon, were posing a grave danger to the administration not only of the Usuthu, but of Zululand. 'I am anxious therefore to prevent Solomon as far as possible from acquiring a following. If any indication in this direction is not nipped in the bud, I foresee that the Government will have the same trouble with him as experienced with his late father.'[49]

Solomon soon began organising 'progressions' and collections on his own. His application for a pass to visit the Transvaal in 1916 was refused when it transpired that he intended to visit his uncle Franz, who held a supervisory position at the Brakpan Mine, to 'collect money from natives in compounds to enable him to pay his debts'.[50] It is significant that officials regarded the influence of Solomon's 'non-tribal' associates with special disfavour. The CNC held that Solomon might 'confidently be expected to lead a quiet life, unless led away by the headmen and agitators, such as John Dube, Seme and others', while the magistrate at Nongoma referred to Mnyaiza and Franz as 'perhaps the most disloyal people in Zululand'.[51]

*   *   *   *   *

Notwithstanding the influence of kholwa advisers, the Church and his more worldly royal associates such as Mnyaiza and Franz, Solomon was also the central figure in the world of Zulu traditionalism. Although, as has been argued, this 'traditionalism' was one of form rather than content, the niche that Solomon occupied in this context was of immense social and political importance. Ultimately it was the entire basis of his status. As the administration was only too painfully aware, Solomon had a huge groundswell of support in the rural districts, and for them Solomon was 'king'.

That Solomon had inherited from Dinuzulu a large number of royal homesteads, dotted about the core of the Zulu country, undoubtedly made his presence and influence more widely felt. Apart from Zibindini and Nobamba in the Vryheid district (although David had been given Nobamba for his personal use, it was ultimately the property of the king), there were the Gqikazi, Sikalenisenyoka, Mahashini and Ekubuseni royal homesteads in the Nongoma district, and Nsindeni in the Mahlabatini district. Not surprisingly, the Natal NAD saw this scatter of royal homesteads as a problem. The cluster of royal graves, Emakhosini, in the Vryheid district was also of great significance. Dinuzulu had recently been buried on the farm 'Koningsdal'. Jama and Senzangakhona were buried on neighbouring 'Welgekozen', Ndaba and Mageba on 'Pandasgraf', and Punga on 'Heel-goed'. The gravesites were held to be the sacred preserve of the Zulu people, and it was one of Solomon's first political preoccupations to get them out of the hands of white landowners and into his own, as the representative of the Zulu nation. Harriette Colenso strongly supported Solomon in this cause and, although he was unsuccessful, his campaign itself did much to reinforce his royal status.[52]

In Zululand, Solomon surrounded himself with *izinduna* and *izinceku* of prestigious birth and rank, all of whom had historic claims to positions of responsibility in the Zulu royal house or Zulu national affairs. Virtually all had either themselves held positions under past Zulu kings, or were descendants of men who had done so. As sons of King Cetshwayo's powerful brothers Ndabuko and Shingana, both of whom had distinguished themselves as military leaders, Solomon's uncles Mnyaiza and Franz fitted this bill. Being blood members of the Zulu royal family's inner circle, neither Mnyaiza nor Franz could be described as an *induna*; they were nonetheless very influential in their roles as informal 'in house' advisers.

Until his death in the mid-1920s, the aged yet redoubtable Mankulumana – who had previously served Dinuzulu – was Solomon's principal *induna*. Considerable tension had existed between Solomon and Mankulumana for the first few years after Solomon's succession, however, as a consequence of Mankulumana's support for David during the succession dispute. Solomon had then resolutely refused to allow Mankulumana any role in the settlement of Dinuzulu's estate, and instead delegated the matter to Mnyaiza and Seme. By 1917, Mankulumana was nonetheless securely back in his long-held position as respected and powerful royal adviser, appearing alongside Solomon at virtually all important gatherings, often dressed simply in a *beshu* (loin skin) and necklace of leopard's claws. Solomon also had another *induna* of high rank: Gilbert kaNgcongcwana Zulu, who was a member of a collateral branch of the Zulu royal family which traced its descent back to Jama. Gilbert's father, Ngcongcwana, had accompanied Cetshwayo to London for an interview with Queen Victoria shortly after the Anglo-Zulu War. Subsequently, back in Zululand, he was killed by the Mandlakazi in 1883. Shortly after the NAD officially recognised Solomon as chief of the Usuthu, Solomon appointed Mankulumana and Gilbert, together with the lesser-ranking Nkunzi Buthelezi, as *izinduna* with official authority to try civil cases arising in the Usuthu ward.

Gilbert never rose to such status as Mankulumana, even after the latter's death, partly because in the later 1920s Solomon came to rely increasingly on kholwa advisers. Equally important, however, was Solomon's decision to revive the tradition – which had fallen into abeyance following the disagreement between the Usuthu and Buthelezi in 1888 – whereby the head of the Buthelezi acted as prime minister to the Zulu kingship. Mnyamana kaNgqengelele Buthelezi had held such a position during

Cetshwayo's time, and indeed had been the most powerful man in the country after the king, and before him his father Ngqengelele had held a similar position under Shaka. Mnyamana's grandson, Matole, was to be the successor to this tradition under Solomon from the mid-1920s, and his voice was to carry more weight than that of Gilbert.[53]

Among Solomon's personal attendants or *izinceku*, Maphelu kaMkhosana Zungu occupied the most senior position as Solomon's chief personal bodyguard. He had acted in a similar capacity under Dinuzulu, and had been implicated in the 1906 rebellion. However, perhaps because of his age, his extensive knowledge of history and custom, and his status as a loyal servant of Dinuzulu who had shared many of his late master's trials, Maphelu had an influence that exceeded the usual powers of an *inceku*. Although he held no public position, he had Solomon's confidence and ear at all times, and in practice his advice was sought on matters beyond the royal homesteads – which worried those Natal NAD officials who remembered the 1906 rebellion all too vividly.

An *inceku* also consistently close to Solomon was Zazeni kaLokhotwayo Mngadi. Lokhotwayo had been *inceku* to Dinuzulu, and Zazeni succeeded his father as *inceku* and body servant (*insila*) to the king. The term *insila* refers to the 'essence' of an individual, which in traditional Zulu belief is held to attach to body matter (hair, sweat and urine) and personal property. If this matter fell into the wrong hands, the individual's health and security was at risk. As Solomon's *insila*, Zazeni was thus in a position of some ceremonial and physical responsibility.[54]

One year after Dinuzulu's death, the occasion of Dinuzulu's *ihlambo* ceremony, the ritual meeting of the *amabutho* to symbolise the end of the period of mourning, illustrated Solomon's role within the world of Zulu traditionalism, and simultaneously revealed what a danger he posed to the existing administrative arrangements in force in Zululand. For many reasons, the NAD was appalled by the prospect of large numbers of Zulu gathering together, as a nation, to pay final respects to Dinuzulu and to perform the requisite traditional rites. Most obviously, the *ihlambo* would free Solomon from the fetters of mourning that had so far inhibited his political activities. Moreover, it would be a national festival, presided over by Solomon. The NAD considered that such a demonstration would pose a threat to the white population not only by eroding the operation of indirect rule in Zululand: there were also fears that there was to be another Zulu rebellion. Long before the *ihlambo*, there was persistent and widespread consternation that, contrary to strict instructions, Solomon was inviting men from all over the country to attend the ceremony. Writing to the SNA, the CNC (Addison) stated that it was clear that the *ihlambo* would not be a 'local matter', and that the 'loyal Mandlakazi tribe' might be attacked. He proceeded to outline the linkage between the *ihlambo*, the World War and the Boer rebellion against South Africa's participation on the side of Britain. The Boers in Northern Natal, intelligence reports indicated, had informed the Zulu that they would be better off under German rule.[55] The magistrate at Vryheid, Colenbrander, who was normally a calm and sympathetic official, similarly expressed 'great apprehension' at the prospect of the *ihlambo* 'in view of the present rebellion [Boer] in the Union'. Despite instructions, large numbers of Zulu were already proceeding to Nobamba, and already rumours of an imminent 'native uprising' were spreading among whites. He felt certain that when the *ihlambo* took place there would be 'a panic in this district'.[56] The CNC arranged for a military detachment – the 'Vryheid Commando' – to remain in the vicinity of Nobamba during the *ihlambo*.

These fears say much more about the Natal NAD and the local white population than about the intentions of the Zulu royal family. The *ihlambo* was a peaceful and highly disciplined ceremony, and there was no hint that anything sinister lay behind it. The *ihlambo* did prove, however, that the NAD's existing application of indirect rule was severely threatened. Furthermore, by lifting the veil of mourning from Solomon and his advisers, it inaugurated the 'reign' of Solomon. Soon the NAD was to find that its administrative arrangements were absolutely unworkable.

Solomon and Mankulumana had indeed sent for people from all over Zululand and Northern Natal to attend the *ihlambo*. It was a scrupulously traditional ceremony; Mkhosana kaZangwana Zungu, who had been an adviser to Cetshwayo and had accompanied him to London after the Anglo-Zulu War, was especially brought from the Mahlabatini district to preside over the ceremony, since he was an expert on ancient custom. Because he was aged and frail, Solomon sent Mankulumana with a wagon to fetch him. A number of royal cattle were slaughtered to provide food for the assembly. While the meat was being prepared, the *izinyanga* (herbalists) prepared ritual medicines for the purification of Solomon at Dinuzulu's grave, and for the *amabutho*, numbering some five thousand men, who crowded into the cattle kraal. Once they had expressed their final devotions and praises to Dinuzulu, the assistant magistrate at Babanango addressed the gathering and emphasised the government's goodwill to the Zulu, as shown by its gift of fifteen head of cattle. In order of ascending rank, he named the 'friends of the Zulus' in the government: J.Y. Gibson (DNC, Zululand), R.H. Addison (CNC, Natal), E. Dower (SNA), and General Louis Botha (Prime Minister and Minister of Native Affairs). He concluded by reminding the chiefs present that it was their duty 'to see that Solomon does not get into trouble by keeping your men in hand, whom you have brought here . . .'[57]

In accordance with the *ihlambo* custom, there was to follow a ritual hunt (*inqina*) to 'wash the spears' of the nation. The NAD had already forbidden this, but, faced with the question at the *ihlambo* itself, the assistant magistrate at Babanango felt that 'tact' was called for and allowed the hunt to proceed. At sunrise the following morning the hunt began. Solomon cut a dashing figure among the *amabutho*, riding a horse and carrying a rifle. He personally, with the royal dogs, was responsible for many of the slain buck that were brought back to Nobamba at sunset, carried on the shoulders of members of the various *amabutho* as they sang 'great songs of Zulu kings'.[58] Before the *amabutho* dispersed, they constructed a cattle kraal for Solomon at Zibindini: the reign of the new king was well and truly under way.

The *ihlambo* was the first traditional national ceremony over which Solomon presided. The adherence to custom that was such a feature of the ceremony had been arranged by Solomon himself when he summoned Mkhosana to prescribe proceedings. Solomon, together with the Zulu royal family as a whole, represented continuity with the past, national unity, and a sense of independent identity. Solomon's role as an embodiment of tradition was vital in establishing his social and political status. At ceremonies such as the *ihlambo*, men were drawn together from all sections of the Zulu people and they grouped themselves together not in the 'tribal' units that the NAD prescribed, but in their *amabutho* – wherein the criterion for membership was age rather than lineage or territorial origin. The activities of the *amabutho* at the *ihlambo* focused on the Zulu royal family and in so doing, made a strong appeal to nationalist sentiments. In such a context of tradition and custom, Solomon was undeniably the king of the Zulu. In this light, Solomon's confirmation by the Bishop of Zululand in February 1914 and his appearance a few months later in his late father's cattle kraal, virtually naked while being washed down with ritual medicines, were not contradictory. Solomon, it seemed clear, was deliberately drawing on both the old and the new, both Zulu tradition and western modernity, in his attempt to unite as many Zulu as possible under himself as a symbol of Zulu national unity.

The function of the *ihlambo* had not only been to complete the period of mourning for Dinuzulu. While the burning of the bones after the feast in Dinuzulu's cattle kraal was a symbolic farewell to the past, the work of the *amabutho* in building a new cattle kraal for Solomon was a symbolic gesture towards the future. Solomon was no longer the 'nation's comfort' for the loss of Dinuzulu; he had become its new leader.

NOTES

1. Account of Maphelu, p. 99; and Report of Socwatsha and Nongejeni, evidence of Chief Nqodi, p. 5. These were my two principal sources for Dinuzulu's funeral ceremony and the succession dispute (see Prologue footnotes 11 and 21). Other sources are noted in the text. See also C. de B. Webb and J. B. Wright (eds), *The James Stuart archive*, vol. 1 (Pietermaritzburg, 1976), p. 172, statement of Hoye kaSoxalase, 20/9/1921.

2. Report of Socwatsha and Nongejeni, evidence of Mhlutshwa, p. 2.

3. This royal salute can only be given once the heir has been formally nominated; prior to this, he may only be saluted with 'ndabazitha', to which all members of the Zulu royal family are entitled. Webb and Wright (eds), *Stuart archive*, vol. 1, p. 172.

4. Account of Maphelu, p. 100.

5. She was subsequently reprimanded for doing so. By taking David by her right hand rather than Solomon, it was thought that she favoured David: the lineage segment that was to bear the heir was referred to as the 'right-hand house'.

6. Fuze, *Black people*, p. 90.

7. CNC 144, 1985/1913, CNC to SNA, 30/11/1913. See also Report of Socwatsha and Nongejeni, p. 2.

8. Pers. Comm. Ndesheni kaMnyaiza Zulu, Nongoma district, 10/11/1981, Part II, pp. 4–5; and Pers. Comm. Princess Mkandandhlovu kaDinuzulu Zulu, Nongoma district, 15/12/1981, pp. 6–7.

9. CNC 144, 1985/1913, G. W. Kinsman, Assistant Magistrate, Babanango to CNC, 28/10/1913, reporting occurrences at Dinuzulu's funeral. Mankulumana's speech caused alarm and controversy in the NAD, and extensive correspondence on the issue is to be found in the same file.

10. Account of Maphelu, p. 102.

11. *Ibid.*, pp. 103–4.

12. CNC 144, 1985/1913, B. Colenbrander, Magistrate, Vryheid to CNC, 12/12/1913.

13. CNC 54, 97/1912, notes of interview between Magistrate, Nongoma and Nobiyana, 5/12/1911 (quotation); and DNC, Eshowe to CNC, 12/1/1912.

14. Report of Socwatsha and Nongejeni, evidence of Chief Zombode, p. 4, and Dukuza, p. 8.

15. *Ibid.*, p. 5. See also CNC 144, 1985/1913, Magistrate, Nongoma to CNC, 11/12/1914.

16. Report of Socwatsha and Nongejeni, pp. 9–10.

17. Natal Archives Depot, Zulu Society Collection, File IV/5/6, typescript entitled 'A discussion between the Zulus and Zibhebhu', 23/12/1898.

18. My sources on the history of the Mandlakazi leadership after 1905 were CNC PMB 73, 57/18, Native Commissioner, Nongoma to CNC, 29/6/1932, enclosing typescript *re* the 'Mandlakazi Tribe'; and statement of Mciteki before Native Commissioner, Nongoma, 30/9/1933.

19. CNC PMB 72, 57/29, quoted in intelligence report of Lt. C. von Keyserlingh, 3rd SAMR, 1/11/1917.

20. CNC 144, 1985/1913, CNC to SNA, 29/11/1913, commenting on the reports of NAD 'confidential messengers' in Zululand. 'Mahashini' means 'place of the horses', which commemorated the combative role played by horses in Dinuzulu's successful attacks on the Mandlakazi during the Zulu civil war. See also the *izibongo* of Mahashini, in unpublished collection of Zulu praise poems.

21. MS LUG 1.09, MS 1406, 'Documentation of Nobamba', by Charles Mpanza; and CNC 144. 1985/1913, T.R. Bennet, Magistrate, Nongoma to CNC, 12/11/1913.

22. Unpublished collection of Zulu praise poems, 'Izibongo sika okaNtuzwa uNina kaMaphumuzana' and 'Izibongo sika uMaphumuzana kaDinuzulu'.

23. CNC 144, 1985/1913, CNC to SNA, 28/11/1913, commenting on Manzolwandle's history; and notes of interview between Chief Manzolwandle and CNC, 27/11/1913.

24. Report of Socwatsha and Nongejeni, evidence of Mbiwa, p. 6 (quotation). See also CNC 219, 1481/1915, CNC to DNC, Zululand, 7/8/1915; CNC 144, 1985/1913, Magistrate, Eshowe to DNC, Zululand, 17/11/1913; and DNC, Zululand to CNC, 12/8/1915.

25. This takes into account that David would pay the rental for the huts he used at Nobamba. Dinuzulu's widows and dependants had 27 huts on 'Koningsdal', at £3 per hut p.a. CNC 144, 1985/1913, notes of interview between SNA and Mankulumana, 12/12/1913; and CNC to DNC, Zululand, 22/1/1915.

26. 'Indlunkulu', which literally means 'great homestead', refers to the wife of a king. This title emphasised how wives were closely identified with the productive and reproductive units of the kingdom: the homesteads. Wives were not, however, usually referred to by their first names, but as 'she who is the daughter of . . .' – hence 'okaNtuzwa' and 'okaQethuka'. My historical sources were C. Faye, *Zulu references* (Pietermaritzburg, 1923), p. 51; *The Net*, June 1933, p. 4; Pers. Comm. Princess Magogo kaDinuzulu Zulu, KwaPhindangene, Zululand, 6/1/1982, Part I, pp. 1–6 (the interviewee was okaNtuzwa's fourth child, conceived at Eshowe when Dinuzulu returned from exile in 1898); and typescript of speech by Chief Mangosuthu Gatsha Buthelezi, Chief Minister of KwaZulu and president of Inkatha, at the ceremony to unveil Dinuzulu's tombstone at Nobamba, 29/8/1981, p. 39 (the speaker was the son of Princess Magogo, she having married Chief Matole kaTshanibezwe Buthelezi).

27. Pers. Comm. Magogo, Part I, pp. 2, 6.

28. Fuze, *Black people*, pp. 132–33; and KCAL, Harriette Colenso Collection, MS 13083, notes *re* Harriette Colenso by Alice Werner, June 1932, p. 8.

29. Pers. Comm. Magogo, Part I, p. 3.

30. Fuze, *Black people*, p. 135; and *The Net*, June 1933, p.4.

31. In response to my question 'Was he a Christian – did he go to church?', Princess Mkandandhlovu replied 'He was a believer . . . there was no one who wore traditional dress (*obincayo* – 'those who wear traditional dress') in our family.' Pers. Comm, Mkandandhlovu, p. 18. The following interchange with Ndesheni is similar: *NC*: 'Was he a real Christian?' *Ndesheni*: 'He was a Christian.' *NC*: 'Even though he had many wives?' *Ndesheni*: 'He didn't wear a loin skin. Moreover, his brothers were also Christians. Even though they were not Christians in the sense of observing the rules of the Church, still they conducted themselves in a Christian way.' Pers. Comm. Ndesheni, Part I, p. 6.

32. Princess Magogo, who would have been about five years old at the time, remembered being carried away at night on someone's back to be hidden. Pers. Comm. Magogo, Part I, p. 7.

33. Unpublished collection of Zulu praise poems, 'Izibongo sika uMaphumuzana kaDinuzulu'.

34. R. H. Reyher, *Zulu woman* (Columbia, 1948), pp.33–34. Having first toured Zululand in the 1920s, Rebecca Reyher returned in 1934 to conduct research for a book on the life of Solomon's great wife, Christina Sibiya, who was her main interviewee. Oswald Fynney, the magistrate at Nongoma during the 1920s, and Sir Charles Saunders put her in touch with a wide number of royal sources, while the CNC assisted by introducing her to NAD officials. See CNC 509, 17/2, CNC to L.E. Oscroft, 14/1/1924. Although it was written as an historical romance, Reyher's *Zulu woman* is based on solid factual foundations.

35. These were Christina Sibiya's impressions of the royal hut when she first entered it in 1915. *Ibid.*, p.54.

36. *The Net*, September 1914, p.9; and see also June 1933, p.4.

37. CNC 144, 1985/1913, report of Nongejeni Zuma, Natal NAD messenger, 2/1/1914.

38. *Izindaba Zabantu*, 15/1/1914, editorial, private translation.

39. *Izindaba Zabantu*, 1/8/1915, private translation.

40. T. Karis and G.M. Carter (eds), *From protest to challenge*, vol.1 (Stanford, 1973), doc.19, 'A talk on my native land' by the Revd J.L. Dube, 1892, pp.68–69. In outlining Dube's career until 1913 I have drawn heavily from Shula Marks, 'The ambiguities of dependence: John L. Dube of Natal', *Journal of Southern African Studies*, vol.1, no.2, April 1975.

41. Marks, 'Ambiguities of dependence', p. 175. For the Natal kholwa view on tribal life, see also Marks, *Ambiguities of dependence*, pp. 45ff; and the evidence of Natal kholwa before the South African Native Affairs Commission, 1903–5, and Natal Native Affairs Commission, 1906–7.

42. Faye, *Zulu references*, record of meeting between J.L. Dube and the Zulus, Eshowe, 30/11/1912, pp. 80–89; and KCAL, Sir Marshall Campbell Collection, File 4, KCM 32590, notes by Carl Faye on the same meeting.

43. Natal Archives Depot, Colenso Collection, Box 76, Harriette Colenso to Mr Dube, 5/12/1913; and see also the report in *Izindaba Zabantu*, 15/1/1914.

44. CNC 144, 1985/1913, NC, Piet Retief to SNA, 9/1/1914.

45. CNC 144, 1985/1913, Seme to Dr Bok, Prime Minister's private secretary, 8/12/1913; and notes of interview between SNA and Mankulumana, 12/12/1913.

46. CNC 144, 1985/1913, NC, Piet Retief to SNA, 9/1/1914.

47. CNC 144, 1985/1913, Magistrate, Nongoma to CNC, 11/2/1914.

48. CNC 144, 1985/1913, notes of interview between CNC and Mnyaiza, 19/2/1914.

49. CNC 144, 1985/1913, CNC to SNA, 18/3/1914.

50. CNC 254, 1557/1916, Detached Assistant Magistrate, Babanango to Magistrate, Vryheid, 21/9/1916. See also CNC to SNA, 3/10/1916; and SNA to CNC, 12/10/1916.

51. CNC 144, 1985/1913, CNC to SNA, 3/11/1913; and Magistrate, Nongoma to CNC, 25/11/1913.

52. Information on the royal gravesites and Solomon's campaign to repossess them, including correspondence from Solomon himself, is contained in CNC PMB 72, 57/29. See also Natives' Land Commission Report, UG22–16, evidence of Harriette Colenso, 19/5/1915, pp. 522–23.

53. My sources on Solomon's tribal advisors were CNC PMB 72, 57/31, O. Fynney, Magistrate, Nongoma to CNC, 9/5/1917; CNC 144, 1985/1913, CNC to DNC, Zululand, 16/1/1915; Guy, *Destruction of the Zulu kingdom*, pp. 31–32, 250; Pers. Comm. Ndesheni, Part I, pp. 1–2; and Pers. Comm. Zephaniah Mahaye, Zulu oral historian, Hluhluwe, 11/11/1981, p. 6. Mahaye's description of Gilbert as an *inceku*, p. 7, is incorrect.

54. My sources on Solomon's personal attendants were CNC PMB, 92, 64/3, notes of interview between CNC, Magistrate, Nongoma, Solomon, Mankulumana and Mnyaiza, 31/4/1920; Reyher, *Zulu woman*, p. 44; Pers. Comm. Ndesheni, Part I, pp. 17–18; and *Ilanga lase Natal*, 17/3/1933. For further details on the meaning of '*insila*', see H.C. Lugg, *Life under a Zulu shield* (Pietermaritzburg, 1975), p. 14.

55. CNC 144, 1985/1913, CNC to SNA, 2/11/1914 (quotation); and CNC to SNA, 6/11/1914.

56. CNC 144, 1985/1913, Magistrate, Vryheid to CNC, 5/11/1914.

57. My sources on the *ihlambo* were Account of Maphelu, pp. 104–107 (Mkhosana kaZangwana Zungu was, incidentally, Maphelu's father.); CNC 144, 1985/1913, report by Assistant Magistrate, Babanango, 16/11/1914 (quotation); and Lt. C. von Keyserlingh, 3rd SAMR, Vryheid to District Commandant, Dundee, 18/11/1914.

58. Account of Maphelu, p. 106.

3

Solomon's appointment as Chief of the Usuthu

The retirement of Dick Addison as CNC in 1916, and his replacement by Charles Wheelwright, was to mark a crucial change in NAD policy towards the Zulu royal family. Addison, who in 1888 had personally witnessed the devastating Usuthu attack on the Mandlakazi near the magistracy at Nongoma, had long been dogmatically opposed to the influence of Zulu royalty and the Usuthu. Under his administration, Solomon was officially treated as no more than a private individual while the Usuthu were parcelled out among four chiefs. In public, Addison ignored Solomon in so far as was possible, though his departmental correspondence proved that he was in fact obsessed by Solomon's growing influence. The major crisis of Addison's administration came in early 1916, on the eve of Addison's retirement, when Solomon called a ceremony to enrol the first *ibutho* (age-set regiment) of his 'reign'. Wheelwright inherited a Zululand administration which was to some extent in a state of panic. Having begun his career in Zululand in 1890, Wheelwright was not an outsider to the Natal NAD's administrative traditions in regard to Zulu royalty. He had, however, spent the fourteen years prior to his appointment as CNC outside Natal, as a colonial official in the Soutpansberg district of the northern Transvaal. Partly for this reason, perhaps, he was able to apply himself to the 1916 crisis in the administration of Zululand with a dispassionate pragmatism that had eluded his predecessor. It was soon to become apparent that Wheelwright's personal style in any case leant towards diplomacy, compromise and accommodation, and shied away from administrative heavy-handedness.[1]

* * * * *

After Dinuzulu's funeral ceremony, the Usuthu had in practice reconstituted themselves around Solomon in defiance of their official partition. In 1914, even before the *ihlambo*, the threat this posed to the administration had led Addison to instruct the DNC for Zululand, J. Y. Gibson, to make a report on the matter. The case of Mankulumana was also to be considered – Addison was piqued that NAD head office in Pretoria had unilaterally sanctioned Mankulumana's repatriation from exile in the Transvaal at KwaThengisa. In his report, Gibson recommended that Mankulumana be regarded as no more than a private individual, and be separated from the royal house by removal to a magisterial district distant from the royal epicentre. More broadly, Gibson reported that the four chiefs appointed to rule over the Usuthu – Moya Ndwandwe, Mpikanina Zulu, Muzimubi Buthelezi, and Mciteki Zulu (of the Mandlakazi) – could not be relied on to defend their positions against 'any recrudescence of Royal pretensions'. Chief Moya, he observed, had been 'habituated since childhood to be deferential to the Royal family', and further it 'might naturally be supposed that his uncle Mankulumana could dominate him'.[2]

Like Chief Moya, the other chiefs appointed over the Usuthu found that their authority was simply being overridden. Referring in 1915 to the Usuthu people placed under Chief Muzimubi, the magistrate at Mahlabatini described their disposition towards 'Dinuzulu's second son as the rightful heir . . . he pays periodical visits to the district and invariably the chiefs disapprove of this very strongly; they say their influence is being taken away by "the boy", who always gets a large following from the tribes'.[3] Chief Mpikanina for his part had virtually no control over the Usuthu in his ward. Solomon never visited him, and did not keep in touch with 'his chief' even by messenger. Mnyaiza, who had also been placed under Mpikanina, moreover repeatedly disobeyed him and refused to visit him even when requested to do so.[4] The only chief on whom the NAD felt it could rely to counter the influence of Solomon was Chief Mciteki of the Mandlakazi. Yet the NAD realised that to back the Mandlakazi against the Usuthu in the existing political climate would be futile, and might well provoke another Zulu civil war.

Solomon's 'roaming about' was reportedly causing various other Zulu chiefs to lose control over their followers, who were 'declaring their allegiance to Solomon'.[5] In a vain attempt to bolster the administration after the *ihlambo*, in early 1915 the CNC informed all Zulu chiefs that 'Solomon holds no official position in Zululand or elsewhere, and he has no right to summon them to any meetings, and they must not attend'.[6] Ironically, since Solomon held no official position, the NAD was almost powerless to take disciplinary action against him. Instead, acting on Gibson's report, the Natal NAD took out its frustrations on Mankulumana, who had in fact maintained a very low profile since Dinuzulu's funeral ceremony. It ruled that

Mankulumana had to remove from the Nongoma and Mahlabatini districts, and live in the Eshowe district. Mankulumana seemed deeply upset that he would no longer be able to act as guardian of Dinuzulu's sons, and repeatedly asked to know what wrong he had committed. Addison replied that Mankulumana should look on 'his being allowed to reside in Zululand at all as a distinct concession'.[7]

Since the NAD did not recognise his status, Solomon was understandably truculent with officialdom. Solomon refused, for example, to assist the magistrate at Nongoma to draw up a list of Dinuzulu's dependants so that the NAD could fairly distribute the government allowance for their subsistence. The magistrate had first spoken to Mankulumana and Mnyaiza on the matter, and Solomon held that he and no one else should have been consulted in the first instance. Subsequently, in 1916, Solomon arrived uninvited in the middle of an *indaba* between the Governor-General and Zulu chiefs at Eshowe, and ordered the *induna* attached to the Eshowe magistracy to interrupt proceedings to introduce him personally to the Governor-General. When the *induna* refused, Solomon rode off abruptly and angrily, causing a disturbance. Indeed, as the *induna* later reported, the prevailing opinion among the Zulu at the *indaba* was that Solomon should have been introduced.[8]

Solomon was not simply obstructive with officialdom, however. During 1914 and 1915 he also pressurised Addison's administration for permission to meet officially with the Prime Minister, General Botha. This came to a head in January 1915, soon after the *ihlambo*, when Solomon requested official sanction to gather forty-one representatives of the Zulu royal family and of Zulu chiefs and headmen from districts all over Zululand and Northern Natal, and proceed to Pretoria for a joint meeting with the Prime Minister, the SNA, the CNC and all Zululand magistrates. The scale of the meeting, and evidence that the whole proposal had been carefully planned, suggested that Solomon intended to broach the subject of his unaccommodated political status. Indeed, Solomon's list of proposed delegates to Pretoria included men who had long been regarded as leading opponents of the Usuthu. Manzolwandle was named, as were two of the chiefs appointed over the Usuthu, Mpikanina and Muzimubi. Also on the list were Msenteli kaZibhebhu of the Mandlakazi (Chief Mciteki's brother), Kambi kaHamu of the Ngenetsheni, and Mtonga kaMpande Zulu who had defected to colonial Natal prior to the Anglo-Zulu War.[9]

The agenda for this proposed meeting, as Solomon had outlined to the Natal NAD, included the dispersal of Dinuzulu's property at KwaThengisa, the welfare of Dinuzulu's dependants, and the education of Solomon and David – which NAD head office had offered to pay for, soon after the news of Dinuzulu's death. The Natal NAD concluded, with justification, that a delegation of this scope was not necessary to discuss the topics Solomon had outlined, and that Solomon had a hidden agenda. In a printed circular to all magistrates in Zululand and Northern Natal, the CNC declared that the request was not granted and that Solomon had no right under any circumstances to summon chiefs in this manner. The magistrate at Melmoth, expressing his opinions to the DNC for Zululand, encapsulated the general attitude of the Natal NAD:

> The whole movement should most unmistakably be nipped in the bud
> . . . No further communications as to deputations should be entered
> into, but Solomon should be sent for at once . . . and be informed that
> his future position (status) is that of a commoner and the Government
> is determined for all time never to place any of Dinuzulu's
> descendants in charge of any tribe or section thereof.[10]

Even after the 1915 deputation crisis faded, Solomon's activities still regularly featured in Natal NAD correspondence. The CNC and DNC for Zululand routinely exchanged information ostensibly to 'correct any false rumours that may be in circulation', but were always faced with evidence that Solomon's influence was, if anything, increasing.[11]

In April 1915 Solomon visited the paramount chief of Pondoland, to the west of Natal, and came away with one of his daughters as a prospective wife. For the Natal NAD this was a disturbing contact, for tribal rule remained strong in Pondoland and the territory was administered similarly to Zululand, but, unlike Zululand, Pondoland had a paramount chief. Solomon's visit to Pondoland was in fact a part of a far larger tour, which included visits to Natal's two principal cities, the capital city of Pietermaritzburg and the commercial port of Durban, and various places in the Transvaal. This was Solomon's first visit to Durban, where there was a large concentration of Zulu migrant labourers, and clearly he established his support in the city. According to the magistrate at Nkandla he was given 'quite a royal reception, the Natives contributing coins for his support'. If the tour as a whole was designed to induce Zulu-speaking people to regard Solomon as their 'paramount head, instead of merely an ordinary person', as the magistrate believed, it would appear that Solomon achieved considerable success.[12]

Early in 1916, Solomon called a large gathering for the purpose of enrolling the first *ibutho* of his 'reign'. Since it was a practice expressly forbidden by the NAD, Solomon had requested official permission merely to hold a hunt – the *inqina* (ritual hunt) was an integral part of the *ukubuthwa* ceremony – in the hope of screening his real intentions. He went ahead with arrangements for the ceremony even though permission for the hunt was refused, and instructions were issued to Zulu in north-western Zululand, particularly young men of enrolling age, to gather at his Sikalenisenyoka homestead in the Nongoma district. NAD officials hastened to countermand Solomon's instructions, making particular efforts to prevent members of the wards of Chiefs Moya, Mpikanina, Muzimubi and Mciteki from attending.

In January 1916 a police patrol, sent to investigate an intelligence report of a gathering at Sikalenisenyoka, discovered about two hundred young men 'giyaing' (*ukugiya* – to perform competitive and demonstrative dances) in front of Solomon. The evidence that Solomon was in the process of enrolling a new 'regiment' was confirmed when it emerged that the young men intended not only to join the hunt but also to reap Solomon's fields – an important element of the *ukubuthwa* ceremony. Although administrative intervention prevented, or at least postponed, the *inqina* from taking place, Solomon nonetheless succeed in enrolling a new *ibutho* during January and February 1916 under the noses of local officials. This new *ibutho* bore a name with nationalistic overtones, 'Nqabakucetshwangabesizwe' (or Nqabakucetshwa), meaning 'the-will-not-be-betrayed-by-foreigners'.[13] J.Y. Gibson, the DNC for Zululand and one of the most perceptive of Zululand officials, identified the significance of the ceremony:

> The act amounted to an exercise of authority over tribes in various parts of Zululand and the Vryheid District. It amounted to the exercise of superior authority over Chiefs in charge of those tribes. The response has amounted to a recognition of such authority.

The whole affair, Gibson observed, had done the NAD a 'great deal of harm'.[14] From Solomon's point of view, on the other hand, reviving such traditional national ceremonies as the *ukubuthwa* was a crucial means of establishing his political status among the Zulu-speaking people.

Events during the past two years had shown that Solomon was now widely recognised as successor not only to Dinuzulu but also to the Zulu kingship. When Solomon succeeded Dinuzulu in 1913 he had had virtually no personal wealth, and since then he had not held any official position. What authority he now held in Zulu affairs had been voluntarily accorded him from below. This posed difficulties for the NAD, because indirect rule was essentially a method of overrule, and depended on a strong element of consensus between the rulers and the ruled. Following the *ukubuthwa* ceremony, Gibson in effect identified that the NAD administration in Zululand would be undermined so long as Solomon was not incorporated into it. Gibson and Colenbrander, the magistrate at Vryheid, were however the only officials stationed near the royal epicentre who held realistic and pragmatic views on the Zulu royal family. The magistrates at Nongoma, Mahlabatini, Babanango, Melmoth (Emtonjaneni district) and Nkandla held views similar to those of the CNC, Dick Addison. In 1916 these dominant Natal NAD views on the Zulu royal family were apparently confirmed by evidence that Solomon's attempted 'hunt' was a front for something even more threatening than an *ukubuthwa* ceremony.

The *ukubuthwa* situation appeared doubly alarming to the NAD because it coincided with a proliferation of seditious rumours among the Zulu in north-western Zululand and Northern Natal. These rumours took account of the British involvement in the Great War, and linked the Zulu royal family with an impending rebellion to retake Zulu independence while the imperial forces were otherwise engaged. It was also rumoured that the Zulu royal family was to receive military support from both German East Africa and local Boer commandos – which to the NAD seemed not altogether unfeasible, because there had recently been a Boer rebellion in South Africa, directed against the South African government's decision to make an active contribution to the British war effort. Immediately before the *ukubuthwa* took place, the magistrate at Nkandla informed the Chief Intelligence Officer at Pietermaritzburg of reports that certain whites 'chiefly of Dutch descent . . . indulge in seditious talk with the Natives, and tell them that Germany is sure to win . . . the Natives must join with them and overthrow the British power'. The same magistrate subsequently reported Zulu rumours that the Germans were to approach from the east coast to 'conquer this country and assist the Natives by restoring the Royal House of Zululand'.[15] Various reports were also received by the magistrate at Nongoma, and one received through a Zulu police constable showed how some Zulu had connected the *ukubuthwa* ceremony with the prospective rebellion. People as far afield as Basutoland and Swaziland had been notified of the *ukubuthwa*, the constable had heard, and the purpose of the *inqina* was to 'hunt down the Black Umfolosi [river] and there they would meet the Germans who would hand Dinuzulu back to them'.[16]

The use of Dinuzulu's name suggested that, in 1916, there were some in rural Zulu society who were reawakening memories of the 1906 rebellion. As in the case of Dinuzulu in 1906, there was no evidence that Solomon in 1916 in some way associated himself with the prospect of a rebellion. Yet the high incidence of rumours implicating the Zulu royal family in a plot to liberate the Zulu from the yoke of white rule was not meaningless: it was as clear an index to the existence of civil unrest as it had been in the months preceding the 1906 rebellion. Especially in the wake of the 1913 Land Act, moreover, social and economic conditions among rural Zulu provided ample cause for civil unrest, as had been the case in 1906. It was significant that in January 1916, while the *ukubuthwa* ceremony was under way, the CNC telegraphed all magistrates in Natal to report that numerous telegrams had been sent

> by Natives recalling friends and relatives working Johannesburg and other Transvaal labour centres on pretext of illness or death in family. Please keep watch on exit and ingress Natives from and to your Division and report anything unusual.[17]

As Addison knew only too well, this was the pattern immediately before and during the 1906 rebellion, when relatives were recalled from urban areas to assist in the rural revolt.

In a lengthy memorandum to the SNA on Solomon's role, particularly in regard to the *ukubuthwa* ceremony, Addison did not mince words:

> Solomon . . . holds no responsible position under the Government, and I hope he never will. He is a menace to the peace of the country and it is time that measures were taken against him which will be sufficiently severe to have a salutary effect on his ideas and aspirations.

He advocated 'swift punishment' and urged that this be dealt out by the highest possible authority: the Governor-General in his capacity as Supreme Chief. Since no criminal charge could be brought against Solomon, Addison recommended that the Governor-General use his autocratic powers to inflict a 'heavy fine' on Solomon and to detain him in Pretoria until it was paid.[18] These recommendations, made in late January 1916, were Addison's parting shots to the Zulu royal family.

*   *   *   *   *

Charles Wheelwright, Addison's replacement as CNC, in effect dismissed the whole *ukubuthwa* affair by merely reprimanding Solomon and emphasising that Solomon should ensure he had official authority before holding any future ceremonies. As soon after his appointment as possible, in April 1916, Wheelwright presided over a large meeting at the Nongoma magistracy to lay the issue to rest. The Acting DNC for Zululand and the magistrates at Nongoma, Mahlabatini, Vryheid and Ngotshe were in attendance, together with most of the chiefs in these districts, as well as Solomon. Despite official attempts to minimise the attendance of 'commoners', some three hundred or more nonetheless congregated outside the magistracy.

The whole spirit in which the new CNC approached the meeting contrasted with the bureaucratic and repressive approach of his predecessor. At the outset Wheelwright carefully explained the governmental changes that the declaration of Union in 1910 had brought about: Zululand was now an 'integral part of the Union', which had one government, the administrative centre being in Pretoria and the legislative centre being in Cape Town. Apparently such an explanation had not been given before. Having reprimanded Solomon for attempting to hold a hunt after it had been forbidden, the CNC reassured the chiefs whose authority had been overridden by Solomon's calling the hunt, saying that they had the government's support. His address then broke into two sections: first he read the 'message of the government', and then he gave his personal views.

The message of the government, as read by the CNC, expressed 'displeasure at the attitude [Solomon] was assuming', and warned that the government had the power to 'keep him out of harm's way . . . if his conduct does not shew improvement'. It also stressed that 'the Government has not at any time recognised Solomon as chief' and that 'the question of his relations with the Government must depend on the manner in which he behaves himself'. Despite the CNC's claim, the message was patently not the precise words of the government. The CNC had expressed the message in such a way as to emphasise that General Botha was the head of the Union government, and that he, the CNC, was Botha's *induna* over the Zulu people. The message had begun: 'General Botha directs that you [the CNC] . . .' These subtleties of approach were a consistent feature of the address.

Similarly, the CNC's personal address appealed to his audience's sense of reason to persuade them that Solomon's activities were inappropriate and dangerous. It was no longer necessary for the Zulu to form 'regiments' (*ibutho*), he said, because the government was prepared to keep the peace, and moreover, because the 'whole aspect' of Zululand had changed.

> We now have railways, mines, sugar industries and numerous other indications of a different aspect which formerly did not exist . . . The object of the people today is to attend to work and to peaceful methods of living. They have to earn money to pay taxes, to buy clothing, to feed themselves . . . And yet in the same breath we hear of the formation of a new regiment by Solomon. Who is this regiment to be used against? What is its purpose?

He concluded by reminding the present generation of Zulu that thirty-seven years previously the Zulu kingdom had been defeated while at the zenith of its power.[19]

In response to the CNC's address, Solomon admitted that he had enrolled a new *ibutho*, but not with the object of war: 'I was just gathering the men together.' As the CNC wrote in his personal report of the meeting, Solomon and the chiefs present 'expressed their gratitude at the manner in which the Government had seen fit to treat this matter'. He also identified that 'there was a pretty general feeling of sympathy on the part of all the Chiefs present towards Solomon'.[20] Indeed, various chiefs at the meeting expressed thanks to the CNC for the warning that he had given Solomon. As Headman Nkunzi of Nongoma put it, 'when we slip the Government assists us and picks us up. [Solomon] has slipped and the Government today picks him up.' Several attributed Solomon's 'lapse' to the fact that 'he has no elders to advise him'.[21]

The rumours that Solomon, in collusion with local Boers and with the support of the Germans in East Africa, was planning a Zulu rebellion had not been the sole cause of official alarm over the 'hunt' affair. It had also been suspected that Solomon's intention was to gather an *impi* (military force, comprising *amabutho*) to attack the Mandlakazi. The fears of both the Natal NAD and Chief Mciteki of the Mandlakazi, when confronted with the prospect of a rebellion led by Solomon, are recorded in Solomon's *izibongo* as having been not only undignified, but groundless:

> Tree-fern that overcame the judges at Nongoma,
> On the day the Royal One made them sit on one log
> Like hadadaws contending for worms.
> Starer whose eyes are red,
> Who looks at a person as if he is angry.
> Looking at the authorities in Nongoma,
> The buttocks of the authorities trembled.
>
> . . . .
>
> The Royal One armed as he betook himself to the forest,
> And the bowels of the authorities were excited;
> Mciteki's became excited,
> He who was born of Zibhebhu.
> Whereas the Royal One
> Had quarrelled with no-one,
> He was going to hunt the game
> On the hill where the lion lived.
> Even the weather feared the storm.
> Black darkness of Phunga and Mageba
> Which was seen by Mthusheyana who said
> 'The Royal One is making an attack!'
> Whereas he was merely going to hunt game.[22]

For the Natal NAD, the public conclusion of the 'hunt' affair was by no means the end of the 'Solomon question'. The hunt had merely thrown into relief several aspects of the more general problem of Solomon's political status. It had been associated with rumours of rebellion. It had revealed the influence that Solomon had, even over Zulu who lived in distant districts and under chiefs unsympathetic to the royal cause, and thus the disruption that Solomon could cause to the administration in Zululand and Northern Natal. Moreover, it had shown how little control the NAD could exert over Solomon, precisely because it refused to accommodate him. All these issues had confronted Wheelwright when he assumed office in March 1916, and they were as yet unresolved.

From his assumption of office, Wheelwright focused his attention on two interrelated aspects of the broader 'Solomon question'. On the one hand, he aimed to provide Solomon with a domicile more permanent and secure than the present Zibindini, which fell on white-owned land. On the other hand, he aimed to define officially Solomon's 'status' within the structure of indirect rule in Natal. In both these endeavours Wheelwright had been prompted by Solomon himself. In a letter carefully timed to arrive on the CNC's desk precisely when the new CNC assumed office, and which had been submitted with meticulous observation of the bureaucratic procedures of the NAD, Solomon made two requests. He explained that as Dinuzulu and all his ancestors had been chiefs and kings of the Zulu, he had hoped he would also be so. He had thus far been disappointed, but now wished to be 'relieved of the suspense' and be informed if he could hope for a chieftainship. Solomon's second request was that the land on which Nobamba and Zibindini lay, presently white-owned, be given to himself and his people as it was their 'old home' and where their kings were buried.[23]

Wheelwright's negotiations with the SNA to find a solution to the 'Solomon question' were conducted against a background of persistent rumours of an imminent Zulu rebellion, which, if anything, had become more threatening since his assumption of office as CNC.[24] Wheelwright nonetheless paid little attention to such rumours, which had so disturbed his predecessor, Addison, and which continued to disturb local officials. He regarded the question not as one of potential treason but simply as one of administrative disorder, and this he clearly expressed in a memorandum drawn up in April 1916. Solomon's frequent journeys between his rented properties near Babanango and his late father's homesteads in the Zululand reserves, Wheelwright felt, placed the region's appointed chiefs in an 'invidious position'. 'Solomon and his adherents continue to intrigue against the tribal authority of such chiefs [who] are faced with a strong sentimental and actual opposition in Solomon's favour.' The solution that the new CNC proposed was to purchase for Solomon and his relatives the lands on which the royal gravesites lay, Emakhosini, near Babanango. The corollary was that this would 'do away with the late Dinuzulu's kraals in Zululand', and so remove 'the necessity of Solomon's constant visits' to the Zululand reserves and minimise his disruptive influence there. The only problem he foresaw was that Solomon would not accept the arrangements.[25] Wheelwright's proposal was reportedly received by Botha with some favour, but the SNA, Edward Dower, whose knowledge of the Zululand situation had been gained under Addison's tutelage, foresaw complications. The SNA argued that the funds used to buy 'the sacred lands' would have to be repaid, since officially Solomon was no more than a private individual, and the national collections Solomon would undoubtedly arrange to do so would give the impression that he had government support. The real difficulty, the SNA realised, was that Solomon was 'not formally recognized in any position and we have no hold over him'.[26]

Directly after the meeting at Nongoma to lay the *ukubuthwa* issue to rest, the CNC had held a private discussion with Solomon which he emphasised was strictly confidential – a condition which Solomon thoroughly appreciated. Here he tentatively outlined his proposal to Solomon, to which Solomon 'unhesitatingly replied that such a course of action would be most unacceptable'. The CNC subsequently remarked that he 'never contemplated that [Solomon] would willingly be prepared to abandon the kraals in Zululand Proper, which form such a convenient stepping-stone to his aspirations to become the Paramount Chief of the Zulus'. Notwithstanding Solomon's response, Wheelwright still held to his proposal that Solomon be redomiciled outside the Zululand reserves, near Babanango.

The discussion had also turned to the issue of Solomon's official status. The CNC made a serious appeal to Solomon to 'patiently await the time when the Government could consider his application for the definition of his status'. Although Solomon's demeanour was impeccable, the CNC recorded that

> he kept repeating 'I do not ask these people to follow me and to show me any sort of respect; wherever I go they recognize me as the representative of the Zulu House, and accord me the respect due thereto'. He kept impressing on me that [such respect] was gratuitously given on the part of the Natives.

This the CNC believed to be true. 'I do not hope for a moment', he commented, 'that the best of us will ever be able . . . to eliminate the inherent sentiment and attachment to the Zulu House and to Solomon as its direct representative'. The CNC felt strongly that 'action of a definite nature must be taken to establish the man's status once and for all'.[27]

Despite the priority that both the CNC and the SNA gave to the resolution of the 'Solomon question', for eight months no action was taken. Instead there followed lengthy correspondence and a number of official discussions in which clarity of vision was blurred by a marked reluctance to make a commitment to any particular course of action, and an equally marked preoccupation with any red tape that might possibly raise impediments. During this period, Solomon constantly pressed the CNC for a formal interview. After a delay of over three months from Solomon's first application, an interview eventually took place. Solomon did not pursue the matter of his status, but concentrated on the matter of his domicile. He requested, first, a 'permanent domicile', and second, relief from tax due on the huts of his father's dependants. Mnyaiza, who had accompanied Solomon, added a request that Solomon be permitted to re-establish the Usuthu royal homestead to the west of Nongoma. The CNC supported Solomon's requests, especially the first. But he strongly disapproved of Mnyaiza's suggestion: he was determined that it should be the NAD and not the Zulu royal family which specified the location of Solomon's domicile.[28]

The CNC's discussion with the SNA of Solomon's representations proved inconclusive, even though the CNC reiterated the urgency of the question and resubmitted his April proposal in revised form. He rather cleverly turned the argument that the SNA had previously used so that it now supported his proposal: if the government did not buy land on which to settle Solomon, including the royal grave sites, Solomon would conduct collections to buy the land himself and through his own efforts, so building up his status as national leader. Despite the forceful way in which Wheelwright argued his case, in the last instance he was still inclined to prevaricate: almost as an afterthought, and presumably with Solomon's strong objections in mind, he observed that the government could lose Zulu goodwill if it insisted that Solomon abandon all royal homesteads in Zululand. Perhaps, then, 'for the time being', he should be permitted to retain the latter.[29] Wheelwright's proposal had, however, always been based on the desirability of removing Solomon from the Zululand reserves and confining his influence to a circumscribed area in Northern Natal. In its attempts to resolve the 'Solomon question', the NAD had clearly lapsed into a state of paralysis.

*   *   *   *   *

Solomon was unaware of the mental exertions he was causing within the NAD, and could only assume that the polite requests he had made through letters or at the interview with Wheelwright were having no effect. He now adopted a different strategy, making use of an opportunity which arose in August 1916, when the government decided to recruit a South African 'Native Labour Contingent' to assist the Allied war effort in occupied France. Solomon's strategy was, in a nutshell, to hinder the Natal recruitment campaign so long as the government showed no sign of accommodating him. The issue of Solomon's role in the recruitment for the Natal Native Labour Battalion was significant in many respects. It threw light on relationships between Solomon and his kholwa advisers, Solomon and the Zulu rank and file, Solomon and the NAD, and the NAD and the Prime Minister. Moreover, it was the issue that precipitated the government's recognition of Solomon as chief over a reunited Usuthu.

The Prime Minister, General Botha, was both the initiator and the driving force behind the Native Labour Contingent scheme. Some white Natalians, however, censured the prospect of the Zulu assisting the war effort, being fearful that the Zulu experience of war in Europe might stir Zulu militarism at home. The most reactionary elements of Natal colonial society went further, and through letters to the Editor of the *Natal Mercury* expressed fears that the experiences of the recruits overseas, where the Allied troops might regard African servicemen more as comrades than as labourers, would upset the delicate structure of unequal social relationships in Natal. One correspondent predicted that 'the respect for the white man would go' as a consequence, while another, evidently perturbed that French women might not adhere to the strict social codes of Natal colonial society, foresaw 'unthinkable horrors when those natives return'.[30] Although illuminating, these sentiments were not broadly illustrative of white Natalian opinion. Wheelwright himself felt it would 'be a great pity if the Zulus cannot be got to Europe . . . since the educational influence of the trip would be lost'.[31] Botha nonetheless emphasised in parliament that all recruits were to be strictly confined to compounds while in France, and that they would never take up a combatant role.[32]

In Natal, immediately the scheme was publicised, Wheelwright received a telegram from Pixley Seme stating that he and Solomon wished to discuss the prospect of the Zulu 'helping the Empire'. Regarding this as another of Solomon's ploys to elevate his status, the CNC replied that he would not discuss the matter with Solomon, but was prepared to discuss it privately with Seme.[33] In fact the evidence indicates that Seme was acting independently, without Solomon's sanction, being concerned that Solomon's image in the eyes of the NAD had been tarnished by the *ukubuthwa* affair and rumours of rebellion. For John Dube there was similarly no question of how Solomon and the Zulu should respond in this matter. He published an emotional plea for volunteers in *Ilanga lase Natal*: 'Arise ye Zulus', he urged, 'Don't bring shame over us.'[34]

Individuals like Seme and Dube were not infrequently to claim to speak for Solomon when they had no authority to do so. Although the kholwa strategy of *hamba kahle* politics ('go carefully', meaning moderate and non-militant) deeply influenced Solomon, and indeed largely accorded with his own personality, the political approach adopted by Solomon and his tribal advisers tended to have its own unique characteristics. While on the one hand they were inclined to adopt a posture of subjection, describing their relationship with state authorities in the images of father and child, on the other hand they were on occasion inclined to be more forthright than the niceties of the *hamba kahle* posture would allow.

Shortly after the discussion between the CNC and Seme, the CNC instructed the magistrate at Mahlabatini, in whose district Solomon was at the time, to 'get in touch with Solomon and to use him as far as he [the magistrate] considered advisable and necessary'. This was precisely the sort of attitude that Solomon rejected. Thus, as the magistrate's report of the meeting recorded, Solomon 'blew hot and cold', frequently changed his mind, and was evidently not willing to assist in recruitment.[35] Maphelu, Solomon's principal *inceku*, reported how Solomon had informed the magistrate that the 'Government knows well that I don't rule anyone. If I had people I would let them go to help the Government.'[36] While Solomon was quite bluntly not prepared to lend the government his unconditional assistance, he was nonetheless prepared to play a delicate political manoeuvre: he would only use his influence to assist the government under conditions that served his own political objectives. By recruiting Zulu for the Native Labour Contingent on his own terms, he could demonstrate to the Zulu people that he was their paramount head, and emphasise to the NAD that if it wanted anything from the Zulu it would have to work through him.

The Natal NAD soon became embarrassed that of all the provinces of the Union the response of Natal and Zululand to recruitment had been the poorest. It started to step up its recruitment campaign. The desperation of those identified with the Natal NAD was illustrated in a poem composed in Zulu by R. C. A. Samuelson to urge the Zulu to enlist, of which these extracts give the tone:

> The rallying call of Bayede, King George,
> Has reached all parts of the world seen by the sun.
> All have responded,
> But the Zulus and Natal remain.

Answer an urgent call,
Manhood of Zulu and Natal,
That disgrace may not befall you,
You scions of a Black Race!

This is for you, our warring men!
Bayede, King George is calling you.[37]

Solomon was meanwhile getting on with his own affairs. When, however, he applied for a permit to visit the Transvaal shortly after obstructing the magistrate at Mahlabatini's attempts to recruit Zulu, the SNA refused: Solomon could better employ himself assisting recruitment than going on a 'begging expedition to the mines'.[38] In early September, Seme once more contacted the CNC. Solomon now wished to call a meeting of Zulu chiefs at Nobamba to prevail on them to co-operate, Seme said, and added – as the CNC related to the SNA – that this would be 'the only way' of getting Zulu recruits. It was at this stage that the CNC realised the intricacies of Solomon's stance. Although Solomon's request had not yet been formally submitted, Wheelwright immediately wrote at length to the SNA stating that 'the failure to recruit Natives from the Zulus has been largely, if not entirely, [due] to the scheme and influence of Solomon', and demanding an immediate resolution of the whole 'Solomon question'. Realising by now that the SNA was unlikely to take action, Wheelwright suggested that his letter be referred to General Botha 'so that he may see our position'.[39]

A few days later, Solomon's official request to convene a meeting of chiefs came through and was transferred to the SNA. The SNA immediately telegraphed the CNC: The Prime Minister regarded it as a matter of duty that the Zulu respond to the king's call for overseas service, and that 'any assistance rendered by Solomon . . . will naturally be placed to his credit'. The telegram continued, 'Government is quite unprepared to treat with him [Solomon] on the basis of a bargain.'[40] For Solomon, to provide immediate assistance for a possible future reward was to put the cart before the horse. In contrast to the SNA, the CNC knew that the NAD was now not in a position to prescribe to Solomon, but had to bargain. The CNC's memorandum to the SNA, which had now been referred to Botha, analysed the situation pragmatically and with clinical clarity:

> The more one sees of it the more one realises the influence [Solomon] possesses . . . over the people. To permit him to hold such a meeting and to conduct recruiting would without doubt be a recognition of the position of Solomon as head of the Zulus. I believe he would get the Natives required, but he had undoubtedly chosen the opportunity –

which is that of a lifetime – to try to re-establish himself. We cannot get away from the fact of his influence – it is unquestionably there. The question is, is it to be harnessed or is it to be left?[41]

Within a matter of weeks, Solomon, Mnyaiza and other royal advisers were summoned to Pretoria to appear before the Prime Minister, General Botha, and the SNA, the Under-SNA and the CNC. Solomon and his advisers had no idea why they were being summoned, and showed their apprehension in the course of the train journey into the Transvaal. Botha had taken the initiative. At the meeting, in the Union Buildings on 25 November 1916, Botha announced that Solomon was to be recognised as a chief, his ward was to be the reunited Usuthu people, and his domicile would be in the Nongoma district.

Overall, the emphasis of Botha's address was that Solomon was now a servant of the government. Botha instructed Solomon to go back to Zululand with the purpose of serving the NAD and the Zulu people. He was to be chief over the Usuthu only, and was to abide by the dictums of his local magistrate 'no matter what orders he may give you'. He was not to raise 'regiments', but was to maintain the peace, especially with the Mandlakazi and the Ngenetsheni. If he did anything wrong he would be removed from Zululand without hesitation, but if Solomon behaved correctly Botha hinted that his status would be officially elevated.

> I want peace now – rest for the Zulu nation; and if you go back with that purpose – to assist in maintaining peace and good order – then you will become a big man in Zululand.

Botha concluded by particularly emphasising two points. First, the government stipend of £300 per annum would make Solomon an official, 'and it will therefore be your duty to act as an official'. Second, it was the government's intention to place a school near Solomon's new domicile, and 'when the school is started, I want you to take a personal interest in it and so stimulate the Zulu people to take an interest in it'.

Solomon was effusive in his thanks and expressed these in deferential fashion. 'I am your child', he said, 'you have treated me with the greatest consideration.'[42]

*   *   *   *   *

The funeral ceremony, the *ihlambo*, the *ukubuthwa*, the rumours of rebellion and Solomon's disruptive 'wanderings' about the country had led to indirect conflict between Solomon and the Natal NAD. The latter's attempts to recruit for the Native Labour Contingent had brought about direct confrontation for the first time. The Natal NAD had attempted to use Solomon's influence in Zululand for its own ends; Solomon, however, had shown not only that he was not prepared to co-operate but that he was prepared to use his influence to frustrate its objectives. In this confrontation, Solomon had emerged as the victor.

The recognition of Solomon as chief of the Usuthu was a significant reversal of past Natal policy of 'divide and rule'. No longer were the Usuthu parcelled out into the wards of four separate chiefs: they were recognised as a coherent group and their hereditary head was recognised as their chief. The administration had in effect been forced to do so. The Natal NAD as a whole – including Wheelwright – still favoured 'divide and rule' as the prescription for administrative success, and especially so in the case of the Zulu royal family. However, the restoration of the Zulu royal family to Zululand had made this dictum unworkable in practice. Solomon had attracted widespread loyalty, and moreover the enmity that had previously existed between his father and the Mandlakazi and Ngenetsheni sections – enmity that had been 'grist to the mill' of the local administration – was clearly ebbing. The recognition of Solomon was not the rash 'experiment' that some Natal newspapers feared it to be, but rather a rational response intended to bolster the administration's powers of control.

Solomon's recognition might nonetheless not have occurred when it did but for the more flexible and perceptive stance adopted by Wheelwright. In contrast to Addison, Wheelwright had consistently been tolerant towards the Zulu royal family. This was no doubt partly related to a difference in temperament – Wheelwright was a far more fair and generous-minded person – but also had much to do with Wheelwright's clearer administrative vision. His attitude was again in evidence immediately after Solomon's recognition in the way he arranged for the government to intervene in Solomon's tenancy problems, and to settle the debts he had accrued in this regard. Furthermore, quietly and without fuss, Mankulumana was allowed to leave his place of exile in the Eshowe district and re-establish himself in the Usuthu heartland, the government paying his relocation expenses. Despite Wheelwright's attitude, however, it took the swift and decisive action of an 'outsider' in the person of Botha to break departmental paralysis and implement the requisite administrative reform.

While relations between the Zulu royal family and the Natal NAD at the beginning of 1916 were extremely sour, by the end of 1916 they were very amicable. A vital change in Natal NAD posting soon improved relations even further. Oswald Fynney was appointed magistrate at Nongoma, in charge of the district in which Solomon's new domicile, Mahashini, was situated. While his predecessor, T.R. Bennet, had been obstructive to the Zulu royal family, Fynney transpired to be a supporter of the royal cause.

Relations between the Natal NAD and white Natalian opinion-makers at the end of 1916, on the other hand, were anything but rosy. Natal newspapers disapproved of the secrecy in which the 'unexpected and incomprehensible departure in Union policy' had been carried out. Fears were expressed that Solomon's appointment could unite the Zulu, and fears were also expressed that it could accentuate divisions within the Zulu. Whatever the details of their arguments, all commentators condemned the change and, in the rhetoric of the day, were 'apprehensive of a recrudescence of native effervescence in Zululand'. A public meeting held in Eshowe forwarded an 'emphatic message' to the government that Solomon's appointment would 'jeopardize the security of the country' and should therefore be cancelled. The scheme was attributed to Wheelwright, and the NAD head office was held to have acted on his recommendations without even informing the Union cabinet or the 'older' and 'more experienced' officials of the Natal NAD. Strong criticisms were expressed in a lengthy article in the *Natal Mercury* by J.S. Marwick, who as a labour agent had attended Dinuzulu's funeral ceremony but was now manager of the Durban municipal Native Affairs Department. He condemned the appointment as indicative of government weakness.[43] Government policy was not deflected. At a meeting at the Nkandla magistracy in January 1917, Solomon's appointment as chief of the Usuthu was officially confirmed by the Governor-General, Lord Buxton, in his capacity as Supreme Chief.

During the early months of 1917, the Natal NAD vigorously resumed its efforts to recruit Zulu for the Native Labour Contingent, treading various paths in an attempt to ensure that this time the recruitment campaign was successful. An appeal for assistance was made, for example, to the Zululand Diocese of the CPSA. But official hopes hung heavily on Chief Solomon, who, appreciative of his new-found official recognition, now agreed to lend the recruitment campaign his support. To this end he authorised Mnyaiza to make an official visit to Cape Town, at government expense, so that Mnyaiza could personally report back to the Zulu about conditions on troopships bound for France. The campaign came to a climax with a large meeting at Nongoma in mid-1917, attended by several thousand Zulu men and women, and presided over by Chief Solomon, Mnyaiza and local NAD officials. This meeting was an absolute failure: not one Zulu came forward to enlist. On the contrary, various Zulu rose to proclaim unambiguously their opposition to the scheme, and the assembled Zulu thereupon dispersed leaving untouched the very substantial feast that had been provided for them. Asked subsequently whether the Zulu refusal to partake in the feast was symbolically 'repudiating Solomon', Wheelwright replied 'No. That was repudiating us. They thought that if they touched the meat they would be sent . . . overseas.'[44]

Though Wheelwright was to a very large extent correct in his analysis of the fiasco, the Zulu response also clearly spelled out to the recently-appointed Chief Solomon that he could not count on Zulu support if he was henceforth to act merely as a government mouthpiece. This was especially true in regard to issues as widely unpopular as the recruitment campaign following news of the fate of the African troopship *Mendi*: it was sunk by a mine in March 1917 before reaching Europe, and the majority of the African recruits on board perished at sea. For Solomon the fiasco had been a harsh lesson on the ambiguities of his new position as chief of the Usuthu. On the one hand he had to be seen to represent the aspirations of not only the Usuthu but Zulu royalists in general, on whom he depended for political support and who saw in him a symbol of Zulu independence. On the other hand he had to be responsive to the wishes of his political superiors in the Natal NAD and the Union Government. In many ways Solomon's political future depended on the way in which he balanced these frequently contradictory responsibilities.

*   *   *   *   *

The state initiative did not stop short at recognising Solomon as chief of the Usuthu. Steps were taken to place Solomon in contact with influences thought to be desirable, and the co-operation of the Anglican church establishment was readily secured. After Dinuzulu's *ihlambo* ceremony, Harriette Colenso's position as missionary and most trusted white adviser to the Zulu royal house had rapidly fallen into abeyance. This was not simply because her closest acquaintance in the royal house had been Dinuzulu. As she remarked in 1915, 'I am getting almost too old for excursions into Zululand and such proceedings.'[45] The CPSA, Natal's second Anglican church alongside the late Bishop Colenso's Church of England in South Africa, was quick to fill the position from which Harriette had retired. The Zululand Diocese of the CPSA had first established an outstation in the Isikwebezi valley, near Nongoma, in 1898. There the Revd F. W. Walters had begun work among the Usuthu. He initially found himself 'up against a stone wall', which he ascribed to the negative influence of Dinuzulu, but Walters' work began to make more progress after Dinuzulu's trial and exile to KwaThengisa.[46] At the time of Dinuzulu's death, therefore, the CPSA had a base from which to bring its influence to bear on Solomon – who, it seemed, might prove more sympathetic to Christianity than his father.

Following Solomon's and David's confirmation in 1914, the Revd David Ntombela took up work at St Phillip's, the new outstation near Mahashini. In the same month that he confirmed Solomon, the Bishop of Zululand had written to the Minister of Native Affairs (MNA) urging that the royal youngsters be educated at KwaMagwaza, the CPSA mission school near Melmoth. His exertions had not been rewarded during the period of Addison's administration: the Zulu people, the Natal NAD had informed the Bishop, did not want Solomon and David educated, and the royal youngsters themselves were 'content as they are'.[47] Addison clearly felt uncomfortable with kholwa politicians, as was reflected in his views on Dube and Seme, and in the light of his views on the Zulu royal family he was hardly likely to support a project to educate its young heir.

By the end of 1916, the Natal NAD attitude had been reversed. The closer relationship that had developed between the CPSA and the Zulu royal family laid the foundations for co-operation between the Natal NAD, under Wheelwright, and the CPSA soon after Solomon's appointment. Both were keen to 'guide' Solomon and make use of his influence. Thus the Bishop of Zululand was approached to 'co-operate with the government and the CNC about the future of Solomon'. The Revd L. E. Oscroft was requested to move to Nongoma 'to be near Solomon [as] a kind of European adviser to him', and also to consider the feasibility of establishing a school at Solomon's new domicile at Mahashini. These developments caused great excitement in the CPSA. 'So much may come of this', enthused the Bishop, 'that I think it best to say no more, but to wait for the guidance of God in the matter.'[48]

It was Wheelwright who put the school project in motion, and in doing so he had the fullest support of General Botha. From the outset it was clear that the proposed school would be no ordinary school, but an initiative unique not only in Natal but the whole Union. The Zululand National Training Institution (commonly known as the ZNTI) was established specifically and exclusively for the education of the sons of Zulu chiefs and headmen. It was designed to prepare its students for the tribal administrative tasks that they were expected to take up as NAD chiefs. The CPSA knew exactly where the interests of the NAD lay in the matter, and took care to maintain NAD enthusiasm. The Zululand Diocesan Synod unanimously carried a motion urging the government to go ahead with the ZNTI, since chiefs 'frequently fail through lack of knowledge and incompetence to carry out . . . the various duties they are called upon to perform'. The motion was merely one of encouragement, because Oscroft, Fynney and Wheelwright had already made concrete plans.[49]

An issue of some significance arose early in negotiations: the question of who should be Oscroft's employer, and hence to whom Oscroft would be primarily responsible. Although the church in the early twentieth century was not the outspoken critic of state policy that it was to become later in the century, there were many points on which church and state differed in regard to 'native policy'. An example lay in the issue of 'Ethiopianism', which had provided the ideological underpinnings of the African independent church movement. While the NAD aimed to repress it at all costs after the 1906 rebellion, the CPSA went so far as to support it. The journal of the Diocese of Zululand, *The Net*, saw Ethiopianism as a religious reflection of the emergence among Africans of 'progressive' secular aspirations: 'as in State, so in Church, they wish to have a voice'. This was precisely why the state ópposed it. Another area in which church and state differed was land policy. Although in early 1917 Archdeacon Johnson of Zululand described himself as in principle 'thoroughly in sympathy with the Government in its scheme of segregation', when details of the proposed land delimitation came out the CPSA strongly felt it was inequitable. In 1920 an article published in *The Net* portrayed the delimitation proposals for Zululand as violating the two commandments 'Thou shalt not steal' and 'Thou shalt not covet'.[50]

While the Bishop pronounced that 'our main aim is to assist the Government' in the ZNTI project, the real attitude of the CPSA was expressed in its stance on the question of Oscroft's future employer. The Bishop's Council recommended that Oscroft 'should not be a Government official' and that he 'be paid chiefly by the Diocese' – despite its constant shortage of funds.[51] Ultimately, however, when Oscroft moved to Nongoma to take up his new post, it was the government that paid the salary for Oscroft's work as educator and adviser to the Zulu royal family. The ZNTI was to be a state and not a mission school. Oscroft was appointed principal of the ZNTI in 1918 (although it only opened in 1920), and during his principalship the government emphasised to him that he was a civil servant first and foremost.[52] In the cases of both Solomon and Oscroft, the NAD had succeeded in co-opting influential individuals whose influence stemmed from a base outside direct NAD control.

By the end of 1920 the construction of the ZNTI was complete. It was situated at a place called Evuna, named after a nearby stream, some fifteen miles from Nongoma and in the ward of Chief Solomon. There was a house for the principal, a hostel, a school building, and tracts of arable and grazing land for practical instruction in agriculture. Aptly described as a 'Civil Service College for Natives', it was a school purely for the tribal elite, and the syllabus that the sons of chiefs and headmen followed there was carefully designed to prepare them for the posts they were to occupy under the system of indirect rule. When General Smuts, Botha's successor as Prime Minister, visited the ZNTI in 1922, he advised the school's thirty students that 'a people without leaders cannot possibly ever become a people, and to be good leaders whom the people will always follow you must keep ahead of your people'.[53]

The policy initiated by the government when it appointed Solomon as chief of the Usuthu, which included the ZNTI project, was a fundamental departure from previous policy – and a successful one. From 1917 until the early 1920s, Solomon's activities were mentioned only sporadically in NAD records. With the exception of Solomon's interminable problems with white landlords in Northern Natal, there seemed to be no official correspondence regarding Solomon either important or voluminous enough for the CNC's clerk to justify establishing a separate file to contain it. Before 1917, by contrast, there had been a number files dealing with different aspects of the 'Solomon question' running concurrently.

*   *   *   *   *

Following his appointment, Solomon's main tasks were to settle into his new domicile at Mahashini and his new duties as chief of the Usuthu. While the NAD had defined his political constituency as the Usuthu ward alone, however, he clearly had wider aspirations. Solomon certainly had a keen sense of what image a twentieth-century Zulu king should present. He was naturally athletic and, of all Dinuzulu's children, was regarded as one of the best looking. Being an able horseman, he was in the habit of riding between his various homesteads in Zululand, clothed in khakis cut in the British military style and sporting a leopard-skin sash – the symbol of Zulu royalty. The royal dogs would run beside him.[54]

Although Solomon and Zulu royalists clearly felt the status of mere chief to be insufficient for Solomon, they expressed their feelings in a way which did not unduly alarm the Natal NAD. When the Governor-General held an *indaba* with the Zulu at Nkandla in July 1918, officials noticed that the Zulu saluted him only with 'Nkosi', as though he were simply a chief. In his reply to the Governor-General's address, furthermore, Mankulumana requested permission for the Zulu to salute Solomon publicly with the royal salutation 'Bayede'. Officials also took note that Solomon occasionally interfered with the jurisdiction of other chiefs, thus indicating that he was to be regarded as *de facto* paramount chief. Indeed, Solomon was in the habit of using a rubber stamp on his correspondence which bore the legend 'Inkosi Yamabandhla Onke' ('King of All Assemblies') beneath his name. Administrative action against him was almost nonchalant. When asked later what action had been taken for these 'misdemeanours', Wheelwright replied that he had merely sent a message through Oscroft to Solomon, to the effect that Solomon should not be 'a silly ass'.[55]

Solomon nonetheless did emphasise his status in more concrete ways. Most importantly, in 1918 he once more summoned young men to Mahashini to complete the *ukubuthwa* ceremony that had been initiated in early 1916, but not completed on account of administrative pressure. The *ukubuthwa* of 1918 in fact proved to be a complete ceremony in itself, and far larger and better organised than that of 1916. Although the ceremonies of 1916 and 1918 enrolled essentially the same *ibutho* (the time between enrolments was usually seven or eight years), those enrolled in 1918 were given a slightly different name. Whereas the enrolment of 1916 had been named the 'Nqabakucetshwa' ('the-will-not-be-betrayed-by-foreigners'), the enrolment of 1918 was given the more confident name 'Nqabakucasha' ('the-will-not-hide-from-foreigners').

The *ukubuthwa* of 1918 demonstrated how important such traditional ceremonies were in establishing Solomon's social and political status. As in 1916, Solomon sent messages out to chiefs and *izinduna*, who in turn called large meetings in their districts to announce arrangements for the journey to Mahashini. Young men were instructed to congregate fully armed with sticks and shields, and in full traditional dress. Each was to be accompanied by a bearer – either a younger brother or a cousin. When the groups of young men from the various districts arrived at Mahashini, the *umpathi* (organiser) of each group handed them over to the direct control of one of Solomon's *izinduna*. Their initial work was to build temporary huts to accommodate themselves during the *ukubuthwa* period. Thereafter, every morning, they congregated around the royal cattle kraal at Mahashini to be issued with instructions for the day's activities, all of which centred on the person of Solomon: collecting firewood, repairing fences, ploughing and sowing the royal fields and, most importantly, constructing a new royal homestead. This was named KwaDlamahlahla and became Solomon's principal residence. Apart from these practical tasks, there were routine daily ceremonies. Every day songs and dances were performed in the royal cattle kraal, usually presided over by Solomon, who was accorded the royal salute 'Bayede' whenever he appeared or took his leave. The young men were also given instruction on the need to observe customs and tradition, to maintain personal discipline, to abide by moral codes, to respect elders and tribal authority, to work hard and to honour responsibilities towards relatives. The purpose of the *ukubuthwa* ceremony was therefore not only to foster a sense of unity under Solomon, but also to inculcate in the conscripts a set of tribal attitudes of mind and codes of conduct. These attitudes, on which loyalty to Solomon personally was superimposed, were a crucial foundation of Solomon's political power.[56]

Surprisingly, there is no record of the CNC having been aware of the 1918 *ukubuthwa*. This may have been because Mahashini needed to be reconstructed as Solomon's new domicile and the new administrative centre of the Usuthu, which justified Solomon's having large numbers of 'labourers' there. Moreover, the new magistrate at Nongoma, Oswald Fynney, who had already established a personal friendship with Solomon, would have been unlikely to file reports that would land Solomon in trouble.

Immediately after the *ukubuthwa* ceremony, Solomon opened the issue of unpaid *lobolo* cattle due on women who had been members of Cetshwayo's *isigodlo* (royal seraglio) and who had married subsequent to Cetshwayo's death. Manzolwandle had attempted to settle the same issue, unsuccessfully, in 1913. In doing so, Solomon evidently aimed to emphasise his claim to the status of Zulu king, and at the same time build up the wealth of the royal house. Solomon accordingly called a number of meetings between early 1919 and late 1920 in the Nongoma, Mahlabatini, Vryheid and Emtonjaneni districts. In contrast to Manzolwandle's attempts, Solomon's right to claim *lobolo* cattle on behalf of the late King Cetshwayo's estate was not disputed. The response he received from the Mahlabatini district affirmed that 'there are many cattle belonging to the King in the neighbourhood . . . if they are required they will be produced'.[57] Chief Somkhele reportedly transferred sixty head of cattle to Solomon in settlement of the *lobolo* 'debts' claimed from him alone. The magistrate at Nkandla described Solomon's activities as 'tyrannical', and urged action to prevent any further transfer of cattle.[58] The NAD, however, took no action other than to refuse Solomon government assistance in securing the *lobolo* 'debts'. In contrast to Natal NAD policy prior to Solomon's appointment, the administration now seemed to take the attitude that Solomon could make whatever claims he wished on the Zulu people, and it was up to the Zulu to accept or reject them. Thus far, with the notable exception of the Native Labour Contingent recruitment fiasco, the Zulu had always seemed very willing to comply.

*   *   *   *   *

Solomon did not establish a clear political role in the context of 'new generation' African politics, where the more established procedures of the Congress movement were increasingly being challenged by trade union militancy, until the mid-1920s. By 1920, however, there were already signs in Zululand that Solomon's adoption of the role of Zulu unifier in accordance with the traditions established by pre-conquest Zulu monarchs, would not contain the new divisions that were evolving in Zulu society. In that year an atmosphere of unrest developed in the north-western districts. This was clearly related to attempts on the part of David to reopen the succession dispute of 1913, and challenge Solomon's position. The rural unrest in Zululand of 1920 can only be understood in a broader political context, however, since it was also related to an undercurrent of vital new influences at work in African politics throughout the Union.

Before and during the war years, the national congress organisation, the SANNC, had adopted 'moderate' and 'conciliatory' methods of protest. It expressed itself mainly through giving evidence to government commissions and select committees, and sending petitions and deputations to various authorities. After the war these methods no longer dominated African political representation, and there came a wave of 'direct action' in the form of civil disobedience campaigns and strikes. A new generation of African political leaders had emerged, usually of kholwa origins like those of Congress, but with militant political programmes. Elements of the more repressed urban African middle class had become 'radicalised', and began to appeal to the increasingly restive constituency of urban African workers, giving direction to their grievances.[59]

The move towards militancy was reflected in changes in the leadership of the SANNC itself. John Dube, the essentially conservative Natal leader who had caused a stir through not opposing the principle of territorial segregation, was ousted from presidential office in 1917 by Sam Makgatho of the Transvaal. Makgatho thereupon infused a more aggressive spirit into Congress activities. Inspired by Mahatma Ghandi's passive resistance campaigns, the Johannesburg branch in 1918 organised a civil disobedience campaign against the pass laws. In 1919, the Bloemfontein branch held a successful wage strike. These actions were part of a broader movement among urban Africans towards militant industrial and political action, spearheaded by radical worker organisations. In 1918, following the work of the International Socialist League among the African workforce, the pioneering 'bucket strike' of Johannesburg's sanitary workers took place.

The Industrial and Commercial Workers' Union (ICU) was formed in Cape Town in 1919, and in the same year led the dockworkers into strike action. In Natal, which of all the provinces of the Union was least affected by these new developments, the rickshaw-pullers of Durban came out on strike in 1918, and in 1919 so too did African workers on the Northern Natal coalfields. In 1920, the activities of the Port Elizabeth branch of the ICU culminated in a clash with police which resulted in twenty-one deaths – the first martyrs to the new strategies of African political protest. In February 1920, this groundswell of militancy was brought to a head through the combined efforts of the International Socialist League and the SANNC: the Johannesburg gold-fields were virtually brought to a standstill by a wage strike of 71 000 African miners, which incidentally put 8000 white miners out of work. This was the largest and most effective instance of worker protest South Africa's prime industry had yet experienced.[60]

The events of 1906 in Natal and of 1916 in Zululand had demonstrated the close relationship that existed between the African rural and urban areas in times of civil disturbance. The relationship had been expressed on these occasions by the return home of migrant workers on hearing news, directly or indirectly, of unrest in the rural areas. In 1920 the relationship was manifested by the spread of sinister rumours in Zululand relating to Dinuzulu, Solomon and David soon after the gold-fields strike, and by the severely strained relations that developed between Solomon and David. In this context, three points should be borne in mind. First, the overwhelming majority of Zulu proceeding to Johannesburg did so to work on the gold-fields, where they formed the Zulu royal family's most important urban constituency – and in a financial sense they were the Zulu royal family's most important constituency altogether. Soon after his succession, Solomon had established the pattern of Zulu royalty maintaining contact with Zulu mineworkers, either personally in the course of what the NAD described as 'begging expeditions to the mines', or through royal representatives such as Franz and Mnyaiza. From the point of view of the mineworkers, however, the monetary tribute they paid their royal visitors placed an obligation on the royal house to provide political leadership and a means whereby grievances might be redressed. Second, it must be remembered that by nature Solomon tended to be humble and conciliatory, whereas David was uncompromising, aggressive and even violent. The third point is better expressed in the form of a question: How did David in 1920 have sufficient confidence and support to challenge Solomon, when he had acquiesced to both his deposition in 1913 and his subordinate position until 1920?

In August 1919, Solomon completed an extensive tour of the Johannesburg mining areas, visiting the labour compounds of no less than seven mining companies, including the Brakpan Mine where his cousin Franz worked as labour supervisor. In each compound many grievances were laid before him, the main and universal complaint being low wages; complaints about the pass laws and pass arrests ranked next in importance. Solomon had each set of grievances for each particular mine transcribed. Before leaving Johannesburg he called on the city's Director of Native Labour to make representations, and handed over the lists of grievances he had compiled. In response, the Director of Native Labour instructed inspectors to investigate the complaints and make reports. On the matter of wages, the reports made no recommendations for increases. On all other matters they simply denied that the grievances were justified or else gave reasons why they could not be remedied. The inspectors' reports were then forwarded to Solomon through the CNC and the magistrate at Nongoma, and there, evidently, the matter ended.[61]

Although their respect for the Zulu royal family was unquestionable, it was patently clear that in the militant mood of 1920, Zulu mineworkers could not find in Solomon the leadership they wanted. Seven months after Solomon's visit and futile attempts to redress their grievances, the mineworkers took matters into their own hands and came out on strike. During the period in which the strike took place, Solomon was in Zululand, involved in his attempts to claim *lobolo* for Cetshwayo's *isigodlo* women. David, however, was in Johannesburg.[62] The purpose of David's visit to Johannesburg was, following the pattern set by his younger brother, to visit the mine compounds and collect revenue. The militant atmosphere within the workforce which David met accorded well with David's style; and if in this mood Zulu mineworkers sought royal leadership, there is little doubt that David rather than Solomon would have appeared the more attractive rallying point.

Prominent among the rumours circulating in Zululand in the first half of 1920, which included the 'old' rumour that Dinuzulu was not dead but was soon to return to liberate his country, was the notion that David was soon to usurp Solomon's position. It became evident that David had the support to do so, which reflected hostility towards Solomon's mode of leadership. These rumours were accompanied by factual reports of friction between Solomon's and David's homesteads, and of strange occurrences at Solomon's homesteads. Several of Solomon's livestock had been stabbed to death, for example, and organs of ritual significance had been removed from them. Mankulumana bluntly stated that these occurrences signified a challenge to Solomon; the magistrate at Ngotshe added that some Zulu now saw David as the true heir, and they had prevailed on David to lead the 'discontents against Solomon's order'. In May 1920, Solomon reported to the magistrate at Nongoma, Fynney, that members of the Sikalenesinyoka royal homestead had twice recently tried to poison him. Then – and this caused severe unease in the Natal NAD – it was reported that David was holding 'political meetings' in the Nkandla district, had visited Cetshwayo's grave there, and was collecting money to provide the 'sinews of war'.[63] At this stage the Natal NAD became convinced that the reopening of the 1913 succession dispute was symptomatic of a deeper malady.

In response, the CNC chaired an inquiry into the matter at Nkandla in May 1920. David was not present to account for himself, and the inquiry turned into a farce: witnesses were prepared to reiterate the rumours and confirm that David's meetings had taken place, but refused to divulge what had been discussed there. Exasperated, the CNC announced that he knew very well that important matters had been discussed, since news of David's intentions had 'thundered through the country [and] had been talked about hundreds of miles away'. Eventually he concluded by warning those present that they 'had learned one lesson during the [1906] Rebellion and now they are deliberately courting trouble again by becoming mixed up with royal youngsters'.[64] It was clear that the Natal NAD suspected a rebellion to be imminent, not simply against Solomon but also against the government, and that David was preparing to lead it.

The outbreak of rebellion that threatened in 1920 ultimately never happened. By the second half of the year the rumours had died away, David settled down in the new homestead he had constructed near Nobamba, and never again did he challenge Solomon's position. For Solomon, however, the events of 1920 in Zululand were of crucial significance. A militant mood had taken hold in important quarters of Zulu society, especially among migrant labourers, and Solomon had lost support as a consequence. David, by contrast, had exploited the situation to his advantage, tapping the support of those who had become disillusioned with Solomon's conciliatory stance. More clearly than the Native Labour Contingent recruitment fiasco of 1917, the year 1920 revealed that Solomon could not assume that his dynastic status entitled him to the unconditional loyalty of the Zulu people as a whole. The approach that he took on issues of importance to the Zulu rank and file, such as wage levels and working conditions, in both urban and rural areas, was vital to his political status. It had by now emerged that Solomon was unlikely to endorse open rebellion against colonial rule, or indeed any militant form of protest, even though elements of his followers clearly hoped he might. Nor had he identified himself with an alternative political initiative that stood to catch the imagination of his followers and offer them hope for the future. The events of 1920 suggested that Solomon needed to do so if he were to consolidate and extend the base of his support.

NOTES

1. For Addison's earlier career, see in particular Laband, 'Dick Addison'; for Wheelwright, see NEC Box 4, evidence of Wheelwright, 25/9/1930, p. 1721, and below.

2. CNC 144, 1985/1913, report by J. Y. Gibson, 5/8/1914.

3. Natives' Land Commission Evidence, UG22–16, p. 623.

4. CNC 219, 1488/1915, Magistrate, Nongoma to DNC, Zululand, 3/2/1915; and CNC 262, 1926/1916, Magistrate, Nongoma to CNC, 11/11/1916.

5. CNC 226B, 25/1916, Magistrate, Mahlabatini to DNC, Zululand, 19/1/1916, and enclosures.

6. CNC 144, 1985/1913, CNC to DNC, Zululand, 20/2/1915.

7. CNC 144, 1985/1913, Magistrate, Nongoma to CNC, 9/2/1915; DNC, Zululand to CNC, 8/3/1915; and CNC to DNC, Zululand, 10/3/1915 (quotation).

8. CNC 144, 1985/1913, Magistrate, Nongoma to DNC, Zululand, 9/2/1915; and, for the incident at the 1916 *indaba*, CNC 219, 1488/1915, report of political messenger, Nongoma, 20/7/1916; and evidence of Sijulu Tabete, NAD *induna*, Eshowe, 26/7/1916.

9. See CNC 144, 1985/1913, G.N. Godley, Under-SNA to Solomon kaDinuzulu, 27/7/1914; Solomon kaDinuzulu's list of delegates for proposed deputation to Pretoria, n.d.; and CNC's circular to all magistrates in Zululand and Northern Natal, 28/1/1915, citing Solomon's request of 6/1/1915.

10. CNC 144, 1985/1913, H.T. Colenbrander, Magistrate, Emtonjaneni to DNC, Zululand, 2/2/1915 (quotation); CNC's circular, 28/1/1915; and Magistrate, Ngotshe to CNC, 23/1/1915.

11. CNC 144, 1985/1913, DNC, Zululand to CNC, 3/5/1915.

12. CNC 144, 1985/1913, Magistrate, Nkandla to DNC, Zululand, 30/4/1915 (quotation); and CNC to DNC, Zululand, 5/5/1915.

13. CNC 219, 1488/1915, NAD summary of all correspondence on the 'hunt', unsigned, n.d., reports of DNC, Zululand, 18/1/1916; and Magistrate, Nongoma, 17 and 19/1/1916. Regarding the names of the *ibutho*, see Faye, *Zulu references*, p. 51.

14. CNC 219, 1488/1915, DNC, Zululand to CNC, 25/1/1916.

15. CNC 219, 1485/1915, Magistrate, Nkandla to Col. Leuchars, Chief Intelligence Officer, Pietermaritzburg, 22/12/1915; and Magistrate, Nkandla to DNC, Zululand, 23/3/1916.

16. CNC 219, 1488/1915, Magistrate, Nongoma to DNC, Zululand, 3/2/1916, forwarding transcripts of various interviews.

17. CNC 219, 1488/1915, CNC telegram to all magistrates in Zululand and Northern Natal, 24/1/1916; see also attached copies of numerous Zulu telegrams. For the parallel in 1906, see Marks, *Reluctant rebellion*, p. 230.

18. CNC 219, 1488/1915, CNC to SNA, 27/1/1916.

19. CNC 219, 1488/1915, memorandum of meeting, Nongoma, 28/4/1916, regarding Solomon kaDinuzulu's attempt to hold an unauthorised hunt, pp. 2–4.

20. CNC 219, 1488/1915, CNC to SNA, 4/5/1916.

21. CNC 219, 1488/1915, memorandum of meeting, Nongoma, 28/4/1916, pp. 5–6.

22. Unpublished collection of Zulu praise poems, 'Izibongo zika Solomon kaDinuzulu'.

23. CNC PMB 72, 57/29. This letter, dated 25/2/1916, was summarised in English in Assistant Magistrate, Babanango to Magistrate, Vryheid, 17/3/1916.

24. See CNC 219, 1488/1915, reports of Native Constable at Nongoma, 3–20/7/1916; Magistrate, Ngotshe to CNC, 25/7/1916; State Archives, Pretoria, Archives of the Commissioner of the South African Police (hereafter SAP) 36, 6/592/18, Chief Dhlangyaan Ngema, Wakkerstroom District, to Director of Prisons, Pretoria, 26/6/1918, relating earlier events; and SAP 35, 6/499/17/2, Ben Machumela, Rosebank, Transvaal, to Solomon kaDinuzulu, 9/3/1917, translated by CNC's office, Natal.

25. CNC PMB 72, 57/29, CNC to SNA, 4/4/1916.

26. CNC PMB 81, 58/7/1, SNA to CNC, 28/4/1916.

27. CNC 219, 1488/1915, CNC to SNA 4/5/1916, pp. 3–5.

28. CNC PMB 72, 57/29, CNC to SNA, 19/7/1916.

29. CNC PMB 72, 57/29, CNC to SNA, 17/8/1916.

30. *Natal Mercury*, 3/10/1916 (quotations) and 7/10/1916.

31. CNC 261, 1881/1916, CNC's memorandum to SNA, 3/11/1916.

32. *Cape Times*, 21/3/1917.

33. CNC 248, 1254/1916, Pixley Seme to CNC, 11/8/1916 (telegram); and CNC to Pixley Seme, 12/8/1916.

34. MS MAR, Newscutting Book, KCM 3196, p. 46, *Natal Advertiser*, reporting Dube's open letter to the Zulu people published in *Ilanga.*

35. CNC 261, 1881/1916, CNC's memorandum to SNA, 3/11/1916.

36. Account of Maphelu, p. 108.

37. MS MAR, File 21, KCM 3185 (b), H.C. Lugg's translation, 27/6/1917, of Samuelson's Zulu original. For Natal NAD embarrassment, see CNC 261, 1881/1915, CNC to SNA, 3/11/1916; and the derisory comments made about Natal by Transvaal members of the House of Assembly, *Cape Times*, 5/4/1917 and 21/4/1917.

38. CNC 254, 1557/1916, SNA to CNC, 12/10/1916.

39. CNC 261, 1881/1916, CNC to SNA, 3/11/1916 pp. 2–3.

40. CNC 261, 1881/1916, CNC to Magistrate, Vryheid, 13/11/1916, quoting SNA's telegram.

41. CNC 261, 1881/1916, CNC to SNA, 3/11/1916.

42. Faye, *Zulu references*, pp. 90–96, record of meeting between General Botha and Solomon kaDinuzulu, Pretoria, 28/11/1916. Carl Faye travelled with the royal party from Natal and acted as interpreter during the meeting itself.

43. *Natal Mercury* 18/12/1916 and 27/12/1916 (quotations); *Natal Advertiser*, 3/1/1917; and *Natal Mercury*, 5/1/1917.

44. *Natal Mercury*, 6/5/1927, evidence of C.A. Wheelwright in the libel case brought by Solomon kaDinuzulu against the newspaper. Other sources on the recruitment fiasco of 1917 include CPSA Records, Diocese of Zululand, Eshowe Diocesan Offices (hereafter DZ), 5/2c, minutes of Diocesan Synod, 26/6/1917; Account of Maphelu, pp. 108–109; Pers. Comm. Ndesheni, Part I,

p. 12; and, most important, Marks, *Ambiguities of dependence*, pp. 33–35, whose perceptive account of the recruitment fiasco has led me to alter substantially the conclusions reached in my doctoral dissertation.

45. Swart, 'Harriette Colenso', pp. 149–52.

46. *The Net*, September 1926, p. 9, history of CPSA activites at Nongoma; see also B. B. Burnett, *Anglicans in Natal* (Durban, 1956), pp. 62–123; and C. Lewis and G. E. Edwards, *Historical records of the Church of the Province of South Africa* (London, 1934), pp. 659–704.

47. CNC 144, 1985/1913, Bishop of Zululand to Minister for Native Affairs, 5/2/1914; DNC, Zululand to Bishop of Zululand, 9/1/1915 (quotation).

48. *The Net*, June 1917 and March 1918 (quotations); and DZ/M/4, *Zululand Mission Report*, 1916, p. 4.

49. DZ/S/2c, meeting of Diocesan Synods, 26/6/1917 (quotation); see also DZ/B/3, Minute Book of Bishop's Council, 20 and 22/3/1917.

50. *The Net*, June 1912; SNA II/5/2, evidence of Archdeacon Johnson, Nqutu, 17/3/1917; and *The Net*, December 1920 (quotations). Apart from the inequitable apportionment of land, the Church opposed the restrictions imposed on African land purchase.

51. DZ/B/3, meeting of Bishop's Council, 20 and 22/3/1917.

52. See *The Net*, March 1918; DZ/B/3, meetings of Bishop's Council, 20, 23/3/1920, and 8/12/1920; CNC PMB 102, 73/46, Bishop of Zululand to CNC, 11/3/1919; and Pers. Comm. Mr Basil Oscroft, son of the Revd L. E. Oscroft, letter dated 24/11/1981. The CPSA continued to pay Oscroft for his missionary work in the Nongoma district.

53. *The Net*, December 1922. See also DZ/B/3, meeting of Bishop's Council, 13/3/1918; *The Net*, March 1918; and DZ/M/4, *Zululand Mission Report*, 1920.

54. Account of Maphelu, p. 109; and Pers. Comm. Magogo, Part II, p. 8.

55. *Natal Mercury*, 6/5/1927 (quotation). Wheelwright made this statement while giving evidence in the libel action brought by Solomon against the Natal Mercury in 1927. See also CNC PMB 84, 58/7/4, CNC's historical memorandum for the Minister of Native Affairs, 15/8/1932, p. 4.

56. My principal source on the 1918 *ukubuthwa* was G. W. K. Mahlobo and E. J. Krige, 'Transition from childhood to adulthood amongst the Zulus', *Bantu Studies*, vol. 8, 1934. The authors' sources were Zulu men enrolled in 1918; their reconstruction of the *ukubuthwa* needs to be read with care, however, on account of its anthropological – and ahistorical – approach. The homestead name 'KwaDlamahlahla' literally means 'The place where the branches were devoured', and commemorates a nearby engagement between Natal Government forces and Zulu rebels during the 1906 rebellion. The Zulu took cover in a forest, and the bullets meant for them merely 'devoured the branches' overhead. Pers. Comm. J. K. Dladla, Cultural Affairs Organiser, KwaZulu Government, Ulundi, 10/11/1981.

57. CNC 349, 453/1919, notes of interview between Magistrate, Mahlabatini and Nyosana Tshangase kaMasipula, 23/1/1920.

58. CNC 349, 453/1919, Magistrate, Nkandla to CNC, 22/2/1919.

59. See P. Bonner, 'The Transvaal Native Congress, 1917–1920: the radicalization of the black petty bourgeoisie on the Rand', in Marks and Rathbone (eds), *Industrialisation and social change*, pp. 270ff.

60. For the broad details of post-war African political militancy, see Edward R. Roux, *Time longer than rope*, (Madison, 1964), especially chs. 12 and 15. Regarding Natal, see Report of the Native Affairs Department, 1919–1921, UG 34–22, pp. 4–10; and SNA II/5/5, J.S. Marwick, Durban Municipal Native Affairs Department, to Mr Clayton, Natal Local Land Committee, 16/4/1918.

61. CNC 359, 1558/1919, Mr Pritchard, Director of Native Labour, Johannesburg, to CNC, 7/8/1919, and enclosures.

62. SNA I/9/5, notes of interview between CNC and Joel Maduna, representative of David kaDinuzulu, Babanango, 25/5/1920.

63. CNC PMB 92, 64/3, Magistrate, Nkandla to CNC, 10/5/1920; and Magistrate, Nongoma to CNC, 20/5/1920 (quotations). See also Magistrate, Ngotshe to CNC, 3/5/1920; Magistrate, Eshowe to CNC, 10/5/1920; and SNA I/9/5, notes of interview between Chief Manzolwandle and CNC, 24/6/1920. While agreeing to use his influence to stop the rumours, Manzolwandle added 'John Dube does not represent the responsible people of Zululand. He was not born to represent people'. Although Dube was certainly not associated with the rumours, this comment indicated Manzolwandle knew the rumours issued from outside Zululand – from the townspeople, whom Dube represented principally, rather than rural Zulu.

64. SNA I/9/5, memorandum of CNC's inquiry into David kaDinuzulu's visit to Cetshwayo's grave, Nkandla, 24/5/1920.

Harriette Colenso with Dinuzulu's wives and children. David Nyawana is seated at her feet.

Solomon on his accession.

Mnyaiza kaNdabuko Zulu

Left to right: Ndabankulu kaLukhwazi Ntombela, Mankulumana kaSomaphunga
Ndwandwe, Somcuba kaMqundane Jama

Solomon addressing a Zulu gathering in the 1920s. Behind him to the left is John Dube, suggesting that this may have been an Inkatha meeting.

KwaDlamahlahla, Solomon's principal residence

Local History Museum, Durban

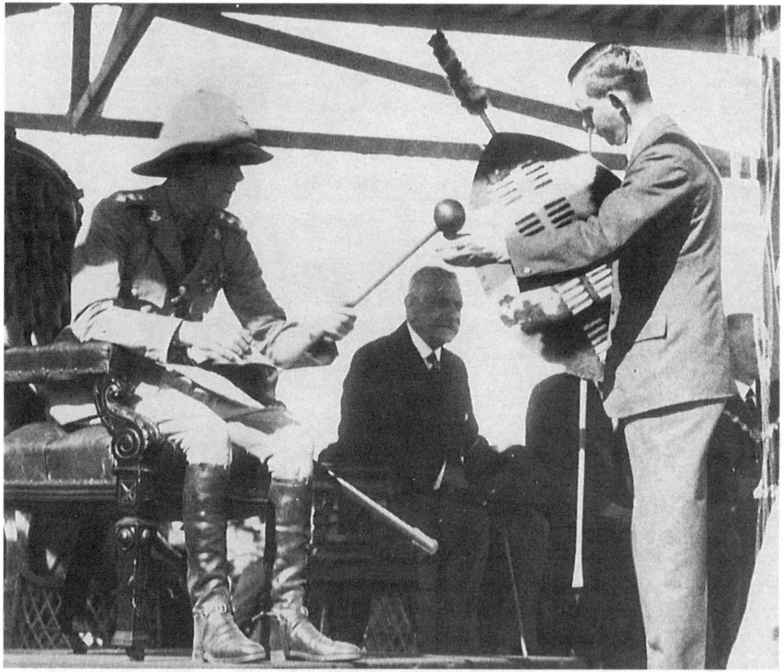

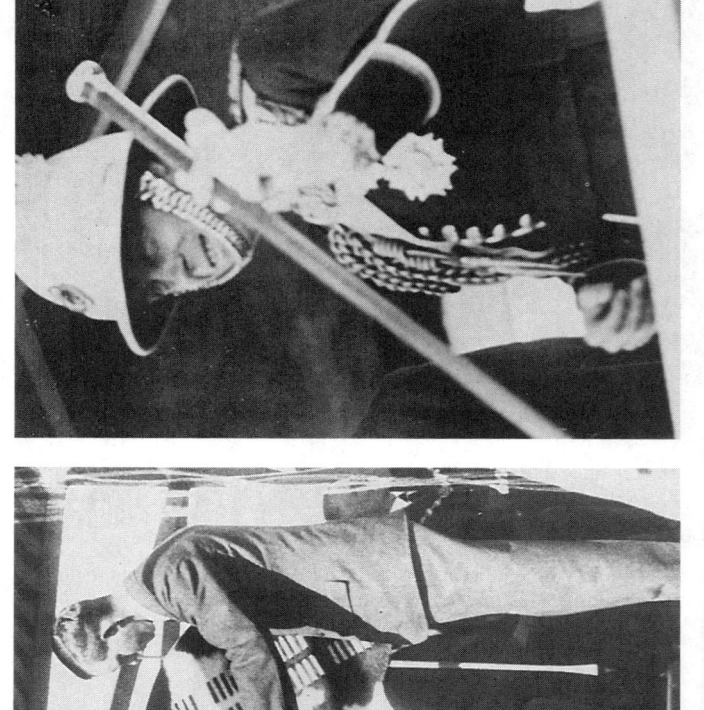

Edward, Prince of Wales, at the Eshowe *Indaba*, 1925. On the right he is seen in formal attire presenting ceremonial sticks during the morning session. On the left he is informally dressed, receiving the assegaais and shields which he requested as souvenirs during the afternoon proceedings.

4

The formation of Inkatha

From 1920 and throughout the decade that followed, class divisions within Zulu society were to become more and more pronounced. They did so both objectively, in terms of economic activity and lifestyle, and subjectively, in terms of self-perception, class consciousness and political expression. Associated with the occupations of minister of religion, teacher or clerical worker, for example, were 'life experiences' and social and political aspirations very different from those of rural labour tenant or urban wage labourer. Politically, from 1920, Solomon and the Zulu tribal establishment came to associate more and more with the Zulu-speaking kholwa establishment, a small elite made up of relatively prosperous kholwa families. The political distance that the year 1920 revealed between Solomon and radicalising elements within the Zulu rank and file, which was principally made up of the 'commoners' of tribal society and the 'working class' of the fast-developing industrial society, was to widen. If in the early years of the 1920s Solomon clearly needed to identify himself with a new political initiative, thus consolidating and extending his support among a people undergoing rapid social change, intellectuals of the aspirant middle class were in a strong position to guide him.

Since his succession in 1913, Solomon had maintained cordial yet distant relations with the 'progressive' world of the Zulu-speaking kholwa. His confirmation by the Bishop of Zululand in 1914, together with the support he had given to the ZNTI project for the education of the sons of Zulu chiefs, had done much to allay kholwa fears that Solomon might define his political role as a reactionary defender of the Zulu tribal order. So too had the 'respectable' manner in which he had chosen to furnish his personal living quarters at Zibindini and then at Mahashini, and the taste he had shown for clothing tailored in the British military style. Solomon, had, moreover, kept in contact with leading individuals of the Zulu-speaking kholwa establishment. This was especially true with regard to Pixley Seme, the

Natal-born but Johannesburg-based lawyer who, having returned to South Africa after completing his studies in New York and at Oxford, had been the driving force behind the formation of the SANNC in 1912. It was also true with regard to John Dube, unquestionably the most influential spokesman for Natal's conservative kholwa elite, who had distinguished himself as an educationist, minister, journalist and local politician before being elected in 1912 as first president of the SANNC.

Having previously been content simply to maintain cordial contact with Solomon, from 1920 kholwa leaders made great efforts to formalise a closer relationship with Zulu royalty – efforts which were eventually to bear fruit in the formation of a political organisation, Inkatha. The forthcoming political 'marriage of convenience' between the leaders of the old and new Zulu elites was symbolically heralded in May 1920 by the marriage of Pixley Seme to Phikisile Harriette Zulu, Solomon's sister. Phikisile was regarded as perhaps the most beautiful of the royal youngsters, and was apparently also one of the better educated.[1] It was however of more than symbolic significance that in early 1920, precisely when Zulu mineworkers were participating in the massive strike on the gold-fields, John Dube was in Zululand to discuss with Solomon the 'organisation of a proposed mission of congratulation to the Throne on the successful issue of the war, with which Solomon and his people were in full sympathy' – a nicety distant indeed from exigencies facing the masses.[2] This was the first in a series of attempts made by Dube to involve Solomon directly in the kholwa political world and the Congress-style political process.

Kholwa approaches to Solomon in the post-war period were made not only by such leading lights as Seme and Dube. Solomon was also called upon to associate himself with smaller kholwa bodies which, while being products of western educational and missionary endeavour, were anxious to establish their independence from their mentors. In 1919, for example, Gardener Mvuyana, a Zulu cleric from Ifafa on the Natal south coast who had recently broken with the American Mission, established an independent church at Doornfontein on the Rand. He requested Solomon to lay the foundation stone of the new church, which he wished to be known as the 'National Zulu Church'. In correspondence with the NAD, the Bishop of Pretoria commented that Mvuyana was associated with the 'young nationalist crowd' of the SANNC.[3]

Why this blossoming of interest in Solomon among Zulu-speaking kholwa in the early 1920s? This is a question crucial to an understanding of the origins of Inkatha, an organisation always dominated by Christian and educated individuals of the Zulu-speaking middle class, and one which was gradually to assume the status of 'official' party for Zulu royalists.

* * * * *

In his inaugural address as first president of the SANNC, John Dube expressed some key elements of contemporary kholwa thinking:

> Upward! Into the higher places of civilisation and Christianity – not backward into the slump of darkness nor downward into the abyss of the antiquated tribal system. Our salvation is not there, but in preparing ourselves for an honoured place among nations.[4]

Such invectives against the African past reflected the extent to which Natal's kholwa landowning establishment, Dube's immediate constituency, owed its origins and character as a self-consciously distinct social group to nineteenth-century missionary endeavour. Indeed, the Zulu-speaking middle class as a whole, which ranged from rent-paying cash-crop cultivators through clerks and traders to qualified professionals, shared similar origins. Scattered erratically between urban and rural areas all over the province, kholwa communities were generally congregated around local mission centres: in Natal proper, where the more established and prosperous communities were based; Northern Natal, where communities such as the Vryheid East Township had developed rapidly since the Anglo-Boer War; and even in Zululand, which of all the regions had been the most resistant to missionary enterprise. They were loosely connected through their common ideological roots – Christianity and Victorian bourgeois liberalism – and it was this that assured Dube's inaugural SANNC address of an appreciative reception.

In the wake of the 1913 Natives' Land Act, however, kholwa communities were more tightly connected by a common urgent need: land. The 1913 Act had effectively prevented further African purchase of freehold land, the desirability of which represented almost an article of faith among the kholwa. It also undermined all other African options to labour tenancy on white farmland.[5] If there was one overriding issue which prompted the Natal kholwa to redefine their policy directions in the early 1920s, thus embarking on negotiations with the most influential of the region's tribal authorities, the Zulu 'king', it was the land issue. Indeed, it was the urgent desire for purchaseable land in Northern Natal kholwa circles that was to act as the first spur to the formation of Inkatha – this was during the very first years of the 1920s. Inkatha was formally established only in 1924, however, when representatives from the more established kholwa communities in Natal proper also involved themselves in the fledgeling organisation. Significantly, they similarly did so partly because a *rapprochement* with the rural tribal elite seemed a potential route towards private land ownership and commercial agricultural production at a time when other routes were being closed down.

The land issue was also related to the formation of Inkatha in a more indirect way. Because the 1913 Act hit hardest among the younger generation of kholwa, who had not yet established themselves either in their careers or in terms of property ownership, it promoted social stratification and the development of profound tensions within kholwa communities. These tensions were also closely related to the radicalisation of African worker politics in the immediate post-war period, as was expressed in the civil disobedience campaigns and strikes that took place all over the Union. Identifying and associating with the new radicalising constituency of African workers in the urban areas, elements of the new and marginalised kholwa generation expressed themselves politically, first in the Transvaal and a few years later in Natal. In doing so they dispensed with the doggedly constitutional and *hamba kahle* modes of protest favoured by the kholwa establishment.[6] Indeed this new stratum overall showed greater interest in the methods and objectives of the worker movement, whose Bolshevik representatives in Russia were then making great progress, than in those of Victorian bourgeois liberalism.

The political consequences were soon felt by the kholwa establishment. These were presaged by the ousting of John Dube from the SANNC presidency in 1917, and the election of the more militant Sam Makgatho, president of the Transvaal branch of Congress, as his replacement. Makgatho was a man more in touch with the growing and increasingly volatile urban African population on the Rand. Dube responded by breaking ties with the national organisation and retracting to his original political home in the NNC.[7] From that base he did all in his power to prevent African politics in Natal from following the route recently taken in the Transvaal.

Natal's relative immunity from the militancy of the 1918–20 period was largely a reflection of the successful way in which Natal's *hamba kahle* leadership countered local radicalism. In 1918, indeed, there were clear signs that Durban's African workforce was radicalising. In April the rickshaw-pullers came out on strike, for example, while in August the staff of the Royal Hotel in Smith Street successfully struck for higher wages. As a response to these developments, Dube convened mass meetings with Durban's African workers in July and August 1918. His audience was urged 'not to do this sort of thing. When there is a request for a rise in wages, work must not be stopped . . . no trouble should be caused'. He then distributed copies of a petition addressed to 'The Government, Municipal Authorities and Employers of Labour Generally' and signed by Dube 'For the Native Workers'. It opened by requesting 'your assistance . . . in such a direction as you in your wisdom may deem proper'. The focus of the grievances listed was the inadequacy of wage levels in Durban, especially since prices had rocketed during the war; other grievances related to evictions following the 1913 Act, rental increases on white farms, and various restrictions imposed by government laws and municipal regulations. By way of conclusion, Dube's petition emphasised that Durban's African workforce 'desire particularly to contradict allegations in the Press that they are working in accordance with the Socialistic Movement taking place in Johannesburg or elsewhere'.[8] Yet, ironically, the very reason for Dube's intervention was that local workers had already clearly shown their sympathy with the 'socialistic movement'.

Dube's return to the leadership of his local political constituency in Natal, severed from the national Congress organisation, was thus not an easy homecoming. In the post-war period, at national level and in Natal, Dube was alerted to the existence of a new and radicalising generation of potential Congress members, concentrated mainly in the urban areas. And if in Natal the African workforce became radicalised and was represented in the NNC's body politic, as had happened in Congress's Transvaal branch and in the national executive, Natal's kholwa establishment was in danger of losing its political base and influence, and hence being left less able to defend either its relatively privileged position in African society or its particular view of the course that African 'modernisation' should take. In the post-war period, Natal's kholwa establishment was thus thrown into a search for new political allies, a new political constituency, and, as later developments were to indicate, a new base in the rural areas. These developments, which in Natal came to a head in 1924, were crucial to the formation of Inkatha.

The increasing segregationism of the South African state in the post-Union period also played an important role in nudging the Natal kholwa establishment towards a *rapprochement* with the rural tribal elite. Indeed the drift of legislation since Union tended to dash kholwa hopes of being enfranchised and incorporated as equal members into a non-racial South African middle class. 'The law' had an immediate and practical importance for kholwa political leaders, since it was ultimately responsible for defining their room for political manoeuvre. The Native Affairs Administration Bill of 1917, introduced to parliament by the Prime Minister, General Louis Botha, was the first state attempt to entrench political as well as territorial segregation in South Africa. Though this Bill failed to pass into law, because it depended on consensus over the final delimitation of 'black' and 'white'

land under the 1913 Land Act, some of its key principles were soon
embodied in the Native Affairs Bill which became law in 1920. The architect
of the 1920 Native Affairs Act was General Jan Smuts, who had succeeded
to the office of Prime Minister following Botha's death in late 1919.

Apart from setting up a 'constitutional outlet' at national level for African
'views and grievances',[9] which took the form of an annually convened
Native Conference and a permanent extra-parliamentary Native Affairs
Commission, the 1920 Act more significantly made provision for the
establishment of African local councils in rural areas. These local councils,
whose members could be appointed or democratically elected, were to have
considerable powers in the administration of local rural communities and the
land on which they lived. On the one hand, by tying local councils to the
reserves and by placing both the local councils and the Native Conferences
under the control of the NAD and the extra-parliamentary Native Affairs
Commission, the state emphasised that both urban areas and the central
government were to be the preserve of 'white South Africa'. On the other
hand, however, Smuts affirmed in parliament that the 'principle of
self-government for natives' was part of the 'law' of segregation:

> The white parliament would always remain the sovereign power in the
> country, but [Smuts] did not see why a certain amount of self
> government . . . should not be allowed to the natives so that in their
> own territories they would be able to attend to their own domestic
> affairs.[10]

The corollary to the displacement of African politics from the realm of
'white South Africa', as was prescribed by the 1920 Act and soon afterwards
by the 1923 Natives Urban Areas Act, was that African political institutions
were to lie in African rural areas.

One of the principal objectives of the 1920 Act was to divert the
aspirations of educated African leaders away from 'white South Africa',
where the unabated urban conflicts were directly attributed to the influence
of 'detribalised agitators', and towards 'their own people' in the rural areas.
To certain Natal kholwa thinkers, the more thoroughgoing policy of political
and territorial segregation initiated by the 1920 Act seemed to offer some
potential advantages, and even suggested a potentially long-term way out
from current kholwa political and economic difficulties. For the first time
since Union, Natal kholwa interests welcomed a new piece of 'Native
legislation'. Dube was almost euphoric:

> I support the Bill with my whole heart. This is what we have always
> been wanting the Government to do. We have no voice . . . in the

administration of our interests, and these councils will meet that general need.

The 'difficulty', Dube added significantly, was that 'the chiefs may think that their power is going to be undermined'.[11] This, then, provided another reason for the initiation of a more formal political interchange between kholwa and tribal leadership. The first kholwa initiatives in this direction in early 1921, which led eventually to the formal establishment of Inkatha, came explicitly as a response to the local council provisions of the 1920 Act. However, Dube and his closest political associates in the NNC, which was based mainly in Natal proper, were to become directly involved in Inkatha only in 1924.

The formal establishment of Inkatha in 1924, following intensive kholwa initiatives, cannot be understood solely in terms of the influences mentioned so far: the increasing need in Natal kholwa circles for greater access to land, especially after the 1913 Act's clamp-down on African land purchase; the rising tensions within post-war Natal African society, most notably in urban areas, which provoked severe insecurities for Natal's wealthier kholwa establishment; and the state's growing commitment to segregation as a practical policy, which included certain notions of African self-government. The decision taken in 1924 by the NNC's 'old guard' leadership to involve themselves directly in Inkatha also reflected – and further developed – important changes that were taking place in the sphere of kholwa ideology.

An important influence on the ideological changes taking place in the kholwa world was the concurrent ideological shifts occurring within the white establishment which, in part, were reflected in the evolving state policy of segregation. During the 1920s increasingly less credence was given to liberal democratic ideas by members of of the white ruling elite, even among white 'liberals' and 'friends of the natives' with whom kholwa leaders maintained close contact. With growing confidence at state level through the 1920s, the policy of segregation was presented as being in accordance with the immutable logic of positivist social science (most specifically in regard to the 'cultural pluralism' of contemporary social anthropology) and also as morally 'correct'. These ideological developments, away from Victorian 'universalism' and liberal democracy, exerted a subtle influence on certain members of Natal kholwa society who through literacy kept closely in touch with 'advances' in the field of 'scientific knowledge', which was seldom regarded as derivative or value bound, and the pulse of white political thought.[12]

There was, however, another – and apparently more weighty – ideological influence. This issued from black American intellectuals and the developing ideology of world-wide black consciousness. Dube in particular and the educated African elite of which he was a part had long been influenced by black American leaders, especially Booker T. Washington who held that black advancement towards socio-political equality with whites could best be achieved through black education, industry and self-improvement. These conciliatory doctrines of black-white 'racial co-operation' and black 'racial self-help', as opposed to black political agitation, remained influential after Washington's death in 1915. They had a resurgence of popularity after the South African tour in 1921 of James Aggrey, an American-based West African educationist who similarly advocated black 'progress' through 'enlightenment'. But in the post-war period overall, it was the more assertive doctrines of the American-based W.E.B. DuBois and Marcus Garvey that were more influential in the national and provincial Native Congresses in South Africa.[13]

DuBois advocated the stirring of black nationalism as a political force in the struggle for equality with whites. Publicising the slogan 'Africa for the Africans', he envisaged the establishment of an independent black state in Africa based on the industrial democratic model. Garvey, a Jamaican resident in New York, whose populist and somewhat messianic 'Back to Africa' movement swept post-war black America, was more radical. He criticised DuBois's movement saying he did not aim for integration and social equality but black 'race purity' and 'race dignity'. The differences within the Pan-African movement should not however be overemphasised – DuBois was, for example, impressed with Garvey's idea of a 'self-sufficient black economy' as an element of black liberation. The evolution on the international scene of a separatist black nationalism seemed also to be linked to the European post-war concepts of 'self-determination' and 'reconstruction' for 'nation states'.[14]

Although until the mid-1920s the NNC was dominated by representatives of Natal's conservative kholwa establishment, who have been held to have rejected Garvey's radicalism as unambiguously as they rejected socialism, in October 1920 a black American exponent of Garveyism addressed a large and attentive meeting of the NNC in Durban. Significantly, John Dube keenly questioned the visiting speaker on the progress of Garvey's ideas in America.[15] Dube subsequently attended the London session of the 1921 Pan-African Congress, largely organised by DuBois, which was perhaps 'the most radical of the [Pan-African] Congresses'. Delegates from francophone Africa at the subsequent Brussels session refused to endorse the resolutions drawn up in London, entitled 'Declaration to the World', on the grounds of their 'radicalism' and racial 'separatism'.[16] Solomon Plaatje, a

Kimberley-based SANNC stalwart of Dube's generation who was then touring America, where he addressed meetings of both DuBois's and Garvey's movements, presented an address *in absentia* to the 1921 Pan-African Congress.[17] Dube was evidently very struck by the proceedings of the London session, and felt them to be of immediate importance to African politics in Natal – particularly in regard to the role of the officially unrecognised Zulu king, Solomon kaDinuzulu. Following his return to South Africa, Dube said as much to a meeting of the NNC in Durban in 1922.[18]

Dube and Plaatje, together with others of their older, more conservative generation of Congress members, without doubt felt uncomfortable with the more radical aspects of post-war black consciousness. Clearly, however, they did not feel entirely alienated from the developments that were occurring in international black political thought, nor from the new energy that was fuelling them. Indeed, for Dube in particular there seemed to be some aspects of post-war black consciousness that converged with aspects of his own thinking, and from this convergence there emerged new inspiration for African politics in Natal. In this context it seems significant that there was a proposal contained in the London session's 'Declaration to the World' which foresaw

> the rise of a great black African State, founded in Peace and Goodwill, based on popular education, natural art and industry and freedom in trade, autonomous and sovereign in its internal policy, but from its beginning a part of a great society of peoples in which it takes its place with others as co-rulers of the world.[19]

There were certain points of overlap, although very problematical, between the separatism of contemporary black consciousness and anglophone Pan-African nationalism, on the one hand, and South African segregationism on the other. It seems that this offered an ideological climate, and also some space for political manoeuvre, which was conducive to a revision of policy directions within Natal's kholwa establishment. This revision of policy directions was reflected in the formation of Inkatha, an organisation which aimed to achieve some measure of Zulu 'self-rule', under 'progressive' leadership, so as to implement a programme of Zulu 'modernisation' in the fields of education, commerce and industry.

*   *   *   *   *

The first moves towards the formation of the 'Zulu National Congress' (later renamed 'Inkatha') issued from 'prominent and progressive Natives' who

lived mainly in the Vryheid district. Influential among them was the Revd
Samuel D. Simelane, who lived in Chief Matole Buthelezi's ward in the
Nongoma district (in Zululand) but worked mainly in the neighbouring
Vryheid and Ngotshe districts (in Northern Natal). Having been educated at
Amanzimtoti Training Institute (in Natal proper), he was subsequently
ordained into the Dutch Reformed Mission Church. In February 1921,
accompanied by Solomon's closest royal adviser, Mnyaiza kaNdabuko
Zulu, Simelane requested official permission to discuss with the CNC,
Wheelwright, how the Zulu could respond to the 1920 Native Affairs Act. At
this meeting in March 1921, Simelane took pains to emphasise that his
proposals had Solomon's fullest support. It was 'our wish', he said, to
organise an 'annual meeting' in accordance with the 1920 Act to discuss
'matters that will tend to promote the welfare of the people'. More
specifically in this context, he requested permission for the establishment of
a 'co-operative agricultural scheme' in Zululand.[20]

The proposals were essentially an attempt on the part of local Zulu
kholwa, living near the royal epicentre, to co-operate with tribal chiefs to
take advantage of the 'progressive' provisions of the 1920 Act. The intention
of the agricultural scheme was to buy land and farm it for commercial
purposes. Inkatha was in this way initially seen as a means through which
commercial agricultural production could be set under way on land
ostensibly bought by a 'tribe' – non-tribal land-buying syndicates having
been practically outlawed since the 1913 Natives' Land Act.

From the outset, however, there was more behind the formation of
Inkatha. Dube had already been in contact with Solomon, urging him to
associate himself with NNC activities. On the same day in March 1921 that
Simelane was presenting his proposals to the CNC, Albert kaTshingana Zulu
was also in Pietermaritzburg. He had come to attend the annual NNC
meeting, in compliance with the NNC's request that Solomon 'send
someone to listen for him'.[21] Solomon's tentative acknowledgement of the
NNC, however, sharply contrasted with the importance that the NNC
attached to Solomon's support.

The NNC's interest in Solomon was clearly underpinned by the black
consciousness ideas that were spreading among the educated African elite.
In the Natal context, where the search for 'roots', a black identity and a sense
of proud independence turned almost inevitably to the Zulu royal family,
these ideas imparted to Solomon an undefined and somewhat mystical role
of leadership. The June 1922 NNC meeting in Durban strikingly exposed
how these ideological influences were being interpreted. Dube had recently
returned from London, where he had attended meetings of the Pan-African
Congress. There, Dube reported in his presidential address, it had been

argued that 'if any native in any part of the world was oppressed or living under hardships that such conditions should move every black man throughout the world.' As if to further emphasise the international character of this black solidarity, Dube also added that he was shortly to leave for America 'as a result of an invitation of prominent Negroes' in that country. However, Dube significantly went on to intimate that

> he was not prepared to expose the very important matters that had been discussed at the Pan African Congress . . . He desired to meet the Paramount Chief of the Zulus, 'Solomon ka Dinuzulu' to whom he would make a full report . . . [This report] could only be submitted to 'Solomon' and no other man.

Dube reiterated these views the following day at an NNC meeting in Pietermaritzburg.[22]

If the NNC aimed to establish Solomon as its ideological centrepoint, Solomon proved to be a highly elusive quarry. At a meeting at Mahashini, Solomon's principal residence in Zululand, two months after Dube's report-back to the NNC, Solomon made it clear that he was not prepared to link himself openly to the activities of Natal's 'Congress People'.[23] Before 1924, all that existed of Inkatha was a 'Zulu National Fund' whose function was primarily to accumulate money for the proposed agricultural and land projects. Simelane, as secretary, was the driving force behind this fund. The 'acting chairman' was Mnyaiza, and the treasurer was the aged Mankulumana kaSomaphunga Ndwandwe, previously Dinuzulu's principal headman. These details appeared on publicity leaflets dated February 1923, which called for contributions from the Zulu public on the basis of a sliding scale:

Chiefs	£5.10. 0.	Teachers and	
Indunas	£2. 5. 0.	educated natives	£1.10. 0.
Ministers	£2. 5. 0.	Kraal people	£1. 1. 0.

However, although Mnyaiza's support for the venture was unquestionable, both Solomon and Mankulumana 'repudiate[d] any association with the fund'. To Oswald Fynney, the magistrate at Nongoma who had established a close relationship with the Zulu royal house, Mankulumana protested that the treasurership had been foisted on him. And when attempts were made in 1923 to formally establish a 'Zulu National Congress' as well as a fund, Solomon informed Fynney that he was 'opposed to its creation other than under government auspices'.[24]

Although Solomon's unenthusiastic statements to NAD officials must be read with some caution, it was nonetheless evident that Solomon felt himself to be under some pressure from kholwa interests, and that he baulked at their political ascendancy in 'his' preserve. Solomon was at this stage mainly preoccupied with healing the vertical divisions – 'tribal' and dynastic – within the Zulu that had nourished the civil war of the 1880s, and had since poisoned Zulu national unity. Although he defined himself less as a reactionary than as a reformer of the 'tribal system', Solomon's political objectives were still cast in the 'tribal' mould and hence were distinct from the 'detribalised' and 'progressive' political objectives of the driving forces behind Inkatha. His aim was essentially to resuscitate Zulu national unity, together with Zulu respect for their tribal elders, their chiefs, and their royal family, and to defend tribal rights to the land.

In calling for more land to be made available to the Zulu people, Solomon seemed not to have in mind a nation of Zulu landowners holding individual title deeds and engaged in commercial agricultural production. On the other hand he would undoubtedly have welcomed the opportunity to allocate new tracts of land to those chiefs who he deemed to be worthy, so that they in turn might redistribute it among those of their followers who they deemed to be needy. The power to allocate land in the reserves, where land was held on the basis of communal tribal tenure, was perhaps the prime material support of the rule of chiefs, and was thus to be defended at all costs. That Solomon personally was in the process of buying real estate in Johannesburg (through Seme) did not mean that he supported private ownership of land by 'commoners' in the rural areas. For Solomon, land ownership on the Rand was a buttress to his status as Zulu king at a time when the cultural climate of Zulu leadership was undergoing change. The indaba between the Governor-General, Prince Arthur of Connaught, and the Zulu at Nongoma in July 1923 offered tribal authorities a forum for voicing their land demands. Such 'royal interchanges' were the manner in which Solomon preferred to deal with his white rulers; here it was his role to express Zulu loyalty and make appropriate gestures with the utmost decorum – on this occasion he presented the Governor-General with a loin skin, a meat mat, a beer strainer, and an autographed portrait of himself. Mankulumana, however, whose role it was to be more pithy, dwelt on the lands that had been alienated from the Zulu, and called for more reserve lands to be set aside for them.[25]

It was nevertheless also apparent that Solomon was more attracted to the alliance proposed by the NNC, as embodied in Inkatha, than he was prepared to admit to NAD personnel. A Zulu National Congress could certainly contribute to Solomon's drive for recognition as Zulu king, and so too could the skills of highly educated advisers. Solomon's reticence in regard to Inkatha was in part because he was well aware that such recognition had to come ultimately from the South African Government. Thus he wished to be associated with the organisation only when he had ascertained that it had gained NAD approval.

From the point of view of the Zulu-speaking middle class, apart from demands for better educational facilities and longer-term aspirations for the franchise, there were two immediate and urgent political goals. Both were related closely to the ethos of private ownership and individual accumulation to which the kholwa adhered, and which did not easily accord with the tribal world-view. First, there was the desire to promote African business pursuits in both urban and rural areas. The obstacles here were trading licences (white trading monopolies were sanctioned by law even in the African reserves) and insufficient capital. At the 1922 annual SANNC meeting in Bloemfontein, a decision was made to create a fund to purchase and run a number of trading stores. These were to remain SANNC property and profits were to return to SANNC coffers, but they were to be managed by individual members who would benefit from the 'respectable' employment and business experience they gained. Josiah S. Gumede, the only member of the NNC executive committee to maintain contact with the SANNC after its radicalisation, was a prime mover in this scheme.[26] The 'business interest' was strongly represented in the NNC by the chairman, William Foshla Bhulose, who had been born in Inanda and educated at Amanzimtoti. He had entered storekeeping 'at an early age' to become 'one of the most progressive businessmen in Durban'.[27]

Second, there was the desire for private land ownership, both as a matter of cultural and ideological principle and with a view to commercial agricultural production. William Washington Ndhlovu had been a long-standing member of the NNC, and was a member of the committee that drew up the SANNC constitution in 1919. Like Dube, Ndhlovu of Vryheid East Township had distanced himself from the radicalised SANNC and had reverted to his original political home in the NNC, where he succeeded Seme as treasurer. The attitude of the NNC leadership as a whole on the land question accorded with that of Ndhlovu, as was indicated by the NNC meeting of October 1923. Addressed by Dube, Bhulose and Gumede, this meeting focused on the issue of how the 'Native population was generally held back, more especially in respect to owning land and property'.[28]

These two immediate and urgent political goals were reflected in Simelane's proposed agricultural scheme, which was the only area in which the early Inkatha took practical action. Like the SANNC's scheme for business pursuits, its envisaged advantages were twofold: first, to generate profits which would build up Inkatha funds and, second, to provide a functioning model of 'progressive' agricultural techniques to assist those who wished to pursue careers in commercial agriculture. In addition to the

Zululand-based Zulu National Fund, Simelane established another fund based on the Rand, called 'Imali yo Umpini' (literally 'money for the hoe handle'), to further the agricultural scheme. He also began negotiations with a Vryheid solicitor, Horace Guy, with a view to buying a farm. This venture was ultimately to be blocked by the government, which insisted that land should be bought only by 'definite tribal bodies' rather than an 'irresponsible general fund'. The SNA instead suggested that Inkatha use its funds for 'philanthropic purposes, such as an asylum for the crippled and destitute'.[29] Ironically, with the quickening pace of evictions from white-owned land, an asylum for the destitute was soon to be much needed in the Vryheid district, and an agricultural co-operative might have been the most constructive form that it could have taken. Inkatha's agricultural scheme, however, was not conceived to be of benefit to those who were destitute.

During interviews with Fynney, Solomon and Mankulumana made it clear that they saw little value in – and were not even fully informed of – Simelane's scheme. Solomon held that the 'campaign is entirely unauthorised so far as [I am] concerned'.[30] Significantly, the fund was publicised in the Vryheid district and not in the Nongoma district which lay in the Zululand reserves. Equally significantly, it was publicised by way of printed posters rather than by word of mouth through the network of tribal leaders. Non-literate Zulu seemed only to have the vaguest awareness of the existence of an agricultural scheme, and much less of an understanding of what it was all about.[31]

It was during 1923 that the fledgeling organisation led by Simelane came to be known as 'Inkatha' – a name charged with royal and national associations. The original Zulu *inkatha* of the nineteenth century was not an organisation but an artefact: a sacred coil containing substances of metaphysical significance, bound circularly in woven grass. It had customarily hung from the roof in the Zulu king's residence, representing the unity of the Zulu nation and embodying the spiritual essence (*insila*) of the Zulu people. It had also served as a symbol of state, and of the 'supreme power' of the Zulu kingship. The *inkatha* had been passed down from king to king, until 1879, when it was destroyed as British redcoats fired King Cetshwayo's principal residence at Ondini (Ulundi). According to Baleni kaSilwana, speaking in 1914, the purpose of the *inkatha* had been

> to keep our nation standing firm. The binding round and round symbolises the binding together of the people so that they should not be scattered.[32]

For Natal's kholwa establishment, the need to keep the Zulu nation 'standing firm' behind its present political elite became an urgent political issue in mid-1924. The reasons for urgency lay in the radicalisation of African political consciousness in Natal proper, which was soon to be spearheaded by the ICU. Since the NNC was practically the only African political organisation in Natal at the time, and since it defined its political constituency as all-embracing, the NNC was in the first instance susceptible to currents of political opinion that took hold outside the ranks of the kholwa establishment. The latter was strongly represented in the NNC by not only Dube but also Bhulose (businessman), Ndhlovu (lawyer's clerk), Chiefs Stephen Mini, Walter Khumalo and Dirk Sioka (all 'kholwa chiefs' – one of the anomalies of indirect rule in Natal) and, although he held no office in the NNC, Simelane (minister). What happened in 1924, with consequences that were all the more devastating for the NNC kholwa old guard, was in the nature of a palace revolt: certain members of the existing NNC personnel became radicalised, identified with the moods of popular militancy, drew the rank and file into the NNC's body politic, and toppled the NNC's existing leadership. At the annual NNC meeting in April 1924, at Estcourt, the core of the NNC's *hamba kahle* leadership was not returned to office. John Dube himself, as well as William Bhulose and W. W. Ndhlovu, were not re-elected to the executive.

The new president of the NNC was Josiah Gumede, a long-standing member of the NNC whose political ideas were dramatically radicalised in the mid-1920s. In the space of the preceding year, so the police report of the 1924 NNC meeting maintained, Gumede had risen to become 'the most prominent speaker in Native meetings in Maritzburg . . . an extremist [whose] utterances disclose a bitter hatred of the European'. The police report also observed that 'although he has attained a certain amount of popularity among the Native hotheads, he carries very little weight with the older men'. Another 'hothead' elected to the NNC executive committee was Alexander Maduna, who had been noted for his fiery speeches alongside Gumede during the previous year. Reporting back to the NNC in Pietermaritzburg after the Estcourt NNC meeting, Maduna announced that Dube had been 'thrown out' and Gumede was 'now supreme', and hence 'Natives must now get their money ready as the Government would now be attacked and told what the Natives wanted.'[33] It was in this way that the NNC's old guard was displaced from leadership of the organisation that they had in practice regarded as their own.

Gumede's presidential address to an NNC meeting in August 1924 revealed that a battle for 'royal patronage', or at least some evidence of support from Solomon, was an aspect of the political struggle between Natal's kholwa establishment and radicalising rank and file. While emphasising the NNC's 'bounden duty to help the ICU organise Native

Labour in Natal and Zululand', Gumede went on to announce that the NNC would pay special attention to land alienation in Zululand (presumably he meant Northern Natal) and to assisting Inkatha.[34] Apart from the more ethereal significance that kholwa ideologues attached to the person of Solomon, his support was vital in a practical sense since it would serve to impart a broad legitimacy and thus a populist character to the political movement with which he was identified. In this respect, Solomon in 1924 held the key to African politics in the province of Natal – and there was little doubt that Dube's movement rather than Gumede's would be favoured with royal patronage.

*   *   *   *   *

The first real meeting of the Inkatha organisation took place at Solomon's principal residence, Mahashini, in October 1924. Solomon still shied away from completely open involvement in Inkatha, for he remained out of sight during the public part of the meeting, but for the kholwa establishment it was enough that he had permitted the 1924 meeting to take place at the very heart of royal Zululand. At this crucial meeting, Inkatha's executive committee was enlarged to include the two most prominent conservative kholwa leaders who had just been displaced from the NNC. John Dube and William Bhulose became joint chairmen of the new executive committee, and Inkatha in effect became the 'old guard' NNC in new and potentially much more influential form. Apart from the Revd Timothy Mathe (an associate of Simelane, evidently from the Vryheid district), the balance of the new executive was made up of the existing office holders: Simelane (secretary), Mankulumana and Mnyaiza.[35]

The coexistence of prominent tribal and kholwa leaders on the Inkatha executive committee, the 'peaceful and decent character of proceedings', and the instance in which a speaker who 'tried to create a sensation concerning the [cattle and goat] Dipping Levy. . . was called to order', all suggest that the elitist alliance had been consummated with some success.[36] However, the proceedings provided a wealth of evidence that the alliance was very tenuous. The meeting had been called at the instigation of kholwa leaders and with kholwa interests in mind. It had been advertised in Dube's Zulu-English newspaper, *Ilanga lase Natal*, with notices being circularised to Natal's *abafundisi* (teachers or educated people) personally, and the majority of those who assembled had travelled from urban and peri-urban areas in Northern Natal and Natal proper, and from Johannesburg. Zulu chiefs had simply not been called to the meeting; the only local Zulu present were those 'who through coincidence merely, were at Mahashini', among whom was Chief Mthethwa of the Qulusi.[37] The Revd L.E. Oscroft, principal of the ZNTI and Solomon's closest white confidant alongside the local magistrate, Oswald Fynney, concluded that 'the meeting was certainly not representative of Zululand or even Natal and Zululand'.[38] Mnyaiza, Chief Mthethwa and Mankulumana all strongly censured Simelane for being 'most concerned for the attendance of outside natives', and at the outset Mankulumana announced that any resolutions passed could not be regarded as those of the 'Zulu nation' since its chiefs were not there to represent it.[39]

Before the public meeting got underway, a private meeting took place between Solomon, his court advisers and the Inkatha executive committee. The three main issues on this meeting's agenda revealed how kholwa issues predominated: first, 'that Natives should be admitted to the Franchise'; second, a project to erect a church at Mahashini where 'the nation' could worship; and third, the significance of the 1920 Act's provisions for the establishment of local councils.[40] Once these discussions had ended, Solomon played no further part in the 1924 Inkatha meeting.

While the franchise issue was not raised during the public meeting, the church question was discussed at length. It transpired that the project was to establish not an interdenominational place of worship, but an independent African church on the Ethiopianist model. Situated at Mahashini, it could not fail to be of an explicitly nationalist character. The practical details were delegated to a special subcommittee of five members, all of whom were from outside Zululand, who proposed that the church be known as the 'African National Church' – instead of 'Shaka Zulu's Church' as previously mooted. The proposal met with strong opposition from local Zulu, particularly Solomon (whose objections were made in private) and his courtiers Gilbert, Franz and Mnyaiza, and from Bhulose. The whole project was shelved as a consequence.[41] A related project to erect a memorial on the site of Shaka's grave was set underway, however, and a separate fund was established for this purpose.

Regarding the 1920 Act, the public meeting passed a remarkable resolution against its application in Zululand, and resolved that 'the present means of government through Solomon should not be interfered with'. Seeking to explain this about-face, Oscroft argued that the church fiasco had

> helped harden local [viz. tribal] feeling [against] the 1920 Act and national [sic] councils for it is felt that they will injure the name and power of the present heads of the Zulu race . . . certain natives from outside Zululand want to acquire gradually the leadership in all native matters.

Natal's kholwa establishment had always supported the local council scheme, and, indeed, Simelane had from the outset intended Inkatha to be a local representative organisation that would seek state recognition under the 1920 Act. That kholwa leaders were prepared to retract on this issue and even support the resolution illustrated the extent of their determination to ally themselves with the Zulu tribal elite – which clearly felt threatened by the prospect of democratically elected local councils. If the alliance was to succeed, some political compromises were necessary. It is also important to remember, however, that kholwa leaders did not wish to undercut the status of the Zulu aristocracy at its very heart, Zululand, when its existence was becoming so central to kholwa ideology. Significantly, Inkatha's resolution on the 1920 Act was opposed to its application only in Zululand, and not in the rest of the province. Oscroft remarked, with perception but also some exaggeration, that the growth of Inkatha was an element in a broader, modern development whose 'real aim [is] the uniting of all the black races of the Union . . . They are casting around for a rallying point – a central figure – and that would seem to be Solomon.'[42]

The question of unity was similarly a prime consideration for Inkatha's tribal office holders. However, for them the question was a Zulu one and not a Union-wide or pan-African one. During the meeting, Mankulumana rose to lament the divisions within 'the Zulu house' which prevented the Zulu from being a true nation. It was thereafter resolved that 'the two streams [Usuthu and Mandlakazi] must be made one'.[43] This resolution highlighted another feature of the royal drive for national unity: it was directed principally towards healing the vertical or dynastic divisions in Zulu society (like those between Usuthu, Mandlakazi, Buthelezi and Ngenetsheni) rather than horizontal or class divisions. Integral to the royal drive for Zulu national unity was, of course, the resuscitation of the institution of Zulu kingship. The financial fortunes of the Zulu royal house, which was severely in debt at the time of Solomon's succession, had to be set on firmer foundations if this was to be achieved. An extravagant lifestyle was apparently seen as an essential element in the image of a twentieth-century Zulu king – and for Solomon the means were to be provided by Inkatha. This, from Mahashini's point of view, was one of Inkatha's most immediate attractions.

During the 1924 Inkatha meeting the purpose of Simelane's scheme for a commercial agricultural co-operative was presented with a different emphasis: the Imali yo Umpini fund was 'for the purpose of buying implements and growing crops for the subsistence of Solomon, his children, and those who come to Mahashini'. There was also the clear implication, as the CNC subsequently noted, that any 'profits [were] to go to the benefit of Chief Solomon'.[44] Solomon was indeed soon to be totally dependent on the revenue he received by way of Inkatha. In the course of the 1924 Inkatha meeting it was revealed that Inkatha's funds stood at £3000, banked at the National Bank at Vryheid (shortly afterwards they were estimated to be £5000), and there was considerable discussion as to how these funds should be administered. Evidently, however, these funds were eventually invested directly in Solomon's name, and in practice Solomon treated Inkatha money as his own. Speaking in 1981, Solomon's son, Thandayiphi, recalled that there seemed to have been 'no difference [between] Solomon's personal money and Inkatha'.[45] At the time of the 1924 Inkatha meeting, Solomon was already heavily in debt to the Denny Dalton liquor store in the Vryheid district, and 'embarrassed' on account of his land investments in Johannesburg through Seme. Directly after the 1924 meeting, however, Solomon paid £500 for a new car and hired a chauffeur.[46]

The 'confusion' that existed between Solomon's personal finances and those of Inkatha was, however, a problem for the future. Despite the internal strife at the 1924 Inkatha meeting, which was in any case to characterise Inkatha throughout its existence, a working relationship between the Zulu-speaking kholwa and tribal elites had been created, and to an extent their interrelationship and political objectives had been clarified. The meeting unquestionably established the kholwa elite as the social group most favoured by Zulu royalty and most able to manipulate royal influence. It also demonstrated that the tribal elite could not remain aloof from 'new generation' politics and its kholwa leaders; the latter had the organisational skills and political awareness that the twentieth century demanded. Inkatha moreover provided Solomon with a far greater source of support and a far more efficient means of collecting tribute than he otherwise could muster. The 1924 meeting thus formally established Inkatha as the organisation within which the alliance between Natal's kholwa and tribal elites would develop, and henceforth Inkatha was to take on the role of political mouthpiece of the 'Zulu nation' – which Inkatha's leadership defined as including all the Zulu-speaking people in the whole Province of Natal. Indeed, since it directly associated the best-known kholwa Zulu leaders with the Zulu royal house and the tribal aristocracy, the formal establishment of Inkatha played an important role in boosting Solomon's political profile and in resuscitating the notion that there was a 'Zulu nation' to which Zulu-speaking people could belong. Comparatively few Zulu, especially in rural areas and north of the Thukela river, would have consciously identified Dube as an opponent of popular interests, as did Gumede and Maduna.

*   *   *   *   *

Following the 1924 Inkatha meeting, the interdependence and co-operation – albeit uneasy – between the kholwa and tribal elites in Natal were consolidated, and the former made every effort to involve the latter in the 'modern' political process. Significantly, only a couple of weeks after the Inkatha meeting a tribal chief (as opposed to a kholwa chief), and a high-ranking one from Zululand moreover, for the first time participated directly in the 'modern' political world: Chief Matole Buthelezi of the Mahlabatini district went to Pretoria to attend the annual Native Conference called under the 1920 Act. His colleagues in the Natal delegation were John Dube (greater Durban) and W. W. Ndhlovu (Vryheid East Township).[47]

The single area in which Inkatha took immediate action was the scheme for a commercial agricultural co-operative. Here too, it was significant that the aged and highly respected royal *induna enkulu*, Mankulumana, now took up an active role; he was to die, in fact, while attending to his fund-raising duties in Johannesburg in 1926. By contrast, the chairman of the Imali yo Umpini agricultural fund, which was based in Johannesburg in accordance with financial good sense, was a notably progressive man. Emmanuel Peter Mart Zulu owned property on the Rand and was a member of the Alexandra Township Ratepayers' Association, a representative body dedicated to the defence of private landowners' rights and the maintenance of the township's respectable character. The agricultural fund was administered by an organisation named 'Umpini ka Zulu', which presented itself as the 'Transvaal branch' of Inkatha representing 'practically all of the Zulus on the Witwatersrand'.[48] Evidently, however, its main support issued from the Rand-based Zulu middle class, for it had virtually no support in the mining compounds. Interestingly, Umpini made special efforts to represent itself at the 1926 Native Conference to state its opposition to the establishment of local councils in the Zulu reserves, since these would 'weaken the power of chiefs in Zululand'. Similar to the Natal-based middle class, it apparently wished to preserve in Zululand a tradition of authentic 'Zuluness' which all could revere. Mankulumana and Daniel Vilakazi, a kholwa from the Vryheid district who at one stage had been Dinuzulu's private secretary, would periodically come up from Zululand to assist in the Umpini collections, and take the money back to Inkatha headquarters at Mahashini.[49] Nevertheless, as already mentioned, the government ultimately blocked Inkatha's attempts to use its Imali yo Umpini funds to purchase a farm in the Vryheid district, and Inkatha's commercial agricultural co-operative thus never materialised.

The only role which the rank and file played in the formation of Inkatha was a negative one: it was through its militancy in Natal proper that conservative kholwa leaders were displaced from the NNC in mid-1924. In

Zululand, after the rebellious rumblings of 1920, the rank and file had lapsed into a period of quiescence that was hardly ended by the few rumours of rebellion that circulated shortly after the 1924 Inkatha meeting: some young bloods, it seemed, chose to believe that the recent spate of Inkatha collections was to buy arms and ammunition for some sort of uprising.[50] The earlier half of the decade for Zululand was one of recovery, if not prosperity. No further land alienation had taken place since the declaration of Union, and the flush of evictions from white farms in Northern Natal after the passage of the 1913 Act had slowed to a trickle during the post-war depression. The rains were consistently good, and there were no serious locust depredations. And however much the Zulu bemoaned the state's livestock dipping regulations, by 1920 these had succeeded in controlling the various diseases – most importantly east coast fever – which had decimated Zulu cattle herds between the 1890s and 1913. Indeed, Zulu cattle herds had been so successfully replenished by the late 1920s that over-grazing and consequent soil erosion were important causes of the ensuing economic crisis. Moreover, apart from the high incidence of venereal disease among migrant workers and hence in the rural areas, after the post-war influenza pandemic the Zulu were relatively disease-free until the malaria epidemic of 1930.[51] The Inkatha organisation was thus formed during a period of relative calm and well-being in Zululand.

If, in the context of Inkatha, 1924 had proved to be the golden year of Natal's kholwa elite, 1925 was to prove to be the golden year of the Zulu tribal elite. In the period 1920 to 1925, Solomon's main sphere of activities lay quite separate from Inkatha. In June 1925, when Solomon and Edward, Prince of Wales and heir apparent to the British throne, met publicly in the course of an elaborate royal *indaba*, Solomon's drive for Zulu unity and his own recognition as Zulu king was to reach a peak. This royal and tribal side of the story now needs to be considered.

NOTES

1. CNC PMB 92, 64/2, minutes of interview between CNC, Magistrate, Nongoma, and Solomon, Mankulumana, Mnyaiza and others, 31/5/1920.

2. CNC 379, 3265/1919, NC, Nongoma to CNC, 2/3/1920; and see also entry for 29/11/1920 in CNC PMB 84, 58/7/4, CNC's memorandum, 15/8/1932, p. 5. The proposed mission to England undoubtedly had more pithy objectives as well.

3. CNC 332, 2337/1918, Bishop of Pretoria to CNC, 21/5/1919; and see also CNC to Bishop of Pretoria, 27/4/1919. Although the NAD believed that its efforts to

persuade Solomon to shun Mvuyana were successful, the church was none-theless erected complete with foundation stone claiming Solomon's patronage. It was still standing at Doornfontein in 1988, in a dilapidated state, being used as a workshop for a burglar-guard manufacturing business.

4. Quoted in Marks, *Ambiguities of dependence*, p. 53.

5. See Chapter 1 above for more detail on the Zulu-speaking middle class, and the consequences of the 1913 Act.

6. See Helen Bradford, 'Mass movements and the petty bourgeoisie: the social origins of ICU leadership, 1924–1929', *Journal of African History*, vol. 25, 1984, p. 310; and Bonner, 'The Transvaal Native Congress, 1917–1920', pp. 271–72 and 305–6.

7. Willan, *Sol Plaatje*, pp. 211ff; and Marks, *Ambiguities of dependence*, pp. 65–66.

8. State Archives, Pretoria, Archives of the Secretary of Justice (hereafter JUS) 270, 4/267/18, report of meeting called by John Dube, 18/8/1918, and enclosed copy of petition; see also SNA II/5/5, J.S. Marwick, Municipal Native Affairs Department to Clayton, Natal Local Land Committee, 16/4/1918.

9. *Cape Times*, 27/5/1920.

10. *Cape Times*, 3/6/1920.

11. Select Committee on Native Affairs, 1920, SC6A–'20, evidence of J.L. Dube, 14/6/1920, pp. 11–12.

12. It is significant that Natal kholwa leaders and state segregationists seemed to speak the same language of 'race', especially in the later 1920s, as will be illustrated later. For more on the ideological development of segregation, see Saul Dubow, '"Understanding the native mind": the impact of anthropological thought on segregationist discourse in South Africa, 1919–1933' (paper presented at the Workshop on Class, Community and Conflict, University of the Witwatersrand History Workshop, 1984); 'Holding "a just balance between white and black": the Native Affairs Department in South Africa, c.1920–33', *Journal of Southern African Studies*, vol. 12, 1988; and 'Race, civilisation and culture: the elaboration of segregationist discourse in the inter-war years', in Shula Marks and Stanley Trapido (eds), *The politics of race, class and nationalism in twentieth century South Africa* (London, 1987).

13. Shula Marks, 'Ambiguities of dependence', pp. 167ff; *Ambiguities of dependence*, pp. 52–53; and Robert Hill and Gregory Pirio, '"Africa for the Africans": the Garvey movement in South Africa, 1920–1940', in Marks and Trapido (eds), *The politics of race, class and nationalism*, pp. 233ff.

14. Apart from Hill and Pirio, my principal sources are T. Couzens, 'Moralising leisure time: the transatlantic connection and black Johannesburg, 1918–1936', in Marks and Rathbone (eds), *Industrialisation and social change*, pp. 315ff; Willan, *Plaatje*, pp. 229–79; and J. A. Langley, *Pan-Africanism and nationalism in West Africa, 1900–1945* (Oxford, 1973), pp. 35, 41–70. For other references to black American influence, see Helen Bradford, 'The Industrial and Commercial Workers' Union of Africa in the South African countryside,

1924–1930' (Ph.D., University of the Witwatersrand, 1985), pp. 120, 364; Shula Marks, 'Patriotism, patriarchy and purity: Natal and the politics of Zulu ethnic consciousness' (African Studies Institute seminar paper, University of the Witwatersrand, 1986), pp. 27–28; and Peter Walshe, *The rise of African nationalism in South Africa: the African National Congress, 1912–1952* (London, 1970), pp. 89ff.

15. Hill and Pirio, 'Africa for the Africans', pp. 211–12.

16. Langley, *Pan-Africanism*, pp. 71, 76 and 79–80.

17. Willan, *Sol Plaatje*, pp. 272–73.

18. CNC PMB 92, 64/2, CID report, Johannesburg, 12/6/1922, regarding NNC meeting, Durban, 7/6/1922. See also below. For an analysis of the parallel situation in Nigeria, where elements of the educated Christian elite took an interest in Garveyism during the post-war trade crash, see Gavin Williams, 'Garveyism, Akinpelu Obisesan and his contemporaries: Ibadan 1920–22' (unpublished seminar paper, St. Peter's College, University of Oxford).

19. Quoted in Langley, *Pan-Africanism*, p. 77.

20. CNC PMB 92, 64/2, NC, Nongoma to CNC, 14/2/1921; and CNC's memorandum of interview with Simelane, 31/3/1921.

21. CNC PMB 92, 64/2, CNC's memorandum of interview with Albert Zulu, from Chief Solomon, 31/3/1921.

22. CNC PMB 92, 64/2, CID report, 12/6/1922, of NNC meetings in Durban, 7/6/1922, and Pietermaritzburg, 8/6/1922.

23. State Archives, Pretoria, Archives of the Department of Native Affairs (hereafter NTS) 7205, 20/326, CNC to SNA, 10/11/1923, quoting earlier correspondence with the NC, Nongoma.

24. *Ibid.*; and SAP 41, 6/953/23/4, SNA to Dep. Comm. SAP, Pretoria, 28/2/1924. For the publicity leaflets, see NTS 7205, 20/326, NC, Nongoma to CNC, 14/1/1924.

25. Natal Archives Depot, Carl Faye Papers, Box 12/29, 'Account of the visit of HRH Prince Arthur of Connaught, Governor-General of the Union, etc. etc., to Zululand, 15–23/7/1923' (Faye was the interpreter), pp. 10–12.

26. CNC PMB 92, 64/2, Inspector CID, Johannesburg to Dep. Comm. SAP, 12/6/1922, reporting Gumede's SANNC address, 11/6/1922; and see also various other CID reports and Congress circulars in this file and SAP 41, 6/953/23/4.

27. CK 9A, 2:XB16:91, biographical notes on Bhulose.

28. SAP 41, 6/953/23/4, report by CID Detective Sergeant Arnold, Durban, 13/10/1923, on NNC meeting, Durban, 1/10/1923. See Chapter 1 above for Ndhlovu and his views on land ownership.

29. NTS 7205, 20/326, SNA to CNC, 2/10/1925.

30. NTS 7205, 20/326, NC, Nongoma to CNC, 14/1/1924, reporting interviews with Solomon and Mankulumana.

31. See NTS 7205, 20/326, CNC to SNA, 10/11,1923, quoting earlier correspondence with the NC, Nongoma; and SAP 41, 6/953/23/4, T.H. Hedges, District Commandant, SAP, Eshowe to Dep. Comm., Natal SAP, Pietermaritzburg, 6/9/1923.

32. Webb and Wright, *Stuart archive*, vol.1, evidence of Baleni kaSilwana, 17/5/1914, pp.40–41. Further details on the *inkatha* are recorded in my doctoral dissertation, pp.161–62 and notes 19–22.

33. CNC PMB 92, 64/2, Senior Inspector to Dep. Comm., Natal SAP, 23/4/1924, regarding recent NNC developments; and see also SAP 41, 6/953/23/4, various reports on NNC meetings during 1923. The three kholwa chiefs, incidentally, were returned to the NNC executive committee in 1924. For more on Gumede, see Francis Meli, *South Africa belongs to us: a history of the ANC* (Harare, 1988), pp.74ff; and for more on Maduna, see Paul la Hausse, 'The message of the warriors: the ICU, the labouring poor and the making of a popular political culture in Durban, 1925–1930' (unpublished paper, University of the Witwatersrand History Workshop, February 1987), pp.17, 23.

34. *Natal Witness*, 19/8/1924, report on NNC meeting.

35. My main sources on the 1924 Inkatha meeting were two reports made by local NAD officials: SAP 41, 6/953/23/4, report of 'Nkata ka Zulu' meeting, Mahashini, 8–10/10/1924, by the Revd L.E. Oscroft, ZNTI principal, 13/10/1924 (hereafter 'Oscroft's report'); and report of Inkatha meeting by O. Fynney, Magistrate, Nongoma, n.d., enclosed in CNC to SNA, 3/11/1924 (hereafter 'Fynney's report'). Other sources will be noted in the text.

36. SAP 41, 6/953/23/4, CNC to SNA, 3/11/1924 (first quotation); and Fynney's report (second quotation).

37. Fynney's report.

38. Oscroft's report.

39. Fynney's report.

40. SAP 41, 6/953/23/1, Dep. Comm., Natal SAP, to Secretary, SAP, Pretoria, 25/11/1924, *re* Inkatha meeting; and Oscroft's report.

41. Oscroft's report. While it was apparently not a direct outcome of the Inkatha meeting, a new independent African church called 'Shaka Zulu Church' came into being in 1924. It was a secession from the Zulu Congregational Church (itself a secession from the American Board Mission) which had flourished during the apogee of Ethiopianism at the time of the 1906 rebellion. See B.G.M. Sundkler, *Bantu prophets in South Africa* (Oxford, 1961), p.45 and p.53 for Sundkler's comments on the nationalist character of 'congregational offshoot' churches.

42. Oscroft's report.

43. Fynney was requested to assist the reconciliation with the Mandlakazi, of whom no representative attended the meeting. *Ibid.*; and Fynney's report.

44. Oscroft's report (first quotation); and NTS 7205, 20/326, CNC to SNA, 10/7/1925 (second quotation).

45. Pers. Comm. Thandayiphi kaSolomon Zulu (Solomon's declared heir until his deposition in 1946 following a succession dispute), Isikhwebezi valley, Nongoma district, 10/11/1981, p.6. Regarding the estimates of Inkatha's finances and the questions surrounding their investment, see NTS 7205, 20/326, T.J. Robinson, Sub-Inspector, SAP, Vryheid to Divisional CID Officer, Pietermaritzburg, 19/1/1925; CNC to SNA, 10/7/1925; and Oscroft's report.

46. SAP 41, 6/953/23/4, T.H. Hedges, District Commandant, SAP, Eshowe to Dep. Comm., Natal SAP, 6/9/1923 (*re* debts); and SAP 41, 6/953/23/1, Dep. Comm., Natal SAP to Secretary, SAP, Pretoria, 25/11/1924 (*re* car).

47. Report of the Native Affairs Commission, 1924, UG40–25, p.20.

48. NTS 7205, 20/326, SNA to Director of Native Labour, Johannesburg, 9/7/1926 (quotation), and enclosed copy of Umpini ka Zulu literature. See also NEC Box 8, evidence of E.P.M. Zulu, Johannesburg, 15/5/1931, pp.7914–16.

49. NTS 7205, Acting Director of Native Labour to SNA, 14/8/1926, enclosing J.T. Boast's report on Umpini ka Zulu, 12/8/1926.

50. See NTS 7205, 20/326, F.E. Trenchell, Detective Head Constable, Dundee, to District Commandant, SAP, Dundee, 4/12/1924; and T.J. Robinson, Sub-Inspector, SAP, Vryheid to Divisional CID Officer, Pietermaritzburg, 19/1/1925.

51. This socio-economic overview is explicitly comparative; see Chapters 1 and 6 for more detailed considerations.

5

Solomon and Zulu unity

Although Solomon framed his policies within the tribal mould, he also adapted the role of a tribal leader to the twentieth century. His prime source of wealth lay not in cattle and tribute from Zululand's subsistence farmers, but in money collected from wage labourers on the gold mines; part of his duties thus lay in representing mineworkers' grievances. He was, moreover, closely associated with an educational project for the tribal elite. Solomon's overriding political objective, however, was to reunite the Zulu people as one nation, as they had been in pre-colonial times, and to establish himself as Zulu king, as his grandfather had been. And in pursuing this objective, he made full use of traditional Zulu customs of marriage to forge ties of allegiance to the Zulu royal house.

Solomon fashioned a Zulu 'royal culture' that was very different from that of his dynastic forebears of the pre-colonial period. While his predecessors' world-views, religious beliefs and ways of life in general – the food they ate, the clothing they wore, the type of dwellings they occupied, the sort of furniture they used – were at one with those of Zulu society as a whole, those of Solomon set him apart from ordinary Zulu people. Although he continued to play out his traditional cultural role with great care – his role in ceremonies like the enrolment of *amabutho* continued to be central to his political status – his tastes and habits became increasingly of a middle-class character after 1920. Solomon's cultural eclecticism illustrated the struggle of a tribal leader to maintain a position of dominance during a period of accelerated social change. Tribalism was being assailed by powerful social and economic forces that tended to divide society into two groups: on the one hand there were those who were 'progressive', 'respectable' and 'civilised', and on the other hand there were those who were not. In this new order that was developing, it was clearly the 'black Englishmen' who were the new social and political elite – and they assuredly knew so themselves. If Solomon was to be a twentieth-century Zulu leader, he would in some way have to identify with this class. It must be emphasised, however, that Solomon's increasingly middle-class tastes and habits were in the first instance the trappings of a modern African leader: Solomon was not becoming one of the African middle class.

Solomon was not alone among Zulu tribal leaders in seeking to adapt the image and role of tribal leadership to the twentieth century. Such social and cultural adaptation among the Zulu tribal elite, however, was not merely a matter of appearances: it reflected deeper changes. The trappings of middle-class life were after all expensive, and necessitated substantial private monetary wealth. The trend during the 1920s was for the Zulu tribal elite to distinguish themselves as a separate class, drawing their economic power from their control over land in the reserves, their salaried public office, and their own and their wards' agricultural pursuits in Zululand and monetary earnings in the urban areas.

*   *   *   *   *

There is little need to make out a case for Solomon's definitive role in the context of 'traditional' Zulu culture – 'traditional' insofar as it made connections with the independent Zulu kingdom of pre-colonial times. Significantly, the retired Natal official, James Stuart, called on Solomon to assist him in his project of recording Zulu history and custom. One of the informants Solomon sent Stuart in 1921 was Hoye kaSoxalase, Solomon's *imbongi* (the royal bard, or reciter of *izibongo*), who in many ways could be regarded as the prime custodian of Zulu tradition. Both the context in which Solomon's *imbongi* performed (such as *ukubuthwa* ceremonies) and the content of his performance (the outstanding qualities and heroic deeds of successive Zulu leaders since Shaka) served to identify Solomon as inheritor, embodiment and guardian of Zulu history and custom. This, and the heroic form in which Solomon's own achievements were recited, presented Solomon as a living legend.[1]

However plausibly Solomon played out his traditional role during ceremonial occasions, it was clear that he himself did not fully subscribe to the system of beliefs that defined the king's function in these contexts. The 1918–20 influenza pandemic, which caused considerable loss of life in Zululand, provided the context in which the king traditionally would have played the role of high priest and 'medicine man', assembling the nation's *izangoma* (diviners) and *izinyanga* (herbalists), and presiding over ceremonies to appease the ancestral spirits. Indeed, forms of ancestor possession – *amandiki* or *amandawe* possession, reflecting psychopathic disorders –

were rife in the reserves and cried out for this type of response. As news of widespread illness poured into Mahashini, however, Solomon's response was to act as a dispenser of European medicines and 'comforting delicacies' – tea and sugar – supplied to him by the magistrate's wife, Mrs Fynney.[2]

Such cultural incongruities were expressed in a variety of contexts, and reflected both the contradictions in Solomon's upbringing and the disparate social pressures to which Solomon was subject. Solomon apparently 'pooled' different belief systems and cultural practices, most clearly those deriving from pre-conquest Zululand and imperial Britain, and adopted whatever seemed appropriate for the particular occasion. An example was the way in which Solomon presented himself to the newly appointed Minister for Crown Lands and Irrigation, Denys Reitz, during the latter's tour of Zululand. While Solomon's retinue was clad in skins and ostrich feathers, Solomon appeared in the formal attire of an English gentleman, wearing a frock-coat and top hat. Reitz found Solomon's clothing incongruous at the time, but perhaps more incongruous was a request made by Solomon while so clothed: he reopened the issue of unpaid *lobolo* cattle for Cetshwayo's *isigodlo* women, and asked for government assistance in extracting *lobolo* from the various men who had taken them as wives following Cetshwayo's death.[3]

Solomon's many marriages, however, illustrated that his cultural eclecticism was not entirely incongruous in his own eyes; cultural eclecticism also served his political purposes. Whereas he was reputed to have been a somewhat indefatigable and wide-ranging lover, Solomon's taste in women he wished to marry was quite specific: they should be Christian, 'sophisticated' and 'educated'. In other words, his personal preference (which he could not always indulge) was for women with a mission-station background, for they had learnt at close quarters the habits so essential to 'respectable' living: the serving of tea, the turning down of bedspreads, and a distaste for the forthrightness and frivolity of 'heathen' maidens.[4]

Solomon's first wife – and the one he evidently held most dear, despite their subsequent separation – was born to a kholwa family on a Norwegian mission station near Nhlazatshe in the Vryheid district. When Christina Sibiya was only eight years old, her father, Hezekiah Matatela Sibiya, had 'recanted' and taken two heathen wives with the result that he was disowned by both the mission and his Christian wife, Elizabeth. Perhaps reinforced by this trauma and her family's subsequent poverty, Elizabeth clung to Christianity and her 'superior ways' with a rigour that was remarkable even within the mission community. At the age of ten, Christina left home and moved into the mission house to work as a babysitter to the Revd and Mrs Eckenbren's new baby. Here her days were devoted to domestic duties –

she was taught to sew, knit and embroider – and attendance at school and church. While still a teenager, Christina left this cloistered environment for another: she took up a salaried post as primary teacher at a nearby outstation. Here she caught Solomon's attention.

Because Christina was so shy of both marriage and the Zulu king, Solomon courted her mainly through letters and gifts, which included combs, an ornate brooch and a silk scarf. For permission to marry Christina, Solomon first approached the Zulu pastor at the outstation, then the Revd Eckenbren, and only in the last instance the Sibiya family. She thus left the mission world – and was immediately plunged into a night of beer-drinking and ribald celebration. In the cultural disorientation and trauma that followed, Solomon instructed his senior *inceku*, Maphelu, to be an 'uncle' to Christina, to educate her in the 'customs and laws of my house [that] those Christian women who have brought her up have forgotten to tell her'.[5]

Solomon was nonetheless determined that Christina should retain her 'civilised' image. The first shopping spree at the Denny Dalton store in Babanango to which he treated her, however, proved that her new image was not to be the dull propriety of the mission station but instead the sophistication of a social trendsetter. She was bought selections of flamboyant striped material, which Mrs Dalton made up into a dress, together with a hat and coat. The marriage itself was a traditional ceremony at Christina's father's homestead, but it was subtly blended with western influences. In the course of the ceremony, Solomon and Christina held hands after the European fashion (traditionally the bride and groom never touched during the ceremony, and opposite sexes did not hold hands), Solomon presented Elizabeth Sibiya with dress materials in consideration for the pain she had suffered in bringing Christina into the world (this *ingquthu* transaction was traditionally a beast), and Solomon formally indicated to Hezekiah that he would honour his *lobolo* commitments (no mention was made of the form or value of the *lobolo* and in the event it was never paid).[6] Thereafter followed a ceremonial dance at Zibindini during which Christina was formally introduced as a member of the royal household.

As Solomon's first choice, Christina's appeal lay in the first instance in the refined qualities exhibited in herself and the social station she represented – though there is no doubt that Solomon was genuinely fond of her as a person. Her family's poverty and humble place in tribal society did nothing to recommend her. However, having followed his personal preferences in marrying Christina – and making a social statement in the process – Solomon then proceeded to enter into polygamous marriages in accordance with Zulu custom. This scarified Christina's sensibilities and was the major reason for her subsequent desertion. Lustfulness was not the reason for the number of wives Solomon amassed in his lifetime – variously estimated to be between thirty and seventy[7] – for, as 'king', he was both entitled and encouraged to accommodate as many *isigodlo* women (concubines) as he was able. As much as Solomon himself used the institution of Zulu marriage to consummate important socio-political linkages within his realm, he was subject to great pressure from below to accept the many daughters that were preferred to him. In the tribal context, a marital connection established between a subordinate and a dominant kin group was, for the former, an important means of upward social mobility.

The women Solomon married after Christina shared two characteristics in their social origins. First, despite all the opportunities provided by his extensive travels, Solomon only married Zulu women – as Solomon's sister Magogo expressed it, 'he didn't even want to hear of marrying a foreign girl'. Solomon's concern throughout his life was with the Zulu, and he single-mindedly carried this through to his married life. Second, Solomon married primarily into what the Zulu oral historian, Mahaye, calls the 'hero families' of the Zulu. Speaking of Solomon's wives, Mahaye stated that Solomon 'just loved them according to . . . their grandfathers, they were the heroes who defended Zululand . . .' Thus he married into the families of pre-conquest *izikhulu*, leading *izinduna* and warriors of outstanding merit.[8]

Since the internecine strife in Zululand in the post-conquest period had served to destroy its pre-conquest unity, the arrangement of many of Solomon's marriages required great perseverance. Yet the difficulties Solomon encountered provided the precise reasons why he persevered: through marriage, Solomon could dissolve old animosities and reconcile disaffected sections and lineage groups to the royal house. Thus he married three women from the Buthelezi because of, rather than despite, the tension that had existed between the Usuthu and Buthelezi since 1888. One of these marriages was to Sokwenzeka, daughter of Mbulawa kaMnyamana Buthelezi. Apart from being the son of Mnyamana, Buthelezi chief and principal counsellor to Cetshwayo, Mbulawa had served with distinction against the British at Isandlwana. OkaMbulawa (Sokwenzeka) was destined to become Solomon's highest-ranking wife alongside okaMatatela (Christina). Indeed, when okaMatatela's son, Cyprian, and okaMbulawa's son, Thandayiphi, reached their majority in the early 1940s, they were locked in a five-year succession dispute that only a government board of inquiry was able to resolve. Magogo's account of okaMbulawa's marriage ceremony, given as evidence at the board of inquiry in 1945, testified to its broader political significance: all members of the Zulu royal family from every royal homestead were summoned to be present, the *amabutho* were called up, and

Solomon invited Fynney to attend as witness (Fynney gave the bride a present of two blankets) – all of which was unprecedented.[9]

However, as Mahaye reveals, Solomon did not confine himself to marrying among the descendants of pre-conquest heroes. The turbulent years since conquest had thrown up a new set of individuals who had earned their places in Zulu history in less than heroic ways. Solomon married Malele, daughter of Sintwangu of the Cele, who had been one of Cetshwayo's lesser *izinduna*. However, the reason Solomon married into this lineage group was that Mayatana Cele, Sintwangu's brother, was popularly believed to be the man who had murdered the magistrate at Mahlabatini during the 1906 rebellion. This deed was hardly heroic in the traditional Zulu sense (the open battlefield was the venue for heroism), but it was nonetheless 'the fact that made Solomon marry the daughter of Sintwangu'.[10] With apparent incongruity, at first sight, Solomon also married into the descent groups of those who had made their marks as traitors to the royal cause. Before 1920, Solomon and the Usuthu had reserved a particular animosity for Zulu commoners who had collaborated with the colonial powers. After 1920, however, Solomon embarked on an intensive drive for Zulu unity and attempted to reconcile even traitors to the royal cause – however unpleasant a task this may have been on a personal level. Thus he married the daughter of Shibilika, who had earned infamy as a spy who assisted colonial forces in hunting down Dinuzulu after the civil disturbances of 1888.[11]

Solomon also used marriage as a political device by arranging his sisters' marriages. In accordance with Zulu custom, when Solomon succeeded Dinuzulu he simultaneously inherited the responsibility of acting as 'father' to his sisters with the power to 'advise' them in their choice of husband. Magogo described a meeting, held sometime around 1920, to which Solomon summoned all his sisters.[12] Nearly twenty princesses attended (Magogo was one) and, faced with Solomon and his *izinduna*, each was required to announce the name of her 'sweetheart'. As each sister did so, the merits of her choice were discussed by Solomon and the *izinduna*, and almost without fail the objects of their affections were subjected to hilarity and ridicule. Solomon proceeded to instruct his sisters to put on 'top knots' (headdress signifying eligibility for marriage). With the exception of three, all refused. In effect they were refusing to empower Solomon to assign them to men of his choice. Ultimately, this was not much more than a delaying tactic because, short of absconding, they had to get Solomon's approval for their 'choices'. Apart from the socio-political gains he could make, Solomon also stood to gain the hundred head of cattle (or equivalent) which princesses could command as *lobolo* – and he would only do so if the princesses married men of wealth and rank. He thus had good cause to defend his prerogative.

Magogo agreed to put on a top knot even though she had already developed an affection for a son of Mankulumana Ndwandwe – a choice that would have been highly acceptable to the patriarchs were it not for their political priorities. Magogo was thereafter assigned to Matole, chief of the Buthelezi. This was the most celebrated marriage arrangement Solomon made, and was responsible, more than any other single event, for the reconciliation between the Usuthu and Buthelezi.[13] Magogo was Solomon's eldest and highest-ranked unmarried sister (she was the only daughter of Dinuzulu's great wife, and hence Solomon's only full sister). Moreover, she was highly attractive. Although, as Magogo related, 'I was taken away from my fiancé by Solomon by his own hands', Solomon left it to his Buthelezi wife, okaMbulawa, to persuade Magogo to marry Matole: 'My mother [i.e. okaMbulawa] asked me if I loved Matole, and I said "Yes, since it is your desire".' She also observed that she would have loved Matole in any case. Thereafter Solomon announced:

> Today I am enhancing the prestige of the Buthelezis and establishing a blood relationship between the two tribes, for never since the advent of their ancestor Ngengeleli [sic – referring to the appointment of Ngqengelele, Mnyamana's father, as counsellor to Shaka] . . . has there been any fusion of our blood with that of the Buthelezis: I have merely appointed indunas for them. This is the first time a Royal girl has been given as a bride to them.[14]

That the whole Buthelezi chiefdom, rather than Matole personally, supplied the hundred head of cattle required as *lobolo* for Magogo was testimony to the wider significance of the marriage. As a special gesture, Matole added another eighteen head of cattle to this hundred, plus £40 in cash. For Solomon, the immediate benefit of the marriage was that, by selling the *lobolo* cattle, he was able to buy his first motor car. But the reconciliation between Usuthu and Buthelezi was of far greater and more lasting value.

There were two other marriages of note. While the marriage between Phikisile Harriette and Pixley Seme was not arranged by Solomon, Solomon gave the marriage his fullest support. Indeed, during the 1920s the family connection with Seme was of great value to Solomon as a source of independent advice (Seme never got involved in Inkatha) and a source of legal assistance. And as much as Seme benefited by his association with the Zulu royal family, the Zulu royal family's image among the kholwa elite benefited by its association with such a luminary as Seme. Second, Solomon's sister, Kessie Impiyamaxhegu, was married to Prince Dlamini of the Swazi royal family. This was the only instance in which a member of the Zulu royal family was married to a 'foreigner' during Solomon's time. There is little doubt that Seme had persuaded Solomon of the importance of this marriage. Throughout the 1920s, Seme acted as adviser and legal officer to the Swazi royal family, and there seemed to be no contact between the two dynasties but through the medium of Seme.[15] Moreover, while Solomon's political ambitions lay squarely within the Zulu, it was the kholwa ideologues (of whom Seme was a leading exponent) who were showing interest in the notion of a pan-African aristocratic 'super culture'.

Overall, Solomon's 'marriage policy' reaped advantages in two social contexts. In the tribal context, Solomon employed the Zulu institution of polygamy and his patriarchal authority over his sisters as a central part of his 'reconciliation' and 'reunification' strategy. As a twentieth-century Zulu king, however, Solomon aspired to establish a royal image that would not be outshone by the 'respectable' ways of the new African elite; he thus attempted to ensure that the marriages he arranged also served to 'keep up with the Dubes' and their perceptions of social propriety. Solomon's marriage policy aimed to promote Zulu unity and buttress Solomon's royal status throughout Zulu society, and its incongruities were a measure of the complexity of Solomon's task. Solomon had married Christina knowing that the core of her 'civilised' image lay in a set of religious beliefs that prohibited polygamy. Nevertheless, he not only established himself as a polygamist but also insisted that each woman he married should become a 'Christian' on taking up residence at one of his homesteads.

The term 'Christian' here raises problems. In Zulu, the term *kholwa* has two interrelated meanings: it refers to a person who believes in Christ and the teachings of the Bible, and to a person who wears European clothing. The opposite of *kholwa* is *bhinca*, which describes a person who wears traditional clothing, and who by implication is a 'heathen'. For Solomon, the term *kholwa* was interpreted primarily in a cultural rather than religious sense. Indeed, the Christian veneer he prescribed for his wives was designed for a cultural purpose. Yet Solomon not only required all his wives to dress after the European fashion, but also encouraged their attendance at church.[16] The church, apparently regarded to some extent as an earthly outstation for a great finishing school in the sky, offered vital instruction in European etiquette and 'decorum'. It nonetheless also dispensed the fundamentals of Christian belief, within which lay an injunction against polygamy. Solomon was not permitted to receive Holy Communion because he was a polygamist, but his wives could do so because each had only one husband.[17] Despite all the incongruities, through his problematical relationship with the church Solomon succeeded in forging for the Zulu royal house an image of western respectability even in the midst of a social practice that was its antithesis. The gains he made in the tribal context through the practice of polygamy were thus not incompatible with gains in the 'civilised' context.

Solomon's marriage policy reflected how Solomon was forging a particularly 'royal' culture that drew from the cultural worlds of both Zulu traditionalism and the mission station. During the 1920s, there was a growing trend among the Zulu royal family and other elements of Zululand's aristocratic establishment to associate themselves with the very fount of African 'civilised' counter-culture: the church and education. In 1922, Solomon had given the CPSA a site for a church in a part of his ward within three miles of the ZNTI. In the same year Solomon gave a site for a church and a priest's house at Mahashini itself, and a catechist named Mbuko Mhlongo took up residence there to assist Oscroft in his part-time pastoral duties among royalty and the Usuthu. Mhlongo was ordained at Nongoma in 1924 and thereafter took full responsibility for the Mahashini congregation. In 1929, Solomon gave the CPSA another site for a church and school in a part of his ward that abutted Nongoma – which by then was no longer merely an administrative centre, but a thriving trading centre and European enclave employing its own 'urbanised' labour force. When the Bishop of Zululand blessed the site, he was accompanied by a representative from Solomon, dressed in skins and with a tall feather standing from his headring, in both the service and the procession around the site.[18]

These developments were not peculiar to Solomon. As the secular image associated with Christianity came to be the mark of social excellence and political leadership, chiefs in various parts of Zululand scrambled to consolidate their positions by associating themselves with the church. In 1922, the CPSA established four 'preaching places' among the Mandlakazi, long the most implacable opponents of missionary endeavour in north-western Zululand. Some of these developed into regular outstations with their own catechists in charge, and by 1926 Oscroft had built a wattle-and-daub church at Bangonomo itself – the principal homestead of the Mandlakazi, corresponding to Mahashini of the Usuthu. In 1929, the Bishop blessed a substantial stone church at Emsebe on a site given by Chief Bokwe of the Mandlakazi – after which there was huge feast given by Bokwe and his *izinduna*. Further, in the mid-1920s a new outstation at Emngeni – towards the south of the Nongoma district where it served Usuthu and Buthelezi communicants – was graced with a properly constructed church, and the Revd Cuthbert Buthelezi took up duties there. Chief Silimane kaMkungo, a grandson of Mpande whose ward lay to the east of Eshowe, approached the CPSA in 1923 to build a church at his principal homestead. After it was built, Silimane was not permitted to take Holy Communion in it – but his wives were. In 1925 Silimane requested the CPSA to conduct a special service at 'his' church for the benefit of the souls of those who had died at the battle of Ndondakasuka in 1856 (at which Cetshwayo defeated his rival brother, Mbulazi, so securing the succession to Mpande). Especially in the north-western regions of Zululand, the mission work of the CPSA during the 1920s advanced on an unprecedented wave of success, with many new centres of worship being opened 'at the request of the people'.[19] While the CPSA ascribed these developments variously to the will of God, a spontaneous Zulu rush towards 'the light', or, more plausibly, the influence of the ZNTI on the tribal elite, they were more clearly a consequence of the changing cultural climate within which tribal leaders found themselves.

$$* \quad * \quad * \quad * \quad *$$

Three other elements of Solomon's 'royal culture' deserve special mention: motor cars, liquor, and houses. Collectively, these were the principal causes of the private and public maladies that beset Solomon's later life. They did much to establish a 'fitting' image for a twentieth-century Zulu king, but Solomon seemed powerless to curb his extravagance. By 1925, Solomon already had two cars – and his preference was for the largest, fastest and most prestigious American models: the Buick 'Straight Eight' and Chrysler 'Imperial'. The Buick was soon seized by Charles Adams, an Eshowe storekeeper, on account of debt.[20]

Solomon's tastes in liquor were considerably more catholic: whisky, brandy, beer and wine in order of preference. Reports that he did not always drink moderately date back to as early as 1918.[21] Other members of the Zulu royal family and tribal elite were also great drinkers, very notably so in the case of the young Chief Bokwe, even though the sale of 'European liquor' to Africans was illegal. Their consumption of liquor should not, however, be taken at face value. In the first place, as the 'respectable' anodyne of the white man's leisure time, it had social implications. In the second place, by the 1920s liquor had come to be regarded as the 'drink of kings' and, perhaps heightened by its illegality, a high ranking form of chiefly tribute. Magogo observed that cases of liquor would be brought to Solomon. Perhaps more revealingly, the Revd Oscroft's son, Basil Oscroft, recalled how Solomon demarcated the flower beds alongside his magnificent new house at Mahashini with row upon row of empty bottles of 'hard tack' buried head down.[22] The display of bottles and flowers formed a twin cultural statement.

When Solomon moved into Mahashini after his appointment as chief of the Usuthu, it was no more than a collection of dilapidated huts built in the traditional Zulu 'beehive' style. His initial renovations included building a few rectangular wattle-and-daub 'kholwa houses', set slightly apart from Mahashini, which were called KwaDlamahlahla. Then, in the early 1920s, Solomon set about having a substantial stone house contructed on the site. In doing so he drew on the advice of the Revd Oscroft, who gave assistance not only in designing the house, but also in supervising the Italian builder Solomon had hired. The result was an imposing residence, modelled on the prevalent colonial style, but outstripping it in grandeur. Set on a slight slope on the crest of the Nongoma range, it was encompassed by a deep veranda with dummy turrets mounted above the bay windows. Broad flights of stairs fanned out from the veranda to the grounds, and at the end of each there were pillars bearing large decorative urns in the classical style. In the same period, incidentally, Solomon was in the process of having a five-roomed brick house built in Sophiatown township, Johannesburg, on a freehold stand bought through Seme.[23]

The new KwaDlamahlahla added the final − and most crucial − touch to a unique combination of cultural elements brought together by Solomon at Mahashini. The combination ranged from the original circular beehive huts and royal cattle kraal where traditional ceremonies were performed, through the rectangular wattle-and-daub 'kholwa houses' with the royal stables nearby, through the small church and school where the royal children received their primary education, and finally to the imposing house, KwaDlamahlahla, with the Buicks in the forecourt. There was at least something here with which every Zulu could identify. As much as it was a fitting meeting place for the organisation that aimed and claimed to represent every Zulu − Inkatha − it was the perfect base for Solomon's drive for Zulu national unity.

In this drive, the overriding concern of the Zulu royal house, the little CPSA outstation at Mahashini played an important role. As well as being the centre to which Solomon's *bhinca* wives and all royal children from the various royal homesteads came for baptism, it soon developed into an elite educational centre for the very young. It was Magogo who first gathered the children at Mahashini to teach them the alphabet and the singing of hymns. The Revd Mhlongo then took up duties as a primary teacher, initially holding lessons on the veranda of KwaDlamahlahla while the school building was being completed. On its completion, however, the school taught not only the royal children who lived at Mahashini: royal children from all royal homesteads, together with other children of high birth in Zulu tribal society, came to Mahashini to live and to be taught for extended periods of time. This was the case with Mangosuthu Gatsha Buthelezi, son of Chief Matole Buthelezi and Magogo, who later in the twentieth century was to play a leading role in Zulu affairs. After his birth at Ceza mission hospital in the late 1920s, the young Buthelezi was 'immediately rushed' to KwaDlamahlahla 'as was the custom in those days', where he was to live and complete his primary education.[24] He only went to live at KwaPhindangene, the principal Buthelezi homestead, when he was a 'strapping young boy'.[25]

Of greater immediate importance as a centralising device than 'Solomon's kindergarten', however, was the ZNTI. This elite institution had been popularly regarded as 'Solomon's school' since its inception, partly no doubt because of its close proximity to Mahashini, but perhaps more so because Solomon had always given the venture his fullest support – as General Botha had requested him to do in 1916. Solomon was personally responsible for sending six of his younger brothers there, and moreover he attended the end-of-term concerts and prizegiving ceremonies, often making a speech himself and presenting the prizes. The links Solomon forged through the ZNTI were not, incidentally, confined to the Zulu. The prizes Solomon presented in 1922 were donated by the leading Natal sugar baron, C.G. Smith; and the visit of the Prime Minister, Jan Smuts, and two influential Natal MPs, J.S. Marwick and G. Heaton Nicholls, to the school earlier in the same year had a part in establishing contacts that were to be vital later in the 1920s. The Zulu royal family's main interest in the school, however, was alluded to by Ndesheni kaMnyaiza Zulu: 'the whole [Zulu] country', he commented, came to the ZNTI 'to learn the protocol of the royal household'.[26]

The ZNTI was the means through which Solomon accomplished the most difficult and important tribal reconciliation of his chieftainship: the dispute between Mandlakazi and Usuthu. Since the Mandlakazi leaders were a collateral branch of the Zulu royal family, Solomon could not use intermarriage as a part of his reconciliation strategy. Besides this difficulty, the dispute had had no hope of ending while the fiery Chief Mciteki was Mandlakazi regent. Even once the more moderate Bokwe had assumed the chieftaincy, in January 1922, there was nearly a major conflagration between Mandlakazi and Usuthu during a wedding ceremony in the Nongoma district. Police estimated fifteen hundred combatants would have been involved had officials not intervened. Mnyaiza, who had led four hundred fully armed Usuthu to confront the Mandlakazi, had evidently been the aggressor, and Mahashini's inquiry into the incident resulted in his being personally reprimanded by Solomon. The incident caused such consternation in official circles that arrangements were made to increase the Nongoma police force. There was a further period of tension in 1923.[27]

At the beginning of 1924, however, Bokwe enrolled at the ZNTI as a student and remained there for three years. For the Zulu royal house it was a diplomatic achievement indeed that the Mandlakazi chief should attend 'Solomon's school', and the friendship cemented between Solomon and Bokwe while the latter was at the ZNTI permanently doused any possibility of a resurgence of the forty-year-old family feud. For many Zulu, especially those of Solomon's generation, this was held to be the most memorable achievement of Solomon's lifetime.[28] With the major reconciliations between Usuthu, Mandlakazi and Buthelezi achieved, the stage was set for the massive display of Zulu unity at the *indaba* with the Prince of Wales in 1925.

The other major tribal division Solomon had faced at the time of his succession, that between Usuthu and Ngenetsheni, had gradually resolved itself largely through the disintegration of the Ngenetsheni as a social group. This was consequent on the takeover of Ngenetsheni lands by the Boers, who had claimed much of latter-day Northern Natal as 'payment' for Boer aid to the Usuthu in their war against the Mandlakazi in the 1880s. Solomon's policy towards Chief Kambi of the Ngenetsheni, the son of Hamu who had sided with the Mandlakazi, had nevertheless always been one of goodwill; it was a somewhat ironic measure of its success that Solomon's death in 1933 was to occur while he was at the principal Ngenetsheni homestead, mediating in a dispute between two of Kambi's sons. Kambi's absence from the display of Zulu unity at the *indaba* with the Prince of Wales was not because he did not wish to attend, but because he was so 'old and bedridden' that he could not make the journey to Eshowe.[29]

*   *   *   *   *

The news that Edward, Prince of Wales and British heir apparent, was to visit Zululand threw English-speaking Zululanders into a frenzy of excitement. A public fund was floated to cover the cost of triumphal arches, decorations and celebrations; arrangements were made to present HRH with a farm (abandoned because of the Hertzog government's opposition), a new bridge was built across the Tugela, and a dance hall was especially erected at Eshowe for the Grand Royal Ball. While the reaction of the white settler community was understandable, the reasons why the Zulu felt the visit to be so evocative were less obvious and require some preliminary explanation.

If anything, the Act of Union that vested white settlers with sovereign power in South Africa had heightened the wistful and emotional attachment that Africans in Natal had for the 'imperial connection'. Among educated Africans there had arisen a belief in the colour-blindness of Queen Victoria's rule, founded on Natal's 'exemption clause' (enabling 'exempted natives' to vote) and African land purchase rights before the 1913 Act. The drift of legislation since Union had eroded previous hopes that 'civilisation' would be a more persuasive social criterion than skin colour – and hence the nostalgic appeal of the 'good old days of Queen Victoria'. In the post-Union period, kholwa leaders drew heavily on Victorian liberal democratic ideas in arguing that Africans too were 'His Majesty's subjects' and thus that discriminatory laws were unethical. Their faith in the imperial connection was reflected in the series of deputations to England that were arranged to protest about the 1913 Act.[30]

Even in tribal Zululand there was a strong and romantic memory of the 'Great White Queen'. She, after all, had left the Zulu in possession of their land, if not their king, after the Zulu defeat of 1879. It was the Boers who later had taken the prime lands in the north-west as their 'New Republic', and the colonial settlers who had then parcelled out the remainder of Zululand into Zulu reserves and areas for purchase – in practice by white settlers. When Union was declared, with Dinuzulu in prison and with memories of the way in which the Natal government had suppressed the 1906 rebellion, the Zulu had displayed a marked indifference to the demise of the Natal government and the transfer of power to the new Union government. The death of King Edward VII in the same year, however, occasioned a 'spontaneous outburst of sorrow amongst the Natives of Natal and Zululand'. Zulu condolences to the bereaved British royal family poured into magistrates' offices throughout the Natal countryside.[31]

The British royal family was not directly implicated in the black experience of colonial rule in South Africa and so had an immunity from black protest arising from it. The British monarchy moreover appealed to the monarchical sentiments so ingrained in the tribal world-view, at the heart of which was the notion that political legitimacy was in the first instance imputed by birth. If Solomon naturally stood at the apex of the Zulu social and political order in the imagination of the majority of the Zulu, they also had a more remote and ethereal monarchy in the British royal family. Zulu attachment to Buckingham Palace was very marked in Solomon himself: portraits of British royalty decorated the walls of his principal residence, KwaDlamahlahla. Solomon's meticulous preparations for the *indaba* with the Prince of Wales, reflecting his perception of the importance of the event, were set underway months before the Prince's arrival. These included Solomon's personally equipping an expedition to East Africa, there to shoot an elephant bull with tusks of suitable proportions to make a memorable gift from the royal house of Zululand to the royal house of England.[32]

The sixty thousand Zulu who gathered on the Eshowe golf links to meet the Prince was the first mass assembly of the Zulu since their conquest in 1879. They met as a nation, not as a collection of colonial tribal chiefdoms.

Some had come from as far afield as the Ubombo and Ingwavuma districts and the borders of Portuguese East Africa. Most had marched to Eshowe wearing odd scraps of European clothing, but on arrival they stripped and turned out in traditional ceremonial dress: loin skins, dancing sticks, oval hide shields and plumed headdresses. They furthermore camped in the open and slept on their shields, as was the custom in pre-conquest times on occasions requiring a national assembly. In a remarkable expression of their mutual reconciliation, Solomon and Bokwe had together led the Usuthu and Mandlakazi contingents from Nongoma to Eshowe. On arrival, Solomon received the massed royal salutes from those already encamped, and then pitched his own camp – three tents on a promontory above the Umlalazi river, overlooking the whole assembly. Thereafter he assembled all the tribal leaders present and, once more with Bokwe at his side, led a 'picturesque cavalcade of Chiefs and Zulu notables four abreast' through the streets of Eshowe to confer with NAD officials.[33]

The assembled Zulu quite clearly saw Solomon as their king. Solomon indeed had made efforts to ensure that they did so; in accordance with royal responsibilities, he had made a substantial personal contribution to the fund to cater for the Zulu assembly. At a meeting of all chiefs on the day before the *indaba*, Solomon and Mankulumana were unanimously elected as the representatives who were to address the Prince, and Solomon was to lead the royal salutes. The CNC, too, had placed a special responsibility on Solomon to control the whole Zulu assembly. Most importantly, however, the *indaba* was to prove that the Prince himself had no doubt about Solomon's superordinate status. The agenda for 6 June 1925 was divided into two parts: first, the formal exchange of greetings and gifts between the Prince and the Zulu during the morning, and second, a less formal display of Zulu dance during the afternoon. The Zulu royal entourage was to be seated in front of the crescent-shaped Zulu assembly for the morning ceremony, directly facing the Prince's dais.

Solomon's arrival on the day of the indaba was greeted with a roar of 'Bayede' from the Zulu concourse – a demonstration which certain white observers believed Solomon had engineered as a mass affirmation of his royal status and as a slight to the Prince.[34] He was strikingly presented, his ceremonial dress of British military cut having been specially tailored for the occasion. It was of black cloth faced with leopard skin, a symbol of Zulu royalty, and on his epaulettes and white sun helmet there were brass insignia bearing the elephant emblem of Zululand. Ceremonial sticks and white gloves completed his outfit. So attired, Solomon clearly stood out from the other Zulu dignitaries: Zulu teachers and ministers wore nondescript morning suits, and tribal chiefs presented themselves in various idiosyncratic combinations of traditional and European clothing. Mankulumana was the only other Zulu who was conspicuous, though in a very different way, naked as he was but for a loin skin and a necklace of leopard claws. Solomon's only real rival was the Prince himself, who also appeared in ceremonial dress with a white sun helmet. In keeping with the pomp of the occasion the young Edward was laden with decorations, and his scarlet tunic was traversed by the blue sash of the Order of the Garter. As the Prince arrived to ascend the dais, Solomon led the royal salute 'Bayede' by raising his helmet three times – and it might indeed have been unclear to which royal figure the salute was directed.

In his address, Solomon did not restrict himself to the customary expressions of devotion and great joy, but made a direct political appeal from 'king' to 'king'. The Zulu were a nation, Solomon proclaimed, expressing the kernel of his message, and therefore should have the opportunity to take a part in framing the laws that applied to them. Although noteworthy, Solomon's speech was ultimately of less significance than the four separate occasions during the course of the day on which he spoke to the Prince on a personal basis. Only the first of these was officially scheduled; the rest represented a unique achievement on Solomon's part, for he alone in Zululand was accorded such repeated royal favours.

Following the speeches, the Prince made presentations to ten high-ranking Zulu chiefs. Nine were presented with silver-mounted ceremonial sticks, but to Solomon he gave a gold-mounted ceremonial stick. Having received the presentation, Solomon alone delayed proceedings by making a personal statement of loyalty to the crown – to which he pointedly added that the Prince should 'take that not only from himself but from the whole Zulu nation'.[35] Solomon thereupon made his official presentation to the Prince, two elephant tusks, again indicating that they were presented on behalf of the Zulu nation as a whole. At the close of the morning's proceedings, Solomon was granted a private interview on the royal train at Eshowe station, to which he went accompanied by Mnyaiza, Dube and two Zulu clerics. No account appears to have survived of what transpired there, except that Solomon made further, more personal, presentations: an extravagant gold album of pressed flowers, and a personal letter expressing devotion to the British crown. However, the very privacy of this second meeting gave rise to a rumour that Solomon took care not to quash: by the time the Zulu dispersed from the *indaba* it was 'common knowledge' that the Prince had appointed Solomon as Zulu king.[36]

When Solomon returned to the *indaba* grounds in the afternoon he progressed around the perimeter of the assembly, being acclaimed as he did so, before resuming his seat before the dais. In the course of the dances, the

Prince summoned Solomon with a request for some shields and assegaais as souvenirs. While presenting them, Solomon delayed to converse once more; this third meeting was openly observed by the whole multitude, and was evidently taken as a cue for the climax of the dancing. The performing *amabutho* raised their sticks aloft and charged the royal dais, causing some disquiet among officials. At this point Solomon distinguished himself by taking control of the dancers, driving them back and reforming them into their *amabutho*. Solomon then approached the Prince for a fourth consultation, this time requesting permission for his two thousand horsemen to absent themselves for refreshment. To this the Prince readily acceded, and he thanked Solomon for the magnificent display. The British heir apparent shortly thereafter left, having clearly been impressed by the emotional power of the *indaba*, and by Solomon himself.

*   *   *   *   *

However politically innocent the Prince's intentions were, he left behind him a Zulu throng charged with monarchical and nationalist fervour. Solomon had expertly transformed the *indaba* into a combined Zulu and British royal showpiece, all the while maintaining a fastidious deference to the Prince. He now seized upon this moment to consolidate his achievements: Solomon called the whole Zulu gathering together on his own account and enrolled a new *ibutho*. The full *ukubuthwa* ceremony could not be performed since the location and time available prevented it. But balanced against these deficiencies was the unprecedented size of the Zulu assembly, the new unity Solomon had achieved since the *ukubuthwa* of 1918, and the emotional atmosphere that the royal *indaba* had generated. The new *ibutho* was named 'Phondowendhlovu' ('the tusks of the elephant') in commemoration of the Zulu gift to the Prince – an appropriate symbolic climax to the whole event.[37]

Solomon's high profile during the *indaba* not only intensified national attachment to him, but effectively broadened the geographic and demographic base of his support. Beforehand, there had been Zulu enclaves distant from the royal epicentre which, while occasionally expressing loyalty to Solomon, had never seen Solomon nor in practice looked to Mahashini as the font of Zulu political authority. Of great importance was the rumour – which, in practice, was 'accepted fact' – that the Prince of Wales had appointed Solomon as Zulu king. It was understood that the appointment had deliberately not been made public at the *indaba* because of the presence of South African government officials. It was more in the nature of a secret pact between the Houses of Windsor and Zulu.

The legend of Solomon's appointment was exploited by A.H. Todd and Co., a Durban-based retailer of patent cure-all medicines for the African market. Late in 1925, A.H. Todd issued a 'commemorative' pamphlet bearing portraits of the Prince of Wales and Solomon alongside each other, and including a notice announcing that 'Edward kaNkosi George' ('Edward the son of King George') had appointed Solomon as King. It also included a word from Solomon endorsing A.H. Todd's medicinal supplies.[38]

This, the first instance in which Solomon allowed his name to be used for commercial purposes, represented one of the concrete advantages Solomon gained from his kholwa contacts. The intermediary between A.H. Todd and the Zulu royal house was Simpson Isaac Bhengu. After a childhood in the Natal countryside and a mission education, Bhengu had moved to Durban to sell his literacy on the job market. Shortly after the war he had become secretary of the Durban branch of the NNC, oganiser of the Durban African night schools, and an official of the Football Association. He was employed by A.H. Todd as a clerk in 1922 and, following kholwa initiatives at Mahashini two years later, came into contact with Solomon. Having relocated to Vryheid, by 1929 Bhengu was to hold the dual positions of Solomon's private secretary and secretary to Inkatha. Solomon's endorsement of A.H. Todd's merchandise established a precedent for similar business relationships which, while confirming Solomon in the public eye, constituted an important means through which he could earn additional revenue. By the late 1920s, A.H. Todd's advertisements frequently dominated the front page of *Ilanga lase Natal*, featuring a facsimile of a letter from Solomon, the 'Inkosi Yamabandla Onke' ('King of All Assemblies'). The medicines themselves were marketed as the 'Inkosi Yemiti Yonke' and 'Umuti Wamakhosi' ('King of All Medicines' and 'Medicine of Kings').[39]

These advertisements reflected Solomon's new image among the aspirant middle class. Ten years previously, when newspapers like *Izindaba Zabantu* were bewailing Solomon's basic education and inadequate acquaintance with 'civilization', Solomon's endorsement of European medicines would have been plainly farcical and not commercially viable. The advertisements that appeared in 1925 were thus in a sense a manifestation of the way in which he had redefined the royal image in a suitably 'civilized' manner – while simultaneously remaining at the forefront of a tribal and populist nationalism.

Local officials and white residents soon recognised the consequences of the visit of the Prince of Wales. In a new departure, even those in southern Zululand now found cause to complain that Solomon's influence was disrupting the day-to-day running of their districts. A local resident notified the Defence Force that 'something queer' was afoot in the Gingindhlovu and

Emtonjaneni districts. Zulu had refused to disclose any details, but the local resident had noticed that individual labourers were sending all the money they had to Solomon. Others were selling their mealies and goats to realise further capital for this purpose. The magistrate of Lower Umfolosi district made a similar report, and complained that Solomon had issued instructions to chiefs that they were to attend a gathering of the Zulu people at Mahashini on 6 October 1925 – which was to be the occasion of the annual Inkatha meeting. What perturbed him most, however, was that a 'petty chief' (meaning Solomon) held the power to override his magisterial authority over chiefs in his district – and that the Zulu believed that Solomon legitimately held this power because he had been 'appointed Paramount Chief of Zululand . . . by the Prince of Wales'. He also reported that on the day following the *indaba*, Solomon had addressed the Zulu saying that Zululand belonged to the Zulu and whites should live elsewhere.[40]

The complaints of the magistrate at Eshowe, A.D. Graham, expressed substantially similar sentiments. The notices of the Inkatha meeting, of which he had not been informed, constituted a 'great breach of etiquette', he said, and his own powers and those of 'his' chiefs were being undermined accordingly. In his district it was similarly alleged that Solomon was now paramount chief and that his intention was to drive the whites from Zululand. Indeed, the rumours of Solomon's appointment were so endemic and were expressed with such certainty that some officials came to wonder if it had in fact been made. In a somewhat piqued letter to the CNC, the magistrate at Mtunzini asked that Solomon's status and powers be defined if he now really was the Zulu paramount chief. State officials outside the ranks of the NAD were now openly referring to Solomon as 'the king'.[41]

What officials were observing was a new wave of Zulu nationalism that was unprecedented since 1879. What was different in late 1925, however, was that the role of the Zulu king as national leader was now being supported by such a modern organisation as Inkatha. The *indaba* had brought to a head and fused two parallel political developments both of which centred on the person of Solomon: first, the kholwa drive to formalise Inkatha as a link between themselves and the tribal elite, and second, Solomon's own drive for tribal reconciliation. The sixty thousand Zulu who had assembled at the *indaba* represented all sections of the Zulu people – in both a tribal and a class sense. Together they had seen Solomon in the company of advisers ranging from Mankulumana in his loin skin to Dube in his morning suit, behaving and being treated as a king by all present. The suspicions and divisions between tribal and kholwa Zulu that had hitherto hamstrung Inkatha were nowhere evident in the euphoria of 1925. Riding on the crest of this new wave of adulation, Solomon openly turned to Inkatha's organisational structure to consolidate his success. As the previously mentioned magistrates' reports indicate, the instructions that were being issued within Zululand to attend the forthcoming Inkatha meeting were held to be from Solomon himself. As Solomon now publicly took up his role at the pinnacle of Inkatha, even those Zulu furthest from the royal epicentre were now not only aware of Inkatha as a political force, but regarded the names 'Inkatha' and 'Solomon' as inseparable.

Solomon's new acclaim was reflected in the scramblings of various bodies to associate themselves with him. Similarly, the welcome that Solomon gave them reflected his new confidence in his role as Zulu king. For example, Gardener Mvuyana, who had established an independent African church on the Rand, conducted the 1926 general synod of his church at Mahashini. Isaiah Shembe, the flamboyant and influential leader of the large Nazarite sect based at Ekuphakameni (at Inanda, near Durban), similarly succeeded in forging a link with Solomon. Solomon accepted Shembe's daughter, Zondi, in marriage, a special house was built for him at Ekuphakameni, and a Nazarite hymn soon affirmed the relationship in the following manner:

> King Solomon is called
> He, the son of Dinuzulu,
> And the fame of Jehovah
> Is in Ekuphakameni.[42]

After 1925, Solomon's multifaceted role as Zulu king thus represented a more powerful and pervasive presence in Zulu-speaking society. The institution of Zulu kingship was felt to be functioning once more in a practical sense, and a sense of Zulu nationhood had been recreated.

The Inkatha meeting of 1925 was characterised by buoyant nationalism, in contrast to the tensions that marked the meeting of 1924. The immediate consequence of the *indaba* was the vastly increased weight of tribal representation: whereas one tribal chief had attended the 1924 meeting, twenty-five attended in 1925. They were supplemented by several representatives of chiefs unable to attend, and a number of *izinduna* from all over the Province of Natal. Solomon's role in the meeting was that of a respected and beneficent constitutional monarch, providing the venue, the food, and most importantly, an air of legitimacy by his mere presence.

The resolutions of the 1925 meeting covered a wide range of topics which reflected the broad base of Inkatha's support. The most important related to education and political representation, however, and reflected the dominance of the tribal and kholwa elites in its leadership. A plea was made that the education of the sons of chiefs and headmen be made compulsory; this was effectively a motion in support of the ZNTI. But the meeting also resolved that 'some primary education' should be made compulsory for all African children – and noted that 'much trouble and unrest emanates from the uneducated class of Natives through ignorance'. Turning to political questions, the meeting applauded the establishment of the 'Native Development Account' under the recently legislated 1925 Natives' Taxation and Development Act. However, for Zululand, it again rejected the establishment of local councils under the 1920 Act, which the new 'local tax' of the 1925 Tax Act was intended to support. In a resolution which indicated the increased influence of the tribal elite in Inkatha, it was recorded that 'the time for Native Councils in Zululand has not yet arrived . . . only outside blood would rule the Council', and requested that 'the "Inkata ka Zulu" should be recognised as the official mouthpiece of all the Chiefs of Natal and Zululand'.[43]

Inkatha was indeed already taking up the task of acting as Zulu 'shadow government' to the South African government. Its proceedings and resolutions of 1925 were forwarded to the NAD for its advice and information. The comprehensive report that found its way into the *Natal Mercury* moreover demonstrated the new prominence that Solomon and Inkatha had achieved in white Natal. The new way in which the organisation perceived itself was reflected in its new insignia: two hands clasped in the manner of a European handshake, surrounded by laurels and bearing the legends 'Ukuhlangana ku Ngamandhla' and 'Unity is Strength' – the Zulu and English translations of the Latin *Ex Unitate Vires* of the South African coat of arms.[44]

*   *   *   *   *

Up to 1925 the NAD had adopted a 'neutral' attitude to Inkatha. The CNC and SNA had remained impassive in the face of pressure from Simelane, Mnyaiza, Mankulumana, Solomon, Gilbert and Bhulose for government recognition – meaning, in practical terms, the integration of Inkatha into the system of indirect rule. They had similarly rejected Oscroft's and Fynney's suggestions that, as a preliminary to making more formal use of the organisation, a government official be formally appointed as Inkatha's adviser and bookkeeper.

Until the 1924 Inkatha meeting, the reasons the CNC and SNA offered for their reticence was that Inkatha was a 'political organisation' (the NAD was elsewhere creating political organisations in the form of local councils), it had 'no definite object' (the NAD had quashed Inkatha's main practical objects by refusing it both permission to buy a Vryheid farm and recognition as a form of local council), and it lacked any accredited bookkeeper and system of accounting for its finances (the ultimate in circularity).[45] The essential problem was that, in presenting itself in 1921 as a basis for a local council for north-western Zululand, or a general council for the whole of Zululand, Inkatha had taken the NAD by surprise. The Natal NAD had not yet persuaded itself that such a council was desirable so soon after the 1920 Act, let alone formulated any plans of its own as to what form the council might take. The NAD's response had merely been to identify the ways in which Inkatha was unsuitable for recognition – which overlooked the fact that the early Inkatha explicitly presented itself as a loose organisation that could be fashioned into a local council acceptable to the NAD.

After the 1924 meeting, while inevitably having to take greater cognisance of the organisation, the NAD still resisted recognising Inkatha for four specific reasons. First, both the CNC and SNA were greatly perturbed that the influence of Natal kholwa leaders far outweighed that of local Zulu in Inkatha. Second, the CNC felt that the local councils envisaged under the 1920 Act were unsuitable for Zululand because there the Zulu were more 'tribal' than 'advanced', and moreover the democratic principles underlying the councils would undermine the authority of chiefs on which his administration depended. Third, the 1920 Act was regarded as inappropriate since it provided for the establishment of local councils only in reserve areas – and about 40 per cent of Natal's African population lived on lands outside the reserves. The core of Inkatha's local support was itself split between the Zululand reserves and white-owned land in Northern Natal. Finally, because Inkatha was associated with Solomon, the CNC and SNA had to consider the opposition that would issue from those Natal NAD officials who still held a deep mistrust of the Zulu royal family.[46] Overall, however, NAD inaction regarding Inkatha could be attributed to the ever-present factor of bureaucratic inertia. There was moreover little organic need for administrative change because between 1920 and 1925 the NAD's Zululand administration had functioned with a smoothness it had never previously known.

This was not so, however, after the royal *indaba* of June 1925. Local officials soon found that Solomon's *de facto* power was disrupting the administration of their districts. This mirrored the situation that had existed between 1914 and 1916, except now Solomon's influence was far more widespread; and in response, as in 1916, the NAD began to think more seriously of co-opting Solomon's influence. At the same time, the proceedings of Inkatha's 1925 meeting undoubtedly served to allay NAD fears concerning the predominance of kholwa leaders. Inkatha's opposition to the establishment in Zululand of local councils accorded with the Natal

NAD's own opposition, and the CNC was now beginning to explore the possibility of developing a special form of council for Zululand, based more on the chiefs' councils already in existence in Pondoland than the local councils envisaged under the 1920 Act. There was another factor, however, that contributed to subtle changes of attitude in the Natal NAD. While Solomon's conduct at the *indaba* had infuriated certain Natal NAD officials, others had evidently identified with Solomon and felt a glow of pride that 'their' Zulu king had so visibly impressed the heir to the British throne. That these were the emotional responses of Fynney and Oscroft goes without saying, but more importantly they were also felt by those at Natal NAD headquarters in Pietermaritzburg, including the CNC himself, Charles Wheelwright, and his influential clerk, Carl Faye. There was a similar response, incidentally, at the CPSA's diocesan headquarters in Eshowe.[47]

In October 1925 the CNC wrote to the SNA arguing that the official definition of Solomon's and Inkatha's status was now a priority. His stance had changed dramatically:

> I would be the last to suggest any action that would tend to decry Solomon's influence as the representative of the Zulu Royal House, for I feel that his influence can be made to serve a useful purpose in Native Administration in this Province.

The CNC's new attitude had, by his own account, also been stimulated by Inkatha's acceptance of the 1925 Tax Act (£1 poll tax to accrue to state revenue, plus a 10s local tax in the reserves to provide revenue for local councils). Since it was the imposition of a poll tax that had sparked off the 1906 rebellion, Natal officials had been apprehensive of its reimposition in 1925. 'Had [Inkatha's] decision been otherwise we should have had considerable difficulty in making collections next year', the CNC observed.[48]

The larger question of 'recognition' would take some time to resolve. In the meantime, with immediate administrative concerns in mind, the CNC instructed Inkatha to abstain from making its widespread collections until further notice, and reassured magistrates that Solomon's official status had not changed since his appointment as chief of the Usuthu in 1917 – though he hinted that a redefinition was under consideration. In November 1925 the CNC and SNA met to discuss in broad terms the issue of Solomon's and Inkatha's future.[49] Not knowing of these deliberations, which the NAD was determined to keep secret, Inkatha inevitably interpreted the instruction against further collections as a blunt sign of official disfavour. However, while the overall attitude of the NAD towards Solomon and Inkatha appeared to be hardly supportive, at the close of 1925 it was in fact one of unprecedented interest in their mutual political future.

NOTES

1. Webb and Wright (eds), *Stuart archive*, vol. 1, pp. 167–71. For the role of the *imbongi* and *izibongo*, see A.T. Cope (ed.), *Izibongo: Zulu praise poems* (Oxford, 1968).

2. Reyher, *Zulu woman*, pp. 90–92; Sundkler, *Bantu prophets*, pp. 21–23.

3. D. Reitz, *No outspan* (London, 1943), pp. 27ff, 44.

4. For an excellent account of the influence of missionary endeavour on African women, see D. Gaitskill, 'Wailing for purity: prayer unions, African mothers and adolescent daughters, 1912–1940', in Marks and Rathbone (eds), *Industrialisation and social change*.

5. Reyher, *Zulu woman*, p. 45. This biography of Christina, from which my account was gleaned, was based on Christina's own recollections as told to Reyher.

6. *Ibid.*, pp. 49–52. For traditional Zulu marriage customs, see Lugg, 'The practice of lobolo', pp. 24ff; and Braatvedt, 'Zulu marriage customs', pp. 554ff.

7. Pers. Comm., Thandayiphi, part I, p. 3 (thirty); Magogo, part II, p. 8 (forty); and Mahaye, part I, p. 17 (seventy).

8. Pers. Comm., Magogo, part II, p. 7; and Mahaye, part II, pp. 19–20.

9. MS MAR, File 50, KCM 2761 (d), Zulu Chieftainship Dispute, Inquiry, 7/2/1945–19/4/1945, evidence of Magogo Buthelezi, pp. 103–4. See also KCAL, B. W. Martin Papers, 3.09, KCM 2668, MS autobiography 'Old soldiers never die', pp. 60–61 (Martin chaired the board of inquiry, which decided in favour of Cyprian); and Pers. Comm., Mahaye, part II, pp. 1ff (during the inquiry Mahaye placed his knowledge of Zulu history at the disposal of Mshiyeni, the Zulu regent after Solomon's death, who supported Thandayiphi's claim).

10. Pers. Comm., Mahaye, part I, p. 19. For more on Mayatana Cele, see Marks, *Reluctant rebellion*, pp. 296–98.

11. Pers. Comm., Mahaye, part I, p. 19.

12. Pers. Comm., Magogo, part I, pp. 18–20; part II, pp. 1–6. In the course of her account, significantly, Magogo referred to her brother Solomon neither by name nor as 'the king' as she usually did, but as 'my father'.

13. My principal sources on Magogo's marriage are the accounts she herself gave on various occasions. First, during my interview with her, as cited in the note above. Second, in her evidence to the board of inquiry into the 1945 succession dispute, MS MAR, File 50, KCM 2761 (d), pp. 105–6. Third, J.E. Ndlovu, Secretary of Education and Culture, KwaZulu Government, had heard Magogo tell the same story at various Zulu public events, and my conversations with him in January 1982 added further details. Magogo was not an unproblematical source for she, as a daughter of Dinuzulu who married a grandson of Mnyamana (the disagreement between these two men in 1888 initiated the rift between Usuthu and Buthelezi), refused to admit that any rift had ever existed and therefore that Solomon had any political purpose in arranging her marriage. See the lengthy deadlock during our interview, Pers. Comm., Magogo, part I, pp. 11ff.

Magogo's position was of course unsatisfactory, as her own evidence suggested, as did that of Mkandandhlovu (Magogo's sister who was at Mahashini, aged about eleven, at the time of the wedding), Pers. Comm., Mkandandhlovu, pp. 11–12; see also Mahaye, part II, p. 9.

14. MS MAR File 50, KCM 2761 (d), evidence of Magogo, pp. 105–6.

15. For Seme and Phikisile's marriage, see Chapter 4 above; and for Seme and Swazi royalty, see H. Kuper, *Sobhuza II: Ngwenyama and King of Swaziland* (London, 1978). That Sobhuza II (under whom the 'Swazi National Fund' was established, very similar to the 'Zulu National Fund' that evolved into Inkatha) was formally invested as Swazi king in 1921, incidentally, was undoubtedly a spur to Solomon's concurrent efforts to gain recognition.

16. Having dressed in the European fashion, his wives thus all became 'Christians'. See Pers. Comm., Ndesheni, part II, p. 13; Magogo, part II, p. 10; Mahaye, part I, p. 18; and also the observation in Reyher, *Zulu woman*, p. 33.

17. See *The Net*, March 1928, p. 6; and Pers. Comm., Mahaye, part I, p. 18.

18. *The Net*, December 1929, p. 3. For the ZNTI and Mahashini developments, see *The Net*, September 1922 and July 1925; DZ/B/3, Meetings of the Bishops Council, 1922–1927; and DZ/P/4, *Zululand Diocesan Magazine*, June 1922.

19. DZ/M/4, *Zululand Mission Report*, 1926, p. 2. For the developments concerning the Mandlakazi, see *ibid.* and *The Net*, September 1922 and December 1929; the Emngeni outstation, DZ/M/4, *Zululand Mission Report*, 1924 and 1926; and Chief Silimane, *The Net*, June and September 1923.

20. CNC PMB 84, 58/7/4, CNC to NC, Nongoma, 27/10/1932, referring to Solomon's earlier problems with cars and debts.

21. CNC 341, 3268/1918, Commanding Officer, 3rd SAMR to CNC, 3/10/1918 and 6/10/1918.

22. Pers. Comm., F. B. Oscroft, letter dated 24/11/1981 (Basil Oscroft's childhood home was the ZNTI); and Magogo, part II, p. 3. Professor Eileen Krige, author of the classic *The social system of the Zulus* and a guest at Solomon's *ihlambo* in 1934, held that accepting and drinking European liquor was in fact one of Solomon's royal duties. Pers. Comm., E. J. Krige, Durban, 6/10/1981.

23. For the Sophiatown house, see Kuper, *Sobhuza II*, p. 101; and the incidental references in SAP 41, 6/953/23/4. The description of KwaDlamahlahla is based mainly on my own visit in 1982, and the conversations I had with the caretaker and elderly people living nearby. See also CNC 509, 17/2, various letters from the Revd L. E. Oscroft; Pers. Comm., Ndesheni, part II, p. 16 (Ndesheni emphasised the financial burdens the house imposed); and Mahlobo and Krige, 'Transition', note on p. 185.

24. G. R. Naidoo, 'Buthelezi, the man with the key to Zulustan: the rebel chief of Zululand', *Drum*, May 1964, p. 13, reporting Buthelezi's own account of his upbringing.

25. Pers. Comm., Magogo, part II, p. 16; see also pp. 11–14.

26. Pers. Comm., Ndesheni, part I, p. 5 (Ndesheni himself studied at the ZNTI). For the white guests and supporters, CNC 509, 17/7, the Revd Oscroft to CNC, 3/10/1922 and 21/12/1922, enclosing 1922 ZNTI Report; and *The Net*, December 1922.

27. For the 1922 incident, JUS 575, 9491/30, Sub-Inspector T. H. Hedges, SAP, Nongoma to District Commandant, Eshowe, 18/2/1922; and CNC to Col. Douglas, CID, 26/5/1922. For 1923, SAP 41, 6/953/23/4, various letters dated August.

28. Illustrative statements were expessed in Account of Maphelu, p. 110; Pers. Comm., Mahaye, part II, p. 9; Mkandandhlovu, pp. 10–13; and Ndesheni, part I, p. 5. Since the formation of the later Inkatha in 1976, the most important achievement of Solomon's lifetime has been identified as his role in the formation of the original Inkatha; this has been taught in KwaZulu primary and secondary schools from 1979 as part of a compulsory course entitled 'The National Cultural Liberation Movement'.

29. F. W. Ahrens, *From bench to bench* (Pietermaritzburg, 1948), p. 70. See also *Ilanga lase Natal*, 17/3/1933, reporting Solomon's death; Pers. Comm., Ndesheni, part II, p. 5; and, for Ngenetsheni tenancy problems, Ch. 1 above.

30. See Roux, *Time longer than rope*, pp. 110ff; and CO 879/114, correspondence *re* appeals to the High Commissioner and British Government on the subject of the 1913 Act. For further comment on the 'imperial connection', see Brian Willan, 'An African in Kimberley: Sol. T. Plaatje, 1894–1898', in Marks and Rathbone (eds), *Industrialisation and social change*.

31. NAD Report, U17–1911, p. 18 (quotation) and pp. 335ff.

32. My main source for the Zulu *indaba* with the Prince of Wales was evidence given in court during the libel action Solomon brought against the *Natal Mercury* in 1927. On 13/6/1925 the newspaper had published allegations by the magistrate at Eshowe (A. D. Graham, alias 'Zithulele') that Solomon's behaviour at the *indaba* 'constituted a direct insult to HRH'. The evidence of C. A. Wheelwright (CNC) and C. Faye (CNC's clerk and the Prince's interpreter in 1925) was comprehensively reported in the *Natal Mercury*, 6/5/1927. The evidence of O. Fynney (magistrate at Nongoma) was found in KCAL, Mrs Mary Tyler Gray's Collection of Press Cuttings, Book 4, ref. 19958, unsourced cutting, p. 132. (All these Natal officials gave evidence for the prosecution, contributing substantially to Solomon's winning £600 damages with costs.) Other useful sources included *The Net*, September 1925; G. S. Moberly, *A city set on a hill: a history of Eshowe* (Eshowe, 1970); T. Aronson, *Royal ambassadors in South Africa, 1860–1947* (Cape Town, 1975); and the authorised history of the Prince's tour, G. Ward Price, *Through South Africa with the Prince* (London, 1926).

33. Moberly, *Eshowe*, p. 78.

34. This spontaneous display was the most striking of several occurrences which together persuaded the magistrate at Eshowe that Solomon had acted out of order. Hence his article 'The Royal Visit to Eshowe – Solomon's significant behaviour – Saluting the 'King' – Whole Affair Premeditated' in *Natal Mercury*, 13/6/1925, which prompted Solomon's libel action.

35. *Natal Mercury*, 6/5/1927, Faye's evidence.

36. The rumour was still alive over half a century later. Mahaye, who attended the *indaba* as a youth and fervently believed the appointment to have occurred, embellished the legend; he held, for example, that the real reason for the court case after the *indaba* was to prevent 'the truth' of Solomon's secret new status from becoming public. Pers. Comm., Mahaye, part I, pp. 1–6, 11–12; and part II, pp. 13–14. Ndesheni, who also attended the *indaba*, commented that it was clear that the Prince and Solomon 'were in agreement in their talks about this country. The Prince said something about it belonging to the Zulus and to Solomon.' Pers. Comm., Ndesheni, part I, p. 7. In the late 1920s, the rumour was sometimes expressed with a subtly different emphasis: the Prince had not so much 'restored Solomon to Zululand' as 'restored Zululand to Solomon', with the implication that whites might be turned out. See NEC Box 4, evidence of Sir Charles Saunders, Melmoth, 29/9/1930, p. 1897.

37. The Natal NAD was apparently unaware of the enrolment of the *Phondolwe-ndhlovu*, and the precise circumstances of the *ukubuthwa* remain obscure. Ndesheni, for example, merely reported that it took place 'at the time of the Prince of Wales's visit'. Pers. Comm., Ndesheni, part I, p. 5. It seems a rudimentary ceremony was performed on the day after the *indaba*, before the crowds dispersed.

38. NTS 7205, 20/326, A. H. Todd pamphlet, enclosed in NAD correspondence.

39. *Ilanga lase Natal*, editions during 1929 and 1930. For Bhengu, see CK 9A 2:XB13:91, biographical notes on Bhengu; and MS MAR, File 50, KCM 2761 (d), Zulu Chieftainship Dispute, Inquiry, evidence of Bhengu, pp. 92, 109. Here Bhengu attempted to suggest that he had had nothing to do with Solomon before 1929. He had good cause to attempt to minimise his association with Solomon since he was deeply implicated in the financial scandals that characterised Solomon's later life. The NAD banished him from the Nongoma district in 1934, an action which Mshiyeni, regent after Solomon's death, fully supported.

40. JUS 408, 4/323/25, Capt. L. Smith to District Staff Officer, Pietermaritzburg, 21/7/1925, enclosing correspondence from a 'reliable' source (first quotation); and NTS 7205, 20/326, Magistrate, Lower Umfolosi to CNC, 28/9/1925 (second quotation).

41. NTS 7205, 20/326, Magistrate, Eshowe to CNC, 21/9/1925 (quotation); CNC PMB 84 58/7/4, Magistrate, Mtunzini to CNC, 8/10/192; and see also JUS 408, 4/323/25, Divisional Staff Officer, Standerton to Chief of General Staff, Union Defence Force, 11/7/1925.

42. Sundkler, *Bantu prophets*, p. 103.

43. *Natal Mercury*, 31/10/1925, whose report was my main source for the 1925 meeting.

44. This was featured on the Inkatha leaflet publicising the 1925 meeting, a copy of which is in NTS 7205, 20/326.

45. The key documents were NTS 7205, 20/326, correspondence between the SNA, CNC and Magistrate, Nongoma, October 1923 to February 1924.

46. See in particular NTS 7205, 20/326, SNA to CNC, 12/11/1924 and 6/1/1925; and CNC to SNA, 28/11/1924.

47. For an impression of the CPSA view, see the leading article in *The Net*, September 1925, 'Zululand welcomes the Prince'. For Wheelwright and Faye, see their evidence given in the court case that followed the *indaba*, *Natal Mercury*, 6/5/1927.

48. CNC PMB 84, 88/7/4, CNC to SNA, 12/10/1925. For a basic outline of the 1925 Tax Act, see Rogers, *Native administration*, pp. 99–100. Its purposes were more clearly expressed, however, in the course of debates in the House of Assembly during July 1925.

49. NTS 7205, 20/326, CNC to SNA, 30/11/1925 and 5/2/1926; and CNC's circular to all magistrates in Natal, 21/1/1926.

Part Two: 1926–1933

6

Zulu society during the late 1920s

After the respite of the early 1920s, Zulu in Zululand and Northern Natal entered a period of economic hardship and social dislocation far worse than the one they had endured during the First World War. Similarly, in Natal proper the cumulative effects of a long process of rural impoverishment and social disintegration came to a head in the late 1920s. Over the Province of Natal as a whole, the history of African politics during the decade of the 1920s accordingly falls into two periods. The change came in approximately 1926, when the distress of the Zulu and Natal African 'commoners' or 'rank and file' was given political direction. Throughout the Union, in fact, the period 1927–30 was to represent a high-water mark of African protest. At the forefront of this development was the Industrial and Commercial Workers' Union, the ICU, which appealed to and stimulated a new form of African political militancy in the rural areas. The Natal branch of the ICU established Natal proper as the leading exponent of this new form of political protest. Its 'Bolshevik propaganda' had less appeal in Northern Natal and even less in Zululand, where the tribal hierarchy and tribal traditions were at their strongest, though these regions were by no means unreceptive to the ICU's revolutionary message. The vigorous politicisation of the rank and file in the late 1920s fundamentally restructured the character of Zulu politics – which previously had been dominated by the kholwa and tribal elites.

*   *   *   *   *

During the late 1920s, the existence of sparsely inhabited low-lying areas in the reserves, together with the increasing size of Zulu cattle herds (reflecting the success of the government's programmes against cattle disease), led certain magistrates and local settlers to claim that the Zululand reserves were not congested and the Zulu were prosperous. The Zululand sugar industry's persistent complaints that Zulu prosperity kept them away from wage labour on the sugar plantations was prejudiced and hence not entirely reliable — the sugar industry resolutely refused to accept that poor wages and compound conditions rendered plantation work unattractive to the Zulu. But there was an element of truth in these local white views on the state of the reserves.[1] As a detailed study of agricultural production in the Union's reserves from 1918 has shown, in 1927 the value of agricultural production in the Zululand reserves in relationship to their population was the highest in the whole Union except for the Transkei. Zululand and the Transkei were the two reserve regions most nearly self-sufficient in food.[2]

However, there were two important qualifying factors. First, as the study emphasised, these findings were based on statistics arrived at by dividing the value of agricultural production in the Zululand reserves as a whole by population figures. They did not take into account the distribution of wealth in Zulu society, or, in other words, social stratification. The relative prosperity of many Zulu in the reserves was thus able to mask the fact that many more were becoming acutely impoverished. Second, about one-third of the Zulu did not live in the study's domain of investigation, the reserves, but on white-owned land in Northern Natal — where Zulu poverty was most marked.

In order to provide an idea of social stratification among Zulu in the reserves, the study went on to calculate the social distribution of cattle in selected reserves. The findings indicated that in the Nongoma district in 1945, half of the population in fact owned no cattle at all while 27 per cent owned herds of more than 25. Social stratification was, however, even more marked than these figures suggest, because the average herd size was 36. By comparison, in the Umtata district of the Transkei in 1942, only a quarter of the population owned no cattle at all while, at the opposite end of the scale, only 3 per cent owned herds of more than 25. The Nongoma district, the Zulu royal heartland, represented the most striking instance of inequality of cattle ownership in all the Union's reserves. The next highest disparity was recorded in the Nqutu district, which was the only other Zululand district considered. In contrast, the reserves in which the social distribution of cattle was most egalitarian were those of Natal proper. These findings described conditions approximately fifteen years after our period. The late 1920s, however, were the years in which differences in wealth widened in the Zululand reserves and social stratification became more rigid.

Chiefs and *izinduna* constituted the wealthiest stratum in the reserves. Giving evidence before the Native Economic Commission in 1930, Archdeacon Lee reported that certain individuals in the Zululand reserves had herds of as many as three to four hundred cattle. More tellingly, he commented that 'one of the obstacles in the way of more economic use of land is the land-grabbing by men of importance in the community'. Chief Mgixo kaZiwedu Zulu, a grandson of Mpande, bluntly informed the same commission that 'some are very poor', wealth being 'unevenly distributed' in Zulu society.³ The status and role of chiefs as allocators of land afforded them preferential access to the most fertile areas within their wards for their personal use. Moreover, the tribute that tribal authorities received from their wards, together with the higher sums their daughters commanded for *lobolo*, continually reinforced their material predominance. They also had a regular source of monetary income through the fines they exacted while carrying out their judicial functions under customary law, and through the stipends they received from the state. In the late 1920s, Zululand chiefs' stipends ranged between £250 and £350 per annum, Chief Solomon's being the highest at £500 per annum.⁴ Commoner homesteads had no such financial security. In times of harvest failure, they were forced to divert more of their labour power away from subsistence farming to the employers of wage labour, or resort to selling their cattle for cash. These responses served to undermine the productive potential and resilience of commoner homesteads, and so years of poor crop yields had the effect of widening the divisions of wealth in society.

The comparative wealth of chiefs to headmen was not so marked in Northern Natal, primarily because they had no more control over land allocation than did commoners in their wards. The government's purchase of a farm in the Ngotshe district for Chief Kambi's personal use was an exception. Like every homestead head within their wards, chiefs on white-owned land had to negotiate their separate tenancy agreements with their white landlords. And because every homestead head was beholden to his respective landlord, rather than his chief, for the land on which his homestead lay, and more often than not was required to offer labour service to his landlord, the authority of chiefs was reduced.

Moreover, chiefs on white farms were sometimes subject to the indignity of personally having to provide labour service to their landlords – which tended to act as a social leveller. When the CNC heard that Chief Mshudulwana of Paulpietersburg district had been required by his landlord to perform the 'humiliating task' of wagon leader (normally performed by youngsters), he intervened and attempted to ensure that Chief Mshudulwana was not given such work again. Generally, the erosion of the status of chiefs in Northern Natal perturbed the CNC: it was in the interests of the 'better government of the natives', he argued in 1928, that land be bought for the 'personal occupation of chiefs themselves'. But, as the Revd Mahamba of

Dundee remarked to the Native Economic Commission, Africans were 'abandoning their chiefs' because of the difficulties that all Africans, not only chiefs, were experiencing with land tenure in the white countryside.[5] And indeed, those who had to remove during the wave of evictions in the late 1920s were in effect forced to 'abandon' their chiefs. These factors were compounded by western cultural influences corrosive to the tribal order. Without fail, those individuals mentioned so far as representative of the local Zulu kholwa elite – Revd S. D. Simelane, W. W. Ndhlovu, Christina Sibiya, Daniel Vilakazi, Revd. T. Mathe, Revd. C. Buthelezi, Revd. M. Mhlongo and Simpson Bhengu – either lived, worked, or had originated from that part of the Zulu country which had become the Boer New Republic and, subsequently, Northern Natal.

These conditions had no parallel in the Zululand reserves. The process of social levelling in Northern Natal should not, however, be overemphasised. Most chiefs there were hereditary Zulu chiefs and retained considerable status at the ideological level – they clearly held more sway than those in the white countryside of Natal proper. And, unlike commoners, they could still look to the NAD for financial support and special intervention in their tenancy problems. Chiefs in Northern Natal nonetheless constituted a privileged and conservative component of the rank and file rather than – as in the case of chiefs in the Zululand reserves – an entrenched class of wealthy aristocrats.

* * * * *

Until the late 1920s, the local Zulu middle class (as distinct from that in Natal proper) was comparatively undeveloped and had only really come into being in Northern Natal. Even there, following a period of rapid development after the Anglo-Boer War, its growth had been greatly impeded by the move against African land ownership and the gradual transition from cash tenancy to labour tenancy since Union. By the late 1920s, however, a small middle-class stratum of commercial farmers and trading brokers had developed in the Zululand reserves – and there were many who were struggling to join its ranks. Rather than being well-educated sons of established kholwa families, these individuals were predominantly young men with a basic education who had picked up western ambitions through an experience of urban life. Examples were S. Mncwango, Mkwintye, and T. Kumalo, all commoners resident in the Nongoma district, who gave evidence before the Native Economic Commission representing the Young Zulu Movement. Mncwango made his living as a broker of skins and poultry, and was also keenly interested in commercial agriculture. There were an appreciable number of individuals like Mncwango who traded under hawkers' licences, and they provided the medium through which local commercial farmers sold their produce. Others were taking out licences to open butcheries, and, though prospective shopowners claimed they were being 'held back' by the white monopoly of trading stores, some of Zululand's trading stores were now managed by Zulu. Mkwintye was a successful commercial farmer in Zululand. He employed forty to sixty labourers on a seasonal basis, paying them 1/- a day, the same rate paid for labour on white farms. Notwithstanding the successful few, Mncwango (who lived in Chief Bokwe's ward) observed that prospects for 'progressive agriculturalists' were poor in the reserves because chiefs and headmen refused to allocate them sufficient and suitable land.[6]

'Progressive' individuals living in the reserves throughout the province of Natal were encountering opposition from the tribal elite. Mrs Sibusisiwe Makanya, representing the Bantu Youth League (an association similar to the Young Zulu Movement, but based in Natal proper), told the Native Economic Commission that chiefs held their wards in a 'state of stagnation . . . New ideas coming from people other than chiefs and headmen receive no recognition; the door to individual initiative is closed and thus progress is hampered.' Speaking generally of Natal, Dube observed that tribal commoners opposed 'progress' as much as the chiefs themselves. 'Progress', in Dube's view, meant that 'there must be some people getting ahead of the others', whereas 'the old idea of communal life [means] that all people should stay on the same level'. The conflict between old and new ideas was reflected, as Oscroft expressed it, in a 'growing intolerance between tribal and detribalised' in the reserves. Wheelwright instanced a case in which an individual who fenced 'his' lands, employed labour and produced cash crops was 'got at' by other reserve dwellers through witchcraft. Tribal opposition was as much a reaction against the different social habits and values of 'progressive' Africans as an expression of envy of their private wealth.[7]

The evolution of a small middle class in the Zululand reserves in particular was a significant development. Specifically, it was to lend greater power to kholwa interests in Inkatha. Even more markedly than the African middle class in the white countryside and urban areas throughout the Union, however, the Zulu middle class in the reserves was stunted and repressed. Beneath the comparatively few who did fulfil their 'progressive' ambitions in Zululand, there were many more who were struggling to do so – and in the meantime oscillating between wage labour outside Zululand and the fringes of tribal life at home. This latter group was particularly unstable and in practice formed an important component of that somewhat amorphous underclass, the rank and file.

*   *   *   *   *

The rank and file in the province of Natal was indeed such an amorphous social group that it might best be defined in a negative sense: broadly, it included those who were not chiefs and headmen in the reserves, and were not relatively successful individuals of the aspirant middle class in both the reserves and the white countryside. As a broad rural underclass comprised of disparate elements, the rank and file lacked objective unity. Manifestations of a specifically rank-and-file political consciousness thus tended to be sporadic. Nonetheless, during the late 1920s this underclass developed a certain self-identity, based on a common experience of impoverishment, exploitation and insecurity, together with a shared frustration with 'the system' – whether this was represented by state officials and the laws they enforced, conservative tribal authorities, or demanding family elders, employers and landlords. Moreover, there developed a basis of shared political attitudes: a predisposition to reject established structures of authority and the modes of political representation that worked through them, and a tendency to spurn 'polite pleading' in favour of organisation and action. There was also a marked impatience with piecemeal reforms, and an at times heady enthusiasm for fundamental changes in the distribution of land and political power. During the late 1920s, these attitudes were expressed with varying degrees of conviction throughout the Province of Natal.

The year 1925 represented the watershed between the rank and file's phase of more informal and disunited action (reflected in instances of desertion from employment, 'absconding' to the towns, and attempts to avoid payment of taxes) and its phase of more organised and explicitly class-based action. As the post-war depression lifted and commercial production in the white countryside was reinvigorated, the midlands of Natal proper developed into the storm-centre of rural militancy in the province. Those there who had once numbered among the substantial population of rent-paying tenants had particular cause for grievance, many having been coerced into contracts of labour tenancy at a time when the demands made on labour tenants were becoming increasingly burdensome. Yet more damaging to the African farm population in both Natal proper and Northern Natal, however, was the unprecedented wave of tenant evictions that followed the growth of new markets for wool, wattle bark and cotton in the mid-1920s. White commercial farmers, with an apparent lack of awareness of the severe distress they were causing, evicted numberless tenant families to make more land available for the grazing of sheep and the development of wattle and cotton plantations. Corporate capital flooded into the rural districts, moreover, buying up farms, clearing them of tenants, and engaging African wage labour at low rates. The advent of the plantations greatly accelerated the process of rural proletarianisation.

The politicisation of the rank and file in Natal proper owed much to the leadership of A. W. G. (George) Champion, who in 1925 became secretary of the Natal branch of the ICU. A dynamic character and forceful orator, by 1926 Champion had already spearheaded the rise of the Natal ICU to the role of bastion of the ICU's national network. He was, of course, not solely responsible for the mushrooming of the Natal ICU; he took up office at a time when the post-1920 lull in African political protest was drawing to a close throughout the Union, as was illustrated in Natal by the 1924 radical 'palace revolt' in the NNC. Champion and the radicalised NNC indeed soon established an informal alliance: a meeting of the NNC in March 1926 called on 'all men and women . . . to join the NNC and ICU' for a united offensive against political oppression.[8] Born to a kholwa family on the border between Natal proper and Zululand, Champion had been suspended by the Amanzim-toti Training College for rebelliousness in the middle of his secondary education. Somewhat surprisingly, his first employment was as a police intelligence officer – or spy. He came into contact with Solomon in the course of his surveillance duties in Northern Natal in 1915, and this meeting, Champion subsequently intimated, caused him some discomfort and prompted his resignation from the police force. He thereafter took up employment as a clerk on the Crown Mines in Johannesburg, where he gained his first experience in politics as president of the African Mine Clerks' Association. There he also met Clements Kadalie, general secretary of the ICU, which led to his return to Natal in 1925 as an ICU official.[9]

Although ICU organisers and local activists were often drawn directly from the rank and file, most ICU officials, like Champion, came from kholwa backgrounds. The relationship between them and the illiterate poor that formed the main phalanx of the ICU's support was somewhat problematical. Two months after his return to Natal, for example, Champion established the African Workers' Club in Durban, which hardly catered for ordinary workers: it provided writing tables and rest-rooms, facilities for boxing, dancing, singing and dining, and was rigidly opposed to the consumption of alcohol. Nonetheless, the high-society inclinations of some of those in the upper echelons of ICU leadership by no means undermined the ICU's popularity among urban workers and the rural rank and file. At local ICU meetings in the Natal countryside the rural poor were offered the hope of a thoroughgoing redistribution of wealth and political power. They were also offered inspiration by the clarity of political rhetoric that derived from Marxist ideas of confrontational struggle – which held much promise in the light of the successful revolution in Russia – and was infused with a sharp awareness of connections between race and class oppression. The ICU was moreover prepared to intervene practically, with legal assistance, on behalf of aggrieved workers and labour tenants. It was for these reasons that the ICU grew to be a mass movement at the forefront of popular protest in Natal.[10]

Champion's counterpart in Northern Natal was M. L. E. (Lymon) Maling, an ICU supporter himself, who in 1926 began building up an ICU-style organisation named the Abaqulusi Land Union (ALU) in the Vryheid district. Maling was by nature a flamboyant character, and his forthright approach to politicising the local rank and file soon earned him the image of an 'out of work agitator, exploiting the Natives . . . for his own advancement and selfish ends' in the eyes of the NAD.[11] His qualities of leadership, as in the case of Champion, provided a focus and sense of direction to a constituency that was already mobilising for confrontational political action. During 1925, local NAD officials had already identified an 'entirely new . . . and distinctly defiant' attitude in the Vryheid district, and were convinced of 'impending unrest among the Zulus'. Similar reports had issued from the Zululand reserves. While a local officer of the Union Defence Force felt that this new mood was related to the 'general bearing and conduct of Solomon' (whom he identified as 'the King') after the royal *indaba*, and undoubtedly the surge of nationalism had raised rebellious spirits, there was clearly something more underlying the mood of the Vryheid district. Zulu employees on a newly established local cotton plantation had become 'very insolent' and threatened to strike, and, as the local officer himself reported, 'strike fever' was also 'very prevalent on the [Vryheid] Coal Mines'.[12] These developments reflected the onset of a particularly Zulu rank-and-file militancy, based on modern strategies, which predated Maling's public meetings throughout Northern Natal during 1926, as a consequence of which he established a solid base of support among impoverished labour tenants and farm workers.

Like the Natal ICU, the leadership of the ALU was mainly composed of men of some education who, in occupational terms, stood in the lower echelons of the kholwa establishment. In 1927 the ALU chairman, A. M. Khubeka, and the regional organiser for the Paulpietersburg district, E. H. S. Xaba, both described themselves as 'evangelists' although neither was ordained. Maling himself was born to a Wesleyan Methodist family of Newcastle sharecroppers, but had reached adulthood in the post-Union period when the prosperity and status of the aspirant middle class was being undermined. Although he was an 'exempted' African and well educated, having a good command of English, ornate handwriting and a stylish taste in clothes, he had only managed to penetrate the lower ranks of Vryheid's urban salariat before turning to full-time politics. In these respects, Maling's personal history correlated closely with that of Gilbert Coka, a leading figure in the ICU, whose relatively prosperous Vryheid sharecropping parents had moved off the land soon after Union when their landlord attempted to bind them to labour tenancy. Thus both Maling and Coka came from 'respectable' backgrounds, and, like many others of their generation, found difficulty in fulfilling their own and their parents' aspirations. Indeed, P. Maling, evidently Lymon Maling's father, was a founder member of the NNC and a typical example of the kholwa establishment of 'black Englishmen'. It would appear that it was he who changed the family name from the original Zulu 'Malinga' to the more English-sounding 'Maling'.[13]

Throughout the Province of Natal, a crucial factor in the development of rank-and-file political consciousness was the role adopted by local tribal authorities. As a rule, chiefs saw the growth of popular protest as inimical to their social and political dominance, and it was notable that popular protest was least in evidence in regions in which social stratification was greatest and the rule of chiefs most entrenched. Not surprisingly, the tribal elite in Zululand was very effective in forestalling local militancy and isolating their wards from 'outside agitation'. This perhaps seemed especially necessary now that the Zulu royal house and Inkatha defined the whole Province of Natal as their political domain and all the inhabitants as 'Zulu'; developments in the white countryside of Natal proper thus no longer seemed as distant from Zululand as they once might have appeared. That the power bases of the ICU and ALU lay with the rural poor, resident on white-owned land, was thus not only because the exploitative relations between landlords and tenants, or employers and labourers, caused rank-and-file political mobilisation to be far more urgent. In these regions, the tribal order was more eroded and 'social disintegration' more pronounced. Reflecting the lesser material division between chiefs and common people in the white countryside, chiefs tended to identify more with the rank and file. Rather than deploying their influence to undermine popular struggles, certain chiefs in Natal proper and Northern Natal lent the latter their support – albeit conditionally and, in practice, with the effect of dampening popular militancy.

Although conditions on white farms gave cause for Zulu in Northern Natal to wage their separate struggles against their landlords and the state, the division between Northern Natal and the Zululand reserves should not be too boldly drawn. Not only were the Zulu in the two regions bound together by kinship linkages and tribal political affiliations, but the unprecedented wave of tenant evictions in the late 1920s caused repercussions in the reserves as homeless Zulu poured into them for shelter. This had the twin effects of heightening discontent in the reserves on account of overcrowding and land degeneration, and of introducing into the reserves a body of inhabitants whose political outlook had been shaped by direct experience of political struggle in the white countryside – and by the pronouncements of ICU and ALU leadership.

In Maling's opinion, more evictions took place in Northern Natal between 1928 and 1930 than in the whole history of the region prior to 1928. Local NAD officials were well aware that the socio-economic consequences of – as one expressed it – the 'unscrupulous landlord . . . being unjust to his tenants' were not confined to the aggrieved tenants themselves.[14] While a Vryheid chief's representative recounted how 'people on farms are being scattered and are drifting . . . being deprived of all that home connotes', Chief Mgixo of the Nongoma district, reflecting his different perspective on the matter of evictions, vividly described the border between his reserve land and white farm land as a 'yawning crack that empties forth human beings'. He continued that 'these unfortunate people come along to me and plead with me to accommodate them; after all we are of them and they are of us'. Though Mgixo made efforts to accommodate the people themselves on his already overcrowded lands, he prevented them from bringing their livestock with them. However, the response of the 'unfortunate people' to such additional deprivations was not only, as Mgixo related, to 'just fold their arms and look at me in a sad way'.[15] During the late 1920s, the Zulu tribal elite expended much energy in containing rank-and-file militancy which, to them, was coterminous with the breakdown of the tribal order. As the SNA commented in 1926, perhaps somewhat overemphatically, 'none of this propaganda is being carried out in Zululand. The Zulu chiefs are very strict.'[16]

Apart from the impoverished new arrivals from the white farms, the rank and file in the reserves included numbers of 'detribalised' Zulu. From the tribal establishment's point of view, the latter were the *abaqafi* ('delinquents') who reneged on their tribal and kinship obligations. In 1927 Chief Kula of the Msinga district (in Natal proper, on the south-western border of Zululand) described them as 'irresponsible and disrespectful . . . [they] recognise no authority at all'.[17] More broadly, these people were part of the restive floating population of embittered youth, social 'misfits' and unfulfilled 'progressives'. The most numerous – but least volatile – component of the rank and file in the reserves, however, comprised inhabitants of small and impoverished homesteads with neither cattle nor any hope of generating a subsistence. One response of impoverished homestead heads was to look to their chiefs and headmen to assist them in persuading the *abaqafi* to fulfil their kinship obligations by remitting money from the urban areas. Another, however, was to lend support to militant leadership – alongside restive elements, including the *abaqafi* themselves

– whose promises of more land and higher wages seemed to offer the long term solution.

ICU activists thus found considerable potential support in the reserves, even deep in Zululand, as was reflected in the well-attended meeting the ICU held at Empangeni in mid-1927. The sequel to this ICU meeting, however, illustrated what ICU activists were up against. Soon afterwards, the Empangeni and District Farmers' Association and local NAD officials convened an *indaba* with seven local chiefs and their headmen to discuss how to eradicate the ICU. Col. Tanner, magistrate at Empangeni, and George Higgs, sugar planter and representative of the local Farmers' Association, warned that the main casualty of ICU policy would be the authority of chiefs. There was little sense in listening to 'a man who was nothing', Higgs suggested to the gathering, but who nonetheless 'waved his arms and cast his shadow over [you]'. The chiefs needed little persuasion.[18]

*   *   *   *   *

In Northern Natal, the history of Lymon Maling and the ALU illustrated the difficulties in the path of mobilising the rank and file in a region with strong tribal traditions. Maling's formation of the ALU, an independent and regional organisation, was clearly designed to appeal to those notions of Zulu superiority and exclusivity that formed such a tenacious element in the political traditions of Northern Natal. The name 'Abaqulusi Land Union' was itself significant: 'Land' identified the main political concern of the local inhabitants, and 'Abaqulusi' indicated that the organisation aimed to integrate local tradition with current popular politics. The Qulusi section in the Vryheid district was traditionally a 'royal section' of the Zulu, being administered directly by the Zulu royal house in pre-conquest times. Qulusi menfolk used to mobilise as an *ibutho* separately, and were not conscripted into the usual age-grade *amabutho*. In the 1920s the Qulusi retained their fervently royalist character and keen sense of military heritage. From the outset, therefore, the ALU attempted to come to terms with Zulu political traditions, rather than to present itself as a completely 'new' political organisation with a purely class-based appeal.

The mood of the ALU's constituency in Northern Natal was illustrated in a statement that was drawn up in early 1927 following a number of regional meetings convened by Maling. Rather than dealing with grievances in a fragmentary fashion, the statement went to the heart of the matter: it contested Boer rights to the land in Northern Natal and called for the reversion of the land to the Zulu. Maling went to Cape Town and submitted this statement to A.B. Payn, MP for Tembuland and leading parliamentary philanthropist. Payn arranged for Maling to see the Prime Minister personally, but this meeting served no purpose. On Maling's return to Northern Natal, the ALU's immediate priority was to compile comprehensive and plainly worded statements of Zulu tenants' and farm labourers' grievances, also including indictments of the behaviour of white farmers and the judgments handed down by magistrates' courts. These formed the basis of a petition which was sent directly to the Prime Minister – an action regarded as an open breach of the etiquette of both indirect rule and employer-employee relations. Obviously struck by the directness of the petition, and also very sensitive to the growing power of the ICU in Natal proper, the NAD immediately arranged a thorough inquiry into the allegations.[19] The petition itself, the evidence collected during the CNC's inquiry, and the CNC's subsequent report immediately predated the 1928–30 period of accelerated evictions, and thus focused on conditions of Zulu tenure and employment on white farms.

By the mid-1920s, the payment of cash rent for tenure on white-owned land in Northern Natal had been phased out: labour tenancy was the only way in which Zulu could retain access to land in the region. In the latter half of the 1920s, the move among white landlords to exploit their landholdings more thoroughly for the purposes of commercial agriculture had adverse consequences for labour tenants in two broad respects: the plots of land available to labour tenants were reduced, and labour demands made on tenant homesteads were intensified. Tenants were sometimes required to perform more than the six months' unpaid service that the 1913 Act laid down as the maximum in Natal, and sometimes even children were put to work. Tenant homesteads which would not or could not acquiesce in such demands were liable to retribution from the farmer, in the form of livestock seizure, for example, or at worst eviction. On the newly established large cotton plantations, of which the Candover Estates and the Goss Estates were examples, there was a rash of evictions as labour tenancy was rapidly replaced by wage labour. For the Zulu in Northern Natal, these developments initiated a period of acute impoverishment and disruption of home life.

The ALU petition and the evidence given before the CNC's inquiry emphasised the autocratic and brutal nature of exploitation on white farms. Several complaints of physical assault were made against white farmers. In the course of a detailed investigation into one complaint, the CNC uncovered evidence that on the Goss Estates – comprising twelve cotton farms in the Ngotshe and Vryheid districts owned by a single company – workers were 'disciplined' by farm managers and Zulu 'farm constables' by way of handcuffs, leg-irons, solitary detention, and arbitrary appropriation of personal property. Mtateni Ndwandwe, a labour tenant on a Goss Farm who had been subjected to all these forms of violence and who had provided eighteen months unbroken free service, had not complained to the local magistrate because he 'thought Goss was acting under Government authority'.[20] Generally there was a sense among the rank and file in Northern Natal that state officials and farmers were in collusion: complaints were made that magistrates' courts offered little protection against farmers either breaching the statutory rights of labour tenants or dispensing their own 'justice' and punishment on their farms. Although the CNC felt the accusation of injustice in the magistrates' courts (i.e. that 'Europeans always win') to be unfounded, he did not deny that farmers took the law into their own hands and forced their labour tenants to acquiesce under the threat of eviction.[21]

As in Natal proper, farmers engaged complete homesteads in labour tenancy contracts (which were often verbal and thus easily modified to suit the farmer) under what was known as the 'kraalhead system'. The contract was made with the homestead head and it was he who was responsible for ensuring that all his dependants discharged their 'contractual' obligations to the farmer. The labour contract was superimposed on the tribal hierarchy at the familial level, and, like indirect rule, was predicated on the survival of the tribal order. However, these contracts ultimately undermined the tribal order at its very base. Not only were sons and daughters required to perform six months' free service, but they were often required to continue working on the farm afterwards at the current rate of farm wages (and frequent complaints were made that they were sometimes not paid at all), which meant that they could not seek more remunerative employment elsewhere. Moreover, sons could not look to their fathers or chiefs to provide land for them to establish their own homesteads and families. The high incidence of young men dishonouring their labour obligations and deserting permanently to the towns was a direct consequence of these conditions. Following a desertion, the homestead head was responsible for either providing a replacement labourer at his own expense, or paying 'damages' to the farmer. If the homestead head failed to do so, he faced eviction.[22]

Even when tenant homesteads were not depleted of their labour complement through these desertions, they had difficulty in meeting their subsistence requirements and monetary needs. Since farmers made such stringent labour demands on all members of the tenant homestead throughout the seasonal cycle, little time and labour power was left for tenants to cultivate their own plots. For their subsistence needs tenants became increasingly dependent on cash, which they gained partly from the sale of livestock and partly through remittances sent by members of the homestead in paid employment – outside their six-month period of unpaid service on the farm. Remittances sent home from the urban areas were at best sporadic, reflecting the breakdown of familial unity and the tribal ethos on which it was based. In comparison to the early post-Union period, rural dependants' complaints of the irresponsibility of youth were more forceful and widespread during the late 1920s. Ultimately, many tenant homesteads became dependent on food rations from their landlords and employers. The 'debt' so incurred could be repaid in the form of labour over and above the six-month period of unpaid service.[23]

There was thus a trend in the late 1920s for impoverishment to transform labour tenants into rural serfs almost totally dependent on their landlords for daily survival – and all the more exploitable for it. Conditions on the Goss Estates were particularly harsh: no tenant was permitted, for example, to leave his or her farm of employment at any time 'for any purpose whatsoever without the written consent of the landlord'.[24] Despite the worsening conditions on white farms, Zulu were loath to sever their connections with the land of their ancestors on which they felt they had a right to live, and where, if little else, they could cultivate hollow illusions of past independence. The threat of being evicted, and so having to search for other land on which to re-establish the homestead, was undoubtedly the worst of the labour tenant's various insecurities.

The ALU petition and the CNC's inquiry it provoked brought little material benefit to labour tenants in Northern Natal, even though the CNC's report showed some sympathy for local grievances and called for the establishment of reserves in the region. It was notable, however, that the influence of the ALU on the Goss Estates led forty tenants to go on strike during the CNC's inquiry and represent themselves to the CNC personally in a deputation. The CNC responded by making special efforts to investigate conditions on the Goss Estates, where he prevailed on management not to punish the strikers and to ameliorate the terms of labour tenancy contracts.[25]

While NAD intervention itself contributed to containing more militant popular protest in Northern Natal, the CNC's inquiry highlighted two other important factors. On the one hand, the predominantly Afrikaans-speaking white settlers in the region displayed a marked disregard for the rule of law, and were prone to 'administer' the African inhabitants of their farms in a manner reminiscent of the nineteenth-century frontier tradition. The transition to capitalist relations of production was carried through with a ruthlessness underpinned by a commonplace brutality that seemed not to have been equalled in the countryside of Natal proper. That the rank and file in Northern Natal were subject to more stringent everyday repression, and had every cause to believe that not only their livelihoods but their lives were endangered if they dropped their facade of servility, was certainly a reason why it could not mobilise as openly as the rank and file in the neighbouring Natal midlands, an area in which the white settlers were predominantly English-speaking.[26] On the other hand, and more importantly, the hierarchical nature of Zulu society was reflected in the ALU – which proved to be a profoundly undemocratic organisation. Positions of leadership remained in the hands of unfulfilled 'progressive' men like Maling, and the popular appeal of the organisation relied heavily on the moral support it received from local chiefs. The apogee of rank-and-file radicalism in Natal proper came when 'ordinary people' – with neither educational nor hereditary claims to positions of leadership – adopted the Natal ICU as their own representative organisation and voluntarily became local organisers. By contrast, the ALU's local leadership was never infused by 'ordinary people'. For all their radical and emotive exhortations, both Maling and Champion of the Natal ICU were prone to be less militant in practice than the political constituencies they purported to represent. When the Goss tenants went on strike, for example, Maling immediately 'disclaimed all reponsibility for what they had done' – just as the Natal ICU headquarters disowned the spontaneous strikes that took place in Durban and on the Northern Natal coal-mines during 1927.[27]

Maling's role of leadership among the Zulu rank and file was underpinned by the status and skills that a kholwa background had imparted to him. Even so, despite the inroads that white occupation had made on the status of chiefs in Northern Natal, the Zulu inhabitants did not easily transfer the role of political leadership to 'commoners' like Maling when it came to so weighty a matter as confronting white rule. They still looked to tribal leadership to give sanction to popular protest. However, as the CNC observed, it was a 'significant fact [that] no chief associated himself with Malinga's [sic] representations' or presented himself voluntarily to give evidence before the CNC's inquiry.[28] This was despite the support that chiefs had pledged the ALU before the inquiry. The stance of chiefs in Northern Natal was ambiguous: while they tended to support the political objectives of popular movements, they were extremely hesitant to do so openly. They thus tended to undermine the effectiveness of popular protest from within.

Despite their early similarities, the political priorities of the ALU and Natal ICU diverged during 1927. In the white countryside of Natal proper, the Natal ICU continued to focus on rank-and-file grievances, and its local branch executives were infused by local 'commoners'. But the ALU increasingly devoted its attention in the first instance to tribal authorities, attempting to secure their open and active support. In this it was influenced by the political consciousness of the Northern Natal rank and file itself, which was preoccupied with Zulu chiefs and Zulu nationalism. By late 1927, the ALU had achieved some success in associating itself with chiefs: Chief Sikukuku Sibisi (Paulpietersburg district), Chief Mtshikila Buthelezi (Ngotshe district) and Chief Hali Mdlalose (Vryheid district) were all represented in the organisation. Chief Hali's support was especially important. His ward included most of the Qulusi section in the Vryheid district and, moreover, his representative in the ALU was Zinyo Mdlalose, a brother of Solomon's mother, Silomo Mdlalose, and also one of Solomon's lesser *izinduna*. As soon as the NAD became aware of the ALU's new-found support among chiefs, the SNA instructed that chiefs be informed that their allowing the ALU to represent them would 'lessen their own dignity, abdicate their privilege and acknowledge their inability to perform their functions'. He also suggested that the CNC personally warn Maling that he was 'courting inconvenient consequences to himself'.[29]

Maling's preoccupation with Zulu chiefs and Zulu nationalism served in practice to cripple the effectiveness of the ALU. Not only were chiefs themselves inclined to be considerably less volatile than ordinary labour tenants and farm labourers, but, as state employees, they were more amenable to NAD 'advice' − which inevitably influenced the ALU through the chief's representatives in the organisation. Significantly, when it became known in September 1927 that the Prime Minister, General Hertzog, was to visit Vryheid, Maling called on the magistrate at Vryheid with two traditional Zulu earthenware pots. Each pot bore Hertzog's name, the date 1927, and the initials 'Z.N.' which stood for 'Zulu Nation'.[30] Such a conciliatory and even ingratiating gesture would have been very out of character for Maling in late 1926. Like Inkatha, the ALU had set out to affirm its political legitimacy among the rank and file by presenting itself as a vehicle for Zulu nationalism and also as an organisation that was in some way recognised by the government. The magistrate at Vryheid astutely observed that the prospective presentation of pots was probably a ruse to gain government recognition − and the SNA ruled that they could not be accepted. The ALU apparently dissolved soon after the CNC's inquiry in January 1928, and Maling thereafter turned his attention to working his way into the leadership of Inkatha, an organisation which had hitherto regarded Maling's political activities with disapproval.

*   *   *   *   *

In Natal proper, Natal African society was considerably less stratified both politically and materially, and tribal traditions were not as strong as in

Northern Natal and Zululand. This was notwithstanding the fact that the *hlonipha* code of social etiquette (which affirmed sexual role and social rank) and *khonza* custom (which prescribed obedience to elders and authority) were common linguistic and socio-political traditions. Accordingly, popular protest was very markedly less dependent on the sanction of tribal authorities. During 1927 and 1928, rank-and-file grievances in the white countryside of the Natal midlands were expressed with a rigour that was unprecedented since 1906. Champion's role as general secretary of the Natal ICU was certainly important in this context. But it was the local ICU organisers who, being part of the communities they represented and closely acquainted with the burning issues of evictions, wage levels and labour conditions on white farms, were primarily responsible for disseminating the radical message in the most turbulent districts of Umvoti, Kranskop and New Hanover. Claiming that the land rightly belonged to the black people, and that the whites and white rule were to be driven from the country, they were preoccupied less with the details of labour tenancy than with the eradication of labour obligations altogether. They also spoke the language of Zulu nationalism, urging attendance at separatist rather than white churches, and invoking symbols of Zulu royalty and memories of the 1906 rebellion. Soon after Zabuloni Gwaza became ICU branch secretary in Greytown (Umvoti district) in mid-1927, he personally smashed a wreath on the graves of white policemen killed in 1906, and proudly publicised this deed among local Africans.[31]

In addition to offering a vision of a prosperous future unburdened by white rule, the ICU also provided lawyers to act in court for members who brought evidence of maltreatment or harsh contracts to its offices, and was sometimes successful in reversing eviction orders through legal action. From mid-1927, Champion was also conducting much-publicised negotiations on behalf of the Natal ICU for the purchase of farms in the Natal midlands on which to settle evicted members – which proved unsuccessful, as were those conducted by national ICU leader Kadalie on his visits to Natal. Natal ICU membership mushroomed during 1927, with Africans flocking to ICU meetings in the small towns of the white countryside to buy their 'red tickets'. By early 1928, Umvoti membership allegedly amounted to over 80 per cent of the adult population. The political consequences were soon apparent to white farmers. Many tenants now simply refused to obey eviction orders – and resolutely returned even after they had been forcibly evicted – and farmers increasingly had to go to court to have their eviction orders enforced. Moreover, when good rains provided an unusually good harvest in 1927, farmers all over the Natal midlands found that many in their workforces refused to continue working for less than 8 shillings a day –

the figure currently demanded by the parliamentary Labour Party for white workers. The political impact of this 'strike' became more pronounced as it persisted well into the labour-intensive wattle-stripping season.[32]

Such developments were cause for intense concern among white farmers and the white public at large: the role of the ICU was interpreted as a threat to not only employer interests but also white rule itself, 'white civilisation', and the physical safety of white families in the countryside. As early as September 1926, when the dramatic expansion of the ICU in the countryside had just begun, the *Natal Witness* published an alarmed account of ICU support and activities in the Natal midlands. Headlined 'Watch the ICU', the article expressed a plethora of fears, and called on the government to introduce legislation to combat sedition.[33]

White fears became more widespread during 1927, when the work stoppages on white farms were accompanied by strikes on the Northern Natal coal-mines and at the Durban docks. Farmers' Associations and MPs for the Natal country constituencies made repeated calls for police and NAD reprisals against the ICU, and for the enactment of repressive legislation to enable the latter to carry these out more efficiently. Demands were also made for changes to the Masters and Servants Law which would serve to tighten control over the rural labour force and define breaches of employment contracts as a criminal rather than a civil offence. But rural whites' strategy was not merely to rely on state coercion; one alternative was the widespread 'counter defensive action', as the MP for Weenen described it, on the part of farmers in evicting or refusing to employ any African who was believed to be an ICU member. Such class action, which was made 'official' policy by various local Farmers' Associations in early 1927, took effect in the most troubled midlands districts of Umvoti, Kranskop and New Hanover and also the neighbouring districts of Weenen, Estcourt and Dundee.[34] Furthermore, rural whites mobilised through the medium of 'vigilance associations' – often formed on the initiative of the local Farmers' Association – which were dedicated to the defence of all the ICU was perceived to threaten. Perhaps the most belligerent of these, the aptly-named 'Anti-ICU', was formed in early 1928 in the Umvoti district soon after one hundred gravestones were overturned in Greytown's white cemetery – allegedly by an ICU activist.

In the context of both European and African beliefs surrounding death and the afterlife, the wrecking of gravesites was an act of sacrilege. The desecration of white graves in Greytown in February 1928 occasioned fear, anger and deep personal distress among the white community. Given the mystical ties that Africans traditionally perceived between ancestral spirits, their living descendants, and the land in which ancestors were buried, the desecration could be seen as having a deeper meaning: a repudiation of the right of the white community to become spiritually and physically identified with the land, and perhaps a statement that white occupation was not permanent. The symbolic act in the Greytown cemetery transformed what had been a simmering class conflict into a series of violent confrontations in the countryside. Armed with shotguns, incensed whites first grappled with police guarding the cell containing Zabuloni Gwaza, the ICU official who had been arrested as prime suspect. Thereafter they scoured Greytown and the Umvoti countryside for all traces of the ICU, firing the ICU offices in Greytown and the nearby village of Kranskop despite the defensive efforts of local ICU members and the police. In the five days of violence that ensued, white mobs also attacked ICU property in Bergville, Estcourt, Weenen and Pietermaritzburg itself.

At Estcourt the local magistrate condoned the action taken by the white mobs: who could blame them, he wrote to the SNA, if they 'adopt primitive measures for redress' when the state had taken inadequate action against the 'noxious society' that was the ICU?[35] Tacit support for the white reprisals was widespread both within departments of state and among the white public. Indeed, the ICU assailed almost every aspect of white rule and thus attracted condemnation from almost every quarter of the white establishment. While the organisation's class character and 'direct action' strategy were a threat to property and 'the peace', its ideologues' Marxist-derived denunciations of religion – and Christianity in particular – were an offence to the God that the colonisers had brought with them. In July 1927, the ecclesiastical authorities of the 'Roman Catholic Church of South Africa and Rhodesia' responded in kind to the ICU's ideological warfare by pronouncing that all Catholics who were members of the ICU should be refused the sacraments – an injunction that the Pope subsequently confirmed.[36] In parliament, the eradication of the ICU and the enactment of a more disciplinary 'native policy' was now being presented as the most urgent objective facing the state. W.A. Deane, MP for Umvoti, and, more especially, Marwick and Heaton Nicholls, MPs for Illovo and Zululand respectively, were leading protagonists in this cause.

As the forces that clashed physically in March 1928 were polarising during 1927, the leading exponents of African popular interests had come increasingly from the ranks of local 'commoners' who were mainly young and without formal education. The role of tribal authorities had become increasingly peripheral. Certainly the NAD instructions to local chiefs in mid-1927 to inform their wards that farmers would not be dispossessed of their land, and that tenants would not be freed from their labour obligations, did little to dampen popular support for the ICU. Deane nonetheless looked on African chiefs within his constituency and elsewhere in the province as allies against the ICU – although his statement that they 'prohibited agitators addressing meetings and they did not allow their young men to attend' was an exaggeration of their practical role.[37] There was in fact little evidence that chiefs resident on white farms resolutely and of their own volition took action to undermine the ICU, or that they had the power to do so. Indeed, it seems that at least one openly sympathised with the ICU. A meeting of Kranskop farmers in May 1927 called upon the government to take punitive action against Kranskop Chief Mxamo, since, it was alleged, an ICU meeting that had recently taken place in his ward was both arranged and supported by him.[38]

It is apparent, however, that the different responses of Zulu chiefs in the Zululand reserves on the one hand and in Northern Natal on the other were mirrored in Natal proper. The most vociferous African opponents of the ICU in the Natal midlands were chiefs who were resident on reserve land. In giving evidence before the select committee on Hertzog's Native Bills (Marwick and Heaton Nicholls were members of this committee) in June 1927, Chief Kula of the Msinga district and Chief Swayimana of the New Hanover district delivered broadside attacks on all 'detribalised' elements in African society, and the ICU 'thieves' with whom they were associated. They claimed that ICU activists had not penetrated their wards – even though the latter abutted on the Umvoti, Kranskop and Weenen stormcentres. Both emphasised the disciplinary virtues of tribalism, and felt that 'the proper system of rule was by a king and council', and that 'Solomon is by birth the big chief of the natives in Natal'.[39] It is likely that they were Inkatha members.

In berating the ICU and the class it represented, Chiefs Kula and Swayimana were not merely speaking either for themselves or of their own regions. By the late 1920s, notwithstanding regional differences, the Zulu-speaking population in the province of Natal had become a society made up largely of three social classes: the tribal elite, of which Kula and Swayimana were a part, the kholwa elite, and the rank and file. Each was politically represented, moreover, through the medium of formally established modern political organisations. By far the most significant development was the politicisation of the rank and file and its political mobilisation as a formidable militant force. This was to prove a crucial dynamic in Natal politics, and, more specifically, in the evolution of Solomon's and Inkatha's political position.

NOTES

1. When an official of the International Labour Office toured South Africa in 1928, he similarly concluded that the Zulu were 'under less pressure to work owing to the comparative sufficiency of their lands to meet their requirements'. *South African Outlook*, 2/7/1928, p. 135.

2. C. Simkins, 'Agricultural production in the African reserves of South Africa, 1918–1969', *Journal of Southern African Studies*, vol. 7, no. 2, April 1981.

3. NEC Box 4, evidence of Archdeacon A. W. Lee, Vryheid, 18/9/1930, p. 1414 (first quotation); and Chief Mgixo, Nongoma, 24/9/1930, p. 1690 (second quotation).

4. Reports of the Auditor-General (UG publications), 1925–1930. For more on the powers and duties of tribal authorities, see ch. 4 ('Chiefs and Headmen') of the Natal Code of Native Law (1932), in Rogers, *Native administration*, pp. 319–20.

5. NTS 280, 227/53, CNC's report entitled 'Labour Conditions in Northern Districts of Natal – Malinga' (hereafter CNC's report), 9/2/1928 (first quotation); and NEC Box 4, evidence of the Revd E. A. Mahamba, Dundee, 17/9/1930, p. 1363 (second quotation).

6. NEC Box 4, evidence of Shiyabanye Mncwango, Nongoma, 24/9/1930, p. 1693. See also evidence of C. A. Wheelwright, Mtubatuba, 25/9/1930; Archdeacon Lee, Vryheid, 18/9/1930; Chief Mqwebu, Stanger, 2/10/1930; and Mose Mtuli, Nongoma, 29/9/1930.

7. NEC Box 7, evidence of Mrs V. S. Makanya, Durban, 2/4/1931, pp. 6302–3 (first quotation); J. Dube, Durban, 2/4/1931, p. 6268 (second quotation); NEC Box 4, evidence of the Revd L. E. Oscroft, Nongoma, 22/9/1930, pp. 1635–36 (third quotation); and C. A. Wheelwright, Mtubatuba, 25/9/1930, pp. 1734–35 (fourth quotation). For more on Sibusisiwe Makanya, see Shula Marks (ed.), *Not either an experimental doll* (Pietermaritzburg, 1987).

8. CNC PMB 92, 64/2, J. Gumede, President, NNC to CNC, 17/3/1926, forwarding resolutions of NNC meeting.

9. Two important published sources on Champion are his own writings, edited by M. W. Swanson, *The views of Mahlathi* (Pietermaritzburg, 1983), 'Mahlathi' being Champion's journalistic *nom de plume*; and Marks, *Ambiguities of dependence*, ch. 3.

10. See Helen Bradford, 'Social origins of ICU leadership', p. 295; and 'Lynch law and labourers: the ICU in Umvoti, 1927–1928' (paper presented at the Workshop on Class, Community and Conflict, University of the Witwatersrand, February 1984).

11. NTS 280, 227/53, CNC to SNA, 23/9/1927.

12. JUS 408, 4/323/25, Staff Officer, Standerton to Chief of General Staff, Union Defence Force, Pretoria, 11/7/1925, also reporting the feelings of local magistrates.

13. For P. Maling see Marks, *Reluctant rebellion*, p. 71; and for Gilbert Coka see Helen Bradford, 'Social origins of ICU leadership', pp. 297ff. My main sources on Lymon Maling were NEC Box 4, evidence of M. L. E. Maling, Vryheid,

20/9/1930, pp. 1563ff; C. A. W. Wheelwright, Mtubatuba, 25/9/1930, pp. 1762–64; and NTS 280, 227/53, 'Matters concerning Northern Natal land and labour', which contains considerable official correspondence relating to Maling's activities.

14. NEC Box 4, evidence of E. N. Braatvedt, Magistrate, Melmoth, 29/9/1930, p. 1873(a); see also evidence of Maling, Vryheid, 20/9/1930, p. 1583.

15. NEC Box 4, evidence of Magungwana Zondo, Vryheid, 20/9/1930, p. 1528 (first quotation); and evidence of Chief Mgixo, Nongoma, 24/9/1930, pp. 1685–87 (second quotation).

16. Select Committee on the Prevention of Disorders Bill, Report, SC14–26, evidence of Major J. F. Herbst, SNA, 24/4/1926, p. 15.

17. Select Committee on the Native Bills, Report, SC10–27, evidence of Chief Kula, 15/6/1927, p. 384.

18. *Zululand Times*, 1/9/1927.

19. NTS 280, 227/53, SNA to CNC, 19/9/1927. See also the three ALU petitions to the Prime Minister, General Hertzog: the first undated (approx. April 1927) and submitted via A. B. Payn, MP, and the others dated 31/8/1927 and 1/9/1927. For Maling's meeting with the Prime Minister, see Debates of the House of Assembly, vol. 19, speech by Payn, 9/5/1932, col. 4299.

20. NTS 280, 227/53, CNC's inquiry, 1928, annexure 2, statement of Mtateni Ndwandwe.

21. NTS 280, 227/53, CNC's report, 9/2/1928.

22. See NTS 280, 227/53, ALU petition to the Prime Minister, 1/9/1927; CNC's inquiry, 1928, annexure 1, evidence, and annexure 3, copy of Goss Estates 'Agreement'; CNC's report, 9/2/1928; and also NEC Box 4, African evidence given at Vryheid, 20/9/1930.

23. For the broader significance of these developments, see Morris, 'Capitalism in South African agriculture'; and Bradford, 'The ICU in Umvoti, 1927–1928'. For Northern Natal, see NEC Box 4, evidence given at Vryheid, September 1930.

24. NTS 280, 227/53, CNC's inquiry, 1928, annexure 3, Goss Estates 'Agreement'.

25. NTS 280, 227/53, CNC's report, 9/2/1928, pp. 8–10.

26. For reference to detentions, floggings and culpable homicide, and the use of sjamboks and firearms in 'labour relations', see NTS 280, 227/53, CNC's inquiry, 1928, annexure 1, evidence.

27. For Maling, see NTS 280, 227/53, CNC's report, 9/2/1928, p. 7; and for the Natal ICU, see Roux, *Time longer than rope*, p. 173; and E. Webster (ed.), *Essays in southern African labour history* (Johannesburg, 1978), p. 117.

28. NTS 280, 227/53, CNC's report, 9/2/1928, p. 2.

29. NTS 280, 227/53, SNA to CNC, 4/10/1927 (quotations from two letters of the same date). See also W. Nxumalo, E. H. S. Xaba and M. L. E. Maling to Magistrate, Vryheid, 13/9/1927, naming chiefs' representatives in the ALU.

30. NTS 280, 227/53, Magistrate, Vryheid to CNC, 17/9/1927. See also CNC to SNA, 23/9/1927; and SNA to CNC, 4/10/1927.

31. Bradford, 'The ICU in Umvoti, 1927–1928', pp. 12–13.

32. See *ibid.*, pp.13–22; and Shula Marks, 'Natal, the Zulu royal family and the ideology of segregation', *Journal of Southern African Studies*, vol. 4, no. 2, April 1978, p. 185. For Kadalie, see CNC PMB 81, 58/7/3, A. E. Trigger, CID Johannesburg to Divisional CID Officer, Pietermaritzburg, 22/2/1928.

33. *Natal Witness*, 11/9/1926.

34. See Debates of the House of Assembly, vol. 9, speech by Major G. Richards (Weenen), 20/6/1927, cols 5326–27; and Bradford, 'The ICU in Umvoti, 1927–1928', pp. 21ff.

35. JUS 437, 4/366/27, Magistrate, Estcourt to SNA, 2/4/1928; and see also other correspondence in the same file. My source for the Greytown events was Bradford, 'The ICU in Umvoti, 1927–1928', pp. 1–2, 27–28.

36. *South African Outlook*, 1/5/1928, p. 82.

37. Debates of the House of Assembly, vol. 14, speech by Deane, 26/3/1930, cols 2351ff, during which he referred to the role of chiefs in the recent disturbances in the Natal midlands, and argued that they would welcome a Riotous Assemblies Bill.

38. *Natal Mercury*, 19/5/1927.

39. Select Committee on the Native Bills, Report, SC10–27, evidence of Chief Kula and Chief Swayimana, 15/6/1927, pp. 382ff.

7

Solomon and Inkatha

Soon after the portentous Inkatha meeting of 1925, while the NAD privately and ponderously reconsidered official policy towards the Zulu royal house, Inkatha's kholwa leaders set about drawing up a formal constitution for the organisation. Their object was not only to satisfy their own and – more importantly – NAD conceptions as to what constituted a 'proper' political organisation; it was also to define the specifically kholwa interests and objectives they hoped Inkatha would pursue.

The 1926 Inkatha constitution was finalised in the Durban offices of J. Ray Msimang, a man of legal training and evidently a member of the influential kholwa Msimang family that had already produced several church and political leaders. The preamble to the constitution dwelt on the need for Zulu national unity:

> . . . it is necessary to attempt to have unity amongst the Zulu people now scattered throughout and outside the Union with a view to establishing something tangible and worth the name of the once powerful ZULU NATION and also with the ideas of obtaining a place under the sun and not infinitely to suffer to be [down] trodden and looked down upon by other nations . . .

Inkatha, which had the 'Hereditary Paramount Chief of the Zulu Nation' as its 'Patron', was the organisation which aimed to realise the aspirations of the nation as a whole.[1]

The constitution's statement of Inkatha's aims, however, clearly identified the particular interests that lay behind this broad nationalism. First, Inkatha aimed to 'encourage thrift amongst the Zulus and also establish industries and Trades'. The appended reason for this – to ensure that the Zulu were 'worthy of the name and traditions of their Ancestors' – hints at the ambiguity of the kholwa position in Inkatha: it was a reflection of their cultural disorientation, and more specifically their paradoxical preoccupation with both 'roots' and 'progress'. The second, third and fourth aims all related to the agricultural co-operative for which the Umpini ka Zulu fund had been established. Inkatha aimed to buy or hire farms so as to cultivate sugar-cane and cotton (the plantation cash crops then being cultivated successfully by local white farmers), together with a variety of other fruits and vegetables that 'might prove remunerative to Inkata ka Zulu'. It was emphasised that the produce was for the open market rather than for subsistence. Mention was made, furthermore, of Inkatha's intention to establish itself as a trading broker, buying and selling hides and livestock. The fifth aim was to establish 'Educational and Industrial Schools' for the Zulu, clearly on the lines of Dube's Ohlange Institute. It was hoped that those who qualified in these schools would be able to find employment in Inkatha's own expanding agricultural and commercial concerns.

In accordance with western prescriptions, the constitution mapped out the structure of Inkatha's executive, the powers and duties of its office-holders, the rules of procedure during meetings, the methods by which its activities would be publicised and subscriptions collected, and its financial regulations. Overall, great emphasis was placed on Inkatha's sound foundations according to western criteria, and its loyalty to the South African government and British Crown. Government officials were entitled to attend Inkatha meetings, which were otherwise restricted to paid-up members, and any member giving evidence of a 'spirit of disloyalty to the throne' was to be 'evicted'. Every meeting would open with prayers, and 'regulations for the conduct of Meetings of civilised Races [would] operate at the sittings'. The constitution furthermore laid down that the decision-making process was to be democratic. It stated equally firmly that Solomon's relationship with Inkatha was that of 'Patron', while the executive leader was to be the elected president. The only regulation not based on the democratic principle was that a member of the Zulu royal family would automatically always be the treasurer to Inkatha – in practice this meant Solomon and his heirs.[2]

While the constitution as a whole was foreign to Inkatha's tribal elite, it was the democratic principles enshrined in it that were clearly contrary to their interests. During 1926, Inkatha's tribal elite prepared a petition to the MNA that stood in stark contrast to the 1925 constitution. This petition, co-signed by the two most worldly members of the royal inner circle, Mnyaiza kaNdabuko Zulu and Franz kaDabulamanzi Zulu, was presented to the CNC personally by Solomon in January 1927. It represented an attempt on the part of the Zulu royal family to establish its own concord with the South African government, and reflected the political struggles being waged within the Inkatha leadership.

The 1927 royal petition was, however, also related to two other issues of national importance. First, the *induna enkulu*, Mankulumana kaSomaphunga Ndwandwe, had died late in 1926 while in Johannesburg. He had been in the Transvaal to attend to Inkatha and Umpini matters there, to arrange the collection of royal tributes through Franz at Brakpan Mine Compound, and to visit the NAD head office. As a man who had been a forthright and eloquent national leader throughout the turbulent period since conquest, Mankulumana had been deeply respected by the Zulu (including the Mandlakazi) and whites alike. His death left a very marked gap in the ranks of Zululand's royal and national leadership.[3] Second, the success of Solomon's policy of tribal reconciliation, which had been publicly affirmed during the *indaba* with the Prince of Wales, now needed to be consolidated by the appointment of Mandlakazi and Buthelezi leaders to formal positions of leadership at Mahashini.

The petition began with the bald statement that Solomon's 'present Title, Chief of the Usuthu merely, is misleading to the authorities because he is in fact recognised by the Zulus as head of all the clans which form the Zulu Nation'. The request was that Solomon's title be redefined to 'adequately express his responsibility to the Government and to the people as head of the Zulu Nation'. In practice this request called for the creation of a new central position in the NAD's Zululand administration, that of paramount chief, and the recognition of Solomon as incumbent in accordance with hereditary right — a fact immediately recognised by the NAD. The petition went on to complain that Zululand magistrates were forbidding local chiefs to attend national gatherings at Mahashini, and that the CNC had forbidden the Zulu to continue making contributions to the Inkatha fund.

Two further requests were made. First, that Matole kaTshanibezwe Buthelezi 'be restored to the office of his grandfather Mnyamana' — that is, chief counsellor to the head of the Zulu royal house. The death of Mankulumana provided the petitioners with a tangible pretext for the resuscitation of the national role of the Buthelezi leader, and it was integral to Solomon's own drive for recognition that recognition also be sought for other members of the Zulu aristocratic elite. Similarly, it was requested that Bokwe kaZibhebhu Zulu of the Mandlakazi be appointed to the position of 'Induna of the Nation' so that 'the two of them Mathole and Bokwe [can] assist each other in the affairs of the Zulu Nation, they being next to Solomon, the principal men of the Nation'.

It is interesting that the petition also argued that the Zulu themselves had regarded Solomon as Zulu king since Solomon's installation by the Governor-General, Lord Buxton, in 1917, and had done so because Lord Buxton had then intimated that they should. The Zulu royal house frequently indicated, as in this case, that it regarded representatives of the British royal family, such as Lord Buxton and the Prince of Wales, as holding authority superior to the South African government. Oswald Fynney, incidentally, supported the Zulu royal house's interpretation of Lord Buxton's address.[4]

The NAD response to both the kholwa 1926 constitution and the royal 1927 petition was coloured by the retirement of Fynney from the key post of magistrate at Nongoma. His replacement, H.L. Gebers, was no supporter of the Zulu royal cause. The 1926 constitution had moreover confirmed two of the CNC's earlier fears: that educated men from outside were seeking to 'interfere' with Solomon and so might disrupt the tribal system in Zululand, and that Inkatha did not see itself as an organisation that represented only Zululand, or even only ·Natal and Zululand. The CNC's response was to argue that Inkatha's stated aims were still 'hopelessly indefinite', and accordingly the NAD informed Inkatha that it could not be given official recognition. In regard to the royal petition, the new magistrate at Nongoma feared the 'very powerful combination of Natives under Solomon in Zululand' if the historically 'loyal' (i.e. loyal to the British Crown since conquest) leaders of the Buthelezi and Mandlakazi were allowed to become Solomon's chief counsellors. He was also convinced that there was no room for the office of paramount chief in the Zululand administration. In turn, the CNC's response to being pressed by the Zulu royal family was to retreat from his recent pragmatism. Referring to the conditions of Solomon's appointment in 1917, he advised that Solomon be informed that his jurisdiction was limited to the Usuthu ward alone and was 'still temporary' – an unrealistic response. He went on to argue that if Matole and Bokwe wished to take up posts with Solomon, they would have to renounce their chieftainships of the Buthelezi and Mandlakazi. He seemed especially fearful of the consequences that the unification of the Usuthu and Mandlakazi would have for Solomon's status.[5]

The annual Inkatha meeting of September 1926 highlighted some important features of the organisation and signalled that it was entering a new phase in its history. Most importantly, during the meeting there was an attempt on the part of local militant leadership to redefine Inkatha's political stance, and this introduced a new fissure within Inkatha.

There was a comparatively small attendance at the 1926 meeting; in particular there were very few tribal leaders present. The simultaneous meeting of the Native Affairs Commission at Vryheid, together with the inclement weather, played a role in keeping attendance down. But the main factor was that the recent NAD instructions against Inkatha collections had been interpreted as a sign of the government's disapproval of Inkatha's very existence. The sensitivity of Inkatha's supporters (especially Inkatha's tribal supporters, and NAD-recognised chiefs and *izinduna*) to the wishes of the government, reflected the organisation as essentially compromising and even collaboratory, with a momentum significantly dependent on government approval. The low attendance and the low spirits of the Inkatha leadership (Oscroft spoke of an atmosphere of futility) at the meeting also indicated that Inkatha's impetus and sense of direction in late 1925 had been corroded by discord with its leadership in 1926. The import of the meeting was not, however, purely negative: the way in which Inkatha personnel reacted against the militant element at the meeting showed that there were grounds for an elitist alliance, and that Inkatha had a role to play in representing it.

Solomon chose not to attend any of the proceedings of the 1926 meeting, not even the private executive committee meeting which the 'patron' and 'treasurer' was obliged to attend. He instead remained out of sight in his house for the duration of the deliberations, and it was Inkatha funds that met the cost of catering for the gathering, in contrast to the personal contribution of Solomon in 1925. Divisions were expressed even within Inkatha's kholwa leadership: friction existed between the secretary, Simelane, and the chairman, Bhulose, which was probably a reflection of the differing political priorities of the local Zulu kholwa establishment as opposed to 'outsiders' from Natal proper. It was the kholwa establishment as a whole, nonetheless, that was unquestionably dominant.

The proceedings were almost wholly taken up in discussion of the three new 'Native Bills' that Prime Minister Hertzog had tabled in the South African parliament during the 1926 session. Except for the Native Lands Further Release and Acquisition Bill, which aimed to allow for the release of certain tracts of land abutting on the reserves for African ownership, the bills were of little interest to Zululand's tribal elite. The Union Native Council Bill aimed to establish a council of fifty African representatives, of whom thirty-five were to be elective, as a substitute for the Native Conferences established under the 1920 Act. The Representation of Natives in Parliament Bill aimed to remove Cape Africans from the common voters' roll in the Cape, and as an alternative provide seven white representatives of black interests in the House of Assembly.

The meeting passed two related resolutions. One was an 'appreciation of the life and work of the late Hon. J.X. Merriman', the prominent white defender of the 'Cape liberal tradition'. The other was an expression of 'regret that certain Cape Natives should be deprived of the Franchise, which . . . they have never abused'. These were issues far removed from the political priorities of those tribal Zulu who were present, and the resolutions were passed despite Mankulumana's statement that the meeting had 'no right' to pass any resolutions since the chiefs were absent.[6]

Another delegate also disagreed with these resolutions, but for a very different reason: he believed they were insufficiently forceful. This was Lymon Maling, the educated, exempted, stylish and eloquent political organiser from Vryheid, and founder of the ALU. Although Maling was making his mark as champion of rank-and-file interests in Northern Natal, concerning himself principally with the exploitative relations between labour-tenant and landlord in the districts of Vryheid (including Babanango), Ngotshe, Utrecht, Paulpietersburg and Piet Retief, he had now arrived to address Inkatha, an organisation concerning itself principally with the interests of Zulu social elites. It should be remembered, however, that Maling was attempting to organise in an area where the authority of chiefs was comparatively strong, and where Inkatha had become without question the dominant political organisation; he thus needed in some way to establish a relationship with Inkatha. It was also to become apparent that Maling personally held a reverence for Solomon, and was by no means insensitive to the emotional power of Zulu royalty and Zulu nationalism.

In addressing the meeting, Maling chose to focus on what seemed to be the issue of the day: Hertzog's 'Native Bills'. Supported by a group of followers from Northern Natal, he used his considerable oratorical skills in a rigorous denunciation of state policy. 'His views obviously appealed very strongly to the gathering', Oscroft reported, and would have led the assembly to pass a resolution in strong condemnation of the bills had it not been for the intervention of Inkatha's conservative rulers. Oscroft was deeply impressed by the way in which Mankulumana and Mnyaiza rose to 'counteract the influence of extremists . . . a striking illustration of the powers of leadership still retained by the headmen of Zululand'. Mankulumana and Mnyaiza were firmly supported by the chairman, Bhulose.[7]

This incident set the shape of Inkatha politics for the rest of its existence (this, the first Inkatha organisation, disintegrated in the early 1930s). Whatever the differences between Inkatha's kholwa and tribal elites, and however strongly these were contested, kholwa and tribal leaders were to unite solidly against rank-and-file radicalism and militant leadership. From 1927, Zulu politics resolved into a struggle between three classes: the kholwa elite, the tribal elite, and the rank and file, the dominant cleavage being between the two elites on the one hand and the rank and file on the other.

The fissure between the kholwa and tribal elites nonetheless continued to hamstring Inkatha, as did the dismissive attitude the NAD had adopted. Inkatha was virtually inactive during 1927, and the annual meeting of

October 1927 clearly reflected its near-moribund state. Following tension between Simelane and Bhulose, Simelane ceased to act as Inkatha secretary with the result that the meeting was poorly organised. Because of an adminstrative 'oversight', Oscroft was for the first time since 1924 not invited to attend as government observer. The meeting itself was notable for three absences. First, the absence of the tribal elite: only three chiefs attended, and Solomon himself was absent. Second, the absence of the leading kholwa representatives, including Dube and Bhulose. The meeting was chaired by the Revd Mathe, a low-ranking Inkatha official who was an associate of Simelane. The third absence was of any sense of purpose and conviction.[8]

* * * * *

Until August 1927, neither Solomon nor Inkatha had made any public comment on the struggles that were being waged in the countryside under the ICU banner. In that month, however, Solomon made a bitter attack on the ICU, and this was publicised through the columns of *Ilanga lase Natal*. Solomon complained that the ICU was obviously not the 'town movement' that he had originally understood it to be, since it was now in the countryside, including Vryheid and Babanango. At no stage, however, had ICU leaders reported to him. He reminded readers what had happened to the white miners who had 'tried to do things unconstitutionally' in 1922 – when their strikes had been quelled by force of arms. The Zulu people were being misled by propaganda, he concluded, and it was the duty of chiefs and headmen to 'kill the ICU in their tribes'.[9]

In a tract published in English, the editor, Dube, applauded Solomon and added his own observations on the ICU: 'The leaders are irresponsible, they do not understand the relations of capital to labour, the need for investment'. He emphasised the threat that the ICU posed to Natal's kholwa establishment, and questioned whether African landowners and employers would pay the 8 shillings a day that the ICU was then demanding for farm labour. 'How about that for the men of Groutville, Amanzimtoti and Ifafa! Are they prepared to pay their employees that wage? How long can they raise cane at a profit if they pay such wages?'[10]

These twin statements expressing unity between Inkatha's tribal and kholwa elites against the ICU – which Champion described as an 'underground political plot of a gang of Bantu political traitors' – evidently had not been solicited by either the NAD or white farmers' representatives. They alerted the latter, however, to the role that Solomon and Inkatha could play in combating the ICU. In Zululand, ironically, white farmers had been perturbed by the claims of local ICU officials that they had Solomon's sanction. Twelve days after Solomon's and Dube's views were published in *Ilanga lase Natal*, the anti-ICU meeting mentioned in the previous chapter – between George Higgs (Empangeni and District Farmers' Association), Col. Tanner (magistrate at Empangeni) and local chiefs and headmen – took place at Empangeni. At the close of the *indaba*, Higgs introduced to the assembled chiefs a man named Saul Gumede, who proceeded to read out Solomon's recently published opinions. None of the tribal leaders present had heard of Solomon's instruction to 'kill the ICU in their tribes', and it evidently had a great impact on them. As one chief remarked, 'the position had now been made clear, and [we] know what to do'. For the *Zululand Times* reporter who attended, the attitude adopted by the chiefs at the *indaba*, and the influence that Solomon's words had exerted on them, 'generated the wish that the old days were back again and the ICU could be dealt with by the Chiefs themselves'.[11]

Shortly afterwards, a similar but far larger *indaba* took place on the Campbell Sugar Estates in Mount Edgecombe in Natal proper, inland of Durban. It was presided over by William Campbell, leading Natal sugar baron, and the most prominent personnel of the Zulu royal family and Inkatha: Solomon, Mnyaiza, Dube and Bhulose. The proceedings took the form of an 'anti-ICU festival', nine head of cattle and beer having been provided for the large workforce that attended.[12]

In an attempt to counter the propaganda disseminated at such meetings, Champion published a pamphlet entitled *The Truth about the ICU* in which he condemned the Campbell *indaba* in characteristic style: 'The workers' minds were set thinking of a new economic gospel . . . [and] many glasses were consumed to make them forget the new gospel . . . there was an organisation to be killed and the ICU lamb was there to be slaughtered all to the honour of one who is of the royal blood [Solomon].' Despite the fact that Solomon had by then clearly announced himself to be antagonistic to the ICU, Champion studiously avoided any criticism of Solomon personally for attending the Campbell *indaba*. Instead, Champion sought to suggest that Solomon was not in full agreement with the proceedings, and had attended somewhat unwittingly and only on the advice of Dube – who was there in the capacity of church minister 'to bless the occasion' and as 'mouthpiece of the son of Dinuzulu'. Thus Champion heaped scorn on Dube:

> When [educated] men who are the accepted leaders of the people play the role of Mr Facing-both-ways, when they go so far as to mislead ignorant chiefs, members of the royal blood, when ministers of the gospel of Christ stoop so low as to take advantage of the weak . . . the position becomes deplorable and outrageous.

He emphasised that Solomon merely 'sat still, with the marked feelings as of one who realised the seriousness of the occasion . . . [Solomon] maintained his silence, to the amazement of the crowds.'[13]

The two anti-ICU gatherings, presided over by representatives of white farmers, the NAD, Zululand's tribal elite and Natal's kholwa establishment, and following shortly after Solomon's and Dube's denunciations of the ICU through the columns of *Ilanga lase Natal*, signified that new class divisions and alliances were being made explicit. These were soon to be reflected in the reconstitution of Inkatha in 1928.

* * * * *

By early 1928, African politics in the province of Natal had entered a period in their history when class divisions within African society were reflected at the political level more clearly and with greater emotional power than ever before. There were direct parallels between the way in which African politics had developed during 1924 – when class divisions were also clearly represented at the political level, following the rise to prominence of militant leaders who appealed to the rank and file – and the period from late 1927 to early 1928. In both periods, the importance that popular consciousness attached to the role of the Zulu royal family was highlighted, as was the practical political role played by the Zulu royal family. It is illuminating to outline the similarities between these two periods, both of which led to the reorganisation and formalisation of Inkatha as an alliance of elites which opposed rank-and-file militancy.

In 1924, before the ICU became a significant political force in the province, the NNC had become radicalised when key members of its conservative kholwa leadership, Dube and Bhulose, were deposed and militant leaders, Gumede and Maduna, were elected to the NNC executive committee. Although ultimately with less success than Maling and Champion in the later period, Gumede and Maduna in 1924 adopted the role of political representatives of the rank and file. The political trends reflected in the rise of Gumede, Maduna, Maling and Champion respectively to positions of political influence met with the disapproval of the tribal elite and particularly the kholwa establishment, which of all elements of African society was the most distanced from the basic issues of evictions, unhealthy working conditions and inadequate wage levels. In their attempts to consolidate their political standing among the rank and file, however, all these militant leaders at their respective historical 'moments' sought to associate the Zulu royal family or Zulu nationalism with popular protest. All were well aware that the rank and file increasingly looked to the Zulu royal family to raise political morale in times of militancy – as 1906 had demonstrated so clearly. In both 1924 and 1928, an important area of struggle between militant leaders and their political opponents was the battle for 'royal patronage'.

Thus Gumede had announced in one of his first presidential addresses in 1924 that the 'new' NNC was to work together with both the ICU and the nascent Inkatha organisation, and would pay particular attention to land alienation in Zululand. Subsequently the NNC invited Solomon personally to attend NNC functions.[14] Similarly, in early 1928 Maling was once more to attempt to find a niche in Inkatha, having failed to do so in 1926, and also having failed to associate himself independently with Zulu nationalism despite his appropriation of the name 'Abaqulusi' and his contacts with Zulu chiefs. Also in early 1928, and far more significantly, Kadalie, the national ICU leader, and Champion were separately attempting to forge concrete links with Solomon, as will be related below.

In 1924, the radicalisation of the NNC lent urgency to the attempts of the kholwa establishment to make a political alliance with Solomon and the tribal elite. It succeeded in October 1924: Inkatha was transformed from little more than a moribund 'Zulu national fund' into an active political organisation under the joint chairmanship of deposed NNC leaders Dube and Bhulose. Thus it was made clear that, under pressure to make a 'choice', the Zulu royal family was more disposed to ally itself with representatives of the kholwa establishment than with a militant rank and file, and that it favoured a moderate rather than confrontational political strategy.

Similarly, the activism of the Natal ICU during 1927 acted as a catalyst to unite all those anxious to counter rank-and-file militancy. For the latter, Kadalie's and Champion's approaches to Solomon in early 1928, which, it was feared, would provide an immeasureable boost to the ICU's image if seen to be successful, further emphasised how urgent it was that Solomon should publicly reaffirm his antagonism towards the ICU. The much-publicised June 1928 Inkatha meeting, which resolved to accept a new 'official' constitution drawn up by leading Durban solicitors, Nicolson and Thorpe, provided the required reaffirmation. Indeed, it signified that a new and stronger alliance around the figurehead of Solomon had taken shape, and this covertly included representatives of white landowner and employer interests and had the qualified approval of the Natal NAD. In both periods, therefore, rank-and-file militancy played a negative yet leading role in strengthening Inkatha as perhaps its leading opponent – even though the alliances within Inkatha were themselves problematical.

The negotiations between the various interest groups that were to comprise the new Inkatha alliance of 1928 took place at a time when Zulu nationalism was coming to play an increasingly important role in the articulation of popular protest in the province of Natal. Speaking in 1930 about Africans from all over the province, including the towns, who had rejected the authority of 'their' chiefs, Oscroft remarked that 'it is an amusing thing when you see these detribalised natives coming to the Zululand National gatherings how they konza [sic] to the [Zulu] chiefs, especially Chief Solomon. It is very marked.'[15] State officials, white farmers' representatives, kholwa leaders and rank-and-file leaders alike were well aware that the act of *khonza*'ing to Solomon was not merely a politically innocent expression of personal devotion. To them, Solomon represented a key means by which popular consciousness could be politically manipulated. During the period 1927 to 1930 – which was a high-water mark of popular protest in the province – Solomon was for this reason subjected to unprecedented pressure by diverse political organisations and interest groups to use his influence to support their respective political objectives.

In this period, the rank and file increasingly felt the need to perceive themselves as 'Zulu warriors' (popular protest was conducted almost exclusively by males at this time) when confronting white employers and state or municipal authorities. Leaders like Champion, therefore, grappled with popular consciousness by appealing simultaneously to popular class interests and popular 'Zuluness'. In Durban, which was Champion's most important urban constituency, African workers had long interwoven traditional Zulu 'warlike' customs into popular culture. This was particularly reflected in the *ngoma* dance groups (the dances derived directly from the *giya*'ing performed by *amabutho* and clan groups) which were an important form of popular association and entertainment in the city. The way in which traditional Zulu symbols and concepts were employed in the late 1920s to serve contemporary popular economic and political objectives were especially clear during the disturbances surrounding the 1929 boycott of the Durban Municipal Native Affairs Department beerhalls – whose monopoly over the sale of *utshwala* (beer) to urban Africans financed African administration in the city. *Utshwala* was referred to as 'Zulu beer', Champion pointedly spoke of 'Zulu workers', and when addressing their supporters, ICU leaders used phrases that the royal *izinduna* had used when giving instructions to the *amabutho* at national ceremonies in times of old.[16]

In early 1928, Solomon was 'courted' with unusual persistence by ICU leaders Champion and Kadalie – particulary the latter who, as an outsider to the Natal ICU, was more distanced from Solomon's wrath. The reason for this sense of urgency, of which police and NAD officials were unaware at the time, was that Kadalie, the general secretary of the national ICU, and Champion, secretary of the Natal provincial branch, were waging a personal battle with each other for the leadership of the Natal ICU. When Kadalie returned to South Africa in November 1927, after having spent about five months making contacts with leading trade unionists in Britain and Europe, the Natal ICU had already established itself as the politically and financially most powerful provincial branch of the ICU in the Union. From Kadalie's point of view, Champion presented a threat to his position as national leader; there were also political differences between them, since Kadalie was intent on reorganising the ICU on 'proper' trade union lines and affiliating it with white South African trade unions and overseas labour organisations. On the grounds of alleged financial corruption within the Natal ICU, a national ICU disciplinary tribunal suspended Champion as secretary for Natal.

Before the ICU annual congress met in April 1928 and confirmed Champion's dismissal, however, Champion had rallied Natal branches to his personal support. As a result, the 'ICU *yase* Natal' was formed, a separate Natal organisation with Champion in charge. The secession of the Natal ICU can in part be attributed to Champion's personal ambition; but it was also designed to appeal to the sense of 'Zulu' superiority and exclusivity that was so prevalent in the province even south of the Tugela river. Kadalie explicitly referred to these two factors in mid-1928 when he was attempting to entice Champion and the ICU *yase* Natal back into the national fold: 'what is self to be compared with the great cause [?]', he wrote to Champion, and continued, 'To day Durban is talking about the Great Zulus to stand [sic] alone and have nothing to do with greater South Africa. Are we going to allow this?'[17]

In the midst of the power struggles that resulted in the formation of the ICU *yase* Natal, Kadalie visited Natal in a desperate attempt to save the province for himself. While in Natal during February 1928 he adopted two strategies. On the one hand, he toured the Natal countryside with Mr Glass, the white bookkeeper Kadalie had employed to asssist in the 'cleansing' of the ICU, presenting himself as the leader of a 'proper' trade union, the revamped national ICU. In the Natal midlands he indicated that he was specially interested in buying land for evicted tenants, and gave out that the policy of the national ICU in this matter would be to buy as much land as possible in one area rather than having pieces scattered all over the province. On the other hand, Kadalie sought to affiliate himself with Solomon; if he could present himself as, in a sense, Solomon's *induna*-in-charge of labour matters, this would be possibly his greatest asset in his drive to secure the leadership of the ICU in Natal. Thus one of Kadalie's first actions on arrival in Natal was, with something of a flourish, to intercept Solomon's car on the road between Nongoma and Durban. Kadalie was accompanied by Mr Glass, whose presence, as a white and professional person, might perhaps persuade Solomon that Kadalie's ICU was not the 'riff-raff ICU' which was causing havoc in the Natal midlands. The police inspector at Eshowe was unable to ascertain what transpired at this roadside meeting, but felt that any further developments in this regard should demand the 'closest attention of the Government'. In the personal opinion of the inspector, however, an ICU-Solomon affiliation was unlikely for two reasons, first, because of Solomon's public stand against the ICU, and second, because of Solomon's 'financial difficulties', the cause of which was that 'contributions to the Nkata have fallen off, particularly among the Tribes of Natal proper, since the rise of the ICU'.[18]

Yet unbeknown to the inspector at Eshowe, Kadalie was already making plans to exploit Solomon's financial problems as a means of drawing Solomon towards the ICU. Kadalie knew, apparently, that Solomon was especially sensitive about the way in which ICU popularity had recently reduced the Zulu royal revenue. The Johannesburg CID had succeeded in finding an informant among Kadalie's personal staff, and this source reported in late February 1928 that two meetings of Kadalie's cabal, then in Natal, had focused on the 'matter of enlisting the sympathies of Dinuzulu [meaning Solomon]'. Kadalie and Glass, it was resolved, were to proceed to Mahashini as soon as they had finished issuing instructions against Keable Mote, the ICU 'Lion of the Orange Free State', who, like Champion, was then attempting to break away from the national ICU. At Mahashini, they would 'offer Dinuzulu a certain percentage of the contributions of the ICU members, in order to secure his support'.[19]

Solomon made a short visit to Durban during February 1928, and Champion, for his part, used this visit as an opportunity to court Solomon, attempting to make his own arrangements with the Zulu royal house. In the light of reports that Champion was in contact with Solomon, coinciding with reports of Kadalie's initiatives, official consternation deepened. The Natal NAD immediately requested that the CID undertake a special investigation although it was clear that NAD and police officials already feared – as one Zululand police officer expressed it – a 'furtive alliance' between Solomon and the ICU. Solomon's denunciations of the ICU could not be trusted, the same officer reminded the police Deputy Commissioner at Pietermaritzburg, since Dinuzulu had publicly denounced the rebellion in 1906, but was subsequently found to be sheltering rebels.[20]

These fears were in fact groundless. The CNC, Wheelwright, who by then had known Solomon for twelve years and was well informed of Solomon's movements in early 1928, at no stage succumbed to them. In early 1928, so the magistrate at Vryheid notified the CNC, Solomon's attention was in the first place focused on festivities at Mahashini in celebration of his important marriage to a daughter of Chief Manziyekofi Sithole of the Nkandla district. Manziyekofi's late father, Chief Matshana Sithole, had been a man of some standing in tribal society and in official circles had been suspected of assisting the rebels in 1906.[21] Indeed, left to his own devices, Solomon was as a rule far more disposed to the making of public tribal alliances – which were innocuous from the official point of view – than the making of 'furtive' alliances with the likes of Kadalie or Champion.

Nonetheless, in visiting Durban Solomon was indeed in the process of making a 'furtive alliance'. Officials knew nothing of it despite the close watch that was being kept on Solomon's movements, but had they known they would have been relieved of their anxiety. The reason Solomon visited Durban in February 1928 was to keep an appointment with Mr J.H. Nicolson, a respected Durban solicitor who, during the war years, had served as the city's mayor. Nicolson was acting on the instructions of George Heaton Nicholls, leading Zululand sugar planter and MP for Zululand, to inform Solomon how he might better use his influence against the ICU and, no doubt, how he might expect to benefit by doing so.[22] Besides Nicolson and Solomon's personal staff, there were only two other people who knew about the negotiations between Solomon and Heaton Nicholls: John Dube, Inkatha chairman, and J.S. Marwick, champion of Natal white farming interests. Both Heaton Nicholls and Marwick were also members of the state select committee on Hertzog's 'Native Bills'.

That ICU leaders were approaching Solomon for support at precisely the same time as Solomon was conferring with the ICU's most outspoken antagonists, in February 1928, was not merely ironic: there was a causal link between the initiatives of, on the one hand, ICU leaders, and, on the other hand, Dube and white Natal MPs. Kadalie's and Champion's determined efforts to appropriate the emotive symbol of Zulu royalty to the cause of militant political action made it clear to the tribal and kholwa elites, along with representatives of white planting and farming interests, that the 'menace' of the ICU was threatening to escalate. The CNC, furthermore, was to the draw the same conclusion as the Zulu-speaking tribal and kholwa elites, and the English-speaking planters and farmers. Though it was a crucial factor, however, the reconstitution of Inkatha cannot be understood solely in terms of a pre-emptive strike on the part of these interest groups against an escalation of ICU power.

*   *   *   *   *

While Inkatha itself was at a low ebb from 1926 to early 1928, the NAD came to see Solomon's and Inkatha's potential role in an increasingly favourable light during the course of 1927. And in spite of the friction between the kholwa and tribal elites within Inkatha, through Natal as a whole the political interconnections between the kholwa and tribal elites were increasing during this period. Both of these trends, which were accelerated by the rising tide of militancy among the rank and file, augured well for the future of Inkatha.

Relations between Solomon and the NAD could hardly have been worse in early 1927. Solomon was, as a rule, punctilious about reporting to the magistrate of a district he was visiting, but in 1927 there were lapses. In March, the magistrate at Melmoth, Emtonjaneni district, who was a not unemotional opponent of the Zulu royal family, concluded with unusual clarity that Solomon's recent lapses in 'paying respects' when passing through his district indicated simply that Solomon had no respect to pay.[23] In July, furthermore, Solomon sent a letter to the Magistrate at Nongoma, for transferral to the CNC, in which he recounted the conditions of his appointment as chief of the Usuthu, as explained to him by both the Prime Minister at Pretoria in November 1916 and the Governor-General at Nkandla in January 1917, and added that the latter had also appointed him as King George's 'induna enkulu' for the Province of Natal. Solomon then correctly recounted Botha's words: if Solomon adhered to the conditions of his appointment as chief of the Usuthu, he could expect his status to be elevated. This letter was evidently a counter to the CNC's response earlier that year to the royal petition: Solomon should be advised that his appointment as chief was 'still temporary'. The CNC promptly replied, through the magistrate at Nongoma, that the NAD 'cannot take cognisance' of a letter not signed by Solomon personally – it had been signed on Solomon's behalf by Solomon's private secretary, Leonard Ncapayi. In a confidential minute to the magistrate of Nongoma, the CNC stated that Solomon knew exactly how the government had defined his status, and that Solomon was possibly the 'victim of flatterers . . . who might gain from Solomon's enhanced position'.[24]

The CNC's stance was modified after Solomon's views on the ICU were published in *Ilanga lase Natal* in August. In September the CNC learnt from the Bishop of Zululand that Solomon was describing himself in writing as 'paramount Chief of the Zulus', and he thereupon wrote to the SNA seeking concurrence with his view that the NAD should take no action to contradict Solomon's new designation of himself, adding that there was 'a spirit antagonistic to Solomon among Europeans, including I regret to say some officials, and it is in the interests of sound administration to keep a check upon it . . .' To the Bishop of Zululand, the CNC wrote that Solomon would be 'paramount chief' in the eyes of the Zulu irrespective of any official assertions to the contrary, and, moreover, that Solomon was currently steering 'quite a good middle course' in the matter of politics.[25]

In April 1928, the CNC received an application from Inkatha for permission to hold a 'formal meeting' for the purpose of passing a new constitution which had been drawn up by Nicolson and Thorpe. He immediately granted Inkatha's request. He also wrote an illuminating confidential memorandum to the SNA, in which he described in detail the 'crisis in the affairs of the ICU in Natal' that had recently come to his notice. He noted Kadalie's frequent attempts to gain Solomon's support, and then reported that a few days previously a large 'Native meeting' in Durban had passed a unanimous vote of confidence in Champion – and the CNC had subsequently learnt that Champion intended once more to make approaches to Solomon. The CNC then alluded to the replacement of the cautious and conservative president of the African National Congress (ANC – the renamed SANNC), the Revd Z.R. Mahabane, with the radical Josiah Gumede (previously president of the NNC) in late 1927: 'despite Gumede's reported repudiation of Bolshevik doctrines', the CNC argued, it seemed that there was now an 'affiliation of the ICU and the Native National Congress [ANC]'. All of these considerations, in his opinion, had to be taken into account when reviewing official policy towards Solomon and Inkatha. Solomon was currently trying to build up the power of Inkatha because he knew that an increase in the influence of the ICU and the ANC would undermine the power of chiefs in general and himself in particular, the CNC opined, and continued:

> . . . I do really feel that at the stage that matters have now reached the question of giving some moral support to the Nkata . . . might well be considered as the most promising counterblast to the ICU.

The CNC concluded by referring to the 'problem' of Inkatha in the context of official local council policy. That Inkatha did not accord with the description of a local or regional council under the terms of the 1920 Act should not preclude the possibility of government 'recognition' for Inkatha: a council could be established alongside Inkatha (which would presumably act as a 'House of Lords'), he suggested, for 'there would be ample work to do for both in their respective spheres . . . [Inkatha] might be made a power for good'.[26] This unprecedented wave of favourable opinion, which was to flow through the ranks of the Natal NAD, was to be of great value to Inkatha in 1928.

The political interconnections between the kholwa and tribal elites during

1926 and 1927 were reflected in a variety of contexts. Chief Matole (Mahlabatini district, who also acted as Solomon's representative) and Chief Msiyane (Lower Umfolosi district) were familiar faces among the Natal provincial delegations to the annual Native Conferences held in Pretoria, as were Dube, Bhulose and Ndhlovu. Of the provincial delegations, Natal's were unique in that about half the delegates were chiefs. These ranged from extremely conservative tribal 'aristocrats', like Chiefs Kula (Msinga district) and Msiyane, to 'progressive' kholwa chiefs, like Chiefs Walter Khumalo and Dirk Sioka (both of whom were from the Natal midlands, and members of the NNC 'old guard' who remained on the NNC executive after the 1924 'coup').[27] Natal's delegations reflected that in Natal in particular, the political division between the old and new elites was crumbling – even if the tribal leaders were somewhat out of their depth during the conferences.

Of greater overall significance was the establishment of the South African Native Chiefs' Convention in April 1927 under the auspices of the ANC. This was a result of the courtship that had been conducted since 1920 between 'Congress people', particularly in Natal and the Transvaal, and chiefs. The ANC president who had called the inaugural Chiefs' Convention in 1927, the Revd Z.R. Mahabane, regarded Solomon as the 'most important' chief. Since only twenty-two chiefs attended, mainly from Natal and the Transvaal, the Chiefs' Convention could not justifiably claim to consist of 'the chiefs of the whole Union'. It was nonetheless regarded as successful by those who attended, and became a permanent body – the 'upper house' within the ANC. From the Province of Natal, prominent members were Chiefs Matole, Walter Khumalo and Simon Majozi, while Solomon was represented by an emissary.[28] The ANC Chiefs' Convention provided a vital medium for contact between kholwa and tribal leaders, and between the chiefs themselves, many of whom were kholwa chiefs. One of the specific consequences of this contact was that Chief Simon Majozi, kholwa chief of the Indaleni Mission community near Richmond, who had hitherto taken no part in African politics in Natal, became interested in Inkatha, and after 1928 he was to be an influential figure in that organisation.

Within the ANC, the Chiefs' Convention acted as an ally of the ANC's conservative kholwa leaders and an opponent of militancy. This was especially clear after Gumede was elected to replace Mahabane as ANC president in late 1927. Gumede's election indicated that the move towards radicalism was becoming more pervasive: it was now penetrating the mainstream of 'establishment' African politics.

In this development, the South African Communist Party (CP) was playing a leading role – indeed, at the time of his election Gumede was consolidating links with Communists in both South Africa and Europe. After 1924, the CP had resolved to divert its focus from white South African workers to the masses. This objective was not easily achieved: the CP received a particularly severe setback when it crossed swords with the ICU over matters of organisation and strategy in 1926, whereafter CP members were expelled from the ICU. But in the ensuing few years the scope of CP activities among African workers and political leaders broadened. In July 1927 the CP moved its headquarters to an African quarter of Johannesburg, and the Communist newspaper, the *South African Worker*, was transformed into a primarily African-language (Xhosa, Sotho and Zulu) publication. And in March 1928 it established the 'South African Federation of Non-European Trades Unions', comprising black trade unions not affiliated to the ICU. These developments were stimulated, if not initiated, by the new policy directives that were being enunciated in the Comintern by Soviet leaders – notably Stalin – after 1926. The principle that an 'independent Native Republic' should be established in South Africa was mooted during 1927, and promulgated as a policy directive at the Sixth World Congress of the Comintern in early 1928. In 1927, James La Guma (previously an ICU leader) and Gumede were nominated by the CP to attend the League Against Imperialism (also named the Congress of Oppressed Nationalities) in Brussels. Both then went on to visit Soviet Russia – where La Guma conferred with Bukharin and Gumede was taken on a tour of the Asiatic regions towards the east. On their return, La Guma was appointed general secretary of the Federation of Non-European Trades Unions, in which capacity he championed the cause of the 'Native Republic', and Gumede set about attempting to convert the ANC to communist principles.

In the ANC, Gumede encountered the concerted opposition of the kholwa conservatives and the Chiefs' Convention. At the ANC Easter conference in 1928, the chiefs passed a resolution disapproving of the fraternisation between the ANC and the CP. Though the chiefs withdrew their resolution following an eloquent appeal on behalf of the CP by Gumede, they continued to act in concert as a powerful opponent of radicalism. Kadalie appeared at the same conference and proposed that the ANC and ICU should establish a loose 'united front'; he somewhat opportunistically addressed the gathering as 'Comrades', to which the chiefs replied with scornful laughter.[29]

During the period 1926 to late 1927, there was much evidence of interchange between Inkatha's kholwa and tribal elites closer to 'home', though this took place outside the context of Inkatha. Two examples will suffice. In mid-1926, Solomon and some of his tribal advisers paid an unexpected visit to a mission school at Inanda; and Dube accompanied them. Solomon addressed the pupils, speaking encouraging words on the value of education. Subsequently, early in 1928, the CPSA's Zululand 'Diocesan Native Conference' was held at the ZNTI. The climax of the four-day session was a visit to KwaDlamahlahla, where the delegates were cordially received by Solomon and conducted a discussion with him.[30] The division between the kholwa and tribal leaders within Inkatha at the time belied the essential interdependence of the classes they represented.

As the spread of ICU power had emphasised, the tribal political process was in danger of becoming anachronistic even in its rural preserves. With the speed with which social, economic and political change was taking place among the African population of the Province of Natal, enmeshing it increasingly in a wider industrialised South Africa, the political issues it faced were becoming increasingly less 'parochial' and 'tribal' in nature. In particular, the political questions of the day demanded a detailed knowledge of legislation, and an informed understanding of the Westminster parliamentary system and the process of law. These were skills possessed by very few tribal chiefs, and they were largely dependent on their kholwa allies to 'educate' and advise them in these matters. For the tribal elite, Inkatha and the Chiefs' Convention played an important role in this context. While the proceedings of the 1926 Native Conference had left tribal delegates plainly flummoxed, those of the 1927 Chiefs' Convention, which also focused on Hertzog's 'Native Bills', did not. Away from the abrasive company of young 'hotheads' and the arcane deliberations of progressive intellectuals, tribal delegates at the Chiefs' Convention were much better able to take part in the discussions. These, nonetheless, were inevitably led by their kholwa-chief colleagues, whose political attitudes were generally in accord with those of the kholwa establishment. Accordingly, the resolutions of the 1927 Chiefs' Convention made frequent appeals to liberal democratic ideology, and could equally well have been drawn up by the likes of the Revd Mahabane of the ANC proper, or the Dubes, Bhuloses and Ndhlovus of Natal.[31]

While tribal chiefs benefited from this increased interchange between the tribal and kholwa elites, so too did conservative kholwa leaders, especially those from Natal. Indeed, the radicalised NNC under Gumede was renamed the 'Natal African Congress' in 1926, which signified a more complete break with the traditions of the old NNC prior to the 'coup' of 1924. (The change in name was also in keeping with the concurrent replacement of the word 'Native' with 'African' in the name of the national congress, the ANC.) Conservatives who had remained on the NNC executive committee after 1924 responded by attempting to establish an independent and moderate provincial congress not affiliated to the national organisation, retaining the name 'NNC', but this was unsuccessful. Gumede's election to the presidency of the ANC in the following year served further to accentuate the Natal conservatives' sense of isolation from the mainstream of African politics, and sense of having been outmanoeuvred. There were several other influences, however, which also served to persuade Natal's *kholwa* establishment that their alliance with the province's tribal elite was of central importance.

After their initial expressions of enthusiasm for the 1920 Act's mechanisms for direct Union-wide inter-racial consultation – the annual Native Conferences and the Native Affairs Commission – even Natal's most *hamba kahle* leaders soon grew disillusioned. The meeting of the Native Conference at Pretoria in December 1925 demonstrated its impotence: Hertzog, in his capacity both as Prime Minister and Minister of Native Affairs, addressed the gathering in regard to the 'Native Bills', but (as the SNA, J.F. Herbst, put it) he did so purely 'as a matter of courtesy'. The delegates were not allowed to discuss the bills. Instead, they were instructed to consider matters concerning 'native administration'; for example, the recognition of customary law and problems relating to *lobolo* transactions. Although it was not made explicit at the time, the state was inviting feedback on what was to become the 'Native Administration Act' of 1927. Such proceedings were hardly congenial to the predominantly kholwa and educated African delegates. John Dube, perhaps the prime exponent of the compliant *hamba kahle* tradition, refused to attend the 1926 Native Conference in protest against the ineffectiveness of such gatherings. Furthermore, after the 1926 meeting – which censured the 'Native Bills' – the government did not call a Native Conference again until 1930; and in 1930 any discussion of the bills was forbidden.[32]

Alongside these alienations and disillusionments, however, a sense of direction was imparted by the current trends in state 'native policy' and the segregationist ideology that informed its formulators; these influences offered further cause for kholwa conservatives to consolidate their alliance with tribal leaders. The *hamba kahle* disposition that was such a feature of the Natal kholwa establishment was more than mere 'strategy': it derived from their adherence to liberal democratic ideology and, in particular, the rule of law. For all the grievances that they voiced through the accepted channels, their political activity was always imbued with an ingrained deference to 'authority' – however illegitimate that authority might be in liberal democratic terms – and a desire to work within the law. Yet the legislation that was enacted and the bills that were being debated during the 1920s led to disillusionment and dashed their hopes of a 'liberal-democratic' solution to the South African 'native question'. The disappointment with the mechanisms for the consultation of African opinion established under the 1920 Act was hardly ameliorated by Hertzog's two 'political Native Bills' of

1926: the 'Union Native Council Bill' and the ironically named 'Representation of Natives in Parliament Bill'. The Chiefs' Convention declared that the bills were unacceptable in view of 'sixteen years' experience of indirect representation of Bantu interests' since Union, and the 1926 Native Conference rejected the bills far more bluntly. During the latter conference, the Revd A. Mtimkulu (an arch-'establishment' Natal man) sardonically observed that he now understood 'development on our own lines' to mean 'send the natives back to tribalism'.[33] All the more reason, therefore, that the key exponents of 'tribalism', the chiefs, should be made more amenable to kholwa interests.

The basic import of Hertzog's 'political Native Bills' was the state's resolve to keep Africans out of parliament. On the other hand, the legislation that was accumulating on the statute book emphasised that first, the state was committed to its local council policy for limited African self-government in the rural areas; and, second, the state did not intend 'tribalism' to die a 'natural death' – particularly in Natal. The 1925 Natives Taxation and Development Act laid down new financial regulations designed to promote the implementation of local councils' policy, and to provide the local councils with the financial means to perform their duties. In 1926 and 1927 respectively, moreover, two crucial amendments to the 1920 Native Affairs Act, which introduced the local councils policy, were enacted. The first referred to local populations whose 'stage of development . . . did not permit of the delegation of the comparatively extensive powers contemplated by the [1920] Act'. In these cases provision was made that the Governor-General, in consultation with the Native Affairs Commission and the Minister of Native Affairs, be specially empowered to issue proclamations modifying the internal structure and operation of the local council, and limiting its powers. In presenting this bill to parliament, Hertzog stated that it was particuarly intended for conditions in Natal. The second specially empowered the Governor-General to proclaim sections of white-owned land adjacent to African reserves as 'a Native area for local council purposes' – hence Africans living on white-owned land were no longer excluded from the operation of the 1920 Act.[34] These two amendments removed the SNA's and particularly the CNC's reservations about the appropriateness of the original Act's local councils in Natal: they now had the legislative basis on which to realise their vision of hybrid 'chiefs' councils' and local councils, on the Pondoland model, spanning the African reserves and white countryside.

The 'retribalising' Native Administration Bill was enacted in 1927. Until 1927, 'native administration' in each of the four provinces of the Union was based on the system that each had inherited from the colonial period. With a view to 'administrative uniformity', the 1927 Act extended the operation of the Natal system of indirect rule to African areas throughout the Union. The Natal system was to be applied complete with the recognition of 'customary law', the employment of chiefs as administrative and judicial officials, and the appointment of the Governor-General as Supreme Chief with the power to rule by proclamation. The 1927 Act thus represented a substantial commitment on the part of the state to the preservation of the tribal order: where no local councils had been established, the autocratic system of rule through Supreme Chief, magistrates and native commissioners, chiefs and headmen was to obtain. Moreover, the Native Affairs Amendment Acts of 1926 and 1927 had provided that local councils were not necessarily incompatible with the maintenance of tribal authorities. For those African leaders who held a particular respect for 'the law' and were particularly disposed to 'work within the law', however onerous it might be, the 1927 Act and the (rural) local councils' Acts together provided them with their legislative guidelines.

Simultaneously, the state was offering new ideological guidelines in direct conflict with the British-derived liberal-democratic notions that the African aspirant middle class had imbibed from its missionary mentors. What so endeared the Natal system of 'native administration' to the state in 1927 was not only that it nurtured the disciplinary virtues that were embodied in 'tribalism', but that it also entrenched a division between white and African political and cultural sytems. The rash of 'Native Bills' that had been tabled before parliament between 1920 and 1927, and particularly between 1925 and 1927, had given legislators in parliament, the select committees and the Native Affairs Commission the opportunity to focus resolutely on the 'native question'. With the exception of a few 'liberals' or 'philanthropists' and Labour Party MPs, these legislators reached consensus that a policy of segregation provided the answer. Hence the importance of the Natal 'Shepstonist' model as opposed to the Cape 'liberal-democratic' model – which envisaged the assimilation of 'non-Europeans' to European civilisation and, through the franchise, to the white political system.[35]

While showing how the policy of segregation was being implemented at state level, the 1927 Act also reflected, more broadly, the evolution of segregation as an ideology. Not only behind but also beyond the portals of the Union buildings in Pretoria and the legislative assembly in Cape Town, there was a climate of ideological reassessment. Social anthropology was rapidly developing as a new academic discipline; and even among white liberals, the 'friends of the natives' who had long espoused the values of Victorian liberal democracy, there were some who now came to see a logical connection between 'cultural pluralism', as anthropologists defined it, and political segregation, as some legislators defined it. Educated African opinion was in touch with such developments, especially through the media of liberal-sponsored institutions such as the Joint Councils and Bantu Social Centres.

In the late 1920s there developed something of a consensus among members of Natal's kholwa establishment that the 'solution' to the 'native question', from their point of view, no longer lay in the pursuit of acceptance into the propertied and professional elite of a colour-blind unitary South Africa: it seemed instead to lie in the 'development of their own people'. This approach accorded not only with some aspects of segregationist ideology, but also with some powerful elements of contemporary black-consciousness thinking, in which the importance of black 'roots' and the benefits of black 'self-help', 'self-sufficiency' and 'self-rule' were emphasised. Hence, while in the first instance it was the consensus of anti-ICU opinion among the Province of Natal's kholwa establishment, leading 'native policy' legislators, white employer interests, the tribal elite and the NAD that led to the reconstitution of Inkatha in 1928, the 'new' Inkatha in fact was to embody far broader, more subtle and more long-term objectives than merely the destruction of the ICU.

* * * * *

Representatives of sugar planters in Zululand and Natal proper played a leading role in the negotiations that led to the reconstitution of Inkatha. George Higgs, who had co-organised the Empangeni anti-ICU *indaba*, was a prominent Zululand sugar planter and well known to George Heaton Nicholls. In 1917, when the latter was president of the Zululand Planters' Union, Higgs and Heaton Nicholls were co-signatories of a Zululand Planters' Union pamphlet in protest against the Natives' Lands Commission's recommendations for enlargement of the Zululand reserves. William Campbell, who had hosted the second anti-ICU *indaba*, was a prominent Natal sugar planter and the managing director of Natal Estates Limited. He was well known to John Dube, for the Campbell family had long taken a special interest in 'native' matters and had been since before Union a keen supporter and financial benefactor of Dube's Ohlange Institute at Inanda. Dube, incidentally, also had close contacts with the Huletts, who were perhaps the most prominent Natal north coast sugar-planting family: in his capacity as president of the SANNC soon after Union, Dube advised Congress members in Natal to refer their legal cases to the lawyer G.H. Hulett. Heaton Nicholls, who was now instructing Nicolson to 'advise' Solomon, had first met Solomon when, accompanied by Marwick, he visited the ZNTI in 1922. Later in the same year, at the ZNTI prize-giving, Solomon distributed prizes donated by C.G. Smith, the leading Natal south coast sugar planter.[36]

J.S. Marwick's involvement in the 'Inkatha negotiations' signified that white motives went beyond protecting the interests of sugar planters. After 1920, Marwick had become the most determined parliamentary representative of white commercial farming interests in Natal proper. Marwick in fact played a vital 'linking' role, for he had built up an extensive web of contacts during his career in 'native administration' and in Natal politics since the 1890s. He had long been well known to members of the Zulu royal family and to Dube. His relationship with the latter before 1920 was not always cordial. In 1917 Marwick had sued Dube for an article published in *Ilanga lase Natal* which denounced 'native administration' in Durban, and also alleged that Marwick was no longer known as 'Muhle' (the good one) but as 'Mubi' (the evil one).[37] Since 1920, Marwick and Heaton Nicholls had co-operated closely in parliament to defend the interests of Natal's rural employers on matters concerning labour, and to expound the Shepstonist or 'Natal view' on 'native affairs'; they continued to act together when both were appointed as members of the successive select committees on Hertzog's 'Native Bills' after 1926. It is perhaps significant that while Marwick was manager of the Durban Municipal Native Affairs Department before 1920, the mayor of Durban was J.H. Nicolson – the same person who, early in 1928, was acting for Heaton Nicholls in negotiations with Solomon.

In early 1928, Heaton Nicholls supplied Solomon, through Nicolson, with a draft speech. Heaton Nicholls wished Solomon to deliver this speech on the occasion of the ZNTI's graduation and prizegiving ceremony for the students of 1927. Nicolson at the same time made arrangements that 'Solomon's address' be given extensive coverage in the *Natal Advertiser*. These arrangements were very confidential. As Nicolson wrote to Heaton Nicholls, 'Of course I have kept your name out altogether [from the newspaper report]. Nobody knows you had any part in it, nor will they know.'[38] On 7 February 1928, the *Natal Advertiser* published a leading article emblazoned with no less than five headlines: 'SOLOMON KA DINUZULU TO HIS PEOPLE: ADDRESS TO 'FUTURE LEADERS OF OUR RACE': WARNING AGAINST 'NOISY BAND OF SELF SEEKERS': ZULUS MUST DEVELOP ALONG THEIR OWN LINES: WARRIORS YESTERDAY, PEACEFUL TOILERS TO-DAY.' The 'Paramount Chief of the Zulus' seldom made speeches, it reported – but the ZNTI prizegiving 'was one of those rare occasions when he lets himself go . . .' 'Solomon's speech' bore the unmistakable imprint of Heaton Nicholls's polemical style and political views. It also included some quaint phraseology similar to that used by Chief Kula, of the Msinga district, while bitterly denouncing the ICU before the select committee on 'native affairs' in 1927. As a member of the select committee, Heaton Nicholls had keenly questioned Kula, and it seems that he subsequently drew on Kula's phraseology in styling 'Solomon's speech'.[39]

The speech began by emphasising that the Zulu had ample cause for 'pride of ancestry' because of their renowned courage, virtue, discipline and imperial might in pre-conquest times. But in 'the quagmires of the new world', Solomon said, many Zulu were no longer under the control of tribal authorities or, indeed, under any control at all. Some had begun to pursue 'strange gods'. The whole nation was crying aloud for guidance which, Solomon continued, could be best provided by hereditary leaders. The ZNTI was specially for the educational 'training of those inherent gifts of leadership' that reposed in the sons of chiefs, so that the 'standards of the tribal system . . . [could] be adapted to meet the changing needs of the times'. Solomon emphasised that the Zulu were a different race to the white people, and it was correct that the Zulu should preserve their separate culture – within which they could attain their own 'high state of civilisation'. The ZNTI stood for the 'maintenance of the tribal system', and indicated that it was also 'the wish of the Government that we should be given a full opportunity to develop along our own lines'. The Zulu were to be thankful that the government was not requiring them 'to abandon a harmonious brotherhood in exchange for a discordant individualism'. Solomon then gave an account of the political activities of certain 'well-clothed new-comers, trading on a little book-education . . .' The latter were working in the towns 'to seduce [the Zulu people] from their tribal allegiance', and were also sowing 'the seeds of discontent in the kraals'. They could only cause 'conflict and darkness', and Solomon suggested that their existence further stressed the urgent necessity for rebuilding the tribal order. Solomon concluded by noting that there were white men who had come to understand the problems that the Zulu nation was experiencing, and that these white men were keen to lend their assistance.[40]

At this stage – in early 1928 – it is evident that Heaton Nicholls had made contact only with Solomon, and not with the leadership of Inkatha. Furthermore, although Heaton Nicholls envisaged making further use of Solomon, the arrangements that had been made between these two figures so far related only to the ZNTI speech. But Dube was working quietly in the background, and it seems that it was he who was responsible for 'opening up' the negotiations to Campbell and Marwick, and to Inkatha personnel. A couple of weeks after the ZNTI speech Marwick received an unexpected letter from Dube. In this letter Dube chose to dwell on the matter of the ICU, undoubtedly because Marwick was the most dedicated and outspoken white opponent of the ICU in Natal. The latter had been so since 1926, when Kadalie sued the *Natal Witness* for libel: Marwick voluntarily assisted the counsel for the defence in building up a dossier on ICU 'sedition', and he was the prime witness for the defence at the court case in 1927.[41] Dube denounced the ICU leaders' 'misleading and dangerous propaganda, their absurd promises, their international socialistic inclinations and communism' which would be 'misconstrued amongst our backward Natives'. He continued: 'We, the moderate section of the Bantu people, feel just as you do that communism, whether among white or black, is a real danger to the community.'

The real purpose of Dube's letter, however, was to ascertain whether Marwick concurred with his views on how the 'native question', in broader perspective, should be resolved. More specifically, it was intended to ascertain whether Marwick would be a supporter of Inkatha – although Dube avoided making this explicit. Thus Dube went on to argue that the victory of 'socialistic' doctrines

> would mean breaking down of parental control and restraint, tribal responsibility and our whole traditions, – the whole structure upon which our Bantu Nation rests . . . We have got to maintain, in my opinion, the sense of paternal and tribal responsibility by Bantu traditions with all its obligations of courage, honour, truth, loyalty and obedience for all we are worth . . . Don't think for one moment I am not progressive. I am anxious as any man could be for the development of my people, but on the right lines.[42]

Just as 'Solomon' had done shortly before, Dube thus affirmed his willingness to collaborate in the evolving state policy of 'development on their own lines'. Dube concluded the letter in an open-ended fashion; it was up to Marwick to decide whether to collaborate with the state's African collaborators.

Although records of Dube's activities are fragmentary, it seems that he was successful during the following month in establishing contact between Heaton Nicholls, Marwick and Campbell on the one hand, and the personnel of the Inkatha executive on the other hand; he and Nicolson acted as the 'middlemen'. The solicitors, Nicolson and Thorpe, then began drafting the new Inkatha constitution. When the draft was complete in mid-April 1928, William Campbell paid a visit to the MNA and requested that Solomon now be recognised as Zulu king. The sugar baron also argued that Solomon was in need of guidance, particularly in view of his financial difficulties, and therefore that 'a retired magistrate' should be appointed as Solomon's private secretary. There was little doubt that the 'retired magistrate' that Campbell had in mind was Oswald Fynney – who later in 1928 was to begin personally petitioning the CNC for the recognition of Inkatha. Campbell further intimated that if the government complied with these requests concerning Solomon, 'friends of his [Solomon's]' would be prepared to settle his debts. The minister replied that he would 'seriously consider' these propositions.[43]

The main strategy of Inkatha's white allies in April 1928, however, was to ensure that the 1928 Inkatha meeting was well attended and had official sanction. Nicolson and Thorpe requested that the NAD be represented at the forthcoming meeting, since the latter was to consider the acceptance of a new constitution. In a remarkable departure the NAD nominated Oscroft to attend in an official capacity – previously NAD officials were instructed not to attend Inkatha meetings except in a personal capacity and then only when invited to do so. Then Nicolson and Thorpe requested that the NAD circularise all magistrates in the Province of Natal, inviting their co-operation in making the meeting as representative as possible. Accordingly, the CNC instructed all magistrates to inform their districts that the government had no objection to the forthcoming Inkatha meeting.[44] In this way, the NAD – or, more specifically, the CNC – played an active role in making the Inkatha meeting of June 1928 the largest in Inkatha's history. But more significant was the role played by leading members of Natal's English-speaking establishment: George Heaton Nicholls, William Campbell, J.S. Marwick and J.H. Nicolson.

NOTES

1. NTS 7205, 20/326, 'Inkata kaZulu, Zulu National Council', constitution dated 5/2/1926 at Durban, authorised by W.F. Bhulose, president-elect, p.1, enclosed in CNC to SNA, 1/3/1926.

2. *Ibid.*, pp.2–5.

3. NTS 7205, 20/326, the Revd L.E. Oscroft's report entitled 'Annual Meeting of the Inkata ka Zulu', 6/10/1926, p.3; and see also CNC PMB 81, 58/7/1, H.M. Taberer, Native Labour Adviser, Johannesburg to Major H.S. Cooke, Director of Native Labour, Johannesburg, 4/3/1930. The Native Recruiting Corporation covered the expenses connected with Mankulumana's death and the return of his body to Zululand – although it subsequently reclaimed £115/14/2 from Solomon. Solomon responded by instructing his uncle at Brakpan Compound, Franz kaDabulamanzi Zulu, to conduct a collection among Johannesburg mineworkers.

4. A copy of this royal petition is to be found in KCAL, George Heaton Nicholls Collection, (hereafter MS NIC) 2.08.1, File 2, KCM 3305(a), addressed to General Hertzog, Prime Minister and Minister for Native Affairs, co-signed 'Mnyaiza kaNdabuko and Franz Zulu, By Authority of the Nation', n.d. NAD correspondence relating to the petition is located in CNC PMB 81, 88/7/1. For Solomon and Fynney on Lord Buxton's address, see CNC PMB 81, 58/7/1, Solomon kaDinuzulu to Magistrate, Nongoma, 4/7/1927; and *Natal Witness*, 17/9/1931.

5. NTS 7205, 20/326, CNC's circular to all Natal magistrates, 8/4/1926; CNC to SNA, 1/3/1926 (first quotation); CNC PMB 81, 58/7/1, memorandum by Magistrate, Nongoma, 29/1/1927 (second quotation); and CNC to SNA, 14/2/1927 (third quotation).

6. NTS 7205, 20/326, Oscroft's report of Inkatha meeting, 6/10/1926.

7. *Ibid.*

8. NTS 7205, 20/326, CNC to SNA, 15/11/1927; and see also enclosed translation of Mathe's report of Inkatha meeting, Mahashini, 31/10/1927.

9. *Ilanga lase Natal*, 12/8/1927, NAD translations located in CNC PMB 81, 58/7/3 and 58/7/1.

10. *Ibid.*, quoted in Marks, 'Ideology of segregation', p. 191.

11. *Zululand Times*, 1/9/1927; and, for Champion's statement, *Udibe Lwase Africa*, September 1927, quoted in Paul la Hausse, 'The struggle for the city: alcohol, the Ematsheni and popular culture in Durban, 1902–1936' (MA, University of Cape Town, 1984), p. 221.

12. See CNC PMB 81, 58/7/3, Inspector T. W. Hedges, SAP, Eshowe to Deputy Commissioner, SAP, Pietermaritzburg, 5/4/1928; and [A. W. G. Champion], *The truth about the ICU* (Durban, n.d., evidently 1927), pp. 26–27, a copy of which is to be found in MS MAR, File 74, KCM 8346.

13. [Champion], *The truth about the ICU*, pp. 26–27.

14. CNC PMB 92, 64/2, D. J. Sioka, General Secretary, NNC to CNC, 19/7/1926.

15. NEC Box 4, evidence of L. E. Oscroft, 22/9/1930, p. 1636.

16. La Hausse, 'Struggle for the city', pp. 222, 273–75. For more on the interweaving of 'Zulu rural cultural practices' with popular politics in Durban, see Paul la Hausse 'The message of the warriors'; and '"The cows of Nongoloza": youth, crime and amalaita gangs in Durban, 1900–1936', *Journal of Southern African Studies*, vol. 16, no. 1, March 1990.

17. [A. W. G. Champion], *Mehlomadala* (Zulu-English pamphlet, n.d.), wherein Champion quotes a letter he received from Kadalie dated 5/6/1928, a copy of which is to be found in the A. W. G. Champion Collection, Documentation Centre for African Studies, Univeristy of South Africa (hereafter AWGC) Box 2: 3.2.2. See also Roux, *Time longer than rope*, pp. 175ff; and P. Wickins, *The ICU of Africa* (Cape Town, 1978).

18. CNC PMB 81, 58/7/3, Inspector T. W. Hedges, SAP, Eshowe to Deputy

Commissioner, SAP, Pietermaritzburg, 5/4/1928 (quotation); and for Kadalie's movements, see A.E. Trigger, CID, Johannesburg to Divisonal CID Officer, Pietermaritzburg, 22/2/1928; and 57/7/3, Head Constable, SAP, Ladysmith to District Commandant, Dundee, 13/2/1928.

19. CNC PMB 81, 58/7/3, A.E. Trigger, CID, Johannesburg to Divisional CID Officer, Pietermaritzburg, 22/2/1928.

20. CNC PMB 81, 58/7/3, Inspector T.W. Hedges, SAP, Eshowe to Deputy Commissioner, SAP, Pietermaritzburg, 5/4/1928.

21. CNC PMB 81, 57/7/3, Magistrate, Vryheid to CNC, 15/2/1928.

22. MS NIC 2.08.1, File 5, J.H. Nicolson to G. Heaton Nicholls, 8/2/1928. See below.

23. CNC PMB 81, 58/7/1, Magistrate, Emtonjaneni to CNC, 9/3/1927.

24. CNC PMB 81, 58/7/1, Solomon kaDinuzulu to Magistrate, Nongoma, 4/7/1927, signed by 'L.N.' on Solomon's behalf (first quotation); CNC to Magistrate, Nongoma, 9/7/1927 (second quotation); and CNC to Magistrate, Nongoma, 13/7/1927 (third quotation).

25. CNC PMB 81, 58/7/3, Vyvyan, Bishop of Zululand to CNC, 3/9/1927; CNC to SNA, 19/10/1927 (first quotation); and CNC to Bishop of Zululand, 8/11/1927 (second quotation).

26. NTS 7205, 20/326, CNC to SNA, 23/4/1928; and see also CNC to SNA, 20/4/1928.

27. See Report of the Native Affairs Commission, 1924, UG 40–'25, pp. 19–20; and 1925–1926, UG17–'27, pp. 13–21, 50ff.

28. Select Committee Report on the Native Bills, SC10–'27, evidence of the Revd Z.R. Mahabane, ANC president, pp.299–300 (first quotation) and Chief W. Khumalo, member of the South African Chiefs' Convention, 1/6/1927, p. 289 (second quotation). News of the formation of the Chiefs' Convention was not welcomed by all chiefs in Natal; see evidence of Chiefs Kula and Swayimana, 15/6/1927, pp.382ff, where Swayimana argues that 'we do not feel the need to keep in touch with Natives in other provinces [or] to listen to these young people'.

29. This overview of the communist role in African politics has been drawn from Roux, *Time longer than rope*, pp. 211–12 (quotations); Davenport, *South Africa*; J. Lewis, '"The new unionism": industrialisation and industrial unions in South Africa, 1925–1930', in Webster (ed.), *Essays in southern African labour history*; and Nathaniel Weyl, *Traitors' end: the rise and fall of the communist movement in southern Africa* (New Rochelle, 1970). Weyl's work takes the form of an anti-communist polemic, in support of Apartheid, which celebrates the triumph of the South African state in defending capitalism and 'parliamentary government'; it nonetheless can be a useful factual source if treated with some circumspection.

30. *The Missionary Herald*, May 1926, p.194; and *The Net*, March 1928, p.6.

31. Select Committee Report on the Native Bills, SC10–'27, 'Resolutions of Convention of Bantu Chiefs', 15/4/1927, pp.292ff.

32. Report of the Native Affairs Commission, 1925–1926, UG17–'27, minutes of Native Conference, Pretoria, 2–6/12/1925, pp.13–18, 21. See also Marks, 'Ambiguities of dependence', p.25; and R.J. Haines, 'The opposition to General J.B.M. Hertzog's segregation bills, 1925–1936: a study in extra-parliamentary protest' (MA, University of Natal, Durban, 1978), p.123.

33. Select Committee Report on the Native Bills, SC10–'27, 'Resolutions of Convention of Bantu Chiefs', 15/4/1927, p.292 (first quotation); and Report of the Native Affairs Commission, 1925–1926, UG17–'27, minutes of Native Conference, Pretoria, 2–5/11/1926, p.72 (second quotation). Although Mtimkulu was then acting as representative of the 'Cape Native Voters' Convention', he was a solid member of Natal's 'old guard'. Generally, whatever attractions the Native Conference saw in the 'Union Native Council Bill' were overshadowed by the impotence of the existing Native Conferences and the loss of the Cape African franchise. See *ibid.*, pp.42–49, 56–84.

34. Rogers, *Native administration*, pp.82–83 (quotations); and Debates of the House of Assembly, vol.7, speeches on the Native Affairs, 1920, Amendment Bill, 17/5/1926, col.3560 (Hertzog quotation).

35. For an illuminating contrast between the 'erosion of the Cape African franchise' and the growth of the Natal-based 'segregation ideal', see Lacey, *Boroko*, pp.59–69, 84ff.

36. See G. Heaton Nicholls, *et al.*, *Report of the Special Committee on the Natives' Lands Commission: £11 000 000 per annum:a permanent asset worth more than the Rand is being thrown away* (published by the Zululand Planters' Union, 1917), a copy of which is stored in SNA II/5/4; MS CAMP, File 4, especially J.L. Dube to M. Campbell, 29/10/1908; and Marks, 'Ambiguities of dependence', pp.172–74, including footnote 50. G.H. Hulett maintained his interest in Natal 'native affairs' into the 1920s, and in the late 1920s he was one of the few 'sugar barons' who opposed the official resurrection of the Zulu monarchy. See NEC Box 4, evidence of G.H. Hulett, Stanger, 2/10/1930, pp.2002ff. For the ZNTI, see ch.5 above.

37. *Natal Advertiser*, 15/8/1917.

38. MS NIC 2.08.1, File 5, J.H. Nicolson to G. Heaton Nicholls, 8/2/1928.

39. See Select Committee Report on the Native Bills, SC10–'27, evidence of Chief Kula, 15/6/1927, pp.382ff.

40. *Natal Advertiser*, 7/2/1928.

41. See MS MAR 2.08.5, File 74, KCM 8338, statement of Cowley and Cowley (for Kadalie) *re Natal Witness*, 11/9/1926; Hawthorn, Cameron and Co. (for the *Natal Witness*) to J.S. Marwick, 21/3/1927; J.S. Marwick to Advocate Carlisle, 16/4/1927; and copies of evidence Marwick assembled for the defence.

42. MS MAR 2.08.5, File 74, KCM 8337, J.L. Dube to J.S. Marwick, 24/2/1928.

43. CNC PMB 84, 58/7/4, SNA to CNC, 7/5/1928, confidential, reporting Campbell's recent interview with the MNA.

44. NTS 7205, 20/326, CNC to SNA, 20/4/1928; Nicolson and Thorpe to CNC, 25/4/1928; CNC to SNA, 30/4/1928; SNA to CNC, 5/5/1928; and CNC's circular to all Natal magistrates, 7/5/1928.

ISAZISO.

ASTOUNDING NOTICE.

□□□□ ····· □□□□··········□□□□□□□□□

A HERCULEAN

Monster Meeting

— OF THE —

INDUSTRIAL & COMMERCIAL WORKERS UNION OF AFRICA I.C.U.

(Durban Branch.)

All Roads should lead to the

☞ Rawat's Bioscope Hall ☜

VICTORIA STREET,

To Join the Great Campaign for Emancipation of the African Workers.

Ladies and Gentlemen,—If we are the Producers and the white men the Consumers then we must be entitle to **EQUAL PAY FOR EQUAL WORK.**

This meeting will take place on Sunday 1st Feb. 1925 in the above Hall at 10-30 a.m.

. . Programme . .

From 10-30 a.m., nKosi Sikeleli Africa and Religious Service till 11 a.m.

1. Communication Report.
2. Appointment of Delegates.
3. Motions for the Conference.
4. Consideration of proposed Native Females medical examination and Pass enforcement.

5. Consideration of proposed uniform Taxation.
6. Presentation and consideration of Congress Resolutions
7. Endorsement of Bloemfontein I.C.U. Resolutions.
8. Special collection will be requested of 1/- from everybody.

There is a likelihood of the General Secretary being present at the Meeting.

The following languages will be spoken with Interpreters:
ZULU, SESUTO, DUTCH and ENGLISH.

Workers of Durban and the whole Coast Belt Industrial Organisation is the only effective weapon to wrong out existing disabilities amongst THE AFRICAN RACES.   "   "   "   "   "

REMEMBER! at the RAWAT'S BIOSCOPE HALL, Victoria Street, Durban, 1st February, 25th.

UHLINGANISO OMKULU WEZI SEBENZI ZASE AFRICA mhla ziu 1st February 1925 e, RAWATS BIOSCOPE HALL, Victoria Street, Durban. Lomhlanzano uyo qala ngo 10-30 ekuseni into yokusuta ngei sifunda ama pepa i Komo uhusulela ku 10-30 kuse kube ngu 11 a.m. Kube sekungena izindaba lezi esikwnala ngo popula usingeni bakitinidaba sinkulu ngoba impilo yomntu Upata kwel tukuruku sake lesi esikulima ngazo Blukanini ima jingaba vesi bcdunto nolsa pisi ubhlanga aba qedd baso noma abaachenini, uma tunjalo sifancle irolo ellilingana nomonkanzi,

By Order of the Executive Committee I.C.U

ALEXANDER B. HHDDDLA, Secretary and Tr—————

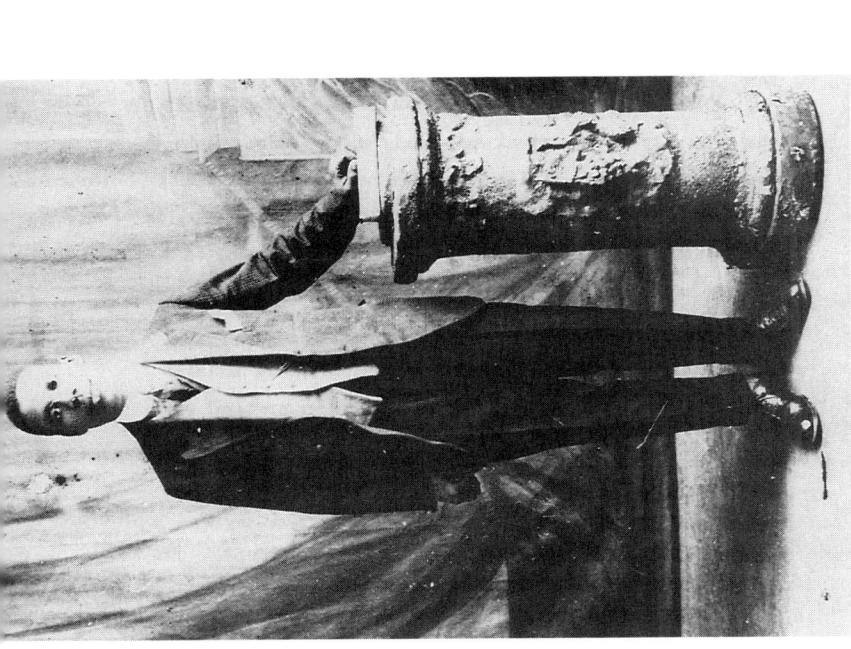

Above: A. W. G. Champion

Right: The rise of the ICU *yase* Natal.

Protocol No.   /1928.

DEED OF TRUST AND CONSTITUTION

of the

INKATA ka ZULU (ZULU NATIONAL CONGRESS).

KNOW ALL MEN WHOM IT MAY CONCERN :

THAT on this the *28* day of *July* , in the Year of Our Lord One Thousand Nine Hundred and Twenty Eight, before me, JOSEPH HENRY NICOLSON of Durban, Natal, NOTARY PUBLIC, by the authority of Government duly admitted and sworn and in the presence of the subscribing Witnesses, personally came and appeared *Alfred Stead, Candidate Attorney,* of Durban, in his capacity as the duly authorised Agent and Attorney of SOLOMON ka DINUZULU, William Foshla HHULOSE, MNYAYIZA ka NDABUKO? Simon Gilbert Evans MAJOSI, JOHN LANGALIBALELE DUBE, NKANTINI ZULU and SILIMANA ZULU under Powers of Attorney duly filed in my protocol with the original hereof.

AND THE APPEARER duly authorised as aforesaid did DECLARE that whereas the Zulu Nation is in danger of becoming a

scattered /

1928 Inkatha constitution

scattered people, with no common responsibilities as a Nation;

★ AND WHEREAS, in proportion to the growth of the danger it becomes daily more necessary to foster by every constitutional means the spirit of unity among the people of the Zulu Nation throughout the Union of South Africa, and to keep alive the Nation' fine traditions, and its sense of the obligations imposed upon it by these traditions, toward the other races of the Union of South Africa both Native and European;

AND WHEREAS it has become expedient to organise the heads of the Nation, and its responsible members in such a manner, and under such constitution as will have the approval and sympathy of the Government of the Union of South Africa;

AND WHEREAS it has been decided by such Heads, and members of the Nation as the result of meetings held from time to time during the last/years, that a Zulu National Congress be constituted, under the patronage of the Hereditary Head of the Zulu Family whose loyal devotion to the best interests, and traditions of his People have been so constantly and practically shown, and that such Congress be known as "INKATA ka ZULU" in other words "EMBLEM OF THE UNITY OF THE ZULU NATION".

AND WHEREAS it is expedient that the objects, constitution, terms and conditions of the Inkata ka Zulu (Zulu National Congress) should be reduced to writing;

AND WHEREAS at a meeting of Chiefs of the Zulu Nation, held at Mahashini, Nongoma, Zululand, on the 22nd day of June, 1928, a formal draft constitution was laid before such Chiefs and approved;

AND WHEREAS at a meeting of Zulu Chiefs and members of the Nation held at Mahashini aforesaid on the 2nd day of June, 1928, the following resolutions were passed, viz:

1. /

George Heaton Nicholls

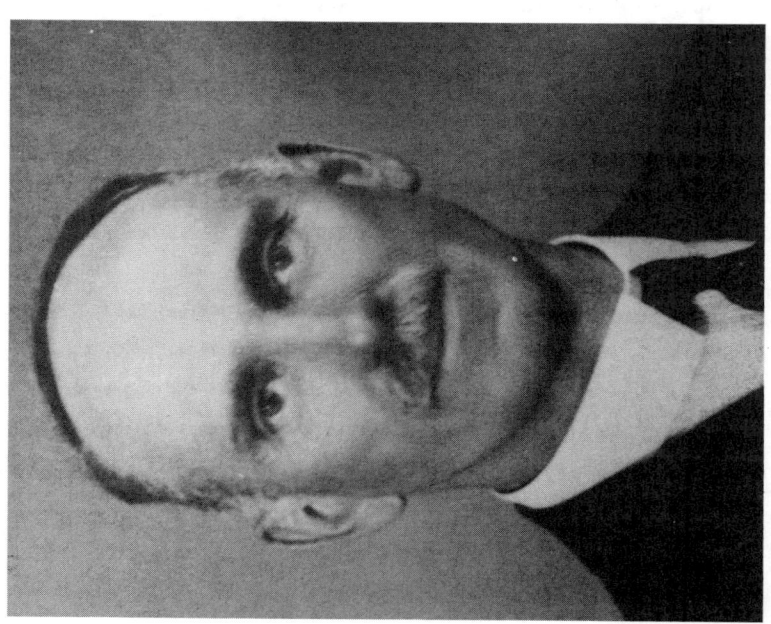

J.S. Marwick, 'Muhle'

8

The reconstitution of Inkatha

Inkatha's annual meeting of 1928 began, as was customary, with a private meeting of the executive committee, which unanimously passed the new draft constitution. Solomon did not attend this meeting, nor the 'open' meetings of Inkatha's ordinary members in the following days, being confined to bed and seriously ill with what the Revd Oscroft described as 'rheumatic gout'.[1] Solomon's taste for liquor, apparently, was starting to take its toll. Apart from Oscroft, the only white people to attend were the lawyer J.H.Nicolson and the ex-magistrate Oswald Fynney; Inkatha's most influential white allies had always intended to remain in the background.

Oscroft estimated that over two thousand Zulu attended the meeting. Among them there were over sixty chiefs and accredited chiefs' representatives, mainly from Zululand and Northern Natal, though some had come from as far afield as Umzinto, Richmond, Harding and Pinetown in Natal proper, and the Ingwavuma district on the border of Portuguese East Africa. The Zulu-speaking kholwa establishment was also strongly represented, and the close co-operation of the old and new Zulu elites was a marked feature of the 1928 meeting in every sphere of its proceedings.

The chairman, William Bhulose, opened the general Inkatha meeting by announcing that the time had come for Inkatha to be 'legally' established 'so that it should obtain the recognition and favourable support of the Government'. He explained the main points of the proposed new constitution, and moved that the latter be formally approved by the meeting. Chiefs Nkantini and Msiyane (who had represented Zululand alongside Matole at the Native Conferences) seconded Bhulose.

There followed many objections from the delegates to the passing of the proposed constitution without a thorough discussion of its contents. The size of the meeting made this impracticable, and a compromise was agreed upon: all the chiefs and ministers of religion present were appointed to form a special committee to discuss the constitution. This special committee, following a day's deliberations, made minor amendments. It also elected Inkatha's office bearers for the forthcoming year: Bhulose was re-elected as chairman; Chief S.G.E. Majozi became vice-chairman; and Solomon was elected as treasurer. Significantly, the appointment of the secretary was left to a later date; it was very likely that Inkatha leaders desired the government to nominate an NAD official for this position. The following non-office-bearing members completed the new Inkatha executive committee: Mnyaiza, Chief Nkantini, Chief Silimane (son of Mkungo Zulu, a brother of Cetshwayo who had fled to the Colony of Natal in 1856), John Dube, and the Revd E.A. Mahamba (a minister of the Free Church of Scotland from the Dundee district). Finally, two patrons of Inkatha were elected: one was Solomon, and the other Oswald Fynney. All decisions of the special committee were subsequently approved by the general meeting, and Nicolson and Thorpe were authorised to legally 'execute' the 'Deed of Trust and Constitution of the Inkata ka Zulu'.[2]

The 1928 constitution was clearly based on the 1926 Inkatha constitution. However, there were certain important differences of emphasis in the 'official' constitution which presented Inkatha in a more favourable light from the perspectives of both segregationist ideology and the local council policy. Thus, the preamble to the 1928 constitution emphasised that it was necessary 'to foster by every constitutional means the spirit of unity among the people of the Zulu Nation . . . and to keep alive the Nation's fine traditions, and its sense of obligations imposed upon it by these traditions . . .' Furthermore, it had become expedient to 'organise the heads of the Nation, and its responsible members in such a manner, and under such constitution as will have the approval and sympathy of the Government of the Union of South Africa'.

The 1928 constitution's statement of Inkatha's aims was essentially identical to that of 1926, but there were important additional aims. Inkatha now dedicated itself to the 'proper development' of the reserves, which probably meant that commercial agriculture, trade and small industries would be encouraged there. And Inkatha would foster the Zulu wish to maintain separate traditions, social discipline and a sense of nationhood. In this context, it was said that Inkatha would

> promote and encourage the development and progress of the Nation along such lines as will naturally be evolved out of the life and traditions of its people and to prepare them for the establishment of their own trade and industries.

Three points deserve special mention. First, no 'agents' or 'collectors' were to be authorised to receive subscriptions; all payments had to be made directly to the secretary who would keep 'proper books'. Moreover, a 'European accountant' would examine Inkatha's balance sheets and financial statements annually. By 1928 it had become widely known in NAD circles that Inkatha's monies were being misappropriated, primarily by Solomon, and these regulations were presumably intended to persuade the government that this would not happen in future. Second, the Inkatha executive committee was empowered to co-opt white people to 'assist in their deliberations', even though whites could not be members of Inkatha. Third, and concerning the relationship of Inkatha to the head of the Zulu royal family, it was laid down that the latter would always be a 'patron' of Inkatha; and 'if possible' a descendant of the Zulu kings would always be treasurer. The executive committee was not bound to act on the resolutions of Inkatha's committee of 'heads of the nation', comprising all chiefs and certain appointed ministers of religion, but in the event of a deadlock between these two bodies the outcome would be decided by a general vote at a full meeting. It was thus envisaged that, under Inkatha, the Zulu nation would be a constitutional monarchy.[3]

The constitutional 'democratisation' of Inkatha was an important development. Solomon had always attempted to superimpose the traditional prerogatives of a Zulu monarch on Inkatha's organisational structure: he had sought to treat the executive committee as a royal *ibandla* (king's council) of which he, and not the elected chairman, remained the executive head. Now the constitution specifically stated that the chairman would be 'in charge' of Inkatha, and would have a casting vote in the executive committee. The conflict of royal and kholwa opinion on this matter had been one of the main reasons for Inkatha's virtual disintegration in 1926 and 1927. In 1928, kholwa interests triumphed. The democratisation of Inkatha also meant that the organisation was now more in accordance with the basic tenets of local council policy – which, even as amended in 1926, envisaged that the internal operation of the local councils would accord with the Westminster-style democratic principle. Moreover, it meant that Inkatha might now be more readily favoured by the Natal NAD, which overall was still vehemently opposed to the resurrection of the historic 'autocratic' powers of the Zulu royal family. In 1928, Oscroft appreciatively reported: 'In the past, Solomon's word was law . . . the Indhlu Nkulu [great house] was supreme. The Inkata existed for the royal house. Under the new Constitution, the position will gradually be reversed, the royal house becoming part of the Inkata . . .'[4]

Apart from approving the new constitution and re-establishing Inkatha as a working alliance between the kholwa and tribal elites, the 1928 meeting was also important insofar as it clearly defined Inkatha as an opponent of militancy. Oscroft's report stated that there was no evidence of 'the slightest connection' between Inkatha and the ICU. In view of the strong suspicions of police and Natal NAD officials during the first half of 1928 that a connection did exist, this statement was not as redundant as it might appear. While no ICU leader dared to attend the meeting, Lymon Maling, the ALU leader, did do so. Inkatha's responses to Maling's appearance at the 1928 meeting and his subsequent attempts to penetrate the 'new' Inkatha not only illustrates Inkatha's role as an opponent of militancy, but also effectively summarises Inkatha's activities between 1928 and 1930.

Oscroft's report of the 1928 meeting recounted that Maling, 'of the agitator type, from Vryheid', attempted to address the meeting: 'Those present were obviously quite hostile towards him, and he was pulled up by the chairman and informed that he had no right to speak as he was not a member of the Inkata. Nothing more was heard of him.'[5] Maling reappeared at the annual Inkatha meeting in June 1929. Bhulose submitted a report of the meeting's resolutions, where it was recorded that the 'most vital question' at the meeting was that of land tenure; the matter had been 'introduced by poor suffering Natives – especially from the district of Vryheid'. No resolution was permitted, however, 'owing to the overheated arguments advanced'. It was thereafter decided to refer the matter to 'a special meeting of Chiefs only' the following month.[6]

Maling attended this special meeting in August 1929, even though it was called for chiefs only. Chief Nkantini took the chair. As it transpired, this was Maling's greatest success in the context of Inkatha: he was elected to represent the Vryheid district on a specially-convened 'Inkatha land committee' which was to accompany Solomon to Pretoria to 'take forward our wail to the Government'. Of the twelve members of this committee, only Maling, the Revd Mathe and Samuel kaDinuzulu Zulu (David's full brother) were not chiefs. In this august company, Maling had to defer to the *hamba kahle* – and ineffectual – political strategies of the Zulu tribal establishment. In contrast to the ALU petitions, which had been forthright in content and were sent directly to the House of Assembly or the Prime Minister, the chiefs' meeting sent a somewhat rambling 'request' to the magistrate at Nongoma, pleading 'to go to hear from our father the Government what it is that we his children have now done that we then should be made mere wanderers in the hills'. The request was routinely rejected.[7]

Because of the support he had come to command among the Zulu in Northern Natal, including important chiefs there, after 1928 Maling could no longer be simply rejected by Inkatha's dominant clique. Once he had gained a foothold in Inkatha, however, it was his political position rather than Inkatha's that was redefined. In 1930 Maling gave evidence before the Native Economic Commission, accompanied by a deputation, and claimed to be the chosen representative of all Zulu in Northern Natal and Solomon's regional official in that area. Evidence suggests that these claims were not unjustified. He spoke almost exclusively on behalf of ordinary labour tenants and farm workers, but the political opinions he tendered before the commission suggested that he was now identifying more with the tribal and kholwa elites. '[Natives] must be given the chance to develop their own civilisation and good things in their customs', he said, the most important of which was the 'showing of respect to elders and those in authority'. He also reported that he had been attempting to establish a Joint Council in Vryheid.[8] There was in fact nothing in Maling's evidence that would not have been heartily endorsed at the Inkatha meeting of 1928.

Between 1928 and 1930, Inkatha played the role of an ideological bulwark against rank-and-file militancy on the one hand, and an ideological bastion of Zulu nationalism and the most conservative elements in Zulu society on the other hand. Apart from the abortive attempt to send a chiefs' deputation to Pretoria in 1929 to 'wail' about evictions, Inkatha took virtually no practical political action during this period. The main purpose of the reconstitution of Inkatha in 1928 had been to formalise Inkatha in such a way as to make it a more attractive ally of the state. In effect, Inkatha was pressing the Union government to implement among the Zulu a more thoroughgoing policy of segregation, allowing for greater powers of self-government, than was currently envisaged in ruling circles. After the 1928 meeting, Inkatha entered a period of paralysis as it awaited the government's response – which was a long time in coming.

* * * * *

The individuals principally responsible for the reconstitution of Inkatha, representing Natal's white rural employers and the Zulu-speaking kholwa establishment, had come together in the first instance because they wished to counter the class threat that the ICU was seen to pose. In the context of the reconstituted Inkatha however, they co-operated not only as opponents of the ICU but also as advocates of 'tribalism', Zulu nationalism, and Zulu 'self-government'. Clearly enough, the aim of fostering those aspects of tribalism that prescribed respect for 'authority' and 'social discipline' generally was not in the interests of popular protest; neither was the cultivation of Zulu nationalism as a *hamba kahle* political force. But the aim of establishing a measure of Zulu national autonomy or self-government –

which was keenly supported by Heaton Nicholls – made it manifest that Inkatha's purpose went beyond the obstruction of popular protest.

Inkatha's white supporters primarily represented the sugar planting interest ('sugar barons' were the most prominent of Inkatha's white supporters) and the Natal commercial farming interest. These two 'fractions' of rural capital in Natal had acted in alliance since 1920 in regard to labour matters and 'native policy'. Their support for Inkatha after 1928 was a further development of this existing alliance – which in the first instance had set out to secure a cheap, tractable and abundant supply of African labour.

The sugar industry had become dependent on Africa labour when the Union government terminated the importation of indentured Indian labour in 1911. But sugar planters soon found that they could not rely on the African reserves for labour; the highly capitalised gold-mining recruitment networks had long held a virtual monopoly over those reserve Africans who were willing to bind themselves to employment contracts. Neither could they draw labour from the African population in the province's white countryside: farmers fiercely defended 'their' labour supply against encroachment by labour recruiters, and, moreover, tended to demand labour service from their tenants erratically throughout the year which prevented the latter taking up 'outside' contract work. In the transition from indentured Indian labour, the sugar industry came to favour a migrant form of African labour and drew its labourers mainly from Pondoland, Tongaland and Mozambique – rather than from within the province.

However, following the rapid expansion of the sugar industry – particularly in Zululand – during the first decade of Union, the industry was afflicted with a chronic labour shortage. The latter persisted although the industry expanded the geographical scope of its recruiting activities in 1918 by establishing the 'Natal Coast Labour Recruiting Corporation (which was based on the model of the gold-mines' Native Recruiting Corporation'). By 1920, the sugar industry had come to realise that the only hope for a long-term solution to its labour shortage lay in the greater exploitation of the labour resources within the province of Natal. This did not bring the sugar industry into conflict with Natal's farmers. The sugar planters sought to employ the inhabitants of the province's reserves as migrant labourers, on a seasonal basis, while the farmers sought to bind the African inhabitants of the white countryside more firmly to labour tenancy contracts.[9]

Soon after their election to parliament in 1920, Heaton Nicholls (who had stood for parliament as a sugar representative) and Marwick (who acted as leader of the MPs for the rural constituencies of Natal proper) established themselves as allies and Natal's leading spokesmen on labour and 'native' matters. Their alliance as representatives of the labour interests of Natal's planters and farmers was clearly illustrated in 1921. In that year, Marwick introduced to parliament a catalogue of proposals – which Heaton Nicholls was the first to support – concerning 'methods of ensuring an increased and more constant supply' of African labour in the country districts. The proposals sought principally to remedy the 'extreme tendency . . . for natives to drift to the towns and labour centres' (Marwick), where there was already 'an enormous amount of wastage in Native labour' (Heaton Nicholls), and where migrant youths came under such a 'strong detribalising influence' that they returned to the rural areas 'utterly demoralised' and incapable of respect for authority (Marwick).[10] Among the measures that were persistently advocated to counter the 'rural exodus' were the revision of the Pass Laws, so that a more rigorous policy of influx countrol could be implemented, and the prohibition of the system of 'advances' which mining recruiters had instituted to lure labour to the compounds. Overall, the aim of the Natal planter/farmer alliance was to retain Natal's rural labour supply in Natal's rural districts. More specifically, the alliance sought to secure 'first option' on the labour resources of Natal's coastal and midlands reserves for the sugar industry, and to bind more securely the labour resources of the white countryside to Natal's white farmers.

Natal's planters and farmers did not only appeal to the state to resolve their labour problems, especially since the state was so slow to respond. They also took action of their own at local level, seeking to use tribalism and tribal authorities (chiefs and homestead heads) as a means of securing better control over the local labour force. In the rural districts of Natal in the 1920s, a particularly Natal-style 'solution' to both the labour and 'native' questions was taking form, based on a loose accord, if not an alliance, between rural employers and tribal authorities.

Natal's farmers strongly favoured a form of labour contract that was based on the tribal order at the level of the family. This was known as the 'kraalhead system', whereby the labour contract was made with the homestead head in his capacity as head of his family, and thus included all members of the homestead. In this way, much of the responsibility of controlling the labour force was conveniently left to the homestead heads. The engagement of whole homesteads as productive units, furthermore, meant that the labour force was able to provide for its own means of subsistence, and hence the costs of food and housing were not incurred by the employer. Farmers strongly felt that the process of 'detribalisation' was a social evil, generally because it undermined the whole 'kraalhead system', and particularly because it increased the likelihood of young labourers deserting the employment to which they had been bound by their tribal superiors or family elders. The chairman of the Ngogo Farmers' Association at Newcastle might equally have been speaking on behalf of tribal authorities when he complained of the tendency among youths to 'defy their parents' and to abscond to the towns where they learnt further 'irresponsible' habits; so too when he painted an idyllic picture of the 'olden days' when chiefs and homestead heads were 'respected and obeyed by everyone in the kraal'.[11]

Throughout the 1920s, Natal's farmers resolutely defended the 'kraalhead system' against the forces of 'detribalisation'. One method was to refuse to pay sons individually for any work performed outside the six-month term of unwaged labour service normally required under the 'kraalhead contract'. Instead, farmers paid an 'aggregate wage' to homestead heads, thus bolstering patriarchal authority and enabling homestead heads to take 'commission' before redistributing the payment among the family. Farmers' representatives also persistently called for the enactment of new legislation to reinforce the 'kraalhead system'. They were rewarded by the 1932 Native Service Contract Act, which for the first time made legal provision for a 'unit of employment' to comprise a married man together with his wives and offspring, thus countering the 'detribalised individualism' of sons who tried to insist on their own separate labour tenancy arrangements. Moreover, the Act laid down that sons could only seek work away from the white countryside with the written consent of their parents and their landlords.[12]

Like Natal's farmers, the sugar planters were well aware that the preservation of tribal order was in their interests as employers of labour. Planters generally regarded the process of detribalisation as closely linked to the increasing incidence of desertion, and knew that it undermined homestead productivity in the reserves on which the cheapness of plantation labour depended. Significantly, they became increasingly concerned about detribalisation at the same time as their demands for Zulu labour were becoming more urgent. Planters also knew that Zulu tribal authorities were similarly concerned about detribalisation, especially in the light of the growing tendency among migrant workers not to remit their wages to the reserves to be redistributed in a tribal fashion. For the planters, the possibility of a 'labour alliance' with tribal authorities became very attractive after 1925, when the secretary of the Zululand Planters' Union, C. W. Dent, described the sugar industry's labour problems as 'acute'.[13]

More Zulu labourers had begun to arrive on the plantations, in fact, in the wake of evictions from the white countryside and as a result of reserve congestion. However, they arrived neither in sufficient numbers nor with any intention of adhering to the six-month plantation contracts, which covered the labour-intensive cutting season. Thus planters sought not only to attract more Zulu labourers to the plantations, but also to devise a system of ensuring that they adhered to their contracts. Various 'experts' – including Dr G. A. Park-Ross (District Medical Officer of Health), C. A. Wheelwright (CNC), and H. S. Fynn (Inspector of Native Labour, Natal) – advised the sugar industry that increased wages and better food, housing and working conditions were the ways to achieve its objectives among the Zulu. The sugar industry nevertheless favoured more coercive strategies, as was vividly illustrated in the proposals the South African Sugar Association made to the NAD, shortly after the NAD began distributing food among the Zulu during the drought of 1931 to 1932. The proposals (which were rejected) were that the NAD should require every homestead head who accepted food to undertake to supply labour to the sugar industry; in return, the sugar industry would contribute to the cost of famine relief.[14]

The main coercive strategy that the sugar industry favoured after the mid-1920s, however, was rather more subtle: it aimed to motivate Zulu tribal authorities to send young men to the plantations. The sugar industry set out to institutionalise a 'deferred pay scheme', under which plantation labourers would receive only small payments while they were working, and a lump sum on the expiry of their contracts and on the eve of their return to the reserves. From the point of view of tribal authorities and workers' dependants, this would ensure that workers would return with six months' wages almost intact. Planters, for their part, could rest assured that workers would not desert before the expiry of their contracts. It was envisaged that tribal authorities would act as the sugar industry's labour agents, altering the pattern of Zulu labour migration away from the towns and towards the plantations.[15] The problem of labour shortage on the sugar plantations was, nonetheless, never satisfactorily resolved during the 1920s.

On more than one occasion, NAD officials protested that the sugar industry was injudicious in its attempts to recruit Zulu labour. This was the case when the sugar baron William Campbell visited the MNA early in 1928, on the eve of the reconstitution of Inkatha, requesting that Solomon be recognised as Zulu king and offering to settle Solomon's debts. While the MNA listened to Campbell's proposals with some sympathy, the SNA immediately and indignantly concluded that the 'scheme' represented 'nothing more nor less than an attempt to get Solomon under the thumb of the employers of labour'.[16] There was considerable foundation for the SNA's views. In 1928, sugar planters had good reason to take such drastic action as offering to settle Solomon's debts, which already amounted to thousands of pounds, in order to secure Zulu labour. Under the terms of the Mozambique Convention that came into force in 1928, it was laid down that Mozambican migrant labourers could no longer take up employment anywhere in the Union except on the gold-mines. Hitherto, labourers from the Portuguese east coast had formed an important component of the planters' labour force, being the only reliable supply of labour that was immune to malaria.[17] Broadly, the move to support the Zulu monarchy from 1928 represented a further development of the Natal planter/farmer alliance of the 1920s, which had always involved the preservation of tribalism and the use of tribal authorities as suppliers and controllers of labour.

*   *   *   *   *

Planters' and farmers' objectives regarding Solomon and Inkatha were, however, not only related to their labour objectives. By 1928, the spread of 'socialistic' propaganda through the African population had persuaded Natal's rural whites that the whole structure of white rule in South Africa was under threat. One response had been to call for more vigorous state repression. The Natal Agricultural Union (principally representative of Farmers' Associations in the province, but also representative of Planters' Unions), for example, made a deputation to the MNA in 1927, pleading for the banning of all 'native meetings' except those conducted with official sanction.[18] Another response, however, was to call for the implementation of a thoroughly segregationist 'native policy' which would meet the expressly political threats that were seen to be confronting white South Africa. Solomon and Inkatha, whose political leanings were both collaboratory and separatist, were regarded as the planters' and farmers' African allies in the pursuit of a segregationist 'settlement' of the 'native question' in Natal.

Natal's rural whites were very disturbed by the tendency among African leaders to adopt 'European' political ideas. 'British' liberal-democratic notions among the African middle class were seen to be almost as revolutionary as 'Russian' socialist notions among African workers. Hertzog's 1926 'Native Bills' were, in influential quarters of white Natal, considered to be giving state encouragement to the 'Europeanisation' of African politics in that they envisaged the establishment of an elective Union Native Council and sought to permit Africans to elect seven white representatives to the House of Assembly. These provisions would give Africans in Natal a voice in the central white government for the first time, and, moreover, would do so on the basis of the democratic principle.[19]

Throughout the 1920s, Marwick and Heaton Nicholls consistently advocated the extension of the powers of chiefs, and, though they approved of the principle of African local self-government and political representation in the rural areas, they opposed the application of the local councils policy in Natal on the grounds that it would undermine tribalism. And in a long and elaborate speech in early 1927, Heaton Nicholls argued that the democratic principles embodied in Hertzog's 'Native Bills' were both dangerous and unnecessary. What was necessary, he suggested, was that a more thorough understanding of 'the psychology of the native' and of tribal law and custom should guide the evolution of 'native policy'. Heaton Nicholls also reminded parliament that Africans had a particular economic role to play in South Africa, since cheap African labour was the foundation on which white South African civilisation and wealth depended. He contended that Hertzog had not adequately considered this fact when formulating the 1926 'Native Bills', and his contention was strongly supported by Marwick.[20]

Marwick and Heaton Nicholls developed their segregationist ideas in the course of supporting the Native Administration Bill, which became the Native Administration Act of 1927. They argued that, by prescribing the political and cultural separateness of Africans from Europeans, the bill was founded on anthropological 'fact'. 'Native customs and usages', Marwick emphasised, were 'invested with a national and civic value'. Heaton Nicholls held that state 'native policy' had to choose between two alternatives: the Cape system which sought to foster 'individualism' and impose European-style democracy on the African population, and the Natal system which sought to maintain tribalism and 'develop the native on his own lines' – as was desired by the 'vast majority of natives in this country'. 'Native policy' had to be based on modern anthropological knowledge and 'the sure foundations of tribal custom and tradition'.[21]

As members of the select committee on the 'Native Bills', which had been tabled in parliament by Hertzog in 1926, Heaton Nicholls and Marwick acted together to represent what they saw as the 'Natal view' on 'native affairs'. By Heaton Nicholls's, own account, they had the full sanction of Natal MPs to do so. In this context, Heaton Nicholls emerged as the leading ideologue, reinterpreting and elaborating the segregationist principles that Natal had inherited from the days of Shepstone. He set out his ideas in a number of memoranda and private letters. In a private letter dated May 1929, he wrote, 'I do not believe that black and white can continue to exist as two separate classes in a South African democracy . . . we cannot long continue as a white aristocracy and a black proletariat'. Whites were faced with a choice between 'a Bantu Nation whose evolving civilisation we can advance and respect, which shall find its national pride in the cultivation of its separateness, or a Black proletariat using all the recognised methods for the complete overthrow of the whites on the basis of class.'[22]

As an alternative to a unitary South Africa with African representation in the House of Assembly, Heaton Nicholls believed that state policy should foster self-governing 'Bantu Nations', founded on tribal rather than democratic principles, in the the Union's reserves. In an unaddressed and unsigned draft letter, probably written in 1929, he wrote:

The policy of a Bantu Nation . . . obviously brings in its train a pride of race. The most race proud man I know is Solomon. He glories in his race and its past prowess; and there is no native in the Union who is so earnestly desirous of maintaining Bantu Purity . . . There is everything to be said for creating the Inkata the Native Council for Zululand.[23]

Although Heaton Nicholls mainly emphasised the importance of chiefs and tribal authorities, he felt that educated Africans had a leading role to play in 'developing' their respective 'Bantu Nations'. In the reserves, Africans were to be eligible for all posts in the civil service, and were to be encouraged to enter the professional and commercial careers that, in practice, were then monopolised by whites. Here were opportunities for the aspirant African middle class.[24]

*   *   *   *   *

There was considerable congruity between Heaton Nicholls's views and those that developed during the late 1920s among intellectuals of Natal's kholwa establishment. The latter, on their own account, had become increasingly anxious to stave off a 'class war' as class antagonisms sharpened both within African society and between black and white. Indeed, hovering uncomfortably in the marginal area between white capitalists and black workers, the African middle class was keenly aware of the insecurities of its position. Dube personally had a foretaste of what seemed to lie in store when, as tension was mounting in Durban prior to the beerhall riots of mid-1929, a 'class skirmish' disrupted his meeting to revive the Durban branch of the old NNC. An '*amalayita* gang', *Ilanga lase Natal* reported, invaded this meeting of 'chiefs and respectable natives' and turned it into a debacle.[25]

During the late 1920s, the ideological mainstream of Natal's kholwa establishment was infused with a powerful new element: a moral indignation against 'foreign' (meaning Russian), 'anti-religious' and 'socially divisive' working-class doctrines. Simultaneously, kholwa ideologues further elaborated the ideology of African or, more specifically, Zulu nationalism that had underpinned their interest in Inkatha from the outset. This ideology came to be more explicitly expressed as one of 'national rebuilding', which envisaged the construction of a 'new African civilisation' on the foundation of its tribal predecessor. Increasing moral value was attached to social unity and respect for hereditary chiefs, whose appeal to vertical tribal loyalties was seen to be the key to the reimposition of 'control' over a society that was fast falling apart at the seams, and, in so doing, was threatening to tear itself away from both its old and new elites.

After 1928 and until the early 1930s, *Ilanga lase Natal* frequently featured articles which were intended to 'warn our people against Bolshevism which is now being freely preached' and counter the 'ignorance that makes our people listen to these foreigners'. Readers were advised against joining Gumede's 'League of African Rights' because 'to hand over the reins of power to the proletariat is for the most savage and ruthless brute . . . to do absolutely what he likes. Such a prospect might be pleasing . . . to one who hates all the moral laws of God.' *Ilanga lase Natal* expected that its readers' respect for both the 'laws' of the Christian God and those of African tradition – which would have been considered incompatible a decade previously – should assist them in their rejection of communism.[26]

The evidence of leading kholwa ideologues before the Native Economic Commission indicated that the rural areas – and more particularly the reserves – were being regarded as the natural domain of 'respectable' African culture. The social influence of the urban areas was seen to be the root cause of African 'social disintegration'; there, it was believed, 'ignorant' and 'uneducated' Africans picked up the worst of white habits. Whereas the kholwa elite had long considered tribal 'barbarity' and 'primitiveness' as the antithesis of mission station 'respectability', great emphasis was now placed on the inherent dignity of hereditary chiefs, their importance as inheritors of African tradition, and the value of tribalism as a means of promoting social propriety. Chief Simon Majozi of the Indaleni mission community, a member of Inkatha's executive committee and a keen tennis player, dwelled on the value of the *hlonipa* custom which prescribed 'respect'. The tribal system was 'in essence representative', he said, as was illustrated in the action that chiefs took against 'agitators'. Chiefs Dirk Sioka and Stephen Mini, kholwa-chief stalwarts of the old NNC, endorsed Majozi's call for the extension of chiefly authority, while Mrs Sibusisiwe Makanya, secretary of the 'progressive' 'Bantu Youth League', felt that tribalism was a remedy for the iniquitous social consequences of labour migrancy.[27]

In all these ideological developments, Natal's kholwa establishment had been influenced by white liberals. After 1925, while communists were developing a network of night schools in the urban areas to offer 'appropriate' education to African workers, Christian or liberal organisations were establishing a variety of educational and social institutions designed primarily to assist the kholwa to take up roles of social leadership. The ideological dissimilarity between CP and liberal night school was very clear. In the former, pupils 'struggled with complicated political doctrines at the same time as they learnt their letters'; by contrast, the Bantu Men's Social Centres offered classes up to Junior Certificate level in the interests of 'development and civilisation', and bookkeeping classes for 'business pursuits'.[28] As African education flourished so too did African newspapers, stimulating an unprecedented spirit of African enquiry into the question of social and political development – which state legislators had been anxious to preserve as their exclusive domain.

The guidance that Christians and liberals offered the kholwa in this context was illustrated in the address that the Revd R.E. Phillips of the Johannesburg Bantu Mens' Social Centre presented to the Natal Missionary Conference in 1929. This address, entitled 'Communism or Christianity: The present-day question for Native youth', was dominated by a measured denunciation of the moral evils of communism. Phillips favoured the promotion of African commercial and agricultural co-operative societies – or 'self-help' schemes – through which Africans themselves were to play a leading role in their own 'social reconstruction' on 'progressive lines'. Similarly, D.R.O. Thomas, tutor of the Durban 'Workers' Educational Association' (a liberal institution), felt strongly that the 'self-help' strategy was particularly appropriate in the African context: co-operative societies were compatible with 'the tradition of the Native people to look to communal prosperity'. This tribal communalism, which was morally laudable, was to be a positive advantage in the transition from a redistributive subsistence economy to one of 'industrial progress' or capital accumulation.[29]

The burden of liberal guidance to kholwa leaders was therefore that they should grapple with the social problems of their day with their own hands, and go out among 'their own people' with the express purpose of building a progressive new African society on the old tribal base. In this context it is significant that J.D. Rheinallt Jones, editor of the anthropological journal *Bantu Studies*, instituted a weekly seminar with the Bantu Mens' Social Centres where the 'African who aspires for leadership among his people' could 'discuss Native Law and Custom and Economics'.[30] Although white Christians and liberals still tended to verbalise a fondness for a liberal-democratic solution to the political aspects of the 'native question', in practice they were now coming to explore a solution that closely accorded with the anthropological/segregationist ideas of Natal's leading 'native policy' legislators.

In 1929, Pixley Seme began a campaign through the columns of *Ilanga lase Natal* to publicise the newly established 'Native Land and Trust Company of Africa, Limited'. This in practice represented part of his political manifesto for his successful election campaign for the presidency of the ANC. And Seme, a Natalian in Johannesburg, largely owed his triumph over the 'red' Gumede in 1930 to the strong support of the Natal kholwa establishment. The purpose of the company was described to *Ilanga lase Natal*'s readership as follows:

> Our main object should be to develop our people and the Native Reserves to the very best extent of which they may be capable, commercially and industrially, and to inspire into our people the spirit of co-operation and self-help to form model modern Townships for the tribal Natives after the style of the Mission Reserves in Natal . . . Then and not until then can we Africans hope to develop a civilisation which shall be our own, a civilisation which shall be more spiritual and humanistic [by implication, than the Europeans'].

Seme argued that if Africans were 'to achieve their economic independence and self-help', they had to have more land than the 'Union Landless Natives Act' (as he described it) had set aside as reserves. More land would also serve to curb the 'drift of landless Natives to towns where they become demoralised'. It was therefore especially important that Africans subscribe to the Native Trust and Land Company 'for the purpose of buying our country back'. Seme begged that all African leaders – including those of the ICU – unite in this matter of rebuilding a land-based African civilisation.[31] It was significant that he used the word 'civilisation' in a purely African context: hitherto it had been assumed that 'civilisation' could only be European.

Throughout the 1920s and until 1929, Seme had played a low-profile role in African politics, concentrating his energies instead on his legal practice in Johannesburg. Nonetheless, he had maintained his personal and professional links with Swazi and Zulu royalty (his wife, Phikisile, of course was Solomon's sister) during this period. And in making his political comeback in the late 1920s, he was to display an inclination to interpret African nationalism less in a pan-Africanist sense than in a narrower ethnic sense. On his election in 1930 to the presidency of the ANC, which supposedly embodied a pan-South African form of African nationalism, he expressed unprecedented personal interest in Inkatha. Although the 'self-help' proposals that Seme publicised through *Ilanga lase Natal* in 1929 did not refer to the 'Zulu people' as a special case, in all other respects they exemplified the main features of Natal kholwa ideology as it had developed in the late 1920s.[32]

The reconstitution of Inkatha, which could be regarded as a Zulu national self-help scheme, made the implicitly segregationist ideology of 'national rebuilding' explicit: Inkatha sought state 'recognition' as the representative organisation of a self-governing Zulu nation. In giving evidence before the Native Economic Commission, representatives of the Natal kholwa establishment clearly outlined the practical objectives that underlay their interest in a more thoroughgoing segregationism. Great emphasis was placed on the desirability of encouraging 'progressive' careers in the African reserves, and ensuring that the career opportunities there should be reserved solely for Africans. In particular, frequent calls were made for the opportunity to trade 'among our own people' — an often repeated phrase. As kholwa Chief Josiah Mqwebu of Stanger complained, Christianity and education 'aroused in certain of the reserve Natives a liking for business pursuits', but they were denied opportunities even in the African reserves because the whites monopolised the trading stores. More bluntly, Seme argued that 'segregation' should mean the dispossession of all white storekeepers in the African reserves. Both W. W. Ndhlovu and John Dube expressed similar views.[33]

Dube's evidence, furthermore, envisaged a thorough 'modernisation' of the reserves: he advocated the introduction of state-assisted irrigation schemes and foresaw the establishment of large-scale commercial agriculture (including sugar plantations), business concerns, and 'centres of industry' (including furniture factories and leather tanneries). Overall, Dube's heaviest emphasis fell on the need for more African land; this was essential if any of his ideas were to be realised. At the same time, he was careful to reassure the commissioners that African labour would still flow out of the reserves, and that African commercial farmers and manufacturers would not set out to compete directly with white business. Turning to the political development of the reserves, Dube stated that he believed in 'the tribal system' — particularly in view of social disintegration. Tribalism was to be a progressive force under 'an educated chief who is open to progress, and educated councillors who are going to support forward movements'. 'Progressive committees' were to be the main decision-making bodies, 'with the chief made a mere figurehead, so that he could not be an obstruction, and the councillors of the chief must be people who are progressive in their ideas'.[34] In effect, Dube's evidence identified why Natal's kholwa establishment was so anxious to secure Inkatha's control over the reserves in Zululand and Natal proper. As a 'progressive committee', Inkatha had laid down in its 1928 constitution that Solomon was to be a 'mere figurehead'. Inkatha's practical objectives were attractive to all of the disparate elements within the Natal African middle class, 'establishment' and 'unfulfilled' alike — including members of the urban middle class who were disillusioned with African prospects and quality of life in the towns, the stifled middle class in the white countryside, and the aspirant middle-class stratum that had developed within the reserves.

The common political ideas among representatives of Natal's white rural employers and Zulu kholwa had been clearly expressed in the context of Solomon and Inkatha in early 1928. The ZNTI speech that Heaton Nicholls had written for Solomon, the letter that Dube had written to Marwick, and the constitution that Nicolson and Thorpe had prepared for Inkatha, all endorsed a tribal-based political and cultural segregation and a reserve-based territorial segregation. All of these statements had applauded the disciplinary virtues of tribalism, but had maintained that the preservation of tribal socio-political traditions did not preclude African political and economic 'modernisation'. Moreover, all had referred to the historical and inherent separateness of the 'Bantu' or Zulu 'nation', and asserted that the latter should 'develop on its own lines'.

The objectives of the reconstituted Inkatha can be summarised as fourfold. First, to inspire a sense of united Zulu nationhood among all African inhabitants of the Province of Natal, thus defusing 'intra-national' class antagonisms. Inkatha's Zulu nationalism was to be underpinned by 'traditional' patriarchal authority and tribal discipline. Second, to entrench the kholwa and tribal elites as Zulu national leaders. Third, to effect fundamental socio-economic and political 'reforms' within the tribal system. The rural areas, and particularly the reserves (which Inkatha aimed to enlarge), were to be the focal point of the 'new African civilisation'.

Fourth and most important, to press the South African state to confer upon the 'Zulu nation', under the figurehead of Solomon and the practical leadership of Inkatha, a large measure of autonomy in attending to its 'own affairs'. Inkatha was not only advocating that a geographically and demographically 'stretched' version of the rural local council policy should be implemented in the Province of Natal: it was also promoting the further development of the ideology and practice of segregation. Whereas the architects of the local council policy tended to regard local councils as administrative instruments of the NAD, the officially-recognised Zulu national council that Inkatha envisaged would be an embodiment of the Zulu nation's desire to maintain its political and cultural separateness – from both whites and other African 'nations' or 'ethnic groups' within the Union. And although it was not made explicit in Inkatha's calls for official recognition, Inkatha ultimately sought greater political autonomy from 'white South Africa' than was currently endorsed by the consensus of segregationist opinion at state level. Inkatha's leading exponents clearly looked on the neighbouring High Commission Territories as attractive models for the 'settlement' of Zululand. Basutoland and Swaziland were effectively Southern Sotho and Swazi 'nation-states', British sovereignty having been superimposed upon the authority of the indigenous monarchs and representative councils.

NOTES

1. NTS 7205, 20/326, the Revd R.E. Oscroft's report of Inkatha meeting, 6/6/1928. Oscroft's report is the main source for the account that follows.

2. For an original signed copy of the 1928 constitution, see NTS 7205, 20/326, CNC to SNA, 16/8/1928, enclosing 'Deed of Trust and Constitution of the Inkata ka Zulu', 28/7/1928.

3. *Ibid.*, pp. 2–14 (all quotations).

4. NTS 7205, 20/326, Oscroft's report of Inkatha meeting, 6/6/1928.

5. *Ibid.*

6. NTS 7205, 20/326, 'Yearly Report of the Inkata Zulu', unsigned (Bhulose), n.d., enclosed in CNC to SNA, 12/8/1929. Somewhat ironically, this same report described Inkatha as the 'widely recognised organisation of all Native human beings in and out of the Union of South Africa'.

7. NTS 7205, 20/326, report and resolutions of Inkatha chiefs' meeting, 16/8/1929, enclosed in NC, ('native commissioner', the term 'magistrate' having been superseded in the Natal NAD in 1929) Nongoma to CNC, 10/9/1929. For thorough reports of this meeting and its appointment of the 'Komiti ukuyo kala ePitoli' (Committee to wail at Pretoria), see *Ilanga lase Natal*, 13/9/1929 and 20/9/1929 (Zulu language reports); for the official response, see NTS 7205, 20/326, CNC to SNA, 18/9/1929 and SNA to CNC, 26/11/1929.

8. NEC Box 4, evidence of M.L.E. Maling, Vryheid, 20/9/1930, pp. 1563–93.

9. This overview of the objectives of white interest groups in allying themselves with Inkatha from 1928 is based mainly on the following sources: Debates of the House of Assembly; Reports (and evidence) of the Select Committees on Native Affairs; evidence given before the Native Economic Commission; the *South African Sugar Journal*; and the G. Heaton Nicholls and J.S. Marwick manuscript collections in the KCAL. The subject is more thoroughly dealt with in my dissertation entitled 'The Zulu royal family under the South African government, 1910–1933: Solomon kaDinuzulu, Inkatha and Zulu nationalism' (Ph.D., University of Natal, Durban, 1986), pp. 311ff.

10. *Cape Times*, 11/5/1921, reports of parliamentary speeches by Marwick and Heaton Nicholls.

11. NEC Box 4, evidence of A. Wood, Newcastle, 16/9/1930, pp. 1180–86. See also evidence of J.A. Graham (spokesman for three Farmers' Associations), Dundee, 17/9/1930, pp. 1257–58.

12. For a summary of the 1932 Act, see Lacey, *Boroko*, pp. 169ff; more specifically, see Heaton Nicholls's parliamentary speeches in Debates of the House of Assembly, 1932, vol. 18, cols 1401–6 and vol. 19, cols 4317–22. Valuable insights into the interconnections between tribal authorities, tribalism, familial unity and Natal's white farmers, as were embodied in the 'kraalhead' labour tenancy contract, are contained in NEC Box 4, evidence of various farmers' representatives during 1930.

13. *South African Sugar Journal*, vol. 9, no. 11, November 1925, p. 741.

14. CNC PMB 97, 68/33, CNC to D.M. Eadie (secretary, South African Sugar Association), 24/2/1932. This scheme in effect was a homicidal attempt at blackmail, since famine relief was being distributed almost entirely in the worst-hit Zululand inland districts where the inhabitants were just as prone to malaria as those of inland districts elsewhere in the Union. The *South African Sugar Journal*, vol. 16, no. 4, April 1932, p. 201, reported at the time that non-immune labourers were 'dying in their hundreds' after working on the plantations. For the opinions of the 'experts' on the sugar industry's labour shortage, see the series of articles in the *South African Sugar Journal*, Congress and Exhibition Number, 1924, pp. 67–78.

15. See NEC Box 4, evidence of G.M. Robinson (representing the Zululand Farmers' Union), Empangeni, 26/9/1930, pp. 1830ff; and Box 7, evidence of D. Saunders (acting chairman, Natal Sugar Millers' Association), 2/4/1931, p. 6214.

16. CNC PMB 84, 58/7/4, SNA to CNC, 7/5/1928 (confidential).

17. For a summary of the 1928 Mozambique Convention, see *Official Yearbook of the Union of South Africa*, no. 14, 1931–1932, p. 906; see also *South African Sugar Journal*, vol. 12, no. 12, December 1928, p. 737, and vol. 14, no. 3, March 1930, p. 153.

18. Debates of the House of Assembly, vol. 10, question by Mr Nel (Ladysmith), 25/10/1927, col. 208.

19. See Select Committee Report on the Native Bills, SC10–27, evidence of William Elliot, Alexander Stone and August Jansen (for the Natal Agricultural Union), 13/5/1927, pp. 86–110; for Natal kholwa opinion regarding these white attitudes, see *Ilanga lase Natal*, 3/5/1929 (editorial).

20. See Debates of the House of Assembly, vol. 8, speeches by Heaton Nicholls (quotation) and Marwick, 28/3/1927, cols 1910ff and 1930ff; and vol. 7, 17/5/1926, cols 3560–61.

21. Debates of the House of Assembly, vol. 9, speech by Marwick, 2/5/1927, cols 2990–97, and MS MAR, File 74, KCM 8343, Marwick's notes *re* Native Administration Bill, n.d. (first quotation); and Debates of the House of Assembly, vol. 9, speech by Heaton Nicholls, 28/4/1927, cols 2921–29 (second quotation). There is a notable similarity between these views and those that Solomon expressed at the ZNTI.

22. MS NIC 2.08.1, Bantu Affairs File 5, G. Heaton Nicholls to J.H. Zutphen, 28/5/1929 (quotation); see also File 2, KCM 3307, fragment entitled 'Native Affairs', n.d.; File 3, KCM 3323, handwritten draft memorandum, n.d. (1930?); and Marks, 'Ideology of segregation', pp. 180–81.

23. MS NIC 2.08.1, Bantu Affairs File 5, KCM 3362, unaddressed carbon fragment, n.d. (1929?).

24. This was most explicitly expressed in correspondence between Heaton Nicholls and Dube in 1930–31, when Heaton Nicholls was soliciting African support for the Natal or 'adaptationist' proposals before the select committee on Hertzog's 'Native Bills'. See in particular MS NIC 2.08.1, Bantu Affairs File 5, KCM 3350 (a), document entitled 'The Land Settlement', n.d.; and KCM 3350 (b),

G. Heaton Nicholls to the Revd John Dube, 11/2/1931. See also Marks, 'Ambiguities of dependence', pp. 178ff, and 'Ideology of segregation', pp. 181ff.

25. *Ilanga lase Natal*, 5/4/1929.

26. *Ilanga lase Natal*, 26/4/1929, 17/5/1929, and 22/11/1929 (quotations); see also 1/1/1932.

27. NEC Box 4, evidence of Chief S. G. E. Majozi, Pietermaritzburg, 9/4/1931, pp. 6709–18 (quotations). See also evidence of Chiefs Dirk Sioka and Stephen Mini, Pietermaritzburg, 10/4/1931, pp. 6772–73; and NEC Box 7, evidence of Mrs V. S. Makanya, Durban, 2/4/1931, pp. 6303–4.

28. Roux, *Time longer than rope*, p. 346; *South African Outlook*, 1/11/1929, 'Bantu Mens' Social Centre: Its Aims, Objects and Activities', p. 215.

29. *South African Outlook*, 1/8/1929, pp. 148–52 (first quotation); and 2/11/1931, p. 209 (second quotation). See also the illuminating article entitled 'Communists and Christians' in the edition of 2/9/1929, pp. 168–69.

30. *South African Outlook*, 1/11/1929, p. 215.

31. *Ilanga lase Natal*, 5/4/1929 and 12/4/1929.

32. For some observations on Seme's ethnic interpretation of African nationalism, see CK Reel 14A, 2:XS14, biographical notes on Seme and newscuttings. Of particular interest are the views of J. K. Ngubane, *Inkundla ya Bantu*, 30/6/1951; R. V. Selope-Thema, *Drum*, July 1953; and Z. K. Matthews, *Imvo*, 25/11/1961. See also Walshe, *African nationalism in South Africa*, pp. 213, 230–31.

33. NEC Box 4, evidence of Chief Josiah Mqwebu (Umvoti Mission Reserve), Stanger, 2/10/1931, pp. 2036–39 (first quotation); and Box 8, evidence of Dr P. kaI. Seme, Johannesburg, 6/5/1931, pp. 7427–28 (second quotation). See also Box 4, evidence of W. W. Ndhlovu, Vryheid, p. 1526; Phillip Mtembu (lawyer's clerk), Dundee, pp. 1358–59; and Mose Ntuli (spokesman of the CPSA 'Committee'), pp. 1902–3.

34. NEC Box 4, evidence of J. L. Dube, Durban, 2/4/1931, pp. 6228–37 (land) and pp. 6252–69 (reserve development and tribalism).

9

The drive for Zulu self-government

Since the realisation of any of the reconstituted Inkatha's ambitions largely depended on the organisation's being given official status, the drive for state recognition was the most crucial of Inkatha's objectives. The way in which the state would respond to Inkatha lay in the hands of the NAD. Under the terms of the then recently amended 1920 Native Affairs Act, and the new 1927 Native Administration Act, the CNC and SNA could call on the Supreme Chief (the Governor-General) to rule by proclamation. And it was in the Supreme Chief's powers to give official sanction to a council such as Inkatha.

By mid-1928, the SNA, J.F. Herbst and CNC, C.A. Wheelwright were aware (or suspected) that white rural employers aimed to use Solomon and Inkatha to secure greater control over African labour, but they were unaware of the broader political objectives being pursued by the leading white and African exponents of the reconstituted Inkatha. This was largely because Heaton Nicholls's interpretation of segregationism was not expressed in public until the 1930s, and the negotiations between white and African leaders that led to the reconstitution of Inkatha had been strictly secret. The NAD was moreover ill-informed of the political ideas current among the African 'intelligentsia' at such institutions as the Bantu Mens' Social Centres. For the NAD, the question of Inkatha's recognition was purely an administrative question.

The NAD had come to regard Inkatha in an increasingly favourable light in the build-up to the crucial June 1928 Inkatha meeting. However, the SNA's attitude had changed dramatically in May 1928 once he had heard of William Campbell's visit to the MNA, at which Campbell requested that Solomon be recognised as king and offered to settle Solomon's debts. Writing to the CNC to express his concern that the drive for the recognition of Solomon and Inkatha was being orchestrated by white rural employers, the SNA went on to argue that these 'outside influences' would seek to subject the Natal NAD to their control. In the light of this possibility, the SNA instructed the CNC to draw up a carefully considered statement on the question of Solomon's and Inkatha's official status. And in doing so, the SNA did not conceal his own opinion that the NAD's council policy in Zululand had not yet 'matured', and that there should not be 'any hurry to give [Inkatha] official recognition'.[1]

The CNC was clearly taken aback by the SNA's change in attitude. He did not reply to the SNA's two letters for nearly a month (by which time the Inkatha meeting was already under way), and, when he did reply, he requested that the NAD postpone discussion of the matter until some two months after the Inkatha meeting. The SNA, however, responded by reiterating his instruction that the CNC immediately draw up a memorandum on policy towards Solomon and Inkatha.

An important reason behind the SNA's determination, undoubtedly, was that Wheelwright was due to retire at the end of 1928, and the SNA did not wish the 'recognition question' to be unresolved when a new CNC assumed office. Wheelwright was the NAD official most responsible for appointing Solomon as chief of the Usuthu in 1917, and had been closely acquainted with Inkatha since its formation. The SNA was also aware that the 1928 Inkatha meeting had already instructed Nicolson and Thorpe to execute the new constitution as a legal Deed of Trust; once this was done, the NAD could expect Inkatha to submit a formal request for official recognition.[2]

In preparing his statement of proposed policy, the CNC was heavily influenced by the opinions that local Natal NAD officials expressed in regard to the 1928 Inkatha meeting. The very favourable report submitted by Oscroft, the NAD's observer and only NAD official to attend, was an exception to the rule. E.N. Braatvedt, the magistrate of Emtonjaneni district, was clearly displeased that the CNC had sanctioned the meeting, and advanced various reasons why Inkatha should be held in suspicion: the organisation's influence directly undermined the authority of local magistrates, its financial practices were under question, and its newly elected executive committee included individuals from all over the province, reflecting Inkatha's expanding ambitions. H.L. Gebers, the magistrate at Nongoma, referred to another source of potential danger: the 'Mandlakazi Tribe' had not attended the 1928 Inkatha meeting, and it seemed that Chief Bokwe had deliberately arranged this conspicuous absence. N.W. Pringle, a member of the CNC's personal staff at the Natal NAD's headquarters in Pietermaritzburg, similarly feared a resurgence of the Usuthu-Mandlakazi feud, and while the CNC was absent from his office for a few days in mid-June, took it upon himself to write directly to the SNA to say so.[3]

In mid-July 1928, the CNC submitted two memoranda to the SNA. The first advised against Solomon's recognition. The second focused on policy towards Inkatha: 'on further consideration', the CNC stated, he was now 'constrained to withdraw' his recent suggestion that Inkatha be given official support.[4]

Regarding Solomon, the CNC reported that General Botha had expressly intended to make Solomon a 'big man' in Zululand if he proved to be a responsible chief over the Usuthu. And Solomon's political conduct had been commendable; he had recently maintained an 'attitude of aloofness' towards various African political organisations, a response which had been of great value to the NAD during a difficult period. However, the CNC felt that Solomon had displayed a number of weaknesses of character. Solomon was now suffering the physical consequences of 'self-indulgence' and the financial consequences of 'spendthrift ways' – two firms of Durban solicitors had been employed to 'unravel the tangle' of Solomon's heavy debts. The CNC offered four further reasons why the Zulu monarchy should not be officially recognised. First, it would be strongly opposed in white Natal. Second, the Mandlakazi absence from the 1928 Inkatha meeting suggested that the Zulu civil war might not yet be over. Third, while it might have seemed feasible to restore the Zulu monarchy following the Anglo-Zulu war, the 'whole idea is now antiquated'. Fourth, 'Native political bodies' and a 'certain small section of the Europeans' had inspired in Solomon a desire to be recognised as king of all the Zulu-speaking people throughout the province of Natal, rather than only in Zululand. The CNC opposed this pan-Natal Zulu unity.

The CNC concluded his 'Solomon memorandum' by suggesting that the NAD attempt to persuade Solomon to renounce all claims to political authority except in Zululand, and to repudiate Inkatha. It was desirable that the NAD establish a single council for Zululand, based on the model of the Pondoland General Council. Solomon's support for the establishment of a Zululand General Council, as opposed to the recognition of Inkatha, could be won if Solomon was informed that such a council would pay him a 'considerable grant' from its revenue, and would accord him the privilege of nominating members by virtue of his royal blood – though Solomon would still not be recognised as king. The CNC also suggested that Solomon and a large deputation of Zululand chiefs be sent to observe the Pondoland Session of the Transkeian 'Bunga' (Transkeian Territories General Council), so as to awaken their enthusiasm for the project. In a personal note to the SNA of the same date, the CNC recommended that the NAD in effect bribe Solomon to undermine Inkatha and support the proposed Zululand General Council by presenting him with a 'blunt offer to take over his [financial] liabilities'.[5]

The CNC's 'Inkatha memorandum' laid particular emphasis on two points: the current drive for the recognition of Inkatha was 'nothing more nor less than a deliberate attempt on the part of the 'die hard' Usutu supporters to build up the power of Solomon', and the 1928 Inkatha meeting had indicated that Inkatha intended to become the General Council for the whole province of Natal. The CNC therefore regarded Inkatha as a 'prime obstacle to the establishment of the contemplated General Council for Zululand'. The CNC recommended that when Inkatha submitted its formal Deed of Trust to the NAD, he should unambiguously reply that Inkatha would not be recognised, and, futhermore, that 'Native Chiefs and people of Zululand should await the [official council] proposals which will be submitted to them in due course'. In the meantime, he recommended that magistrates be reminded of the NAD's ban on Inkatha collections, and that a 'vigorous and intensive campaign of council propaganda' be arranged for Zululand.[6]

During the six weeks between the 1928 Inkatha meeting and the submission of his memoranda, the CNC had unequivocally reversed his attitude towards Inkatha: he no longer defined Inkatha as an ally which should be nurtured and officially incorporated into the NAD's administrative structure, but as an opponent which the NAD should actively attempt to undermine. There were inconsistencies in his arguments. Whereas Wheelwright had previously commended Solomon's role in healing the Usuthu-Mandlakazi dispute, he now, in his 'Solomon memorandum', suggested that the recognition of the Zulu monarchy could rekindle the Zulu civil war. And whereas he had previously complained that 'educated natives' from Natal proper were the dominant influence in Inkatha, he now, in his 'Inkatha memorandum', reported that 'die hard Usuthu supporters' were the prime movers – and this in spite of his own remarks on the role of 'native politicians' in his 'Solomon memorandum'. The fallacies of his assertions were illustrated in August 1928, three weeks after the memoranda were submitted, when fourteen thousand Zulu mustered at Nongoma for an *indaba* with the Prime Minister, General Hertzog. At the forefront of the Zulu mass sat Solomon and Bokwe, the heads of the Usuthu and Mandlakazi respectively, side by side. The leaders of Inkatha too were strongly represented, headed by Dube. And whereas Solomon gave a short speech expressing Zulu loyalty to the government, Dube gave a long political speech 'on behalf of the Zulu people'. Significantly, Dube stressed that the Zulu were wholeheartedly in support of the 'conceptions' of Hertzog's 'Native Bills', since it was their earnest desire to 'develop along the lines of their own traditions'.[7] In his memoranda, Wheelwright tended to conceptualise Zulu politics in an anachronistic tribal mould. This was inconsistent with Wheelwright's understanding, which he had demonstrated during the first half of 1928, that class divisions were the major dynamic of contemporary Zulu politics.

Wheelwright's proposals regarding the establishment of a Zululand General Council would also seem to have been fallacious. Solomon's official status was to remain no more than that of an ordinary chief, and yet he was to have the unique privilege of appointing members to, and being financially supported by, the Zululand General Council. In both memoranda, Wheelwright had emphasised Solomon's personal weaknesses as a reason for refusing to recognise Solomon and Inkatha.[8] However, Solomon would clearly have much greater control over Wheelwright's proposed Zululand General Council than he had over Inkatha. Inkatha's 1928 constitution had defined Solomon's role as that of a 'patron', according him no special right to influence the composition or policies of the executive committee – an arrangement that undoubtedly had been influenced by the recent worsening of Solomon's indebtedness, financial malpractices and addiction to liquor.

It would appear that the main reason why Wheelwright reversed his attitude towards Solomon and Inkatha was that, by doing so, Wheelwright could extricate himself from a difficult position in the bureaucracy of the NAD. In previously proposing official support for Inkatha, he had advocated that the NAD embark on a policy which was unprecedented and somewhat adventurous: hitherto the NAD had been 'creating' councils, as opposed to 'recognising' councils that already existed and therefore had independent power. He had suggested that the NAD conduct its first experiment with none other than Inkatha – when independent Zulu power and the Zulu royal family still conjured up fearsome associations in the corporate consciousness of the Natal NAD. Wheelwright had incorrectly assumed that his previous proposal would be supported by the SNA, but had instead found that it was condemned throughout the NAD. Without doubt he recalled the clamour that had been raised in certain quarters of white Natal, especially the Natal NAD, when Solomon was recognised as chief of the Usuthu in 1916, and foresaw a similar clamour if Solomon were recognised as king in 1928. In preparing his memoranda, Wheelwright was clearly motivated by a strong impulse to retract, like a tortoise, and avoid controversy. He thus simply expressed the corporate Natal NAD views on Solomon and Inkatha, and shortly thereafter retracted yet further into retirement.

Wheelwright's memoranda defined the NAD's policy in Zululand; none of the judgements contained within them were queried by the SNA. When Inkatha's formal Deed of Trust was submitted to the NAD in August 1928, however, it was not accompanied by a request for official recognition. This seems to have been an astute tactical move on the part of Inkatha's leaders and advisers. A direct request would have forced the NAD to give a direct answer, which, if negative, would have acted as a barrier to future negotiations. If the NAD had wished to recognise Inkatha, however, the Deed of Trust would have been sufficient prompt. In the event, the SNA instructed the CNC merely to acknowledge its receipt – and not, as the CNC had recommended, to inform Inkatha that official recognition would not be given. The NAD at no stage divulged its position, despite Oswald Fynney's attempt to glean information on Inkatha's behalf in November 1928, during the course of an unofficial visit to the CNC at Natal NAD headquarters in Pietermaritzburg.[9]

* * * * *

When the new CNC for Natal, T.W.C. Norton, took office in 1929, both he and the SNA immediately acted on Wheelwright's proposals for the establishment of a Zululand General Council. The first step that they took was to send Solomon and a large deputation of Zululand chiefs, in the charge of F.W. Ahrens (magistrate at Nqutu) and H.L..Gebers (magistrate at Nongoma), to Umtata in April 1929 so that they could observe how the council system operated in the Transkei. Although Dube also accompanied this 'Zululand deputation', evidently at the insistence of Solomon, the whole episode received markedly low-key coverage in *Ilanga lase Natal*. The chiefs were under instructions to call a meeting of chiefs and headmen on their return to Zululand, and discuss how council policy should be implemented. The second step taken by the SNA and CNC was to call a conference of all native commissioners in Natal in May 1929. At this conference, the SNA argued that the time was 'ripe' for the implementation of council policy in Natal, and Natal's councils should take the form of the 'chiefs' councils' in Pondoland. The CNC explained that the government wished to form two large councils in the province, one for Natal proper and one for Zululand.[10]

In his 1928 memoranda, Wheelwright had proposed that Solomon and other Zulu chiefs be taken to observe the Pondoland Session of the Transkeian Bunga. By what can only be assumed to have been a gross mistake on the part of the NAD in 1929, the Zululand deputation attended the General Session of the Transkeian Bunga. Thus the Zulu chiefs observed the deliberations of a council that was made up of elected members – and 'new men' rather than chiefs. Some of the speeches were in English and consequently incomprehensible to the visitors from Zululand. On their return to Zululand, Solomon and the Zulu delegates held a large meeting of Zulu chiefs and headmen outside the Nongoma magistracy. This meeting, which was no more than a preliminary discussion of the 'council system', did not support the establishment of government councils in Zululand.[11]

Very ironically for the NAD, the main discussions on this matter took place during the two Inkatha meetings of 1929: the annual general meeting in June, and the special chiefs' meeting in August. Inkatha's leaders, both kholwa and tribal, clearly believed that the government intended to establish in Zululand a council like the Transkeian Bunga – as opposed to the Pondoland General Council. They felt that this would be too 'advanced' for Zululand, and, moreover, that it would cause political division between educated Zulu and tribal authorities. The Inkatha annual general meeting of June 1929, which was chaired by Bhulose, therefore found that the 'council system' was unsuitable – though it did suggest that councils might be introduced at Natal mission stations where Africans 'have an inkling of the western civilisation and are sufficiently educated to follow debating rules'. The report also stated that Solomon had 'personally attended' the meeting, and 'contributed to the deliberations and resolutions herein'. The subsequent Inkatha chiefs' meeting, which was chaired by Chief Nkantini, came to similar conclusions – though it expressed itself in 'chiefly' rhetoric which contrasted strongly with the 'mission station' style:

> It is difficult for us to agree to this Council of the Cape Province at Umtata, we see that this might come right and even be fitted to our children if the Government would teach them so that they understand the procedure of the white people, for ourselves we see that this bead ornament will fit us not at all.

Instead, the chiefs' meeting requested the government to take notice of the 'head' of the Zulu people, Solomon, and 'we [Solomon's] izinduna who support him in his control on behalf of the Government'.[12]

Zulu kholwa and tribal leaders thus united to block the NAD's alternatives to the recognition of Solomon and Inkatha. In the ensuing deadlock, the NAD postponed the implementation of its council policy in the whole province of Natal, even though draft proclamations for the establishment of a Zululand General Council and Natal General Council had already been prepared. Inkatha's leaders, for their part, made no further attempts to 'politely prompt' the NAD into action. By early 1929, it had become clear that Inkatha's drive for recognition required new strategies.

After mid-1929, the leaders of Inkatha adopted two strategies in their drive for the official recognition of the Zulu kingship and Inkatha. The first strategy was somewhat passive: Inkatha affirmed that it still existed despite the NAD's unfavourable attitude, and that it had the power to frustrate any council policy that it regarded as unacceptable. Inkatha affirmed, too, that Zulu kholwa and tribal leaders wished to be the conjoint leaders of the Zulu nation, and, more particularly, that Inkatha and Solomon were inseparable. Inkatha also continued to verify that it was an opponent of militant political action, and to pronounce that it was a loyal servant of the Crown and Union government. All of these points were expressed – implicitly if not explicitly – in the Inkatha's report of its annual general meeting of June 1929, which Bhulose submitted to the CNC.

The second and more significant strategy was to enlist the assistance of Inkatha's influential white allies in taking Inkatha's cause to the highest councils of state. In accordance with the priorities of Inkatha's white allies, Inkatha's appeal for recognition after mid-1929 focused on grounds that were primarily 'political' (Inkatha presented itself as an antidote to the ICU, and an agent of segregationist policy) rather than administrative (previously Inkatha had presented itself as a form of local council, and a potential component of the Natal NAD's rural administration). It was thus to MPs, ministers of state and the Governor-General that Inkatha now looked for recognition, rather than to NAD officials.

As MPs, members of the select committee on 'native affairs' and leading parliamentary spokesmen on 'native policy', George Heaton Nicholls and J.S. Marwick were to be Inkatha's key white allies in this renewed drive for official recognition after mid-1929. There were, however, other important though less influential individuals, most notably Charles Adams, an Eshowe general dealer and arguably Zululand's most prominent businessman. Adams had become involved with the affairs of the Zulu royal house when Solomon fell heavily into debt in 1928, in the first instance because he was one of Solomon's creditors. Having soon adopted the role of Solomon's financial adviser, Adams then took an active interest in Zulu royal politics and became a keen supporter of Inkatha. Evidently at the invitation of Solomon, he attended the mid-1929 meeting of Zulu chiefs and headmen outside the Nongoma magistracy which discussed the Zululand deputation's recent visit to the Transkeian Bunga. Subsequently he addressed the 1929 Inkatha annual general meeting, and, according to Bhulose's report, made 'certain suggestions' which 'encouraged and greatly inspired' the assembly. Adams' evidence before the Native Economic Commission in September 1930 disclosed the principles that underlay his interest in the political future of Solomon and Inkatha: his main emphasis lay on their significance as an affirmation and extension of segregationist policy. As a personal friend of Heaton Nicholls, Adams acted as a vital means of communication between Inkatha's leaders and most influential white allies.[13] In this respect, mention must also be made of the role played by Oswald Fynney, Inkatha's white 'patron' since 1928. Although his contacts and influence lay in the first instance within the NAD hierarchy of which he was once a part, he also had the confidence of representatives of the sugar industry – clearly so in the case of William Campbell.

* * * * *

The strategy of circumventing the NAD was the only strategy that had any hope of success after mid-1929. Solomon's drunkenness and irresponsible habits worsened after his return from Umtata, and this doused any possibility that the NAD would of its own volition reconsider the 'recognition question'. Indeed, even if Solomon had fully supported the NAD's proposals for a Zululand General Council, it is unlikely that the NAD would have proceeded to implement this policy after mid-1929 if it entailed any official extension of Solomon's powers.

Contrary to the prevailing opinion within the NAD, Solomon's personal decline – which can be dated from early 1928 – was not simply indicative of weakness of character, self-indulgence or 'intoxication' with personal power: it was directly related to the frustrations of Solomon's political position which had become acute by 1928. Solomon's main objective, particuarly since the *indaba* with the Prince of Wales in 1925, had been to secure the official recognition of himself as Zulu king and Inkatha as the 'Zulu National Council'. Although Solomon had successfully made great efforts to ensure that the NAD could find no fault with his political behaviour, and both he and Inkatha had provided ample proof of the administrative and political advantages that could be reaped from their incorporation into the structure of indirect rule in Zululand, the overall policy that the NAD had adopted towards them had been one of 'noncommital inaction'. In fact, as when Inkatha collections were banned in 1926, the NAD seemed to want to undermine their influence. The attitude that the NAD adopted regarding the royal petition of 1927 and Inkatha's new constitution of 1928 could only have served to compound Solomon's sense of political frustration.

In addition, the class antagonisms that developed within the Zulu in the late 1920s eroded the populist Zulu national unity that Solomon personally had worked so hard to foster. Solomon had not only been forced to witness the disintegration of his drive for Zulu unity after 1925; he had also found little alternative but to 'take sides' in the newly developed class conflicts, and thus, ironically, to accentuate them further. Solomon clearly saw himself in the traditional role of 'head of the house of Zulu' and as an embodiment of Zulu national unity. He did not perceive his role as that of a politician fighting in the first instance for the interests of a particular class within the Zulu – a role that better fitted men like Champion and Dube. The class conflicts of the late 1920s were not only politically irksome for Solomon;

they were also personally irksome, for Solomon was by nature a conciliator and not a fighter. This nature, by virtue of which Solomon had resurrected Zulu national unity around himself as heir to the Zulu royal house by the mid-1920s, ill accorded with the belligerence between social classes and their representatives that characterised Zulu politics in the late 1920s.

Solomon had clearly lost the initiative in Zulu royal – or 'national' – politics by the late 1920s. Previously, while working to re-establish the position of the Zulu royal family in tribal Zululand and spearheading the broader Zulu 'unity movement', Solomon had managed to retain a large measure of autonomy from 'outside' political influences – mainly the African middle class, acting through the media of the NNC and nascent Inkatha. This was not so after 1927. In 1928, when police and NAD officials were perturbed that Solomon might become a 'tool' of ICU activists, Solomon had in reality already become a 'tool' of two other interest groups: Natal's African kholwa establishment and white rural employers.

That Solomon's fondness for spirits had become a physical illness by mid-1928 must be understood in the context of the tensions, contradictions and frustrations of his public life. In a rather self-recriminatory and desperate letter, significantly written from his sick-bed during the overwhelmingly kholwa-dominated Inkatha meeting of 1928, Solomon had pleaded with the magistrate of Nongoma to be given a permit of exemption from the liquor law (which did not permit Africans to purchase 'European liquor'). Evidently setting aside personal pride, Solomon confided that he needed liquor; he also argued that he would drink less if he had a permit since he would no longer be continually afraid that his illegal supply would be interrupted. Solomon's request was granted.[14] There is no doubt, however, that Solomon's consumption of liquor increased after the permit was issued. And by mid-1929, Solomon's conciliatory, gentle and somewhat self-effacing nature was increasingly less in evidence, in his interaction both with NAD officials and with his 'subjects'.

A series of incidents in the Eshowe district in late 1929 provided evidence of Solomon's deteriorating condition. In September Solomon visited Chief Mehlwana's homestead near Eshowe, having angered the local NAD official for omitting to report his arrival in the district. The police District Commandant reported that Solomon then sent messengers out to a number of Eshowe chiefs' wards to conduct collections for him, so that he could pay an instalment on his car. Solomon also established an illegal supply of liquor (his permit was only valid in the Nongoma district), the District Commandant continued, and was in the habit of having 'immoral relations' with girls sent to him with food. Moreover, Solomon took a number of Eshowe girls with him to Nongoma when he left, on the pretext of intending to marry them, but it transpired that he had not cared for them – with the result that they had become 'destitute wanderers'.

The District Commandant subsequently reported that Solomon returned to the Eshowe district during the following month, accompanied by a party in a number of cars. He visited Chief Mfungelwa's homestead where he addressed a gathering of between two and three thousand, speaking about the benefits of education and the need to avoid 'faction fights'. Although the gathering gave Solomon fourteen head of cattle and £40. 6. 3., Solomon indicated that he felt this was insufficient. That evening Solomon selected two young women from Chief Mfungelwa's ward to sleep with him. When the latter refused to have sexual intercourse, they were required to drink *utshwala* mixed with brandy which induced them to comply.[15]

On being required to explain himself, Solomon wrote to the CNC denying all the allegations regarding his behaviour in the Eshowe district, and added that he had never been under the influence of liquor either in Eshowe or anywhere else. Solomon thereafter called upon the native commissioner at Eshowe and expressed irritation that he had been reported to the CNC. In the course of this interview, however, Solomon admitted that he was indeed at fault. Before leaving, he unsuccessfully asked the native commissioner to supply him with some liquor. Solomon was subsequently permitted to have one bottle on the authority of the District Surgeon in Eshowe.[16]

The official view of Solomon, already at a low ebb on account of the way in which he was treating his 'subjects' in the Eshowe district, together with the administrative disruption his activities were causing (which led the native commissioner at Eshowe to submit a formal memorandum of complaint to the CNC), worsened when Solomon wrote to the CNC simply lying about both his recent actions in the Eshowe district and his problems with alcohol. And official opinion was hardly improved when Solomon approached the NAD six weeks later, in January 1930, with the request that the government settle his debts – which amounted to an admission that even the most reputable legal firms in Durban had been unable to control the spendthrift habits and financial corruption of the Zulu royal house.[17] And significantly, Solomon's alcoholic excesses were also beginning to earn him the displeasure of his own 'subjects'. When in November 1929 the native commissioner at Eshowe held an *indaba* with local chiefs, Chief Mehlwana commented that Solomon had shown by his own actions that he could not be paramount chief of the Zulu.[18] Such an observation, which might have been generally representative of Mehlwana's ward in 1929, would not have been made in 1925.

*   *   *   *   *

In the meantime, an unprecedented upsurge of African worker militancy in Durban was fostering a political climate very conducive to Inkatha's renewed drive for official recognition. For the year following the desecration of the Greytown cemetery in early 1928, which had provoked a violent and even devastating white backlash against ICU branches in the Natal midlands, African political militancy had remained at a comparatively low ebb. But towards the end of May 1928 the boycott of the Durban municipal beerhalls began, co-ordinated – but by no means spearheaded – by George Champion's ICU *yase* Natal.

Durban municipal officials generally ascribed the boycott to the 'agitation' of 'shebeen queens' (independent brewers, whose livelihoods were undercut by the municipal *utshwala* monopoly) and, more especially, the political influence of Champion. The evidence shows, however, that the dockside labour barracks were the cradle of the 1929 beerhall boycott and ensuing disturbances, and that the protests were directed against the oppressive and exploitative nature of the whole 'Durban system' of municipal 'native administration'. Indeed, the decision to boycott the beerhalls, whose revenue financed 'native administration' in the city, showed that the connection between the beer monopoly and the municipal 'native affairs' bureaucracy had been accurately identified. While the ICU *yase* Natal provided workers with an organisational infrastructure, Champion's role in the protests was very ambivalent. He clearly did not identify closely with the workers' cause, and did not support strike action. Indeed, he subsequently opined that the workers were earning a 'very good salary', and that living conditions in the labour barracks were 'good for the class of people they are provided for'. At one stage during the disturbances, when subjected to municipal pressure, he agreed to call off the boycott without consulting the workers. Champion had hoped to garner the support of Durban's militant political constituency, under the ICU *yase* Natal banner, while guiding political action along relatively moderate lines, but the protests assumed a momentum which Champion could not contain. In the eyes of Durban's white population and the Zulu-speaking kholwa establishment generally, however, Champion's image ironically remained that of a dangerous agitator.[19]

A major riot erupted in Durban in mid-June when five hundred white civilian 'vigilantes' – outraged by the large demonstrations of worker solidarity occurring in various parts of the city, which included a clash between police and armed ICU pickets – besieged the ICU hall in the city centre. The besiegers were then attacked by two 'relief columns' of irate workers, and the police found that their intervention was violently opposed by both the conflicting factions. When the two thousand combatants dispersed they left several dead behind them, and over a hundred injured. The speed with which the specially appointed 'De Waal Commission' began its work of inquiring into the origins of the beerhall disturbances reflected the extent of their political impact. While political violence on the streets of Durban died away, the beerhall boycott persisted (with crippling consequences for Durban's 'Native Revenue Account') well into 1930 – sustaining a considerable state of class and race tension in Durban itself, and political anxiety throughout white Natal as well as at state level.

White Natalians, local and even state officials and politicians were not the only groups to be gravely alarmed by the 1929 beerhall boycott and related disturbances; so too was Natal's African kholwa establishment. Immediately after the beerhall boycott came into force, and when worker demonstrations were still comparatively low-key, *Ilanga lase Natal* came out in strong support of 'law and order' and clearly enunciated its disapproval of the 'processions' that were taking place in the streets of Durban. Such protests were not 'constitutional' behaviour on the part of the ICU *yase* Natal, the newspaper's editorial argued: there were many alternatives to the adoption of a 'militaristic and defiant attitude' towards authority.[20] Significantly, this *Ilanga lase Natal* editorial was published in English; its function was not simply to provide a statement of the kholwa establishment's position regarding worker militancy in Durban, but also to communicate this position to its white allies – so as to reaffirm the basis and purpose of their mutual alliance, consummated in the context of Inkatha in early 1928. And, against the background of the beerhall boycott and disturbances, the 'Inkatha alliance' did indeed draw together once more effectively, representing to members of the Union government that official recognition of Solomon and Inkatha would counter the sort of political unrest that was currently exemplified in Durban.

The Inkatha alliance's first move came in early September 1929, while the De Waal Commission was still busy with its investigations, and was initiated by Dube and Marwick. *Ilanga lase Natal*'s coverage of this development was necessarily somewhat oblique and uninformative: both the African and the white political leaders who acted together in the context of Inkatha had always been determined that their relationship with each other should remain secret, or at least understated. *Ilanga lase Natal*'s first edition for September 1929 included a small stop-press report noting that Dube and Marwick had made a deputation to Pietermaritzburg to have discussions with the Minister of Native Affairs. One week later, the newspaper published a report of the discussions that had taken place. The CNC was also in attendance, it was reported, and Dube was accompanied by Francis Xulu and Gilbert Nxaba (evidently members of the resuscitated Durban branch of the NNC), but no mention was made of Marwick's involvement. Significantly, the MNA was the newly appointed E. G. Jansen, MP for Vryheid (Hertzog had relinquished this portfolio after the 'black peril' general election of 1929). Marwick and Jansen had long acted together in parliament – despite their party-political differences – as representatives of Natal farming interests, particularly in regard to control over farm labour. Clearly Marwick had 'pulled strings' to arrange Dube's consultation with Jansen, and while doing so had undoubtedly intimated to Jansen that the political organisations which Dube represented could play a leading role in quelling the resurgence of militancy in Natal.

At this consultation, *Ilanga lase Natal* reported, Dube told Jansen that he had come to speak about what 'was foremost in his mind': 'the state of the people in Durban'. However, not once did Dube mention any of the grievances that caused the disturbances; instead he focused on methods of controlling militancy. While expressing disapproval of the Riotous Assemblies Bill that was then before parliament, he proposed two courses of remedial action. First, the establishment of an African council in Durban. Second, and most important, the appointment of Solomon as 'Paramount Chief' of the Zulu. If Solomon were to be placed in a position where he could influence all Zulu, Dube explained, Solomon would be able to quieten the *umsindo* (literally 'noise', meaning disturbance) and be a 'great help' to the government. Dube made no mention of Inkatha – but in practice the recognition of Solomon necessarily included Inkatha, just as much as the recognition of Inkatha included Solomon. The purpose of Dube's representations, which Marwick had facilitated, was clearly to persuade the new MNA to redefine his department's policy towards Solomon and Inkatha. It seems, however, that Dube's representation did not succeed in doing so – although both the MNA and the CNC reportedly responded to them with considerable interest during the consultation itself.[21]

The Inkatha alliance's second move, which was by far the more important, came in mid-1930 and was spearheaded by Heaton Nicholls. It took place against the background of developments which seemed to indicate that a revolutionary mood was growing within the African population throughout the province of Natal, spanning town and countryside, and embodying a sense of unity and purpose greater than that of the 1906 rebellion. Durban itself became more politically explosive in the months following the meeting between Dube and Jansen, even though a riot comparable to that of June 1929 did not recur. By November 1929, for example, it had become evident that African residents were not only boycotting the municipal beerhalls but also refusing to pay the state poll tax. An armed battalion responded by making African Durban the testing ground for a novel method of social control: the use of tear-gas against civilians. Despite this demonstration of state power, Durban's rickshaw-pullers went on strike in early 1930, so indicating that militant spirits were not to be easily repressed. African political militancy, however, was no longer confined to Durban: it was also developing in the small population centres of the predominantly rural hinterlands. In September, for example, the beerhall at Weenen was attacked by local Africans. At about the same time, the Empangeni branch of the ICU (which had been dormant since the Empangeni 'anti-ICU' *indaba* of 1927) held a well-attended meeting – which was disrupted by the intervention of the local police. Summoned to Empangeni police station, the local ICU organiser was informed that *abelungu bayesaba* ('the whites are frightened') and that the meeting should terminate.[22]

Perhaps most disturbing for the state, however, was the clear evidence of interconnections between the rising tide of militancy in the urban areas on the one hand and the rural areas on the other. The evidence that George Hulett, a prominent Stanger sugar planter, gave before the Native Economic Commission in October 1930 indicated that the rural rank and file was directly in touch with events in Durban and the political doctrines that were being disseminated there. Hulett related how workers on his estate would go into Durban on Sundays to attend meetings at Cartwright Flats near the city centre. The ICU *yase* Natal and the Communist Party's Durban branch (established in 1929) held regular Sunday-afternoon rallies at Cartwright Flats, and it was undoubtedly these that Hulett's employees were attending – although Hulett believed, having been perhaps deliberately misinformed, that they went to Durban to *khonza* ('pay respects to') Solomon.[23] The interconnections between the urban and rural areas were more clearly evidenced in June 1930 when a number of chiefs and headmen from Natal's countryside attended a meeting of the ICU *yase* Natal in Durban. Champion, who had invited them to Durban to discuss a strike among the city's African rickshaw-pullers, shortly afterwards claimed that their attendance 'showed that now the District and Rural areas would combine with them [urban workers] in one general movement'.[24] Champion's statement confirmed the NAD's worst fears.

In July 1930, against the background of these developments, Heaton Nicholls despatched a series of letters to the MNA, E.G. Jansen, arguing that the recognition of Solomon and Inkatha had become an urgent necessity. At the same time he was in confidential communciation with the Governor-General, the Earl of Athlone, to whom – it subsequently transpired – he was expressing similar sentiments. The signs that African worker militancy in the province was to escalate, however, did not comprise the only reason why Heaton Nicholls's representations bore a note of urgency. The Governor-General was to tour Zululand between late July and early August, in the course of which he was to hold an *indaba* with the Zulu at Eshowe. Heaton Nicholls hoped to persuade the MNA and the Governor-General to recognise the potential of the forthcoming 'Zulu *indaba*' at Eshowe, which Heaton Nicholls predicted would be a grand colonial set-piece, as an occasion on which to proclaim the recognition of Solomon as king and Inkatha as 'Zulu National Council'. The Governor-General, in his capacity as Supreme Chief, had the power to make such a proclamation. Heaton Nicholls had always had a taste for drama.

*   *   *   *   *

In practice, the Supreme Chief's powers were normally exercised in response to recommendations from regional NAD officials that had been endorsed by the SNA and MNA. Nonetheless, the 'Governor-General-in-Council' (when in consultation with ministers of state) had the power to override or simply bypass the NAD when proclaiming regional 'native legislation'. Within this body, on such topics as Zulu political reform, the MNA was almost certain to be the most influential individual alongside the Governor-General. The support of the MNA and the Governor-General was thus vital if there were to be any move to introduce changes in Zululand 'native policy' which were not advocated by Natal NAD officials.

Heaton Nicholls could feel assured that both Jansen and Athlone would consider his representations with great care, and even a certain partiality. Jansen, whose Vryheid constituency adjoined Heaton Nicholls's Zululand constituency, had for many years been an active member of the Natal planter/farmer alliance which Heaton Nicholls and Marwick jointly headed. Although Jansen had not frequently addressed parliament on the more theoretical aspects of 'native policy' prior to his appointment as MNA, the occasions when he had done so proved that he adhered to the 'Natal view' on 'native affairs' – of which Heaton Nicholls was the leading spokesman. Athlone, for his part, had long shown a special concern for the interests of agricultural industries in the Union, including the Natal sugar industry. Heaton Nicholls and Athlone were personally acquainted, it seems; and Heaton Nicholls not only arranged Athlone's itinerary in Zululand, but also acted as Athlone's guide and companion in the course of the tour.[25]

Not least important from Heaton Nicholls's point of view, it could be expected that Athlone's tour would inspire in the Province of Natal, among the African as well as the white population, an emotional and celebratory atmosphere similar to that inspired by the Prince of Wales's tour in 1925.

Indeed, a high-ranking member of the British aristocracy himself, Athlone was King George V's brother-in-law and the King's personal representative in South Africa. A spirit of Zulu unity under Solomon, and of Zulu loyalty to the British Crown, was likely to characterise the 'Zulu *indaba*' at Eshowe – which would therefore be an appropriate occasion on which to resurrect the Zulu monarchy and grant the Zulu a measure a self-government.

In his correspondence with Jansen during July 1930, Heaton Nicholls focused on the 'political' advantages that could be gleaned from the incorporation of Solomon and Inkatha into the structure of indirect rule in Natal. The recognition of Solomon and Inkatha, he argued, would appeal to the most 'conservative elements' in Zulu society, and would 'strengthen the chiefs in their fight against communism'. Referring to the recent ICU meeting with chiefs in Durban, Heaton Nicholls expressed the view that some chiefs were beginning to 'imitate the agitator' because the government did not accord either them or their king sufficient status. 'Fearful combinations' were therefore taking shape. Solomon, who stood at the apex of the Zulu tribal hierarchy and who the Zulu perceived as their 'natural leader', was the means by which the state could reassert political and administrative control over the whole Zulu population: 'We can guide the head of the nation when we can do nothing to guide the mass'.

While passionately denouncing the disinclination of NAD officials to change extant policy towards the Zulu royal house, Heaton Nicholls emphasised that his proposal was in line with both official policy towards tribalism, as was embodied in the 1927 Native Administration Act, and the ideology and practice of segregation. It is illuminating that Heaton Nicholls requested the MNA to relocate the main Zulu *indaba* so that it took place at Nongoma, because the Nongoma district was the 'focus of Zulu loyalty', and because 'the emphasis of all native development should be in the native reserve'. Eshowe, by contrast, was a white town.[26]

In his first letter, Heaton Nicholls had proposed that the MNA and the Governor-General should summarily recognise Solomon during the forth-coming Zulu *indaba*. To this the MNA had replied simply that his department had already considered the question of Solomon's official status, and that he was not prepared to depart from the policy the NAD had adopted. Heaton Nicholls then requested that Solomon at least be paid special attention during the Governor-General's tour – with a view to taking action on the recognition issue soon thereafter. On the grounds of these subsequent representations from Heaton Nicholls, Jansen reopened the 'recognition question'. He sent Heaton Nicholls's letters to the SNA, who in turn submitted copies to the CNC. Simultaneously, the MNA informed the NAD that he favoured the establishment of a Zululand Council whose membership was confined to Zulu chiefs and the latter's nominees. While the Governor-General was touring Zululand therefore, the NAD was reconsidering policy towards Solomon and Inkatha.[27]

The Governor-General had keenly espoused the essence of Heaton Nicholls's views and proposals, as was clearly revealed in the 'Athlone memorandum', an expressly secret document which the Governor-General submitted to members of the Union cabinet shortly after his return from Zululand.[28] Athlone's approach contrasted with the red-tape pettiness and nervous inertia of the NAD bureaucracy, and the overblown, sometimes sensational rhetoric of Heaton Nicholls. At the outset, the Athlone memorandum indicated that it would not address itself to Solomon's behaviour, but to 'Solomon's position' in the context of 'native policy' in Zululand. And in doing so, it examined ways in which a redefinition of Solomon's status could, with regard to the administration of the Zulu, revitalise the operation of indirect rule in Zululand, and, with regard to the political life of the Zulu, quell the growth of disrespect for authority and of militancy.

Having made an appraisal of the tribal system and chiefly authority, and their interrelationship with the theory and practice of indirect rule, Athlone questioned whether the policy of refusing to recognise Solomon's status was consistent with its policy of preserving tribalism and chiefly authority. Indirect rule in Zululand involved the use of the Zulu tribal system, 'at the head of which, whether we like it or not, stands Solomon and the Zulu royal house'. Thus he recommended the recognition of Solomon and Inkatha, which he saw as the only basis on which a 'popular Native council' could be established in Zululand. Athlone also considered the spread of 'revolutionary and subversive influences' among the African population, and concluded that the choice seemed to lie between 'the recognition of a Paramount Chief' and the 'disintegration of the Zulu Nation through the influence of the ICU and kindred organisations.'

The Athlone memorandum then went on to propose that the responsibility for administering Zululand be removed from the NAD and vested in the Governor-General in his capacity as Supreme Chief. Similar to the arrangements made for the British High Commission Territories of Basutoland and Swaziland, the Governor-General would then in practice make Solomon and Inkatha responsible for governing the Zulu, only intervening if they did not do so 'reasonably well'. While emphasising that the finer details of his envisaged Zululand policy were subject to negotiation, Athlone summarised his proposals as follows:

[First,] the recognition of Solomon as Paramount Chief, administering the present laws and customs, and responsible to the Supreme Chief for good order and government in Zululand, and watched over by a Government Agent, who would be answerable direct to the Minister of Native Affairs without reference to the Chief Native Commissioner of Natal. Zululand to be regarded as administratively separate from Natal.

[Second,] the institution of a Native Council for Zululand on a foundation of the present 'Nkata, in which the Paramount Chief would preside. Such a Council to have legislative functions, subject to the advice and final 'recommendation' of the Government Agent direct to the Governor-General-in-Council.[29]

Athlone's proposals differed from those of Heaton Nicholls insofar as they effectively advocated that the Zululand administration be made independent from the structure of 'native administration' in the rest of the Union, and that the Zulu be governed more on the model of the neighbouring High Commission territories – by way of a Crown representative watching over the activities of a 'traditional' monarchical political structure. Athlone's proposals were in these respects similar to the 'Basutolandization' proposals made by Zululand's Resident Commissioner Sir Marshall Clarke during the 1890s; the latter, if heeded, would have caused Zululand to be treated along the lines of a High Commission Territory rather than to be incorporated into the Colony of Natal and therefore, subsequently, the Union.[30] Although Heaton Nicholls's special concern was for 'political reform' among the Zulu, as a leading Union 'native policy' legislator he also hoped that the practical application of his 'adaptationist policy' in Zululand would encourage similar initiatives elsewhere in the Union, under state guidance. Heaton Nicholls at no stage seemed to contemplate that control should fall into the hands of a potentially independent authority such as the Governor-General, who might not always be amenable to white settler interests.

The differences between Athlone's and Heaton Nicholls's ideas should not be overemphasised, however. Immediately prior to the Zulu *indaba*, they were clearly in agreement about the central points of their ideas. In practice these meant the official recognition of Solomon and Inkatha as the responsible political institutions of a limitedly self-governing Zulu nation – which accorded precisely with the central points of Solomon's and Inkatha's long-standing hopes. From the point of view of all those who were seriously concerned with how these objectives might be realised, the Zulu *indaba* with the Governor-General scheduled for 24 July 1930 was an event of some promise. It could be expected to be a showcase of Zulu national unity and discipline, of Zulu loyalty to Crown and government, and of the pre-eminent importance of Solomon and his advisers in the political life of the Zulu. And even if the Governor-General were not going to announce far-reaching political reforms for the Zulu at the *indaba*, as Heaton Nicholls had originally hoped, it was his intention to take initiatives in that direction and to pay special attention to Solomon during his tour. Perhaps most importantly, the *indaba* might serve to impress the MNA and the NAD with the value of Solomon's political influence over a large representative assembly of Zulu people. Indeed, the MNA, the SNA and the CNC were the most influential individuals who had yet to be convinced of the wisdom of the 'recognition strategy'.

In late July the Governor-General, accompanied by his wife and daughter, Princess Alice and Lady May Cambridge, and a number of aides-de-camp, entered Zululand to a rapturous welcome from white Zululanders. As Heaton Nicholls related in his autobiography, the tour was quite unlike earlier 'political' tours undertaken by even such nationally and internationally esteemed dignitaries as Smuts; it was more in the nature of a royal progress, similar to that of the Prince of Wales in 1925, punctuated by grandiose social functions at each siding at which the White Train hesitated.[31] Yet the principal engagement of the Governor-General's tour was unquestionably to be his Zulu *indaba* at Eshowe – on the golf links, as the Prince of Wales's *indaba* had been in 1925 – to which every chief in Zululand, with followers, had been officially invited. This event, which was to take place during the afternoon of 24 July, overshadowed the Governor-General's formal reception in white Eshowe during the morning.

Unbeknown to anyone but NAD officials, however, it had become clear in the few days before the *indaba* that the Zulu were unlikely to welcome the Governor-General in the same way as they had welcomed the Prince. It seemed that they regarded the Governor-General less as King George V's representative and 'their' Supreme Chief, and more as a representative of the state which had not long previously tear-gassed their relatives in Durban. In the week prior to the Zulu *indaba*, furthermore, evidence came to light that the royal nucleus near Nongoma was the epicentre of Zulu disaffection. Unaware of the Governor-General's real intentions, Solomon ironically seemed to see the Governor-General as the head of the NAD that had refused to recognise his hereditary position, and was making efforts to ensure that Zulu displeasure was expressed. Contributory to Solomon's attitude, however, was that he was in the midst of a severe bout of heavy drinking.

On 20 July, four days before the Zulu *indaba*, the native commissioner at Nongoma telegraphed his counterpart at Eshowe that, for various reasons, every chief in his district had indicated that he would be unable to attend. In response, the CNC immediately transmitted a personal message to every Nongoma chief, advising them that 'their absence would be regarded as a very serious affront to His Excellency unless unimpeachable reasons for absenting themselves existed' – but this seemed to make no impact. Indeed, when the CNC arrived in Eshowe on 23 July, he learnt from Nongoma that Solomon would definitely not be present. Moreover, he was informed by the native commissioner at Eshowe that a rumour was in circulation among Zulu, to the effect that Solomon would not attend and 'therefore others need not attend'. Since he was aware of the Governor-General's special desire to see Chief Solomon at Eshowe, the CNC made several urgent attempts to communicate directly with Solomon. When NAD messengers called at Mahashini, however, Solomon simply gave out that he was 'ill in bed with gout, and could not move'. The CNC consequently felt that he would have to explain to the Governor-General that Solomon would be absent on account of illness. Privately, however, he was clearly perturbed about the significance of Solomon's absence as an affront to the authority of the state.

On 24 July 1930, the day of the *indaba*, officials were astonished to hear that Solomon and his motorcade had nonetheless arrived in Eshowe. The Eshowe native commissioner was not in his office to receive Solomon, and Solomon, apparently annoyed, thereupon 'disappeared' so far as officialdom was concerned. In the meantime, the other forty-seven chiefs who had arrived to attend, together with over a hundred headmen and six thousand followers, were already assembling at the *indaba* venue. When eventually located by the organisers, Solomon was – in the CNC's words – very 'impudent and truculent' with every official with whom he came into contact, and loudly asserted that he, the Zulu king, alone had the right to summon such large public assemblies of the Zulu. Solomon was also very drunk: it emerged that he had left Mahashini late the previous evening, and had been drinking ever since. A subsequent enquiry into the records of the Nongoma bottle store, incidentally, showed that fifty-five bottles of whisky and brandy had been bought on Solomon's account at Nongoma between 1 and 23 July, while on 25 July 1930, the day after the *indaba*, a further twenty-four bottles of spirits were purchased.[32]

The CNC subsequently explained that the NAD at this stage had no option but to permit Solomon's attendance at the *indaba*, because the assembled Zulu were already expecting him. Once the *indaba* was underway, the Zulu royal party having at last taken their seats at the forefront of the Zulu assembly, Solomon set about openly and repeatedly expressing his anger towards the white authorities at whose instigation the event had been convened. Significantly, his attitude was reflected in the disposition of others in the Zulu assembly. A 'very large number of natives', so the native commissioner at Eshowe reported, shouted 'Bayeza' at the Governor-General (literally 'they are coming', a traditional rallying call) in the place of the royal salutation 'Bayede'.[33] The Governor-General was thus threatened rather than saluted.

Although officials had arranged for a clerk attached to the local magistrate's office to act as interpreter during the *indaba*, Solomon ignored this official interpreter when he rose to address the Governor-General, and instead used his own. The speech as a whole was as a result barely comprehensible to anyone present, Zulu or English speaking, since Solomon was often incoherent in his drunkenness and his interpreter was not fluent in English. Those parts of the speech that were decipherable, however, were of considerable interest. The *Natal Mercury*, whose report was prefaced with the words 'Solomon was understood to say that . . . ', related how Solomon called on members of the British royal family in England to 'assist the country', saying that they were the Zulu's only hope, and requesting that the Governor-General communicate this plea to his relatives in the mother country. Solomon apparently seemed to believe that at that stage it was the British monarchy alone that could cause his hereditary position to be officially recognised. His speech at the same time indicated that he had lost faith in making representations to any quarter of the South African state, and even that he no longer recognised the authority of the South African government. Indeed, whereas it was customary on such occasions to express loyalty to 'the British Crown and the Union government', as though they were inseparably linked, Solomon on this particular occasion was heard only to express loyalty to the former. He also entered into a somewhat convoluted discourse on the merits of monarchs as opposed to elected authorities: they were unequal, Solomon asserted, 'because a King was a member of a royal family and crowned by God and not by any human being'.[34]

Mnyaiza kaNdabuko Zulu, who was the only other Zulu officially to make a speech, reiterated Solomon's request for the intervention of British royalty. Significantly, it was Chief Nkantini and not Solomon who made the presentation of a Zulu knobkerrie and shield to the Governor-General, which could be interpreted either as a reflection of Solomon's incapacitation or of his disaffection.

Solomon also made his opinions readily apparent during the course of the Governor-General's address. He exaggeratedly shook his head at several stages, the native commissioner at Eshowe reported, to demonstrate his disagreement with statements that were being made. This was particularly marked when the Governor-General pronounced that 'in your CNC and NCs you have men to look after your welfare . . . go to them with your troubles and difficulties', and warned the Zulu to beware of 'mischief makers' who denigrated the government's 'good works'.[35] But for the subsequent display of Zulu dancing, which His Excellency and Princess Alice apparently enjoyed, Solomon had succeeded in transforming the *indaba* into a display of Zulu antagonism arguably unparalleled in the history of formal meetings between the Zulu and white authorities.

* * * * *

It was a measure of the Governor-General's determination to keep alive a hope for the recognition of Solomon and Inkatha that he visited Nongoma two weeks after the *indaba*, and held a private interview with Solomon. Here his purpose was not merely to express official umbrage but also to express his personal disappointment with the manner in which Solomon had behaved; and, hinting that the Zulu royal house might yet be rewarded should its image improve, he urged Solomon to 'show yourself worthy of the position you hold in [Zulu] eyes'.[36] Although he secured an apology from Solomon, the Governor-General's attempts to keep open the possibility of 'recognition' were by now futile.

The CNC, T.W.C. Norton, on his return to Pietermaritzburg from Zululand, simply dismissed the reopened 'recognition question'. Referring to the correspondence between Heaton Nicholls and the MNA which had been forwarded for his consideration, he succinctly replied that Solomon's behaviour on 24 July 'was such as to preclude any thoughts of improvement in Solomon's official status'.[37] Neither the SNA nor the MNA questioned this view; indeed, Solomon had been seen to insult the head of state in the full view of a large mass of Zulu people, and had encouraged the antagonistic attitude of the Zulu at the *indaba*. Both the native commissioner at Eshowe and the CNC (the highest ranking NAD officials present at the *indaba*) for these reasons urged that the government severely punish Solomon. The MNA strongly supported them.[38]

The Governor-General had only just returned from Zululand, and was in the process of formalising his 'Athlone memorandum', when the MNA began pressing him to authorise some form of punishment for Solomon. Referring to the suggestions in this regard made by the native commissioner at Eshowe and the CNC, the Governor-General argued that Solomon was 'drunk and *irresponsible*' (original emphasis) at the *indaba*, and that he should not be punished for 'discourtesies' that were a 'natural outcome of his irresponsible condition'. In this view, Solomon's sole misdeed was that he had appeared drunk in public. Moreover, the Governor-General intimated to the MNA, 'I have reasons for not wishing any drastic treatment to be meted out to Solomon' – reasons which were soon to be embodied in the Athlone memorandum.[39] Within a month after the *indaba*, however, the Governor-General had bowed to pressure to punish Solomon: he authorised the cancellation of Solomon's liquor permit and the reduction of his stipend by half for a probationary period of one year. These 'punishments', which were implemented by September 1930, in effect endorsed the CNC's dismissal of the 'recognition question'.[40]

By the time the Athlone memorandum was submitted to members of the Union cabinet ten days later, therefore, the recognition issue was no longer a political reality. The memorandum nonetheless included a 'final resort' clause recommending that, should Solomon's official status remain unchanged after a period of two years, the government should then undertake to reconsider the issue.[41] When the NAD did reconsider the 'recognition question' in 1932, it did little more than routinely dismiss the proposals once more. From the point of view of the Governor-General, Heaton Nicholls, Solomon and Inkatha, and all those who supported their common purpose, the Athlone memorandum would remain simply as a testimony to a lost opportunity.

Solomon's conduct during the *indaba* with the Governor-General in 1930 sharply contrasted with the way in which he had, in effect, taken charge at the *indaba* with the Prince of Wales in 1925. Rising above local officials and NAD policy, Solomon had entertained and consorted with the Prince on a level of royal equality. At the *indaba* of 1930, Solomon eroded rather than enhanced his political status among the Zulu, and frustrated rather than furthered his aim for official recognition as Zulu king. He proved not only that he was physically ill, but that he had lost his sense of political judgement and direction. Ironically, he failed to contain his resentment at the NAD – or to distinguish between the NAD and the Supreme Chief – at a time when his life-long ambition to be recognised as Zulu king was most likely to be realised. The Governor-General and Heaton Nicholls, acting together with such powerful African allies as Solomon and Inkatha, and with the qualified acquiescence of both the MNA and the NAD, would certainly have spearheaded a formidable pressure group in pursuit of the ideal of Zulu self-government. Solomon further demonstrated his political misjudgement in making pleas to members of the British royal family in England, which Solomon might already have realised were very unlikely to intervene in South African politics, while simultaneously rejecting the assistance of his most influential possible allies, in the presence of whom he was then standing. Perhaps most ironically, Solomon failed even to give political direction to the restiveness of the Zulu assembly at the *indaba*.

NOTES

1. CNC PMB 84, 58/7/4, SNA to CNC, 7/5/1928 (personal); and NTS 7205, 20/326, SNA to CNC, 7/5/1928 [official minute].

2. CNC PMB 84, 58/7/4, CNC to SNA, 2/6/1928; and SNA to CNC, 21/6/1928. See also NTS 7205, 20/326, CNC to SNA, 23/4/1928, enclosing draft Inkatha constitution.

3. NTS 7205, 20/326, reports on 1928 Inkatha meeting by E.N. Braatvedt, NC, Emtonjaneni, 11/6/1928, and H.L. Gebers, NC, Nongoma, 4/6/1928; and N.W. Pringle, CNC's office to SNA, 15/6/1928.

4. CNC PMB 84, 58/7/4, CNC to SNA, 17/7/1928 (confidential) [Solomon memorandum]; and CNC to SNA, 18/7/1928 (confidential) [Inkatha memorandum].

5. CNC PMB 84, 58/7/4, CNC to SNA, 17/7/1928 (confidential) [Solomon memorandum]; and, for the personal note, CNC to SNA, 17/7/1928 (private and confidential).

6. NTS 7205, 20/326, CNC to SNA, 18/7/1928 (confidential) [Inkatha memorandum].

7. *Natal Mercury*, 7/8/1928.

8. See also NEC Box 4, evidence of C.A. Wheelwright, Mtubatuba, 25/9/1930, pp. 1728–30, where Wheelwright argued that, as CNC, he had strongly favoured the official recognition of the Zulu monarchy in principle, but had found that Solomon was too unreliable to be recognised. He also complained of white 'prejudices against anything in the shape of Paramountcy in Zululand'.

9. NTS 7205, 20/326, Nicolson and Thorpe to CNC, 2/8/1928, enclosing 'Deed of Trust and Constitution of Inkatha ka Zulu'; CNC to SNA, 16/8/1928, forwarding the above; and SNA to CNC, 3/9/1928. For the CNC's interview with Fynney, see CNC to SNA, 9/11/1928.

10. For the 'Zululand deputation' to Umtata, see *Ilanga lase Natal*, 5/4/1929 and 26/4/1929; and also Ahrens, *From bench to bench*, pp. 81–82. For the Natal NCs conference, see CNC PMB 109, 94/8, Minutes and Proceedings of Native Commissioners' Conference, Durban, 14–16/5/1929 (quotations); and also memorandum entitled 'Local Councils on Locations', n.d. [1933?], which offers an overview of 'council policy' deliberations in Natal, 1929–33.

11. The meeting is referred to in NEC Box 4, evidence of C.F. Adams (Eshowe businessman), Nongoma, 22/9/1930, pp. 1669–70. For Solomon's opinion that the Bunga was too 'advanced' for Zululand, see NEC Box 7, evidence of Chief Solomon Zulu, Pietermaritzburg, 8/4/1931, pp. 6557–58; and CNC PMB 108, 94/8, Minutes and Proceedings of Native Commissioners' Conference, 1929, statement of NC, Nongoma.

12. For the annual general meeting, see NTS 7205, 20/326, 'The Yearly Report of the Inkata Zulu', 1929, enclosed in CNC to SNA, 12/8/1929 (quotations). For the chiefs' meeting, see resolutions of 'Zulu National Council: Inkata Ka Zulu', 16/8/1929 (NAD translation), enclosed in CNC to SNA, 18/9/1929 (quotations); and *Ilanga lase Natal*, 13 and 20/9/1929 (Zulu language reports).

13. NTS 7205, 20/326, 'Yearly Report of the Inkata Zulu', 1929, enclosed in CNC to SNA, 12/8/1929 (quotations). Adams' involvement with the Zulu royal house during 1930–33 is well documented, CNC PMB, 58/7/4. See also G. Heaton Nicholls, *South Africa in my time* (London, 1961), p. 150; and NEC Box 4, evidence of C. F. Adams, Nongoma, 22/9/1930, pp. 1669–70.

14. JUS 448, 4/267/28, Solomon kaDinuzulu to Magistrate, Nongoma, 9/6/1928; Magistrate, Nongoma to CNC, 12/6/1928; and CNC to SNA, 17/8/1928.

15. CNC PMB 81, 58/7/3, District Commandant, Eshowe to Magistrate, Eshowe, 27/9/1929 and 2/11/1929.

16. CNC PMB 81, 58/7/3, Solomon kaDinuzulu to CNC, 30/11/1929; and NC, Eshowe to CNC, 3/12/1929.

17. CNC PMB 81, 58/7/3, Solomon kaDinuzulu to NC, Nongoma, 12/1/1930; and CNC to NC, Nongoma, 23/1/1930. The NAD refused Solomon's request, as well as his request for an increased stipend. For the NC, Eshowe's memorandum of complaint, see NC, Eshowe to CNC, 26/11/1929.

18. CNC PMB 81, 58/7/1, minutes of meeting between NC, Eshowe and Eshowe chiefs and headmen, 8/11/1929, in untitled memorandum *re* Solomon's attempts to gain recognition as paramount chief, n.d. [1932?]. The reaction of Zulu in the Eshowe district against Solomon should not be overemphasised, however; the majority of chiefs at the meeting indicated that they would always pay special respect to Solomon because he was 'the child' of pre-conquest Zulu kings.

19. Paul la Hausse, 'Drinking in a cage: the Durban system and the 1929 beer hall riots', *Africa Perspective*, no. 20, 1982, pp. 70–73 (quotations); Roux, *Time longer than rope*, pp. 190ff; and, for a fuller treatment of the 1929 beerhall disturbances, see La Hausse's 'Struggle for the city'. For white political opinion, see Debates of the House of Assembly, vol. 14, speeches by Heaton Nicholls and Deane on the 'Riotous Assemblies Bill', 26/3/1930, cols 2345–54.

20. *Ilanga lase Natal*, 31/5/1929.

21. *Ilanga lase Natal*, 13/9/1929 (quotations) and 6/9/1929 (Zulu language reports).

22. *Ilanga lase Natal*, 6/9/1929 (quotations); and, for an overview of these political developments, Roux, *Time longer than rope*, pp. 191–92.

23. NEC Box 4, evidence of G. H. Hulett, Stanger, 2/10/1930, p. 2003; and, for meetings at Cartwright Flats, Roux, *Time longer than rope*, pp. 245–46.

24. Report of the District Commandant, SAP, 16/6/1930, quoted in La Hausse, 'Struggle for the city', pp. 222–23. Solomon did not attend this particular meeting, but he did attend an ICU meeting later, in September 1930.

25. Heaton Nicholls relates with some pride his role in the Governor-General's tour in *South Africa in my time*, pp. 154–58. For Athlone, see the *Natal Witness*'s and the *Natal Mercury*'s coverage of his various meetings with white Natalians in July 1930, especially agricultural interest groups, including his attendance at the Royal Show, Pietermaritzburg.

26. This summary of Heaton Nicholls's correspondence, including all quotations, is drawn from CNC PMB 81, 58/7/3, G. Heaton Nicholls to E. G. Jansen, 4/7/1930, 16/7/1930, and 18/7/1930, enclosed in Under-SNA to CNC, 30/7/1930.

27. CNC PMB 81, 58/7/3, E. G. Jansen to G. Heaton Nicholls, 12/7/1930; and the covering letter Under-SNA to CNC, 30/7/1930.

28. Institute of Contemporary History, University of the Orange Free State, E. G. Jansen Collection (hereafter EGJ), File 140, untitled memorandum by the Governor-General, 18/9/1930 [Athlone memorandum].

29. *Ibid.*, pp. 1–8.

30. See Edgecombe, 'Sir Marshall Clarke'.

31. See Heaton Nicholls, *South Africa in my time*, pp. 154–56; and *Natal Witness*, 25/7/1930, report of Athlone's reception in the town of Eshowe.

32. EGJ 140, CNC's report on His Excellency the Governor-General's meeting with the Zulu, for the information of the MNA, 15/8/1930 (all quotations). Other important sources are Athlone's 'Remarks on CNC's Report', 13/8/1930; CNC PMB 81, 58/7/3, NC, Eshowe to CNC, 7 and 8/8/1930; CNC to SNA, 9/8/1930; and NC, Eshowe to CNC, 12/8/1930, enclosing extract from Nongoma Bottle Store records. Shula Marks's recent account of the 1930 Zulu *indaba*, *Ambiguities of dependence*, pp. 15–18, was valuable in reviewing the account given in my doctoral dissertation. My account nonetheless remains different from that of Marks which plays down Solomon's drunkenness and goes so far as to suggest that 'the administration's allegations of drunkenness in 1930 may well have been a convenient fiction for Solomon and the administration alike' (p. 20).

33. CNC PMB 81, 58/7/3, NC, Eshowe to CNC, 8/8/1930.

34. *Natal Mercury*, 25/7/1930 (quotations); and, for the NC, Eshowe's, report of the speech, see Marks, *Ambiguities of dependence*, pp. 17–18.

35. CNC PMB 81, 58/7/3, NC, Eshowe to CNC, 7/8/1930 (quotations); and *Natal Mercury*, 25/7/1930.

36. EGJ 140, 'Address of H. E. the Governor-General to Solomon ka Dinuzulu, Nongoma', 7/8/1930 (quotation); and see also the tenor of the Governor-General's remarks in Athlone to E. G. Jansen, 13/8/1930.

37. CNC PMB 81, 58/7/3, CNC to SNA, 8/8/1930, submitting comments on correspondence between G. Heaton Nicholls and E. G. Jansen, and memorandum on Solomon's official status.

38. CNC PMB 81, 58/7/3, NC, Eshowe to CNC, 7/8/1930; CNC to SNA, 9/8/1930; and EGJ 140, E. G. Jansen to H. E. the Governor-General, 11/8/1930.

39. EGJ 140, Athlone's 'Remarks on Report of NC Eshowe', 13/8/1930 (first quotation); and Athlone to E. G. Jansen, 13/8/1930, enclosing above (second quotation).

40. See CNC PMB 81, 58/7/3, CNC to Dep. Comm., SAP, Pietermaritzburg, 26/8/1930; Acting SNA to CNC, 8/9/1930; and EGJ 140, MNA to Acting SNA *re* 'Ex. Co. minute: Solomon ka Dinuzulu', enclosing official minute, both n.d.

41. EGJ 140, Athlone memorandum, 18/9/1930, pp. 1, 6. For the consequences of this clause, see ch. 10 below.

Itshe lesikumbuzo sika TSHAKA.

Emhlanganweni wesigungu (Executive) eNKATA ka ZULU owa uhlangene eMahashini Royal Kraal ziu 16th December, 1930, kwanqunywa ukuba indaba yokubeka itshe etuneni lika Tshaka kwa Dukuza imelwe ngezinyawo.

Niyazi ke Zulu ukuba kukade ngaqala ngiyibeka pambili kwemiqondo yenu le ndaba noko ingatoli impumelelo.

Namhla ngitanda ukuba nenze into izizukulwana zohlanga lwamaZulu ezohlala ziyi kumbula.

Kulomhlangano ebesi nawo eMahashini ngo December 16, 1930, saketa uChief S. G. E. Majozi wase Indaleni, Richmond, ukuba abe uMququzeli walendaba pakati kwezwe lonke lase Natal nakwa Zulu, nakwezinye izindawo lapo kukona amaZulu. Futi nguye ozopata isikwama sayo yonke imali ezokwenza lomsebenzi, ezo nikezwa amaChiefs nabantu.

Use eseliwe noI-Hulumeni ukuba ukuqogwa kwemali ezokwenza lomsebenzi angakutikimezi Nempjela uHulumeni wali kipa izwi lokuti akali ukuba iqoqwe lemali, nokuba limiswe itshe etuneni lika Tshaka.

NANTSO KE INTANDO ZULU. Auko iuizwe abakulu leso esi ngenzi inikumbuzo ngabo. Natike asenze into eso dunyiswa ngayo yizizwe zonke nabantwana betu.

Iminikelo yabo bonke ebanikelayo yohonakala ePepeni "Ilanga lase Natal" ukuze kuqonde omdala no mncane ututi imali ipetwe ngemfanelo.

Itshe lesikumbuzo se liya buzwa. NgakoKe imali isidingeka kona manje.

Tumelani iminikelo yenu ku :
Chief S. G. E. Majozi,
"DHLOKWAKE HOME",
Indaleni M. S.,
P. O. RICHMOND,
Natal

Yimina, SOLOMON KA DINUZULU.
Mahashini Royal Kraal,
NONGOMA,
April, 1931.

The veiled Shaka Memorial and, right, a notice demonstrating the involvement of Solomon and Inkatha in the Memorial project.

10

Decline and disintegration

Solomon's confrontation with officialdom at the Zulu *indaba* of 1930 in effect terminated his political career, as well as the possibility of 'political reform' among the Zulu during his lifetime. As Solomon's hopes of recognition died in the aftermath of the *indaba*, so too did those of Inkatha, for Inkatha had always defined itself as the Zulu 'royal party' and its political fortunes were inseparable from those of the Zulu royal house. The organisation was now forced to accept that, at least for the foreseeable future, its overriding political objective had been defeated. Solomon had barely two and a half years left to live after the *indaba* debacle and, in terms of practical politics, Inkatha had even less.

At Mahashini, three weeks after the *indaba*, Inkatha's annual general meeting of 1930 proved to be one of the best attended in the organisation's history, comparable in size to the 1928 meeting. It had been widely advertised prior to the *indaba*: printed notices were circulated in the Province of Natal, Johannesburg, the eastern Transvaal and even parts of the Orange Free State. The 1930 meeting had undoubtedly been keenly anticipated by Inkatha's organisers, since it promised to be an occasion on which the populist Zulu nationalism that the *indaba* seemed sure to inspire could be politically consolidated, just as the 1925 meeting had done after the celebrated *indaba* with the Prince of Wales. But in reality the atmosphere of the 1930 meeting was anything but celebratory; its proceedings were instead scarred by dissension and discord, and lacked enthusiasm or even a clear sense of purpose. *Ilanga lase Natal*'s authorised report made no reference to any discussion of the recent *indaba* having taken place during the meeting – at which, significantly, no NAD official or observer was present.[1]

The private deliberations of the general committee (comprising all chiefs and certain appointed ministers of religion) and the executive committee took up the first two days of the meeting, as was customary. Two issues were discussed at length: the need to make representations directly to the Union government rather than to the NAD, and the need to implement a scheme for the purchase of land to alleviate Zulu land pressure. The issue on which greatest consensus was reached, however, related to the deteriorating health of the 'king'. A unanimous resolution advocated that Solomon be sent to England for specialist medical treatment, and noted that 'the change to another place would do him good'. Underlying this resolution, perhaps, was the reasoning that Solomon's absence would certainly do Inkatha good, and more so if he returned a reformed person.

When Solomon appeared before the public assembly on the final day of the meeting, he made a somewhat startling proposal: neither he nor any member of the Zulu royal family, he moved, should continue to hold positions on the executive committee (Solomon personally had been treasurer since 1928). Solomon was evidently acting on the 'advice' of kholwa leaders who foresaw that Solomon would have to be dissociated from the practical affairs of Inkatha if the organisation were to survive. Although this proposal was initially approved by Inkatha as a whole, Chief Matole led sufficiently strong resistance to prevent its being formally accepted. In the ensuing deadlock, the meeting was unable to elect a new executive committee – which, under the terms of the 1928 constitution, was one of the central functions of the Inkatha annual general meeting. Inkatha thus had no legally-constituted leadership after the 1930 meeting.

Another of the central constitutional functions of the Inkatha annual general meeting was to ratify the organisation's annual financial statement. Describing the atmosphere as 'tense', *Ilanga lase Natal* reported how detailed revelations were made regarding unauthorised 'Inkatha collectors', whose collections were not forwarded to Inkatha, and the misappropriation of Inkatha funds. That the unauthorised collectors were able to produce official Inkatha receipts and photographs of King Solomon conclusively showed that the corruption was internal. Although Solomon was not – and could not be – implicated at the meeting, it was clear that he, in conjunction with his private secretary, Simpson Bhengu, who also held the office of secretary to Inkatha, was primarily responsible for both the fraudulent collections and the misappropriation of funds. Mshiyeni, Solomon's full brother who worked as a labour supervisor on the gold mines and, as a practising Christian, identified more with the kholwa than the tribal elite, was especially outraged at the evidence of gross corruption in Inkatha. So too was Bhulose, the chairman, who charged that various chiefs were retaining Inkatha subscriptions for their own use.[2] At the 1930 meeting, it seemed that not only the kholwa elite's relationship with Solomon but its alliance with the tribal elite had become strained. This development, combined with Solomon's accelerated decline, signalled that Inkatha's demise was imminent.

*   *   *   *   *

Ten days after the 1930 Inkatha meeting, Solomon, deeply in debt, went to Durban to consult his lawyers on financial matters. In Durban he also held a meeting with dock workers resident in the municipal labour compounds. On the completion of this meeting at the Bell Street Compound beerhall, one of the institutions that the ICU *yase* Natal had long boycotted, Solomon immediately thereafter attended a meeting of the ICU *yase* Natal.

Solomon's purpose in 'dropping in' on Champion's meeting at the ICU Hall on 3 September was evidently to stake a claim to the organisation's revenue. The ICU *yase* Natal had been wilfully invoking Zulu nationalism at its meetings at Cartwright Flats over the previous year, and much of the tribute that would have been paid to Solomon had undoubtedly been paid in subscriptions to the ICU *yase* Natal. During his discussion with Champion, Solomon advocated that the present division between the ICU *yase* Natal and the NNC should be healed; to this end, he suggested the calling of a conference at which both organisations would be represented, with Solomon himself presiding.[3] Solomon's expressed concern for Zulu unity in this context should not be taken at face value – and not only because it was resoundingly hollow in view of the particular class position he had adopted since late 1927. For Solomon in 1930, the fact that political divisions among the Zulu caused a loss of royal revenue was more immediately important than the political divisions themselves. Indeed, Solomon's decision on 3 September to commit himself to an open association with the ICU *yase* Natal was utterly incompatible with his own and Inkatha's 'anti-ICU' policy since 1927 – a policy which had played a central role in their mutual drive for official recognition. It seemed that Solomon's need for revenue had overcome in him any sense of political purpose beyond cultivating Zulu national allegiance to the institution of Zulu kingship. In meeting Champion, however, Solomon was apparently hoping to reassert not only his own political position, but also the rights of the whole rural-based 'tribal' order together with the values and obligations of 'tribal' tradition, which after all underpinned the political status of the Zulu 'ancien régime'. Explaining to the CNC the reasons why he had met Champion, Solomon stated that he wished to complain that workers in Durban came from 'us' (evidently referring to tribal authorities in the rural areas) to earn money to pay taxes, but then 'you get them'.[4] A weakening of political loyalties to the 'tribal' order as a whole meant a diminished cash flow to the rural areas.

Following their meeting, which caused great excitement in ICU quarters, Champion and Solomon arranged to appear together at a specially convened Zulu mass meeting at the ICU Hall on 6 September. The event was widely publicised by way of ICU handbills, which also advertised that Dube and 'all the educated people of Durban' would be in attendance.[5] This was hardly likely; it was more likely that Solomon had implicated Dube without having consulted him. Significantly, the advertisement published in *Ilanga lase Natal* made no reference to Dube: 'King Solomon will be greeted by the ICU *yase* Natal at a resounding meeting of African workers', it said, 'Come Zulus and see the head of the nation meeting his people.'[6] Needless to say, neither Dube nor any other representative of the NNC attended the meeting. Neither did Solomon. He had one of his increasingly frequent attacks of alcohol-induced illness and refused to leave his quarters at Depot Road Native Location. It was clear, however, that he had also become alarmed about the publicity that the event had attracted, and feared NAD and police retribution. When Champion and three thousand ICU *yase* Natal supporters thereupon congregated outside Solomon's quarters on the evening of 6 September, Solomon remained in hiding, but nonetheless accepted a cash gift. He left for Eshowe shortly afterwards.

The most immediate consequence of Solomon's brief association with the ICU *yase* Natal was the banishment of Champion from the Province of Natal, under the terms of the Riotous Assemblies Act. In calling for this repressive response, the Commissioner of the South African Police informed the Minister of Justice that

> Champion, by reason of his association with Solomon Dinuzulu [sic] and with other Zulu Chiefs, has greatly gained in prestige amongst the natives of Durban, particularly amongst members of the I.C.U. and that he is, consequently, at present a very much greater menace to Law and Order than he has ever been in the past . . . this prestige is bound to increase and a conflict between Europeans and Natives seems to be more than a probability in the near future.[7]

Champion's banishment thus reflected the state's sensitivity to the dangerous political role that Solomon could play – and was not simply a consequence of Champion's involvement in the beerhall protests. The action caused something of a political controversy: the mayor of Durban, the Revd A. Lamont, who was supported by certain 'leading citizens' of the city including the MP for Durban County, A. H. J. Eaton, petitioned the Minister of Justice to delay the banning order until protests had been considered. *Ilanga lase Natal* also objected. These protests, however, were not directed against the banishment of Champion specifically, but against the Riotous

Assemblies Act which was seen to subvert liberal-democratic principles: the rights of freedom of speech and association, the sovereignty of parliament, and the rule of law. Marwick and the *Natal Mercury*, however, vigorously endorsed the banning order.[8]

The banishment of Champion effectively decapitated the ICU *yase* Natal, and the organisation went into an abrupt political decline. Although Champion's provincial leadership in practice had been somewhat moderate, notwithstanding his rhetoric, he had played a vital role in the articulation of popular protest in the Province of Natal. His skills as an organiser and propagandist had been largely responsible for the growth of a mass movement there, and he was a rousing and apparently fearless orator. In the five years since his return from the Transvaal to Natal as provincial ICU organiser, Champion had virtually come to personify popular protest in the region. And although opportunities had long existed for a more radical popular leader to displace or at least to challenge Champion, no one had done so by the time he was exiled in 1930. In early 1931, the Department of Justice was pleased to report that the ICU *yase* Natal had become an organisation of 'little consequence' since Champion's departure.[9]

Champion, meanwhile, lived out his exile in Johannesburg. Irrevocably a Natal-based politician, he withdrew from political life. He nonetheless did occasionally pen self-pitying reflections on his political martyrdom and exile for the ANC newspaper *Abantu-Batho*, while earning a living as a cashier with the Colonial Banking and Trust Company. On his return to Natal, after his banning order was lifted by Smuts in early 1933, Champion occupied himself with political objectives which were fundamentally 'respectable', conciliatory and kholwa in character.[10]

If the ICU *yase* Natal was not to play a significant role in the articulation of popular protest after 1930, it seemed in late 1930 that Champion's absence would enable the Durban branch of the CP to rise in influence as an embodiment of the more radical elements within the spectrum of popular consciousness. Johannes Nkosi, the organiser of the Durban CP, had previously always deferred to Champion as the city's 'elder statesman' of popular protest. Perhaps partly because Nkosi refused on principle to invoke ethnic loyalties, the Durban CP's meetings were never so enthusiastically attended as those of the ICU *yase* Natal. But in the same month as Champion was banished, the Durban CP acquired a new hall; and it was from there that Nkosi orchestrated the Durban workforce's exceptional response to the Communists' Union-wide call for a one-day general strike and pass-burning demonstration. On 'Dingaan's Day' (16 December) 1930, however, the demonstration at Cartwright Flats was attacked by the police, and four Africans including Nkosi were fatally wounded. Many arrests of communist sympathisers immediately ensued, while police forestalled the regeneration of the Durban CP by simply deporting those officials sent by CP head-quarters to replace Nkosi. Durban's Detective Sergeant R.H. Arnold, who had been a prime mover in the banishment of Champion in September, boasted with considerable justification that he was now crushing the communists just as he had crushed the ICU *yase* Natal.[11] Solomon's meeting with Champion, which ironically had seemed to promise much for the popular movement, had in practice set in motion a train of events which ultimately served to repress large-scale and effective popular protest in Natal until the defiance campaign of the 1950s.

The consequence of the 'Solomon-Champion episode' for Inkatha was to increase concern and unease among Inkatha's kholwa leaders. Following so soon after the *indaba* debacle of July 1930, Solomon's association with Champion forced kholwa leaders to the realisation that they could not maintain a working political alliance with so unpredictable and irresponsible an ally. That the Riotous Assemblies Act was first used in Natal as a consequence of Solomon's political behaviour was a cause of great embarrassment to Inkatha: one year previously, Dube had confidently told the MNA and the CNC that such repressive legislation would be unnecessary if Solomon were recognised as Zulu paramount chief. In the month after Solomon's meeting with Champion, *Ilanga lase Natal* published an article which, while ostensibly addressing the question of Solomon's health, in reality expressed the kholwa leadership's disillusionment with Solomon. It was reported that Solomon had been given wise advice by Dube, Bhulose and Seme (the newly elected president of the ANC, who was then taking a special interest in Zulu affairs), evidently to the effect that he should retire from public life so as to convalesce. 'However much they miss him [Solomon]', the article continued, it was not right that Solomon 'lying down and ill should be aroused for our affairs of the Zulu nation'.[12] The article illustrated the anxiety among kholwa leaders generally that Solomon be persuaded to bow out of an active role in Zulu politics.

In fact, however, representatives of the Natal kholwa establishment did not resolutely take action to constrain Solomon's political role. Realistically perceiving that Solomon was barely tractable and that Inkatha was inseparably identified with him, they instead distanced themselves from Inkatha, no longer regarding it as a viable representative organisation for kholwa politics. But because Zulu 'tradition' and the concept of Zulu 'nationhood' remained central to Natal kholwa thinking, the symbols of 'Solomon and Inkatha' were not simply abandoned; they were still perceived as having an important cultural – if not directly political – role to perform as embodiments of Zulu nationalist concepts. Indeed, a 'cultural initiative' was to be launched under Inkatha's auspices and Solomon's patronage towards the end of 1930, focusing on a project to erect a memorial to Shaka as founder of the Zulu nation – and, with hindsight, confirming Inkatha's withdrawal from work of an overtly political nature.

Inkatha's abrupt political decline in late 1930 was hastened by an important factor unrelated to Solomon's political unreliability and the organisation's chaotic financial state: the promise of an alternative political organisation for Natal's kholwa establishment. Pixley Seme, the conservative who had recently replaced the radical Josiah Gumede as ANC president, mounted a campaign in October 1930 to regenerate the Natal branch of the ANC in 'respectable' guise and so firmly bring Natal back into the fold of the national Congress. Following the 1924 'militant coup' in the NNC, the most influential leaders of Natal's kholwa establishment had simply dissociated themselves from their provincial and national Congress organisations and had regrouped in Inkatha. In the late 1920s, moreover, Dube had resuscitated the 'old' NNC, separate from the national Congress, as a small and congenial forum for the most conservative elements of the province's African establishment. The radicalised NNC (later renamed the Natal African Congress, and then the Natal branch of the ANC), though freed from conservative domination, did not develop into an influential political organisation; its promised role in popular politics had instead been performed by the Natal branch of the ICU and, subsequently, the ICU *yase* Natal. The concept of a united Union-wide Congress organisation, which Seme and Dube had played so leading a role in institutionalising in 1912, had thus died in the Province of Natal during the 1920s.[13]

During his 1929 election campaign for the ANC presidency, Seme had expounded an ideology of African national unity, founded on the practical basis of 'co-operation' and 'self-help', which foresaw the reconstruction of an independent 'African civilisation'. This correlated closely with ideas current among the Natal kholwa establishment – though the latter tended to interpret African national unity in a narrower Zulu-ethnic sense. But Seme himself, a Zulu-speaking congressman with a legal practice in Johannesburg, was not insensitive to the appeal of a Zulu ethnic nationalism, as was reflected in his campaign in late 1930 to unite African politics in the Province of Natal under the ANC umbrella – and, by extension, under his leadership. In an open letter to *Ilanga lase Natal* in October 1930 decrying the 'divisions in Natal' and publicising a 'conference' to elect new office-bearers for the Natal branch of the ANC, Seme announced that his wife 'Princess Harriet kaDinuzulu' (Solomon's sister) was to visit Durban 'for the first time in the interests of the African National Congress'. He also expressed respectful concern for the unstable state of Solomon's health.[14]

Seme's efforts seemed to be rewarded when the Natal branch of the ANC was formally reconstituted in October 1930; and Bhulose, who had been Inkatha chairman since 1924 and had acted as a vital mediator between Inkatha's kholwa and tribal elites, accepted a position on the new provincial executive committee. Bhulose nominally remained Inkatha chairman, but he henceforth directed his political energies into the ANC. His shift away from Mahashini reflected a general withdrawal of kholwa support for Inkatha. Yet the Natal kholwa establishment as a whole did not simply transfer its political allegiance to the Natal branch of the ANC along with Bhulose, as Seme had hoped. Dube, the most prominent kholwa leader in the province, remained aloof: having accepted office on the ANC National Executive when Seme became president in April 1930, Dube soon disagreed with Seme's somewhat autocratic style. Dube and many of his most *hamba kahle* supporters thus determinedly retained their independent NNC stronghold – which white authorities appreciated. The third most prominent local kholwa leader after Dube and Bhulose, Inkatha's vice-chairman, Chief Majozi, maintained a low profile in the emerging power struggle between Seme and Dube (although he clearly favoured the latter). Majozi instead focused his attention on Inkatha's 'cultural initiative'.[15]

Seme's frustration with the NNC's obstinate separatism, together with his determination to unite even ICU *yase* Natal supporters under the ANC, was reflected in his attempts to come to terms with Champion soon after the latter's banishment. He wrote to Champion in late October 1930, proclaiming the ANC's drive for African national unity and stating that the ICU *yase* Natal was representative of only 'a section of the community'. In order to present himself as an ally, Seme played on Champion's long-standing antipathy for Dube by intimating that the ANC too wished to 'drive Ilanga out of Natal'. Seme also played on the exiled ICU *yase* Natal leader's insecurity, arguing that the ANC could assist Champion to avoid further disastrous confrontations with the government. 'You must realise that I have written as President General of a senior organisation', Seme wrote, in typical fashion. Champion, in equally typical fashion, rejected Seme's appeal.[16]

The abrupt collapse of Inkatha as a viable political organisation in 1930 had shattered kholwa political unity in the Province of Natal. Many kholwa individuals were left politically homeless, and the divisions within Natal's congressmen remained. Inkatha's sorry state was manifested in May 1931 when the CNC, concerned about the numerous reports from local officials relating to corrupt 'Inkatha collectors', conducted a meeting with Inkatha's chairman and vice-chairman, William Bhulose and Chief Simon Majozi. Seme, at his own insistence, was also in attendance, as was a member of the legal firm J.H. Nicolson and Son (which had drawn up Inkatha's 1928 constitution), attending as Inkatha's solicitor at the insistence of Fynney.

At the meeting it was openly disclosed for the first time that Solomon was misappropriating Inkatha funds. Bhulose informed the CNC that his own position in Inkatha was 'most difficult', and that on one occasion alone a sum of £2000 had been taken from Inkatha to settle Solomon's debts. The CNC noted that, after the formal meeting was over, he was confidentially advised that 'upwards of £10 000 had been disposed of for Solomon's benefit'. When Bhulose agreed to supply the CNC with a written statement that Inkatha had not appointed any itinerant collectors, Inkatha's solicitor intervened to advise Bhulose to be 'cautious in this connection'. It was then revealed that Bhengu, Inkatha's secretary who had emerged as Solomon's right-hand man, had had new Inkatha receipt books printed without Bhulose's knowledge, and that these were being used by fraudulent collectors. The CNC observed that Bhulose 'appeared to know very little of what was going on' in Inkatha. Majozi played little part in the meeting's proceedings, while Seme sat 'mostly shaking his head in disapproval of the disclosures'.[17]

Since Bhulose undertook to terminate Inkatha collections and to draw up a financial statement for submission to the NAD, the CNC decided that immediate intervention was unnecessary. Bhulose, however, was successful in neither of these undertakings. In the first place, he was powerless to halt collections that were being made on the authority of Solomon and his corrupt accomplices. In the second place, it seemed that Dube, perceiving the demand for an unavoidably damning financial statement as part of Seme's drive to discredit his political opponents in the province, took steps to ensure that no such statement was procured. An Inkatha executive committee meeting to investigate Inkatha's financial affairs took place at Mahashini in July 1931. The meeting was delayed for a couple of days while committee members prayed for Solomon's safety: they had arrived to discover that 'the king' had been rushed off for urgent medical treatment, and shortly thereafter had learnt that the royal car had overturned while returning along a precipitous section of the Nongoma road. Although Bhulose chaired the eventual meeting, it was Dube, Majozi and Edgar Mini (kholwa chief of the Edendale community, and veteran NNC member) who dominated the proceedings. No discussion of Inkatha's financial affairs took place – at least according to the meeting's authorised report in *Ilanga lase Natal* – and no financial statement was ever produced.[18]

The NAD for its part took no action when Bhulose failed to submit the promised financial statement. By this stage the NAD had come to realise that the Inkatha executive committee was not responsible for Inkatha's financial and administrative disorders. The fault lay in Mahashini itself, and the NAD therefore brought its concern to bear directly on the Zulu royal house. Inkatha continued to exist, even if only in name and in the minds of those who surrendered contributions to 'Inkatha collectors'. Dube, the most tenacious of Solomon's kholwa advisers, tendered his resignation from the organisation personally to Solomon in October 1932.[19] Inkatha was formally dissolved only after Solomon's death, however, apparently at the instigation of the Zulu regent, Mshiyeni kaDinuzulu, who was embarrassed by and indignant about the image of the Zulu royal house that he had inherited.[20]

*   *   *   *   *

Inkatha's 'cultural initiative' had been set underway in late 1930 in the context of Solomon's and Inkatha's abrupt political decline. The political divisions that then existed within Natal's kholwa establishment were largely superficial, for there was still a strong consensus of opinion on the broad ideal of Zulu 'progress' through unity. Moreover, the 'nation-building' policies that Dube and Seme had separately come to advocate in the late 1920s had been widely understood in terms of Zulu unity and Zulu nationalism in the Province of Natal. The broader purpose of Inkatha's cultural initiative, whose main immediate goal was to organise the construction of a national monument to Shaka, may be summarised as threefold: to nurture, sustain and further develop a sense of nationhood among all Zulu-speaking people; to create an awareness of a Zulu cultural heritage suitable to kholwa sensibilities and conducive to ethnic pride in terms of both traditional and 'western' values; and to define Zulu nationalism as a social force which was rousing yet 'respectable', as opposed to one which was an emotional spur to popular militancy. In celebrating 'Zulu tradition' and 'Zuluness', and through fostering unity in the cosy interior of an inclusive cultural movement, the cultural initiative functioned to deflect attention away from recent political divisions and disappointments. But there was also an underlying present political purpose: to reassert control over the 'Zulu nation' by defining the ideological content of Zulu nationalism.

The 'Shaka Memorial' project was not the only element in Inkatha's cultural initiative, but was certainly the project most energetically and effectively promoted. A separate project, for example, aimed at collecting money to buy the lands in the Babanango sub-district known as Emakhosini – 'the place of the kings', the main burial site for heads of the house of Zulu since the turn of the seventeenth century. The hope was that this sacred preserve of the Zulu would be owned communally by the nation as a whole, and held in trust by Zulu royalty.[21] There had been an earlier unsuccessful attempt to buy the Emakhosini site, led by the Zulu royal family soon after the death of Dinuzulu. The Shaka Memorial project, too, was not an entirely new idea in 1930, since it had been discussed during Inkatha's annual general meeting of 1924.

The decision to put the Shaka Memorial project into practice was made at Inkatha's annual general meeting of 1930 – which proved to be the organisation's last annual general meeting. Subsequently, at a special Inkatha executive committee meeting at Mahashini on 16 December 1930 (by coincidence, the day on which the Durban CP held its fateful pass-burning demonstration at Cartwright Flats), arrangements were made for the launch of the publicity and fund-raising campaign. The 'Shaka Memorial Fund Organising Committee' included William Bhulose, John Dube, William Ndhlovu and Chief Simon Majozi, who held an important position as secretary and treasurer. Writing to the CNC, Majozi emphasised that the Shaka Memorial Fund was independent of any other fund, its account being at the Richmond branch of Barclay's Bank, and offered various assurances on the delicate matter of financial management.[22]

The original project was simply to erect a stone monument dedicated to Shaka, as founder of the Zulu nation, on his grave at Dukuza near Stanger. As money flowed into the fund, however, instructions were given to leading monumental stonemasons to carve monuments not only to Shaka but also to Mpande, Cetshwayo and Dinuzulu (Dingane was not included, undoubtedly because he was Shaka's murderer), and the project was expanded to include the erection of a public building on the site.[23] Plans for an elaborate opening ceremony were initiated at an early stage. The programme was to begin in Durban with a sports event, followed by a concert in the Durban city hall. Thereafter Durban-based Zulu would board trains to Dukuza where, along with rural Zulu and in accordance with pre-conquest Zulu traditions, they would build huts for their own accommodation during the ceremony. There would be addresses by various dignitaries, including the Governor-General, Solomon, two other Zulu chiefs (one from Natal proper and one from Zululand), and a 'representative educated Native'. A 'war dance' would ensue.[24]

Most of the work of fund-raising was carried out by ministers and clerics, whose efforts were enthusiastically publicised through *Ilanga lase Natal* during 1931 and 1932.[25] Although the project had been a kholwa initiative, once under way it seemed to appeal to all strata of Zulu society. The Bell Street labour compound and the ICU *yase* Natal in Durban responded with notable generosity, as did mine labour compounds in Johannesburg; subscriptions also poured in from rural areas.[26] For all, the celebratory atmosphere of the Shaka Memorial project seemed to offer an escape from the political tribulations, repressions and frustrations of 1930. Support also came from white quarters in Natal. The MP for Zululand, George Heaton Nicholls, in particular was to play a vital role in mid-1932, when he approached the NAD and the Governor-General, the Earl of Clarendon, to assist in arrangements for the unveiling ceremony.[27]

The CNC, SNA, MNA and the Governor-General resolved in early 1932 to give formal support to the unveiling ceremony, as was requested by the organising committee, but on condition that Majozi furnished proof that the costs of the monuments had been settled in full. Majozi, however, died suddenly in early July 1932, having just completed a month-long fund-raising campaign in the Transvaal. The CNC then learnt that the stonemasons were still owed £3309 – and the unveiling ceremony therefore was postponed.[28] Within a few weeks of Majozi's death, a meeting of the Inkatha executive committee (which was in practice the Shaka Memorial Fund organising committee), was held at Mahashini to make new arrangements for the administration of the fund. For reasons which cannot readily be understood, the custody of the remaining money in the fund, together with that which was still coming in from local fund-raisers, was handed over to Solomon.[29] The funds thereupon seemed to vanish into thin air. Who precisely was responsible for their disappearance remained unspecified, and no formal inquiry was conducted. As the financial scandal unfolded, Dube simply resigned from the Shaka Memorial Fund organising committee; his resignation was privately tendered directly to Solomon.[30] In late 1932, *Ilanga lase Natal* – which had played a leading role in the project's fund-raising campaign – was subjected to a flood of queries from the Zulu public. After November 1932, however, the newspaper apparently suppressed any further public discussion of the fate of both the fund and the veiled memorial.

The memorial to Shaka subsequently 'remained covered with sheeting for a long time', Heaton Nicholls recorded in his unpublished memoirs, 'until the wind and the rain and the sun rotted [the material] and disclosed a Grecian urn'.[31] The stonemasons, who were still in possession of the monuments to Mpande, Cetshwayo and Dinuzulu, continued to press the government and the Zulu royal house to settle the outstanding debts until the eve of the Second World War. The government disclaimed all responsibility, however; and the Zulu regent following Solomon's death, Mshiyeni kaDinuzulu, indignantly (in the CNC's words) 'kept aloof from the whole business'.[32] The government even rejected a request from the South African Historical Monuments Commission in 1937 to proclaim the Shaka Memorial a protected monument: the issue was a matter of 'delicacy', it was said –

from the points of view of both the NAD and Mshiyeni.[33] From the point of
view of the Shaka Memorial project's organisers, nevertheless, the project
had not been simply an ignominious failure. The publicity and fund-raising
campaigns themselves had done much to propagate Inkatha's ideology of
Zulu nationhood and nationalism; and though Inkatha as an organisation had
disintegrated, its ideas continued to exert an influence on Zulu politics.

*   *   *   *   *

Solomon's last few years until his death in March 1933 were marked by the
disastrous consequences of his alcoholism, physical and emotional insta-
bility, and large cash needs. On a few notable occasions during this period,
however, Solomon was capable of recovering sufficiently to present a public
image befitting his role as Zulu 'king', and to represent the Zulu national
interest (at least as he defined it) to state authorities with both dignity and
clarity. The evidence he gave before the Native Economic Commission in
April 1931, for example, reflected a sensitive awareness of the social and
economic difficulties confronting rural Zulu. Directly after giving evidence,
incidentally, he addressed a meeting of Zulu at a Pietermaritzburg beerhall
and spoke against the influence of the ICU *yase* Natal and communists.[34]
And in September 1931, Solomon took up his traditional role at the head of a
large assembly of Zulu chiefs and people which had gathered at Nongoma
for an *indaba* with the SNA. This *indaba* focused on Zulu local tax arrears –
which totalled £80 000 – and the growing rural famine.[35] But apart from
these occasions, and those on which he publicly gave support to the Shaka
Memorial project, Solomon mainly lived a withdrawn and private life after
1930, at Mahashini. There he sought comfort in alcohol, expensive clothes
and motor cars, and the company of corrupt royal sycophants, while
exploiting Zulu devotion to royalty in a vain attempt to cover the
extravagance of the royal clique.

This period of Solomon's life coincided with a period of acute economic
hardship for rural Zulu. The rural famine that struck Zululand and Northern
Natal between 1931 and 1932 was a consequence of a severe drought,
devastatingly superimposed on the long-term problems of land congestion,
population growth, overgrazing and soil erosion. It was a situation
accentuated by the Great Depression and rising unemployment, when rural
families were less able to supplement their resources from wages earned in
the capitalist and state sectors. Even in the early stages of the drought, the
Natal Witness reported that all that stood between the Zulu and starvation
was 'feeding daily on the dying cattle'. And Ndesheni kaMnyaiza,
reminiscing fifty years later, recalled how a snake could be seen moving

across the other side of a valley in the Nongoma and Mahlabatini districts, for there was no grass left at all.[36] The state of the Zulu became a matter for widespread concern: the MNA and MP for Vryheid, E. G. Jansen, informed parliament that over two hundred thousand Zulu cattle had died in the period June to November 1931 alone; the Bishop of Zululand petitioned the government for the distribution of emergency rations; and the *Natal Witness* gave prominence to Zulu representations for sustenance.[37] In an unprecedented move, the NAD declared the Zululand inland reserves to be famine areas and instituted the distribution of emergency maize rations. For the financial year 1931–32, the NAD spent £35 800 on famine relief in Zululand and Northern Natal – 81 per cent of its total expenditure over the whole Union. It also wrote off £30 000 of the £80 000 local tax arrears that had accrued in the Zululand inland reserves.[38]

Solomon's more controlled extravagance during the mid-1920s, against the background of a period of comparative Zulu prosperity, had served a political purpose. Through his luxury cars, stylish clothing, well-presented wives, magnificent royal residence at KwaDlamahlahla, large supply of liquor, and his generous provision of food and accommodation for the thousands who attended the Inkatha meetings, Solomon had fashioned an image for the Zulu royal house which seemed appropriate to its status. But after 1930, royal extravagance could only be associated with nepotism and corruption, and the personal breakdown of an alcoholic, who now seemed prone to moments of dark anger and despairing nihilism. In July 1931, Solomon appeared in the Melmoth courthouse to answer a criminal charge that he did 'wrongfully and unlawfully, publicly and indecently, expose his penis and whilst dancing around relieved himself' on the forecourt of a local garage. A charge of *crimen injuria* brought by the garage proprietor was also pending. Earlier in the year, Solomon had had a confrontation with Melmoth police when he allegedly refused to stop drinking from a Johnny Walker bottle in public, and attempted to grab a rifle from a policeman.[39] Such reports, together with reports of bouts of dangerously poor physical health, were a feature of Solomon's last few years.

Once Inkatha's funds were exhausted, Solomon's main source of income lay in a network of royal collectors, some of whom seemed to collect as much for themselves as they did for Solomon. The most prominent among these collectors were Simpson Bhengu (Solomon's private secretary); Daniel Vilakazi (a royal *induna* in the Vryheid district, previously secretary to the late Dinuzulu and a minor official in Inkatha); Lymon Maling (previously an ALU leader and chiefs' representative in Inkatha); and two whites, A. S. B. Blackhurst (previously the messenger of the Nongoma court), and Mr Pretorius (a cattle-broker from Babanango). As a consequence of the drought, Great Depression and famine, royal collectors found difficulty in gathering cash tribute in Zululand and Northern Natal. For this reason, the main 'currency' the collectors handled was not cash but cattle – tens of thousands of which were contributed to the Zulu royal house between 1931 and early 1933.[40]

Two separate cattle-collecting schemes were in operation under Solomon's name from 1931. One was organised by Pretorius, a man of dubious character whose career as a small-time entrepreneur in Northern Natal had included periods of employment as Solomon's chauffeur, and Daniel Vilakazi. The latter collected cattle in Northern Natal on Solomon's behalf; the former then sold the cattle and handed over a proportion of the proceeds to Solomon.[41] The more important scheme, which took effect mainly in the Zululand reserves, was organised by Blackhurst. As messenger of the Nongoma court, Blackhurst had first become involved in the financial affairs of the Zulu royal house in the course of serving summonses on Solomon for debt. Blackhurst had arranged for H.J. Brook, a Durban livestock dealer, to advance £2000 to pay Solomon's numerous creditors on the basis of an agreement whereby Solomon would repay Brook's loan in regular instalments. But when Solomon did not honour this agreement, Blackhurst (who was receiving a retainer from Solomon for financial services) began to repay Brook on Solomon's behalf. Then, as writs for debts not settled by Brook's loan continued to flow into Mahashini, and Solomon went on to incur new debts after the 'Brook agreement', Blackhurst agreed to loan Solomon further capital for the settlement of royal debts. Under the terms of a new 'Blackhurst agreement', Solomon would authorise Blackhurst to conduct 'royal cattle collections' throughout Zululand. Blackhurst would then sell the cattle through Brook and other Durban livestock dealers, and the proceeds would go towards the settlement of Solomon's debt to Blackhurst.

It seemed that Blackhurst had initially set out to earn some commission, and to establish himself in a new career as financial agent and cattle dealer among the Zulu, in the course of assisting the Zulu royal house in its financial difficulties. But as Blackhurst had become increasingly entangled in Mahashini's web of financial chaos, his attempts to recoup his losses – and to extract some profit for his efforts – became increasingly desperate and extortionate. It was the famine-stricken Zulu 'commoners' who bore the burden of this exploitation. In the wake of the 1931 drought, when Zulu crops had failed and cattle had begun to succumb to starvation, more and more Zulu had made use of the newly introduced NAD-organised livestock auctions to sell their cattle for money to buy food and pay taxes.[42] But Blackhurst, Bhengu, and the royal *izinduna* Mnyaiza and Gilbert, all of whom acted under Solomon's authority, persuaded many instead to hand over their cattle to Blackhurst, who would sell direct to Durban dealers and so raise higher prices than were obtainable locally. It transpired, however, that Zulu received considerably less for cattle sold through Blackhurst than through the local NAD auctions – it seemed that most of the proceeds went towards the repayment of royal debts, and into the pockets of Blackhurst and his assistant 'middlemen'. There were other indications that the royal cattle collections were being made under false pretences: some Zulu understood that their cattle were to be sold for the benefit of the Shaka Memorial Fund, while others believed that Solomon was establishing a 'national fund' to buy Vryheid farms for the resettlement of dislocated Zulu.[43] But the majority of the Zulu who responded to the royal cattle collections certainly knew that they were contributing towards the repayment of Solomon's debts. And they were generous indeed.

But despite Zulu generosity throughout 1931 and 1932, at the height of the famine, the total debt of the Zulu royal house increased. While writs for pre-1931 debts originally unknown to Blackhurst continued to arrive at Mahashini, new debts were being incurred faster than the old debts were being settled. In May 1931, when royal cash and cattle collections had already discharged some royal debts, Blackhurst informed the NAD that the total debt of the Zulu royal house was £1564. But the NAD ascertained in June 1931 that Eshowe general dealer Charles Adams, who had been attempting to repair the royal house's financial problems since they had become grave in 1928, was separately owed £1300. Then in November 1931, Blackhurst drew up a statement, which was approved by Bhengu as well as by Solomon and Dube, indicating that the total royal debt was £3783. And in July 1932, a statement drawn up by the NAD which took into account neither Solomon's remaining debt to Blackhurst (which Solomon was unable to specify) nor any new debts incurred after 31 January 1932 (which alone amounted to thousands) set the total royal debt at £4174.[44]

Although Solomon personally did not incur every 'royal debt' (some were incurred under Solomon's name by royal advisers), he was evidently responsible for incurring the majority. The largest debts related to Solomon's motor-car expenses. Another major source of debt was doctors' fees and pharmacists' accounts, largely a consequence of Solomon's alcohol-induced illnesses. Liquor costs, incidentally, which might have been the royal house's largest expense, were never reflected because after 1930 royal liquor had to be bought illegally and therefore for cash. Lawyers' fees and court costs were also included in the three largest single sources of royal debt. Some of these legal expenses related to actions arising from Solomon's behaviour (e.g. the public indecency and *crimen injuria* cases of 1931), and others, ironically, arose from Solomon's attempts to forestall his creditors' taking him to court. Other debts were owed to numerous retailers throughout the Province of Natal and the Rand. Such were the royal expenses that the famine-stricken Zulu were attempting to subsidise, and which various white individuals (ranging from Blackhurst and his associates to Charles Adams and George Armstrong), Natal politicians (including Dube and Heaton Nicholls) and NAD officials were attempting to curtail.

The cattle collections proved to be an extremely inefficient method of reducing royal debts. In November 1931, the native commissioner at Nongoma uncovered what seemed to be incontrovertible evidence of administrative and financial malpractice on Blackhurst's part. Not only Blackhurst but also two Vryheid whites named Buys and De Witt, whom Blackhurst employed on Solomon's behalf, drew salaries and 'expenses' from the proceeds of the sale of Zulu cattle. The native commissioner had ascertained that the 'expenses' for a recent consignment of forty-five cattle had exceeded the consignment's market value, and the sale had consequently increased Solomon's debts.[45] However, Blackhurst's dealings overall were apparently to Solomon's financial advantage, and official attempts to restrict Blackhurst's activities among the Zulu did not receive Solomon's support.

Solomon nonetheless was aware of fraud in the royal cattle and cash collections, and denounced several of his Zulu collectors as dishonest – even though he continued to be dependent on their services. On various occasions during 1931, when speaking of his financial affairs to white authorities, Solomon made specific accusations against Leonard Ncapayi and Simpson Bhengu (Solomon's private secretaries), and Lymon Maling (whom Solomon had appointed as royal collector in Northern Natal, alongside Daniel Vilakazi and Timothy Mathe).[46] Solomon's predicament in the last few years of his life was unenviable: he was surrounded by courtiers whom he could neither trust nor afford to dismiss. As royal collections increased during the famine, chiefs in the Zululand inland districts found that their loyalties to the Zulu royal house increasingly conflicted with their traditional roles of 'father' or 'guardian' to their wards – which felt duty-bound to respond to Solomon's appeals for support, despite their poverty. As early as June 1931, the CNC had received reports that certain Zulu chiefs had become 'very perturbed' about Solomon's extortionate activities, and were considering means of imposing some form of discipline on him.[47] It was thus not only Solomon's kholwa support but also his chiefly support that ebbed after 1930.

For its part, the NAD also became increasingly concerned about – even exasperated with – Solomon's chaotic financial affairs and widespread collections. Officials perceived it to be unjust that Solomon was making such impositions on the Zulu people in the midst of a famine, at a time when the NAD was distributing famine relief and Zulu local tax arrears amounted to tens of thousands of pounds. They also had cause to complain that the frequent presence of royal collectors in their districts was interfering with their own and their chiefs' routine administrative work. In addition, somewhat paradoxically, the NAD (including the new Natal CNC, J. Mould-Young, who succeeded T. W. C. Norton in 1931) was apprehensive of the political consequences which might follow the sudden collapse of the Zulu royal house in Zulu public esteem.

As early as May 1931, the NAD considered the possibility of intervening to impose official control over the royal cash and cattle collections, and to offer Solomon guidance in the task of discharging his debts. Such strategies, which were tentatively proposed by the SNA, were initially not favoured by either the CNC or the NC at Nongoma. But after Solomon had personally implored the CNC in July 1931 for government financial assistance, the CNC became more amenable to this idea. The question of official assistance became more pressing when Solomon anxiously informed the NC at Nongoma in October 1931 that 'writs of execution' had been issued against him, meaning that royal property was soon to be attached by the courts. This persuaded the NC at Nongoma, the CNC and the SNA that some form of official assistance was essential; and it was agreed that the preconditions should be that, first, an NAD official should investigate and ratify Solomon's statement of debts, and, second, that Solomon should dismiss Bhengu and appoint a trustworthy private secretary.[48] But the SNA and CNC still procrastinated, unable to agree about the precise form that official assistance should take. It was left to the MNA (whom Heaton Nicholls had petitioned on Solomon's behalf) to dramatically break departmental indecision: 'most important that sale in execution [at Mahashini] is prevented', he telegraphed his department in January 1932. He then immediately authorised the NC at Nongoma to guarantee to Solomon's creditors that the government would settle Solomon's debts. The SNA then arranged for every adult male of the Usuthu ward to pay a £1 annual levy to the government, until such time as Solomon's debt to the government was repaid.[49]

On 7 January 1932, the day on which Mahashini was informed of the government loan to repay royal debts, Mahashini despatched a letter to the CNC expressing Solomon's humble thanks for government assistance. 'My name would [otherwise] have been changed into the mud', said this letter which, though bearing Solomon's signature, was unmistakably in Dube's handwriting.[50] On 8 January 1932, however, Solomon went to Durban and bought a new Chrysler de luxe 8-cylinder, on hire-purchase terms, costing a total of £825. Solomon was soon to be seen at Nongoma, being chauffeur driven in the new limousine. He initially denied that the car was his, but by February 1932 the truth had leaked out. Officials were astonished, and the CNC concluded that Solomon was 'nothing more than a spendthrift and a liar, whose word is not to be believed even at the moment he utters it'.[51]

Although utterly disillusioned with Solomon on account of the car issue, the NAD felt that it had no choice but to go ahead with the government loan to Solomon for the repayment of royal debts: Solomon's creditors had already been informed of the government's undertaking, and the Usuthu ward had already agreed to the levy. The MNA and the NAD did not cancel the government loan even when Solomon refused to abide by conditions that were attached to it, namely to dismiss Bhengu and to submit a full and final statement of royal debts. The minister did, however, insist that the government would not settle any of Solomon's debts incurred after 31 January 1932 – which included the instalments on Solomon's new car. In total, the government was to pay out £4266.19.2 to liquidate Solomon's debts. This reduced but did not remedy Solomon's insolvency, and the cattle collections continued until his death. The government loan was never fully repaid, incidentally: the Usuthu ward continued to pay the annual levy until 1937, four years after Solomon's death, when the Minister of Finance wrote off the remainder.[52]

The official attitude to Solomon, from 1932 until his death in March 1933, was a mixture of concern and contempt – contempt because it was felt that Solomon was exploiting both the Zulu people's loyalty to their royal family and the government's goodwill. In March 1932, in view of Solomon's purchase of a new car and his failure to abide by the conditions of the government loan, the MNA and the SNA decided that Solomon should be officially reprimanded at a special *indaba* attended by Solomon, his advisers, Usuthu tribal authorities and 'tribespeople'. The SNA wished this gathering to be informed that the government was unable to trust Solomon, and would not 'stir a finger' to help him meet any new debts 'even if it involves his detention in gaol under order of civil imprisonment'; and that if Solomon should be imprisoned, the government would have to consider his replacement with a 'reliable chief'. Such a meeting was held at Nongoma in April 1932, and in addition to reading out the 'message of the government' prepared by the SNA, the CNC expressed his own critical opinions about Solomon's behaviour and financial predicament. An abashed Solomon replied simply that he was at fault, and could say no more.[53]

From 1932, there was little that even the most sympathetic of NAD officials could find in Solomon to justify any amelioration of official attitudes towards him. Carl Faye, the long-serving chief clerk and translator at the CNC's offices who had been favourably disposed to the Zulu royal family even in the heyday of Natal NAD antipathy, noted in September 1932 that the 'good' that was in Solomon was somehow 'not dominant in his conduct'. Elaborating, Faye referred to the recent death of Harriette Colenso, a woman who had in a sense been a surrogate 'father' to Solomon during Dinuzulu's imprisonment and exile after the 1906 rebellion, and who had played a leading role in securing Solomon's succession in 1913. Increasingly frail and even somewhat disillusioned during the last years of her life, Harriette had nonetheless clung with affection to the memories of her association with 'Dinuzulu's family'. But, although Solomon had recently indicated that he wished to lay a wreath on her grave, he had over the past few years ignored Faye's repeated suggestions that he should pay her the courtesy of a visit. Solomon had always said that he was too busy, Faye recorded. Faye was similarly disillusioned with Solomon's 'apparent ingratitude' to the many Zulu who had responded to the royal cash and cattle collections.[54]

In the light of NAD attitudes towards Solomon, it may seem incongruous that the 'recognition question' was reopened in the NAD in July 1932 – but it was reopened at the instigation of the MNA, E.G. Jansen, and not the NAD itself. Since the *indaba* fiasco of 1930, Jansen's interest in the ideological aspects of Solomon's recognition had been kept alive by the 'native policy' debates then current in ruling circles; this was a period when Jansen's political party, the ruling National Party under General Hertzog, was making great efforts to develop a segregationist political programme. Jansen was moreover in touch with Zulu royal affairs through his involvement in arrangements for the Shaka Memorial unveiling ceremony. The reopening of the 'recognition question' in 1932 was also prompted by an inquiry issuing from the offices of the Governor-General: the 'Athlone memorandum', drawn up by the Earl of Athlone in his capacity as Governor-General soon after the *indaba* fiasco of 1930, included a clause recommending that, should Solomon's official status remain unchanged after a period of two years, the government should then undertake to reconsider the issue.[55] In the event, although officials went through the motions of reconsidering Solomon's official 'elevation', the NAD decisively blocked the MNA's initiative. Solomon and his advisers played no part in causing the 'recognition question' to be reopened in 1932, but they did get wind that the issue was being reconsidered – which inspired Solomon to make a final attempt to secure official recognition of the Zulu kingship.

At some stage in mid-1932, Solomon received an intimation from Adams, who had recently been consulted by the MNA on matters concerning

Solomon's finances and political status, that the Zulu royal house could expect to be financially and politically rewarded if it redeemed itself in the eyes of the NAD. Evidently acting on Adams' advice, Solomon approached the NC at Nongoma in September 1932, indicating that he wished to reform his behaviour and use his influence to assist the government.[56] As a consequence of these representations, Solomon was granted an interview with the CNC in early October. Before the CNC, Solomon stated that the Zulu delighted in living in harmony with the government, but that he needed greater official powers to be able to guide them to do so. Solomon's approaches to the NAD came too late to influence the NAD's position regarding the 'recognition question', since the SNA, the CNC and the NC at Nongoma had already suppressed the possibility of Solomon's official 'elevation' in late August.[57] But because Solomon had specifically asked that his official powers be extended, which suggested that he had become aware that the 'recognition question' had been formally reopened, the NAD deemed it essential that Solomon be formally reminded of his official status.

It was thus that Solomon, together with his advisers Mnyaiza kaNdabuko Zulu, Gilbert kaNgcongcwana Zulu, Franz kaDabulamanzi Zulu, and Zinyo kaNtuzwa Mdlalose (one of Solomon's maternal uncles), was summoned to Pretoria on 13 December 1932 for an interview with the MNA. In addressing Solomon at this interview, which was also attended by the SNA (J.F. Herbst), CNC (J.M. Young) and NC at Nongoma (E.N. Braatvedt) the minister followed a draft address that the Natal NAD head office at Pietermaritzburg had drawn up specially for the occasion. Accordingly, the minister reiterated the conditions of Solomon's appointment as chief of the Usuthu in 1916, and proceeded to describe how General Botha's advice to Solomon in 1916 had not been satisfactorily heeded: Solomon had not always behaved with chiefly dignity, nor had he consistently paid due respect to NAD officials; he drank too much, and had led so extravagant and unsettled a life that his health had suffered; and he had persistently claimed authority over Zulu outside the Usuthu ward. Moreover, Solomon had fallen deeply into debt, and had failed to reform his financial irresponsibility even when officially instructed to do so at the time of the government loan. Solomon was thus informed that, on the one hand, he had not set a good example to his own people, and on the other hand, he had often been more of a hindrance than a help to the government. At the conclusion of the interview, the minister deviated from the NAD-prepared address and gave out that he still hoped to make use of Solomon in the administration of the Zulu people. Solomon first had to demonstrate to the government, however, that he was worthy of a position of greater authority.[58] So ended Solomon's final interview with white authorities.

After the unfortunate Zulu *indaba* with the Governor-General in 1930, Solomon's attitude towards white authorities and his general conduct suggested that he had given up hope of achieving the ultimate objective of his political career: the official recognition of the Zulu kingship. The news in mid-1932 that white authorities had reopened the 'recognition question', which must have come as a surprise to those at Mahashini, seemed to rekindle in Solomon a spark of hope. The overall tenor of Solomon's interview with the MNA, held in the presence of the most influential members of the NAD hierarchy in regard to policy towards the Zulu royal house, doused this spark. Although the minister had closed the interview on a conditionally positive note, Solomon himself did not expect to live long enough to persuade the government that his expressed desire to reform his ways and 'assist the government' was genuine.

By May 1932, Solomon had already sensed that his death was imminent – even though he was barely forty years old. In a letter of that month replying to Heaton Nicholls's enquiries about the progress of the Shaka Memorial project, Solomon had written that 'if alive' he would certainly be present at the prospective Shaka Memorial unveiling ceremony in July.[59] In November 1932, the CNC had similarly expressed the opinion that Solomon, as a consequence of 'dissolute living' and 'self-gratification', could not be expected to survive for much longer. Solomon would continue 'undermining his constitution', the CNC predicted, 'until he snuffs himself out like a candle'.[60]

Solomon collapsed and died suddenly in the first week of March 1933, less than three months after his interview with the MNA. He died not at Mahashini, but at the homestead of Chief Kambi of the Ngenetsheni, having gone there to act as peacemaker in a dispute between two of Kambi's sons. Particularly in view of the severe antagonism that had existed between the Zulu royal house and the Ngenetsheni before Solomon's succession, the circumstances of Solomon's death reflected Solomon's dedication to the settling of tribal and dynastic disputes which might fracture the unity of all Zulu beneath the Zulu 'king'. Notwithstanding his personal failings during the last few years of his life, and his parasitic activities during the famine, Solomon's funeral ceremony at Mahashini four days after his death was the occasion of a stirring display of Zulu loyalty to the institution of Zulu kingship. *Ilanga lase Natal*'s exclamations on the death of 'Solomon the King of the Zulu' indeed seemed to express a real sense of bereavement: 'We have died, Zulu people! We have no place to hide! He is no more, the honeybird that drinks from deep pools [a line from Solomon's *izibongo*]! The giver of rest [one of Solomon's praise names] has gone!' and, using Christian imagery, 'We are like sheep without a shepherd.' In page after page of appreciative journalism on Solomon's life and work, the only hint of criticism came in the form of an oblique and somewhat self-righteous aside to the newspaper's predominantly kholwa readership. Solomon's fatal liver and abdominal complaints, it was recorded, were symptoms of 'an illness which is not known at Groutville'.[61] Groutville was the name of the long-established and influential kholwa settlement in the Umvoti district of Natal proper, where intemperance, apparently, was not tolerated.

*   *   *   *   *

The phrase 'From Deep Pools',[62] quoted above from Solomon's praise poem, was an earlier choice for this book's title. It was more suggestive and imaginative than the title ultimately selected, but also more oblique if not obscure. This phrase hints, correctly, that the Zulu nationalism of Solomon's generation was drawn from origins deep in the Zulu past, and was reformulated in the 1920s. It also signifies that Solomon's status and role as Zulu leader too had origins deep in the Zulu past: he derived much from his genealogical background while drawing on a depth of advice in contemporary Zulu society. This earlier possibility had a poetic appeal: the imagery of 'Deep Pools' is romantic, yet also tragic, for it is in deep pools that people sometimes drown. However, the present title, 'To Bind the Nation',[63] seemed more suitable not only because it is more direct but also because it encapsulates a dominant theme of the story: it expresses exactly what Solomon and Zulu nationalism set out to do – and did.

NOTES

1. *Ilanga lase Natal*, 5/9/1930, report of Inkatha meeting, 18–20/8/1930 (Zulu language report).

2. *Ibid.*

3. CNC PMB 81, 58/7/3, Detective Sergeant R. H. Arnold, Durban CID to O.I.C., CID, 16/9/1930; and memorandum entitled 'Champion and Solomon Dinuzulu' by the Commissioner of the SAP, Pretoria, for the information of the Minister of Justice, 19/9/1930.

4. CNC PMB 81, 58/7/3, minutes of meeting between CNC and Chief Solomon, Nongoma, 22/9/1930.

5. AWGC Box 2:3.3.4.1., Zulu language handbill headlined 'Inkosi u Solomon ka Dinuzulu', signed by A. W. G. Champion, Durban, 4/9/1930.

6. *Ilanga lase Natal*, 5/9/1930 (Zulu language advertisement).

7. CNC PMB 81, 58/7/3, memorandum by the Commissioner, SAP, Pretoria, for the Minister of Justice, 19/9/1930 (quotation); see also La Hausse, 'Struggle for the city', p. 224; and Marks, *Ambiguities of dependence*, pp. 74ff. Champion himself was aware that he was banished because of his contacts with Solomon, as reflected in AWGC Box 1:1.1., Champion's short manuscript autobiography entitled 'Time is longer than rope in the life of every man', Durban, 1974, p. 4. For the events of 6 September 1930, see CNC PMB 81, 58/7/3, Detective Sergeant R. H. Arnold, Durban CID, to O.I.C., CID, 16/9/1930.

8. See Champion Papers, University of the Witwatersrand (hereafter MS CHAM) A922/A, copy of telegram from Mayor of Durban to Minister of Justice, 26/9/1930; Roux, *Time longer than rope*, p. 193; *Ilanga lase Natal*, 3/10/1930 (Zulu language report); AWGC Box 27:23:1., various manuscripts *re* Champion's banishment, 1930–33; and Champion, *The views of Mahlathi*, pp. 39ff. For the liberal opposition of Eaton and other Natal MPs (notably excluding Heaton Nicholls, Marwick and Deane) to the Riotous Assemblies Bill, see Debates of the House of Assembly, vol. 15, speeches on 15/4/1930 and 1/5/1930.

9. Bulletin of the Department of Justice, 22/4/1931, quoted in Roux, *Time longer than rope*, p. 251.

10. See *ibid.*, pp. 193–94; AWGC Box 1:1.1., Champion, 'Time is longer than rope in the life of every man', p. 5; Box 1:1.3.2., further autobiographical fragments by Champion, *c.* 1974; and Box 27:23.1., various documents *re* Champion's exile from Natal, 1930–33.

11. Roux, *Time longer than rope*, pp. 245–50. For Nkosi's opposition to ethnic politics, see La Hausse, 'Struggle for the city', pp. 196, 274.

12. *Ilanga lase Natal*, 17/10/1930 (Zulu language report).

13. See Walshe, *African nationalism in South Africa*, pp. 228ff; and for the 1924 'militant coup' in the NNC, see chapter 4 above.

14. *Ilanga lase Natal*, 3/10/1930.

15. For these developments, see *Ilanga lase Natal*, 17/10/1930; Roux, *Time longer than rope*, pp. 251–52; and Walshe, *African nationalism in South Africa*, pp. 230–31. Dube's NNC remained separate from the national ANC throughout the 1930s. For Majozi's role in the cultural initiative, see below.

16. CK Reel 15A, 2:XC9:41/14, Dr P. Seme to A. W. G. Champion, 22/10/1930 (quotation); and A. W. G. Champion to Dr P. Seme, 24/10/1930.

17. NTS 7205, 20/326, CNC to SNA, 2/6/1931, reporting on his inquiries regarding Inkatha, February-June 1931.

18. *Ilanga lase Natal*, 17/7/1931, report of Inkatha executive committee meeting, 6–8/7/1931 (Zulu language report).

19. CNC PMB 72, 57/29, handwritten memorandum signed W. R. B. [?], 8/10/1932, referring to Dube's letter to Solomon kaDinuzulu, 6/10/1932.

20. Pers. Comm., Mahaye, part I, p. 13; and part II, p. 8.

21. *Ilanga lase Natal*, 17/7/1931.

22. CNC PMB 72, 57/29, Chief S. G. E. Majozi to CNC, 12/1/1931 and 17/6/1931; and *Ilanga lase Natal*, 12/6/1931, public notice *re* 'Itshe lesikumbuzo sika Tshaka' ('Commemorative Stone to Shaka'), given under authority of Solomon kaDinuzulu. For Inkatha's annual general meeting of 1930, see *Ilanga lase Natal*, 5/9/1930.

23. See CNC PMB 72, 57/29, minutes of interview between MNA, Chief Majozi and Mr Bhulose, 6/7/1931; and CNC to SNA, 17/12/1931 and 18/7/1932.

24. CNC PMB 72, 57/29, unsigned 'Draft Programme' for Shaka Memorial unveiling ceremony, n.d. [Majozi, *c.* December 1931?]; and minutes of interview between MNA, Majozi and Bhulose, 6/7/1931.

25. See *Ilanga lase Natal*, 22/5/1931, editorial, plus the appeal which recurs in subsequent editions; and, for the administration of the fund, see 10/7/1931 (Zulu language reports).

26. *Ilanga lase Natal*'s editions between February and July 1932 published lists of contributors to the Shaka Memorial Fund. In a few rural areas, incidentally, the Shaka Memorial project was popularly associated with preparations for an impending Zulu rebellion. See CNC PMB 72, 57/29, correspondence between NC, Melmoth, Acting NC, Ixopo, CNC and SNA, May-August 1932.

27. For the roles of the Revd L. E. Oscroft, George Armstrong and George Heaton Nicholls, see MS NIC 2.08.1, File 5, KCM 3353(a), Solomon ka Dinuzulu to Heaton Nicholls, 13/5/1932; Oscroft to Heaton Nicholls, 14/5/1932; EGJ 140, Solomon ka Dinuzulu to Heaton Nicholls, 28/5/1932; handwritten memorandum entitled 'Solomon ka Dinuzulu' *re* arrangements for unveiling ceremony [E. G. Jansen?], 28/5/1932; CNC PMB 72, 57/29, Heaton Nicholls to MNA, 8/6/1932; and Oscroft to NC, Nongoma, 7/12/1932.

28. See CNC PMB 72, 57/29, CNC to SNA, 9/4/1932; CNC to secretary, Shaka Memorial Fund, 17/5/1932; and EGJ 140, memorandum entitled 'Solomon ka Dinuzulu', 28/5/1932. For Majozi's fund-raising efforts in the Transvaal, his death, and the outstanding debts, see *Ilanga lase Natal*, 24/6/1932; 1/7/1932; 15/7/1932; and CNC PMB 72, 57/29, CNC to SNA, 18/7/1932.

29. *Ilanga lase Natal*, 29/7/1932 (Zulu language report).

30. CNC PMB 72, 57/29, handwritten memorandum signed W.R.B.[?], 8/10/1932, referring to Dube's letter to Solomon kaDinuzulu, 6/10/1932.

31. MS NIC 2.08.4, File 19, KCM 3833, G. Heaton Nicholls, 'The old Zululand constituency', manuscript, n.d., p. 23.

32. See CNC PMB 72, 57/29, Shaw and Co. (solicitors for Dove Bros, Monumental Masons) to Chief Matole, 15/6/1933; Shaw and Co. to CNC, 4/7/1933; CNC to Shaw and Co., 6/7/1933; CNC to SNA, 24/10/1936 (quotation); and James Crankshaw Ltd (successors to Dove Bros) to CNC, 28/4/1938.

33. CNC PMB 72, 57/29, 'Commission for the Preservation of Natural and Historical Monuments, Relics and Antiquities' to CNC, 7/9/1937; and CNC's reply, 7/10/1937.

34. NEC Box 7, evidence of Chief Solomon Zulu, Pietermaritzburg, 8/4/1931, pp. 6545ff; and CNC PMB 81, 58/7/1, untitled handwritten memorandum *re* Solomon kaDinuzulu, 1927–1932, n.d., entry for 8/4/1931.

35. See *Natal Witness*, 8 and 9/9/1931.

36. *Natal Witness*, 17/9/1931; and Pers. Comm., Ndesheni, part III, p. 21.

37. For Jansen, see Debates of the House of Assembly, vol. 19, 23/5/1932; and for the Bishop of Zululand, see *Natal Witness*, 17/10/1931. See also various editions of the *Natal Witness* and *Natal Advertiser* from September 1931.

38. *Natal Witness*, 8–9/9/1931, 2/10/1931, 22/1/1932; *Natal Advertiser*, 8/9/1931; Debates of the House of Assembly, vol. 18, statement by E. G. Jansen, 9/2/1932, cols 706–7, and speech by A. O. B. Payn, 4/2/1932, col. 669; and Report of the Controller and Auditor-General for the financial year 1931–1932, UG29–32, p. 247. For more on the 1931–32 famine, see my dissertation, pp. 235ff.

39. CNC PMB 81, 58/7/3, NC, Nongoma to CNC, 27/5/1931; and records of the criminal case, Melmoth, 14/7/1931. For the earlier incident, see memoranda by police officers, Melmoth, 3/2/1931; and Dep. Comm., SAP Natal Division, to CNC, 6/2/1931.

40. The activities of the individuals mentioned, between 1931 and 1933, are recorded in voluminous official correspondence on Solomon's financial disorders: CNC PMB 82, 58/7/4; 58/7/5; and CNC PMB 84, 58/7/4.

41. See CNC PMB 81, 58/7/3, Detective L. van Vuuren, CID, Vryheid to NC, Vryheid, 24/6/1932; NC, Nongoma to CNC, 15/6/1932; and CNC PMB 82, 58/7/5, Master of the South African Supreme Court to CNC, 8/1/1935, giving details of Solomon's insolvent estate and financial arrangements.

42. See E. N. Braatvedt (NC, Nongoma, from 1931, who initiated Zulu cattle sales in the reserves), *Roaming Zululand with a native commissioner* (Pietermaritzburg, 1949), pp. 115–16; the extensive NAD correspondence on the matter in CNC PMB 84, 58/7/4; and *Natal Witness*, 16 and 17/10/1931.

43. The key documents concerning Blackhurst and the cattle collections are CNC PMB 82, 58/7/5, NC, Emtonjaneni to CNC, 8 and 15/4/1931; NC, Nongoma to CNC, 15 and 20/6/1931; A. S. Blackhurst to CNC, 13/6/1931; 'Report of Round Table Conference on the Representations of Mr A. S. Blackhurst', Nongoma, 12/8/1931; NC, Nongoma to CNC, 24/11/1931; and CNC PMB 81, 58/7/3, NC, Nongoma to CNC, 6/8/1932, reporting evidence of 'native headman' *re* Blackhurst's representations at a Mahashini meeting in early 1932.

44. See CNC PMB 84, 58/7/4, A. S. Blackhurst to NC, Nongoma, 23/5/1931; NC, Nongoma to CNC, 29/6/1931, 24/11/1931, 7/7/1932; and C. F. Adams to CNC, 29/12/1932.

45. CNC PMB 84, 58/7/4, NC, Nongoma to CNC, 24 and 27/11/1931.

46. CNC PMB 84, 58/7/4, Solomon kaDinuzulu to NC, Nongoma, 10/7/1931; NC, Nongoma to CNC, 24/11/1931 (*re* Solomon's general complaints about fraud); NC, Nongoma to CNC, 15/10/1931 (*re* Ncapayi); NC, Nongoma to CNC, 2/12/1931 (*re* Bhengu); and *Ilanga lase Natal*, 13/11/1931 (*re* Maling).

47. NTS 7205, 20/326, CNC to SNA, 2/6/1931. See also *Ilanga lase Natal*, 17/7/1931 (Zulu language report), which remarks that few chiefs were present at the Inkatha executive committee meeting of July 1931, although all were invited.

48. CNC PMB 82, 58/7/4, SNA to CNC, 13/5/1931; NC, Nongoma to CNC, 15/6/1931; and Acting CNC to SNA, 22/6/1931 (*re* initial NAD position); CNC PMB 84, 58/7/4, Solomon kaDinuzulu to CNC, 10/7/1931; and CNC to SNA, 18/9/1931 (*re* Solomon's approach); NC, Nongoma to CNC, 15/10/1931 (*re* Solomon's further representations); NC, Nongoma to CNC, 24/10/1931; SNA to CNC, 14/12/1931; and CNC to SNA, 24/12/1931 (*re* urgency and preconditions of official intervention).

49. EGJ 140, G. Heaton Nicholls to E.G. Jansen, 19/12/1931; CNC PMB 84, 58/7/4, CNC to NC, Nongoma, 5/1/1932 (quotation – telegram transmitting substance of MNA's telegram); SNA to CNC, 5/2/1932 (telegram); and report of meeting between Solomon kaDinuzulu and Usuthu Tribe, Mahashini, 13/2/1932.

50. CNC PMB 84, 58/7/4, Solomon kaDinuzulu to CNC, 7/1/1932.

51. See CNC PMB 81, 58/7/3, CNC to SNA, 26/2/1932; CNC PMB 84, 58/7/4, Solomon kaDinuzulu to CNC, 19/2/1932; Additional NC, Durban to CNC, 13/2/1932, enclosing copy of Solomon's hire-purchase agreement with 'Colonial Motors Ltd', 8/1/1932; 'Wynne and Wynne' (solicitors for Colonial Motors Ltd) to CNC, 18/2/1932; and NC, Nongoma to CNC, 18/3/1932.

52. See Reports of the Controller and Auditor-General for the financial years 1931–37. For Solomon's failure to abide by the conditions of the government loan, see CNC PMB 84, 58/7/4, correspondence between Oscroft, NC, Nongoma, CNC and SNA, February-July 1932; and CNC PMB 81, 58/7/3, CNC to SNA, 26/2/1932.

53. CNC PMB, 84, 58/7/4, SNA to CNC, 24/3/1932 (quotation); and minutes of meeting between CNC and Chief Solomon and the Usuthu Tribe, Nongoma, 12/4/1932.

54. CNC PMB 81, 58/7/1, handwritten memorandum by C. Faye entitled 'Observations on minute addressed to CNC by NC, Nongoma, 23/9/1932', 5/10/1932.

55. See EGJ 140, Athlone memorandum, 18/9/1930, pp. 1, 6; and unsigned handwritten memorandum [E.G. Jansen?] entitled 'Solomon ka Dinuzulu' (5pp.), 28/5/1932, *re* Shaka Memorial unveiling ceremony and other developments leading to consultation with the Governor-General, the Earl of Clarendon.

56. See EGJ 140, handwritten minutes of interview and accompanying fragments (7pp.) entitled 'Mr Adams', n.d. [E.G. Jansen mid-1932?]; and CNC PMB 81, 58/7/1, handwritten memorandum by C. Faye entitled 'Observations on minute addressed to CNC by NC, Nongoma, 23/9/1932', 5/10/1932.

57. CNC PMB, 82, 58/7/4, Solomon kaDinuzulu to CNC, 12/10/1932 (NAD translation), delivered by Solomon at his interview with the CNC of the same date; and CNC PMB 84, 58/7/4, CNC to SNA, 24/10/1932. For NAD opposition, see especially EGJ 140, unsigned handwritten minutes of meeting between MNA, SNA, CNC and NC, Nongoma, 24/8/1932, *re* Solomon's official status.

58. CNC PMB 81, 58/7/1, unsigned 'Suggested Memorandum' entitled 'Position of Solomon kaDinuzulu', 7/11/1932, being the NAD-prepared draft address to Solomon; and CNC PMB 82, 58/7/4, minutes of meeting between MNA, SNA,

CNC, NC, Nongoma, Chief Solomon, Mnyaiza, Gilbert, Franz, and Zinyo Mdlalose, with Carl Faye interpreting, Union Buildings, Pretoria, 13/12/1932.

59. EGJ 140, Solomon kaDinuzulu to G. Heaton Nicholls, 28/5/1932.

60. CNC PMB 81, 58/7/1, CNC to SNA, 9/11/1932.

61. *Ilanga lase Natal*, 10 and 17/3/1933 (Zulu language reports). See also *The Net*, June 1933, pp. 4–9.

62. Unpublished collection of Zulu praise poems, 'izibongo sika uMaphumusana [Solomon] kaDinuzulu'. The full context of this phrase is as follows: 'The honeybird that drinks from deep pools / If he drank from shallow pools his beak would be muddied . . .'

63. R. C. A. Samuelson, *Long, long, ago*, (Durban, 1929), p. 401. Describing the purpose of the *inkatha*, Samuelson records it was to 'bind the nation in loyalty to the king and even in attracting back to his jurisdiction any of his subjects who may have deserted him for some time'. See also Webb and Wright (eds), *Stuart archive*, vol. 1, pp. 40–41, evidence of Baleni kaSilwana, 17/5/1914, which records that 'The inkatha's purpose is to keep our nation standing firm. The binding round and round symbolises the binding together of the people so that they should not be scattered'.

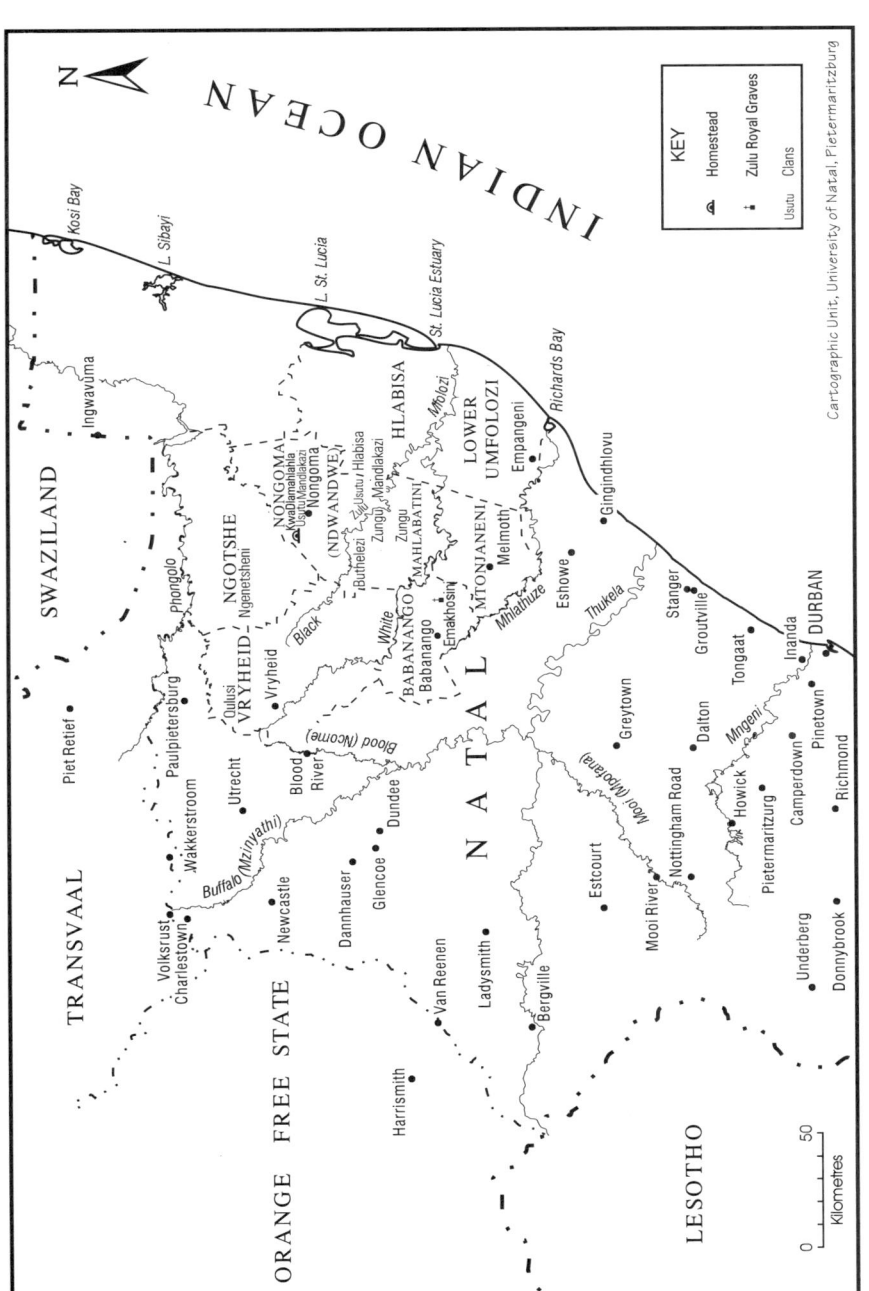

Map of Natal and Zululand

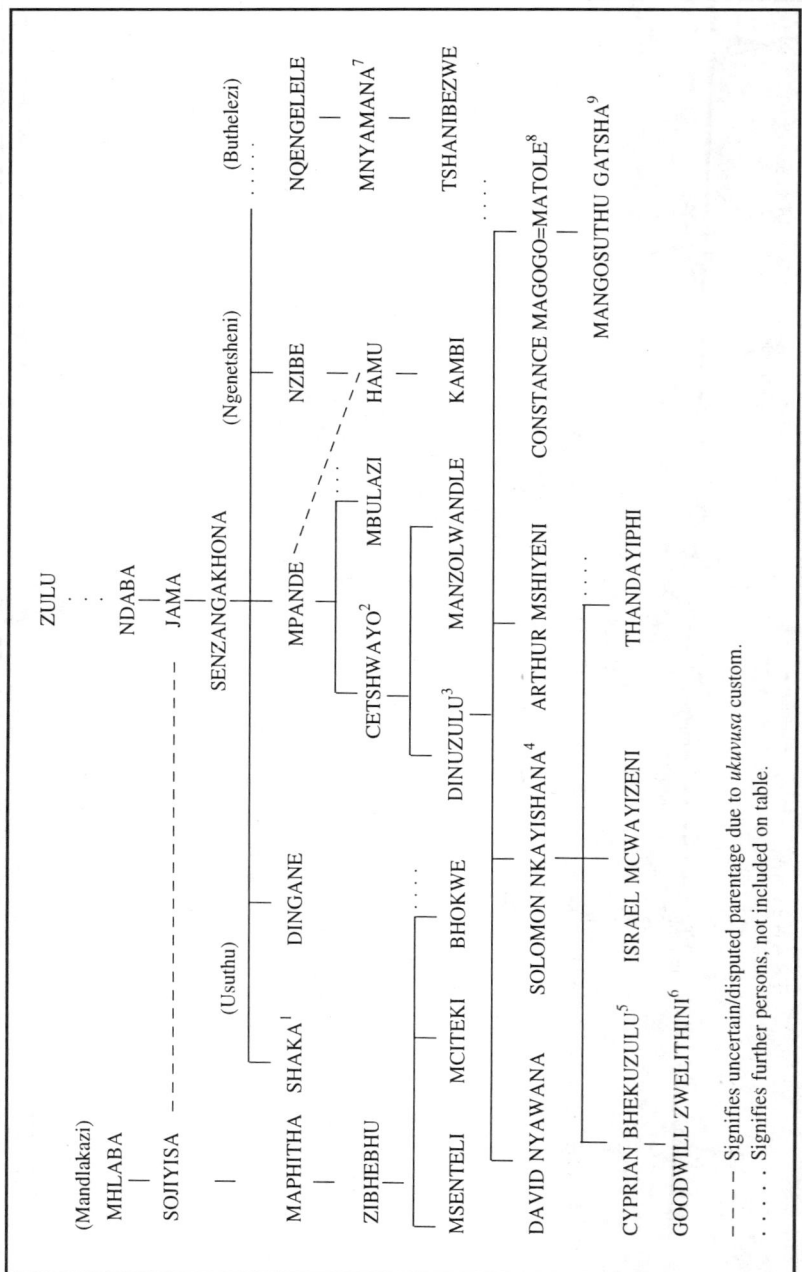

Zulu royal lineage, including collateral branches and the Buthelezi.

Prominent sons, grandsons and great-grandchildren of Mpande ('the root')

Sons	Grandsons	Great-grandchildren
Cetshwayo	Manzolwandle, Dinuzulu	David, Solomon, Mshiyeni, Magogo ($\dagger$)
Mbulazi		
Ziwedu		
Dabulamanzi	Mpikanina	Sithela
Shingana	Franz (France), Manqina	
Siteku	Albert (Halbete)	
	Nkantini, Pika	
Ndabuko	Mnyaiza	Ndesheni
Mahanana	Franz (France)	
Mkungo		
Mtonga		
Mgidlana	Dotela (Dokotela)	
Mantantashiya		
Mandumba		
Sikungu		
Silwana		
Shonkweni		
Dabulesinye		
Somhlawana		

NOTES

1. 1816–28; the founder of the Zulu kingdom.
2. 1872–84; defeated by the British in 1879 and exiled, restored, died during the Zulu civil war.
3. 1884–1913; imprisoned and exiled for his roles in the 1888 and 1906 rebellions, died in exile.
4. 1913–33; officially recognised as chief of the Usuthu but never as Zulu king, patron of Inkatha 1922–33; succeeded by the regent, Mshiyeni, 1933–48.
5. 1948–68; recognised as Zulu king by the Apartheid government; succeeded by the regent, Israel, 1968–72.
6. 1972–present.
7. Chief Minister to the Zulu kingdom, leading royalist during the civil war, chief of the Buthelezi.
8. Chief Minister to the Zulu nation, Inkatha executive committee member from 1928, chief of the Buthelezi.
9. Chief Minister of KwaZulu, president of Inkatha from 1976, chief of the Buthelezi.

Bibliography

PRIMARY MANUSCRIPT SOURCES

OFFICIAL

Natal Archives, Pietermaritzburg
Chief Native Commissioners' Correspondence, 1910–1919
Chief Native Commissioners' Correspondence, 1919–1950
Colonial Secretary's Office. Fourth Interim Report of the Zululand Lands
  Delimitation Commission, 1903, CSO 2844
Prime Minister's Records. Confidential correspondence, 1907, PM 103
Secretary of Native Affairs' Records

State Archives, Pretoria
Archives of the Commissioner of the South African Police, 1901–1960
Archives of the Department of Native Affairs
Economic and Wage Commission, 1925, Evidence
Native Economic Commission, 1930–1932, Evidence
Archives of the Secretary of Justice

UNOFFICIAL

CPSA, Offices of the Diocese of Zululand, Eshowe
Zululand Diocesan Records

**Department of Historical and Literary Papers,
University of the Witwatersrand, Johannesburg**
Buthelezi Speeches, 1972–1976
Champion Papers
Inkatha Records

**Department of Zulu Language and Literature,
University of Natal, Durban**
Collection of Zulu praise poems (*izibongo*) recorded by James Stuart and
translated by D. McK. Malcolm and A. T. Cope.

Documentation Centre for African Studies, UNISA
A. W. G. Champion Collection

Institute of Contemporary History,
University of the Orange Free State, Bloemfontein
E. G. Jansen Collection

Killie Campbell Africana Library, Durban

E. N. Braatvedt Collection
Sir Marshall Campbell Collection
Harriette Colenso Collection
Carl Faye Papers
H. C. Lugg Collection

B. W. Martin Collection
J. S. Marwick Papers
George Heaton Nicholls Collection
F. R. 'Matabele' Thompson Papers
Zulu Society Collection

Natal Archives, Pietermaritzburg
H. E. Colenso Collection
Carl Faye Papers
Zulu Society Collection, 1936–1948

PRIMARY PRINTED SOURCES

OFFICIAL

Pre-Union
Colonial Office Confidential Print (Africa South). Series CO879/41; CO879/104; CO879/114; CO879/116
Report of the South African Native Affairs Commission, 1903–1905. Cape Town, 1905
Report of the Native Affairs Commission, Natal, 1906–1907. BPP. Cd. 3889

Year Books
Official Year Book of the Union of South Africa, 1930/31; 1931/32

House of Assembly
Debates of the House of Assembly, 24/1/1913–16/6/1913; 30/1/1914–7/7/1914; 26/2/1915–21/4/1915
Votes, Proceedings and Annexures of the House of Assembly, 26/2/1915–21/4/1915; 19/11/1915–17/6/1916
The debates of the House of Assembly were not officially published between 1916 and 1924. Comprehensive *Cape Times* Parliamentary reports, covered the period 19/11/1915–19/7/1922.
Debates of the House of Assembly, Vols. 1–23, 1924–1934

Both Houses of Parliament

Joint Sitting of both Houses of Parliament: Representation of Natives Bills JSI–'36, JS 2–'36, 1936

Select and Joint Select Committees

Report of the Select Committee on: Native Affairs, SC6A–'17 [Native Administration Bill]; Native Affairs, SC10A–'20 [Native Affairs Bill]; Native Affairs, SC3–'23 [Natives (Urban Areas) Bill]; Native Affairs, SC6B–'25 [Native Lands (Natal and Transvaal) Release Bill]; the Subject of the Prevention of Disorders Bill, SC14–'26; the Subject of the Urban Native Council Bill, Coloured Persons' Rights Bill, Representation of Natives in Parliament Bill, and Natives Land (Amendment) Bill, SC10–'27; the Subject of the Union Native Council Bill, Coloured Persons' Rights Bill, Representation of Natives in Parliament Bill, and Natives Land (Amendment) Bill, SC19–'27; the Subject of the Natives' Service Contract Bill, SC7–'31.

Reports and Proceedings of the Joint Select Committees on Native and Coloured Persons, 1930–1934 (supplement to JS1–'35)

Commissions

Report of the Commission to make recommendations for the re-organisation of the Departments of the Public Service, UG22–'12

Report of the Natives' Land Commission, Vol. I, UG19–'16

Report of the Natives' Land Commission, Vol. II, UG22–'16

Report of the Local Natives' Land Committee (Natal Province), UG34–'18

Natal Natives' Land Committee, Minutes of Evidence, UG35–'18

Report of the Native Churches Commission, UG39–'25

Report of the Native Affairs Commission, 1924, UG40–'25

Report of the Economic and Wage Commission, 1924, UG14–'26

Report of the Native Affairs Commission, 1925–1926, 17–'27

Report of the Native Economic Commission, 1930–1932, UG22–32

Report of the Native Affairs Commission, 1932–1933, UG3–'34

Report of the Native Affairs Commission, 1935–1936, UG41–'37

Departments of State

Report of the Controller and Auditor-General for the financial years 1917/18–1936/37

Annual Report of the Department of Justice for the calendar years 1914, 1918, 1919, 1928

Department of Mines and Industries, Annual Report, 1913, 1917, 1932

Report of the Native Affairs Department, 1910, 1912, 1913–1918, 1919–1921, 1922–1926

UNOFFICIAL

Books

Webb, C. de B., and Wright, J.B., *The James Stuart archive of recorded oral evidence relating to the history of the Zulu and neighbouring peoples.* Vols. 1, 2. Pietermaritzburg: University of Natal Press, 1976, 1979.

Contemporary pamphlets

Astrup, S.J., *The future of the Zulus*, published by the American Lutheran Mission in South Africa, 1932.

[Champion, A.W.G.], *Mehlomadala*, n.d. [1930s?].

[Champion, A.W.G.], *The truth about the ICU*, published by the ICU, Durban, n.d. [1927?].

Heaton Nicholls, G. et al., *Report of Special Committee on Natives' Land Commission: £11 000 000 per annum: a permanent asset worth more than the Rand is being thrown away*, published by the Zululand Planters' Union, 1917.

Seme, P. KaI., *The African National Congress: is it dead?*, n.d. [1932].

Microfilm

Carter/Karis Collection of South African Political Materials. CK Reels 9A, 13A–15A

Newspapers and Periodicals

Cape Times
Ilanga lase Natal
Izindaba Zabantu
The Natal Advertiser
The Natal Mercury
The Natal Witness

The Net
The South African Outlook
The South African Sugar Journal
Zululand Diocesan Magazine
Zululand Mission Report
The Zululand Times

Collections of Newspaper Cuttings, Killie Campbell Africana Library, Durban
Killie Campbell's Newscutting Books, Nos. 10, 30, 33, 36
H.E Colenso's Newscutting Books, Vols. 2, 3
Mrs Mary Tyler Gray's Collection of Press Cuttings, Book 4
Marwick Papers, Newscutting Books

INTERVIEWS

Interviews conducted under the auspices of the Oral History Project, University of Natal, Durban, 1981–82. The original recordings and translated transcripts are now stored in the Killie Campbell Africana Library, Durban.

Mahaye, Zephaniah.   Born 1913, Emtonjaneni district, Zululand. Zulu oral historian, sometime adviser to the Zulu royal house – particularly during the 1940s – and currently a storekeeper. Interviewed at his store, near Hluhluwe, 11/11/1981.

Zulu, Magogo Sibile Mantithi Constance.   Born approx. 1899, Zululand, died 1984. Daughter of Dinuzulu and Solomon's full sister. Started Solomon's 'royal kindergarten' before being married to Chief Matole Buthelezi in the mid-1920s. Chief Mangosuthu Gatsha Buthelezi's mother. Interviewed at her home, KwaPhindangene, near Ulundi, 6/1/1982.

Zulu, Mkandandhlovu Fundukutholwa Minah.   Born 1913, Zululand. Daughter of Dinuzulu, evidently born shortly after Dinuzulu's death. Lived at the royal homesteads throughout Solomon's chieftainship. Interviewed at her home, Nongoma district, 15/12/1981.

Zulu, Ndesheni Ernest.   Born 1907, Zululand. Son of Mnyaiza. Educated at the ZNTI. In 1939 he took up employment as *induna* at the Nongoma magistrate's court. Ndesheni acted as adviser to Cyprian Bhekuzulu kaSolomon, and acts as adviser to and representative of the present king, Goodwill Zwelethini kaCyprian. He is also consulted on historical matters by Inkatha, and serves on the 'Ondini Restoration Committee' (Cetshwayo's Ondini homestead was burnt by the British in 1879). Interviewed at his home, Nongoma district, 10/11/1981.

Zulu, Thandayiphi Absolom.   Born 1925, Zululand. Principal son of Solomon's marriage to okaMbulawa, a high-ranking woman of the Buthelezi. In the late 1930s Thandayiphi was declared to be Solomon's successor. Following a succession dispute, a government Board of Inquiry in 1945 set aside his claim in favour of Cyprian – against the wishes of the Zulu regent, Arthur Mshiyeni kaDinuzulu. Interviewed outside a liquor store, Nongoma district, 10/11/1981.

Other interviews

Kanyi, [?].   Private secretary to Cyprian Bhekuzulu kaSolomon during the 1960s. Interviewed at his home, Nongoma, 15/12/1981.

Krige, Professor E.J.   Attended Solomon's *ihlambo* ceremony in 1934 as an academic observer. Author of *The social system of the Zulus* (London, 1936). Interviewed at her home, Durban, 6/10/1981.

Mbutho, C.   Zulu oral historian, specialist in the history of Cato Manor, and the Oral History Project's principal consultant for the social history of (African) Durban. Interviewed at the University of Natal, Durban, 20/10/1981.

SECONDARY SOURCES

BOOKS AND ARTICLES

Ahrens, F.W., *From bench to bench: reflections, reminiscences and records of F. W. Ahrens*. Pietermaritzburg: Shuter and Shooter, 1948.

Aronson, T., *Royal ambassadors in South Africa, 1860–1947*. Cape Town: David Philip, 1975.

Ballard, C., 'A "year of scarcity": the 1896 locust plague in Natal', *South African Historical Journal*, 15, 1983.

Bonner, P. et al. (eds), *Holding their ground: class, locality and culture in 19th and 20th century South Africa*. Johannesburg: Ravan, 1989.

Braatvedt, H.P., *Roaming Zululand with a Native Commissioner*. Pietermaritzburg: Shuter and Shooter, 1949.

—— 'Zulu marriage customs and ceremonies', *South African Journal of Science*, 24, December 1927.

Bradford, Helen, 'Mass movements and the petty bourgeoisie: the social origins of ICU leadership, 1924–1929', *Journal of African History*, 25, 1984.

Bromberger, N., 'An exposition and critique of Stanley B. Greenberg's *Race and state in capitalist development*', *Perspectives in Economic History*, 1, 1982.

Brookes, E.H., *White rule in South Africa, 1830–1910: varieties in governmental policies affecting Africans*. Pietermaritzburg: University of Natal Press, 1974.

Brookes, E.H. and Hurwitz, N., *The native reserves of Natal*, Natal Regional Survey, vol.7. Cape Town: Oxford University Press for the University of Natal, 1957.

Brookes, E.H. and Webb, Colin de B., *A history of Natal*. Pietermaritzburg: University of Natal Press, 1965.

Bryant, A.T., *Olden times in Zululand and Natal*. London: Longmans, Green, 1929.

Bundy, Colin, *The rise and fall of the South African peasantry*. London: Heinemann, 1979.

Burnett, B.B., *Anglicans in Natal*. Durban: St. Paul's, 1956.

Butler, J., Rotberg, R.I. and Adams, J.A., *The black homelands of South Africa*. Berkeley: University of California Press, 1977.

Carter, G.M., Karis, T. and Stultz, N.M., *South Africa's Transkei: the politics of domestic colonialism*. London: Heinemann, 1967.

Champion, A.W.G., *The views of Mahlathi*, edited by M.W. Swanson and translated by A.T. Cope and E.R. Dahle. Pietermaritzburg: University of Natal Press, 1983.

Clarke, S., 'Capital, fractions of capital and the state: "Neo-Marxist" analysis of the South African state', *Capital and Class*, 5, 1978.

Cloete, R., 'Black farmers in Natal, 1850–1913', *Africa Perspective*, 4, July 1976.

Cohen, R., 'Class in Africa: analytical problems and perspectives', *The Socialist Register*, 1972.

Collins, R. O. (ed.), *Problems in the history of colonial Africa, 1860–1960.* Englewood Cliffs, N.J.: Prentice-Hall, 1970.

Cope, A. T. (ed.), *Izibongo: Zulu praise poems.* Oxford: Clarendon, 1968.

Cope, John, *South Africa.* London: Benn, 1965.

Cope, Nicholas, 'The Zulu petit bourgoisie and Zulu nationalism in the 1920s: origins of Inkatha', *Journal of Southern African Studies*, 16(3), September 1990.

Davenport, T. R. H., *South Africa: a modern history.* London: Macmillan, 1977.

Davenport, T. R. H. and Hunt, K. S., *The right to the land.* Cape Town: David Philip, 1974.

Davies, H. and Shepherd, R. H. W. (eds), *South African missions, 1800–1950.* London: Thomas Nelson, 1954.

Davies, R. et al., 'Class struggle and the periodisation of the state in South Africa', *Review of African Political Economy*, 7, September–December 1976.

Duminy, Andrew and Guest, Bill (eds), *Natal and Zululand from earliest times to 1910: a new history.* Pietermaritzburg: University of Natal Press and Shuter and Shooter, 1989.

Duerdan, J. E., 'Social anthropology in South Africa: problems of race and nationalism', *South African Journal of Science*, 18, 1921–22.

Edgecombe, Ruth, 'Sir Marshall Clarke and the abortive attempt to "Basutolandize" Zululand, 1893–7', *Journal of Natal and Zulu History*, 1, 1978.

Etherington, Norman, 'The origins of "indirect rule" in nineteenth-century Natal', *Theoria*, 47, 1976.

Evans, I. L., *Native policy in southern Africa: an outline.* Cambridge: Cambridge University Press, 1934.

Faye, C., *Zulu references for interpreters and students.* Pietermaritzburg: City Printing Works, 1923.

Fuze, Magema, *The black people and whence they came.* Pietermaritzburg: University of Natal Press, 1979.

Gann, L. H. and Duignan, Peter, (eds) *Colonialism in Africa, 1870–1960,* Vol. 3, *Profiles of change: African society and colonial rule*, edited by V. W. Turner. Cambridge: Cambridge University Press, 1971.

Garthorne, E. R., 'Applications of Native Law', *Bantu Studies*, 3, 1927–9.

Gluckman, M., 'Zulu women in hoecultural ritual', *Bantu Studies*, 9, 1935.

—— 'Analysis of social situation in modern Zululand', *Bantu Studies*, 14, March (part 1), June (part 2), 1940.

Greenberg, Stanley, *Race and state in capitalist development: comparative perspectives.* New Haven, Conn.: Yale University Press, 1980.

Guy, Jeff, 'Production and exchange in the Zulu kingdom', *Mohlomi*, 2, 1978.

—— *The destruction of the Zulu kingdom.* London: Longman, 1979.

Hahlo, H. R., and Kahn, E., *South Africa: the development of its laws and constitution.* Cape Town: Jutas, 1960.

Harris, R. L., *The political economy of Africa.* Cambridge, Mass.: Schenkman, 1975.

Heaton Nicholls, G., *Bayete! 'Hail to the King'!* London: Allen and Unwin, 1923.

Heaton Nicholls, G., *South Africa in my time*. London: Allen and Unwin, 1961.

Horrell, M., *Action, reaction and counteraction*. Johannesburg: South African Institute of Race Relations, 1971.

Horton, J.W., 'South Africa's Joint Councils: black-white co-operation between the two World Wars', *South African Historical Journal*, 4, 1972.

Hurwitz, N. and Williams, O., *The economic framework of South Africa*. Pietermaritzburg: Shuter and Shooter, 1962.

Isaacman, A., 'Social banditry in Zimbabwe (Rhodesia) and Mozambique, 1894–1907: an expression of early peasant protest', *Journal of Southern African Studies*, 4(1), October 1977.

Jones, J.D. Rheinallt, 'The need for a scientific basis for South African native policy', *South African Journal of Science*, 23, 1926.

Jones, J.D. Rheinallt and Saffery, A.L., 'Social and economic conditions of native life in the Union of South Africa', *Bantu Studies*, 7 and 8, 1933 and 1934.

Kane-Berman, J., 'Inkatha: the paradox of South African politics', *Optima*, 30(2), February 1982.

Kingdon, J.R.L., 'The transition from tribalism to individualism', *South African Journal of Science*, 16, 1919.

Karis, T. and Carter, G.M. (eds), *From protest to challenge: a documentary history of African politics in South Africa, 1882–1964*, vols. 1, 4. Stanford: Hoover Institution Press, 1973, 1977.

Kidd, D., *Kaffir socialism and the dawn of individualism: an introduction to the study of the native problem*. London: Black, 1908.

Kirk, J., *The economic aspects of native segregation in South Africa*. London: P.S. King, 1929.

Krige, E.J., *The social system of the Zulus*. London: Longmans, Green, 1936.

Kuper H., *An African aristocracy: rank among the Swazi*. London: Oxford University Press for the International African Institute, 1947.

—— *Sobhuza II: Ngwenyama and King of Swaziland*. London: Duckworths, 1978.

Kuper L., *An African bourgeoisie: race, class and politics in South Africa*. New Haven, Conn.: Yale University Press, 1965.

Kuper L. and Smith, M.G. (eds), *Pluralism in Africa*. Berkeley: University of California Press, 1971.

La Hausse, Paul, 'Drinking in a cage: the Durban system and the 1929 beer hall riots', *Africa Perspective*, 20, 1982.

—— '"The cows of Nongoloza": youth, crime and amalaita gangs in Durban, 1900–1936', *Journal of Southern African Studies*, 16(1), March 1990.

Lacey, Marian, *Working for boroko: the origins of a coercive labour system in South Africa*. Johannesburg: Ravan, 1981.

Langley, J.A., *Pan-Africanism and nationalism in West Africa, 1900–1945: a study in ideology and social classes*. Oxford: Clarendon, 1973.

Legassick, M., 'Kuper and Smith, *Pluralism in Africa*' (review article), *Economic Development and Cultural Change*, 19(4), July 1971.

Lewis, C. and Edwards, G.E., *Historical records of the Church of the Province of South Africa.* London: S.P.C.K., 1934.

Loram, C.T., 'The claims of the native question upon scientists', *South African Journal of Science,* 18, 1921–22.

Lugg, H.C., 'Agricultural ceremonies in Natal and Zululand', *Bantu Studies,* 3, 1927–9.

—— 'The practice of lobolo in Natal', *Bantu Studies,* 4, 1945.

—— *Life under a Zulu shield.* Pietermaritzburg: Shuter and Shooter, 1975.

—— *A Natal family looks back.* Durban: Griggs, 1970.

Luthuli, A., *Let my people go: an autobiography.* Johannesburg: Collins, 1962.

Mahlobo, G.W.K. and Krige, E.J., 'Transition from childhood to adulthood amongst the Zulus', *Bantu Studies,* 8, 1934.

Maré, G. and Hamilton, G., *An appetite for power: Buthelezi's Inkatha and South Africa.* Ravan: Johannesburg, 1987.

Marks, Shula, 'Harriette Colenso and the Zulus, 1874–1913', *Journal of African History,* 4(3), 1963.

—— 'Natal, the Zulu royal family and the ideology of segregation', *Journal of Southern African Studies,* 4(2), April 1978.

—— *Reluctant rebellion: the 1906–8 disturbances in Natal.* Oxford: Clarendon Press, 1970.

—— 'The ambiguities of dependence: John L. Dube of Natal', *Journal of Southern African Studies,* 1(2), April 1975.

—— *The ambiguities of dependence in South Africa: class, nationalism and the state in twentieth-century Natal.* Johannesburg: Ravan Press, 1986.

—— (ed.), *Not either an experimental doll.* Pietermaritzburg: University of Natal Press, 1987.

Marks, Shula and Atmore, Anthony (eds), *Economy and society in pre-industrial South Africa.* London: Longman, 1980.

Marks, Shula and Rathbone, Richard (eds), *Industrialisation and social change in South Africa: African class formation, culture, and consciousness, 1870–1930.* London: Longman, 1982.

Marks, Shula and Trapido, Stanley (eds), *The politics of race, class and nationalism in twentieth century South Africa.* London: Longman, 1987.

Meli, Francis, *South Africa belongs to us: a history of the ANC.* Harare: Zimbabwe Publishing House, 1988.

Mgabi, S.R., 'Installation of Cyprian as chief of the Usuthu tribe', *Native Teachers Journal,* 28, October 1948.

Moberly, G.S., *A city set on a hill: a history of Eshowe.* Eshowe: Eshowe Rotary Club, 1970.

Molteno, F., 'The historical significance of the Bantustan strategy', *Social Dynamics,* 3(2), 1977.

Moorsom, R., 'Underdevelopment, contract labour and worker consciousness in Namibia, 1915–1972', *Journal of Southern African Studies,* 4(1), October 1977.

Morris, D.R., *The washing of the spears: a history of the rise of the Zulu nation under Shaka and its fall in the Zulu War of 1879.* London: Cape, 1966.

Morris, Mike, 'The development of capitalism in South Africa' (review article on *Source Material on the South African Economy, 1860–1970* by H. Hobart Houghton and J. Dagut), *The Journal of Development Studies*, 12(3), April 1976.

——— 'The development of capitalism in South African agriculture: class struggle in the countryside', *Economy and Society*, 5, 1976.

Mzala, *Gatsha Buthelezi: Chief with a double agenda*. London: Zed, 1988.

Osborn, R. F., *Valiant harvest: the founding of the South African sugar industry, 1848–1926*. Durban: South African Sugar Association, 1964.

Palmer, R. and Parsons, N. (eds), *The roots of rural poverty in central and southern Africa*. London: Heinemann, 1977.

Perrings, C., 'Consciousness, conflict and proletarianization: an assessment of the 1935 mineworkers' strike on the Northern Rhodesian Copperbelt', *Journal of Southern African Studies*, 4(1), October 1977.

Price, G. Ward, *Through South Africa with the Prince*. London: Gill, 1926.

Reader, D. H., *Zulu tribe in transition: the Makhanya of southern Natal*. Manchester: Manchester University Press, 1966.

Reitz, D., *No outspan*. London: Faber, 1943.

Reyher, R. H., *Zulu woman*. Columbia: Columbia University Press, 1948.

Rich, P. B., 'Ministering to the white man's needs: the development of urban segregation in South Africa, 1913–1923', *African Studies*, 37(2), 1978.

Rogers, H., *Native administration in the Union of South Africa*. Johannesburg: Witwatersrand University Press, 1933.

Roux, Edward R., *Time longer than rope: a history of the black man's struggle for freedom in South Africa*. Madison: University of Wisconsin Press, 1964.

Samuelson, R. C. A., *Long, long, ago*. Durban: Knox, 1929.

Simkins, C., 'Agricultural production in the African reserves of South Africa, 1918–1969', *Journal of Southern African Studies*, 7(2), April 1981.

Sklar, R. L., 'Political science and national integration – a radical approach', *The Journal of Modern African Studies*, 5(1), 1967.

Slater, Henry, 'Land, labour and capital in Natal: the Natal Land and Colonisation Company, 1860–1948', *Journal of African History*, 16, 1975.

Southall, R., 'African capitalism in contemporary South Africa', *Journal of Southern African Studies*, 7(1), October 1980.

——— 'Buthelezi, Inkatha and the politics of compromise', *African Affairs*, 80(321), October 1981.

Sundkler, B. G. M., *Bantu prophets in South Africa*. 2nd Edn. Oxford: Oxford University Press for the International African Institute, 1961.

——— *Zulu Zion and some Swazi Zionists*. London: Oxford University Press, 1976.

Tatz, C. M., *Shadow and substance in South Africa: a study in land and franchise policies affecting Africans, 1910–1960*. Pietermaritzburg: University of Natal Press, 1962.

Temkin B., *Gatsha Buthelezi: Zulu statesman: a biography*. Cape Town: Purnell, 1976.

Vail, L., *The creation of tribalism in Southern Africa*. London: Currey, 1989.

Van der Horst, S. T., *Native labour in South Africa*. Oxford: Oxford University Press, 1942.

Van Onselen, C., *Chibaro: African mine labour in Southern Rhodesia, 1900–1933*. London: Pluto, 1976.

Van Onselen, C. and Phimister, I., 'The political economy of tribal animosity: a case study of the 1929 Bulawayo Location "faction fight"', *Journal of Southern African Studies*, 6(1), October 1979.

Vilakazi, Absolom, *Zulu transformations: a study in the dynamics of social change*. Pietermaritzburg: University of Natal Press, 1965.

Walker, Cherryl (ed.), *Women and gender in southern Africa to 1945*. Cape Town: David Philip, 1990.

Walker, O., *Kaffirs are lively*. London: Gollancz, 1948.

Walshe, Peter, *The rise of African nationalism in South Africa: the African National Congress, 1912–1952*. London: C. Hurst, 1970.

Watson, R. G. T., *Tongaati: an African experiment*. London: Hutchinson, 1960.

Webster, E. (ed.), *Essays in southern African labour history*. Johannesburg: Ravan, 1978.

Webster, D., 'From peasant to proletarian: the development/underdevelopment debate in South Africa', *Africa Perspective*, 13, Spring 1979.

Welsh, D. J., *The roots of segregation: native policy in colonial Natal, 1845–1910*. Cape Town: Oxford University Press, 1971.

Werner, A., 'Native affairs in Natal', *Journal of African Society*, 17, October 1905.

Weyl, Nathaniel, *Traitors' end: the rise and fall of the communist movement in southern Africa*. New Rochelle, N.Y.: Arlington House, 1970.

Wheelwright C. A., 'Native circumcision lodges in the Zoutpansberg district', *Anthropological Institute*, 35, 1905.

—— 'Native administration in Zululand', *Journal of African Society*, 24(94), January 1925.

Wickins, P., *The Industrial and Commercial Workers' Union of Africa*. Cape Town: Oxford University Press, 1978.

Willan, Brian, *Sol Plaatje: South African nationalist, 1876–1932*. London: Heinemann, 1984.

Wolpe, Harold, 'Capitalism and cheap labour-power in South Africa: from segregation to apartheid', *Economy and Society*, 1(4), 1972.

THESES AND UNPUBLISHED PAPERS

Ballard, C. and Lenta, G., 'The role of the peasantry in the agricultural economy of colonial Natal, 1844–1909: a reassessment'. Paper presented at the Southern African Studies Seminar, University of Natal, Pietermaritzburg, 1982.

Beall, J.D. and North-Coombes, M.D., 'The 1913 disturbances in Natal: the social and economic background to "passive resistance"'. Paper presented at the Workshop on Natal History, 1910 to 1961, Pietermaritzburg, 1982.

Bradford, Helen, 'Lynch law and labourers: the ICU in Umvoti, 1927–1928'. Paper presented at the Workshop on Class, Community and Conflict: Local Perspectives, University of the Witwatersrand, 1984.

—— 'The Industrial and Commercial Workers' Union of Africa in the South African countryside, 1924–1930'. Ph.D., University of the Witwatersrand, 1985.

Buys, D., 'The negotiations between the Colony of Natal and the Colonial Office leading to the passing of the Annexation of Zululand Act (number 37) of 1897, 1894–1897', BA Hons., University of Natal, Durban, 1980.

Cloete, G.R., 'The social and economic context of African politics in Natal 1907–20: a preliminary research report'. African Studies Institute seminar paper, University of the Witwatersrand, 1974.

Colenbrander, P.J., 'Warriors, women, land and livestock: Cetshwayo's kingdom under stress?' Paper presented at the Workshop on Production and Reproduction in the Zulu Kingdom, University of Natal, Pietermaritzburg, 1977.

Cope, Nicholas, 'The defection of Hamu, 1879'. BA Hons., University of Natal, Durban, 1980.

—— 'The Zulu royal family under the South African government, 1910–1933: Solomon kaDinuzulu, Inkatha and Zulu nationalism'. Ph.D., University of Natal, Durban, 1986.

Dubow, Saul, '"Understanding the native mind": the impact of anthropological thought on segregationist discourse in South Africa, 1919–1933'. Paper presented at the Workshop on Class, Community and Conflict: Local Perspectives, University of the Witwatersrand, 1984.

Duminy, A.H., 'The Natal sugar interest and the Smuts government, 1919–24'. Paper presented at the Workshop on Natal and the Union, 1909–1939, University of Natal, Pietermaritzburg, 1978.

Haines, E.G., 'Natal and the Union, 1918–1923'. MA, University of Natal, Durban, 1976.

Haines, R.J., 'Reflections on African protest in Natal, 1925–36'. Paper presented at the Workshop on Natal and the Union 1909–1939, University of Natal, Pietermaritzburg, 1978.

—— 'The opposition to General J.B.M. Hertzog's Segregation Bills, 1925–1936: a study in extra-parliamentary protest'. MA, University of Natal, Durban, 1978.

Hemson, D., 'Class consciousness and migrant workers: dockworkers of Durban'. Ph.D., University of Warwick, 1979.

Jeeves, A.H., 'Migrant labour in the political economy of the mines: the Native Recruiting Corporation and its rivals, 1903–1919'. Paper presented at the Conference on South Africa and the West, University of Natal, Durban, 1982.

Laband, John, 'Dick Addison: the role of a British official during the disturbances in the Ndwandwe district of Zululand, 1887–1889'. MA, University of Natal, Pietermaritzburg, 1980.

La Hausse, Paul, 'The struggle for the city: alcohol, the Ematsheni and popular culture in Durban, 1902–1936' MA, University of Cape Town, 1984.

—— 'The message of the warriors: the ICU, the labouring poor and the making of a popular political culture in Durban, 1925–1930'. Paper presented at the History Workshop, University of the Witwatersrand, February 1987.

Lekhela, S.M.M., 'An historical survey of native land settlement in South Africa from 1902 to the passing of the Natives' Trust and Land Act of 1936'. MA, University of South Africa, 1955.

Mackenzie, D.J., 'Dube and the land issue, 1913–1936', B.Soc.Sc. Hons., University of Natal, Durban, 1980.

Marks, Shula, 'Patriotism, patriarchy and purity: Natal and the politics of Zulu ethnic consciousness'. African Studies Institute seminar paper, University of the Witwatersrand, 1986.

Reeves L., 'Natal, the Status Bills and fusion: cross purposes'. BA Hons., University of Natal, Durban, 1980.

Swanson, M.W., 'The rise of Clermont', paper presented at the Workshop on African Urban Life in Durban in the Twentieth Century, University of Natal, Durban, 1983.

Swart, L., 'The work of Harriette Emily Colenso in relationship to Dinuzulu kaCetshwayo culminating in the treason trial of 1908–9'. MA, University of Natal, Durban, 1968.

Williams, Gavin, 'Garveyism, Akinpelu Obisesan and his contemporaries: Ibadan 1920–22'. Seminar paper, St. Peter's College, University of Oxford.

Index

Kholwa names are entered under surname, e.g. Dube, John.

All other **African personal names** are entered under the first or given name, e.g. Dinuzulu kaCetshwayo Zulu. The author has sometimes supplied the clan name, e.g. Zulu after the patronymic, e.g. kaDinuzulu. For consistency and to aid identification, this policy has been extended wherever such names could definitely be established by reference to *The James Stuart archive*, vols. I–IV. The *Stuart archive* orthography has been followed where patronymics and clan names have been supplied.

Clan names are listed with no description, e.g. Buthelezi.

Zulu words are entered under the stem and not under the prefix. Thus *amaButho* follows Buthelezi.

Cross references to **organisations** have been abbreviated, e.g. *See* NNC, although all organisations appear under their full name, e.g. Natal Native Congress.